The Fairway of Life:

Simple Secrets To Playing Better Golf By Going With The Flow ~

Rand S. Marquardt

iUniverse, Inc.
New York   Bloomington

The Fairway of Life
Simple Secrets To Playing Better Golf By Going With The Flow ~

Copyright © 2009. Rand S. Marquardt

All rights reserved. No part of this book may be used or reproduced by any means, graphic, electronic, or mechanical, including photocopying, recording, taping or by any information storage retrieval system without the written permission of the publisher except in the case of brief quotations embodied in critical articles and reviews.

iUniverse books may be ordered through booksellers or by contacting:

iUniverse
1663 Liberty Drive
Bloomington, IN 47403
www.iuniverse.com
1-800-Authors (1-800-288-4677)

Because of the dynamic nature of the Internet, any Web addresses or links contained in this book may have changed since publication and may no longer be valid. The views expressed in this work are solely those of the author and do not necessarily reflect the views of the publisher, and the publisher hereby disclaims any responsibility for them.

ISBN: 978-1-4401-2906-3 (pbk)
ISBN: 978-1-4401-2908-7 (hbk)
ISBN: 978-1-4401-2907-0 (ebk)

Printed in the United States of America

iUniverse rev. date: 6/22/2009

Acknowledgments

I am grateful to be connected to God & Life Source, the leading edge extension of pure positive energy, one stream that flows to and through each of us inspiring new rockets of desire, and better feeling thoughts, allowing us to gravitate toward the life of our dreams in being the creator of our own reality. We are all one.

I am grateful to be inspired by the example of Albert Einstein. Because in some far out crazy way I feel a little bit like Einstein chasing this elusive formula for being in The Zone (the purest of positive energy), just like he did with his Theory of Relativity never giving up, always scratching out ways that didn't work that got him one step closer in his pursuit to finding the truth. The more we stay focused upon our desires the closer we come to the true meaning of genius and excellence. It's all right here: within. If you do not go within, you go without.

I am grateful to the many Masters living and passed who have awakened the sleeping giant within me. It is not the one with the most students; it is the one who creates the most Masters. To all who have ears to hear, let them hear: I am most grateful.

To my "perfect" parents...whom *I chose* before I decided to come forth.
John O. Marquardt
Ellie A. Clark
To my sister, Kristi, all is well and you are loved!
Kristina L. Marquardt

I am grateful to my extended family, your lives have all had an affect on me paving the way forward in such a profound manner. To my nieces and nephew Hadley, Claire, and Logan you are brilliant and magnificent kids becoming teenagers. Remember, kids are the ones teaching us adults. To Nancy, you are the catalyst to get me back on my true path, which has led and allowed me to write this book. I love you for being you forever.

I am grateful to all my friends, mentors, and those that have come into my life for a reason, a season, or a lifetime—I acknowledge and honor all of you! Thank you for all the memories. You are all brilliant and magnificent in your own unique way.

I am grateful that this is the first day of the rest of our lives. We are here to ride the wave of eager anticipation following our bliss along *The Fairway of Life*, embracing the highs and the lows along the way.

I am grateful to my amazing professional editor, Christine Belleris, who kept me centered, grounded and to the point as best as she could. For ten years Christine was the editorial director of Health Communications, Inc., the publisher of the Chicken Soup for the Soul series and other self-help, life issues books. When I asked Christine what makes my book *The Fairway of Life* unique? She responded enthusiastically, "Your book offers golfers a philosophy about golf and life that they really can't find anywhere else. Each person, each reader is unique. Thus, you don't offer readers a one-size-fits-all approach to golf, but rather lead them to chart their own course based on their dreams and desires. Your book is about golf and life and how to make the best of both based upon a person's situation. It is about acceptance without abandoning your dreams. You accept where you are but still strive to be better by playing against yourself and not other people!

The beauty in your book is in its simplicity (the Simple Secrets, of course, and the Coaches Notes) and the techniques and exercises--the MEGT (Mental Edge Golf Technique), is certainly not something you would find in any other golf book!"

I am most grateful to you who are drawn to hear this message. Allow the Introduction to be a new foundation; a reflection; and a process leading and paving the way forward to all the good stuff that lies ahead. The intention throughout this text and beyond is meant to wake you up into becoming more of who you really are. May the freedom to fully express yourself in all endeavors be with you the rest of your life!

Advance Praise for *The Fairway of Life*

"What good are your spiritual and life beliefs if you cannot integrate them with your trip to the mall, your time with your children and spouse, who you see when you look in the mirror, or your vision of yourself when you are on the golf course! So many people love reading books and going to workshops, but when it comes to living the principles that inspire them, it is a different story.

The Fairway of Life is a unique, fresh and entertaining way of looking at how we can use our spirituality and understanding of how the world works anywhere. Rand Marquardt uses his humor, wisdom, and, of course, his natural talent and love for golf to teach us how to use some of the most powerful success tools out there.

I worked closely with Rand Marquardt and author Neale Donald Walsch during Rand's participation in the Conversations with God Foundation's Life Education Program. Rand is an inspiring man who is committed to enjoying life and making a difference.

If you want to be more successful in any area of your life, take a look at life from a new perspective. This perspective is fun, engaging, and challenging, and it requires concentration and commitment. But on a clear sunny day there is nothing like playing a round of spiritual golf."

—Rachael Jayne (Kennedy) Groover
Former Director of Education, Conversations with God Foundation

"I recognize and honor Rand's deep commitment, clarity, compassion and leadership as a messenger of the New Spirituality."

—Neale Donald Walsch
Author, *Conversations with God*

"Rand's inspirations have helped me not only with my mental toughness; they are helping me discover who I am as a golfer. He has taught me what I can do on the golf course. As a result of his coaching, my scores have lowered dramatically."

—Jeffrey Mocini
Sophomore, University of Findlay golf team

"Being a golfer of only ten years and stuck in a pattern of shooting high eighties and low nineties, Rand's thought process of staying in the moment, embracing the moment, whatever that moment is, good or bad, has helped me become not only a better person but a much better golfer, dropping my handicap seven strokes in one summer. This stuff really works. If you have an open mind, want to become a better golfer and lower your handicap, then this book is for you. Have fun playing golf and watch your shots become all that you want them to be. I never knew the true powers of the mind as it relates to the sport of golf. Let's face it—we all want to play better, but we often think in a pattern that doesn't allow us to be the golfer we would like to be. Read this book and learn to embrace and relish the moment, good or bad."

—Christopher B. Shepler
America's Cup sailor

"What Coach is hitting on here is so pure and natural, it is a wonder that it is not more prevalent. The challenges in today's world tend to throw people off track. *The Fairway of Life* is a road sign in life, directing all who read it to their own natural pathway toward a more enjoyable and fulfilling life."

—Keith Fitzpatrick
2006 True North Golf Club Champion

"Rand is a dear friend who has been a true inspiration for me. His insight around the game of golf and the game of life has been invaluable. It's priceless. While I do not play on a regular enough consistency to keep a handicap, I have learned to detach from the outcome, the score, and embrace the enjoyment, which is my true purpose for playing this wonderful game. There was a point when I would be so upset during a bad round, that I wouldn't even talk with my comrades afterward. Now, more than ever, I appreciate my time on the course, my friends, and the beauty of the surroundings regardless of what I shoot. *The Fairway of Life* has allowed me this new freedom and understanding to go within. As a result, I am hitting better golf shots on a more consistent basis simply by giving up my ego's need to win. Life is good."

—David Zmikly
Business Entrepreneur

"After paying even closer attention to my son in July 2006, and practicing even more self-control, I no longer swear or throw my clubs. I am no longer a miserable bastard with whom people did not want to play golf. Now I have over forty people in my inner golfing circle that actually do want to play golf with me. That is a fact, that is the truth, and it is a big thing—and it's very important to me. You can paraphrase any of this all you want, but that is the truth. This stuff really works."

—John O. Marquardt
Dad, life-long golf enthusiast

Contents

Acknowledgments   v
Advance Praise for *The Fairway of Life*   vii
Introduction   xiii

PART I – THE INNER GAME OF GOLF ... AND LIFE

Chapter 1	Awaken to Your Magnificence	1
Chapter 2	Dreams	9
Chapter 3	Desire	30
Chapter 4	The Power of Intentional Golf	41
Chapter 5	The Power of Present Golf	76
Chapter 7	Thoughts Create Swings	112
Chapter 8	Golfer's State of Inspired Being	137
Chapter 9	The Zone	155

PART II – THE INNER GAME OF GOLF ... AND CHANGE

Chapter 10	A Game of Integrity	189
Chapter 11	Conquering Self	214
Chapter 12	The Secret to Change	223
Chapter 13	Say Goodbye to Your Fears	294
Chapter 14	Let Time Serve You	355

PART III – THE INNER GAME OF GOLF ... AND BECOMING A CHAMPION

Chapter 15	Creating a Champion's Self-Image	371
Chapter 16	Keep Dreaming Your Dream	390

PART IV – THE GOLF SWING

Chapter 17	The Golf Swing	395
Conclusion		408
References and Resources		417

Introduction

The Fairway of Life
A Revolutionary Life...and Golf Transformation Program

Life: An Investment in Ourselves
Awaken to Who You Really Are

When you are out on the golf course, are you relaxed and happy, or tense and miserable? When you play badly on a hole, do you shrug it off and move to the next one, or beat yourself up and play poorly the rest of the day? Golf is not supposed to be a sport that sends you spiraling wildly out of control to the pharmacy for an anti-anxiety drug. Golf is supposed to be fun. But many of us have forgotten why we started playing in the first place because every time we set foot on the course, we get anxious and uptight, which often leads to frustration and disappointment with our game. This carries through to our lives off the course, and vice versa. Our personal state of affairs affects every aspect of our lives. Our external world is a direct reflection of our internal world.

If you are nodding your head in agreement, if you have found yourself in this situation, I am here to assure you there is a better way to play golf to the very best of your ability and to live a happier life. Allow me to show you how to awaken to your authentic Self, make peace with your life, enjoy your present moment, and build a champion's self-image following your true path that you have come forth to experience.

I am here to help you with a simple yet profound action plan that will show you how to stop beating yourself up and begin to play the best golf of your life—right now, if you will just simply allow yourself to be in alignment and be open to new more empowering perspectives. If you can zero in and clearly define what you want, I can show you how to get it. All it takes is a simple shift in perspective.

In the process of transforming and changing your golf game for the better, you will also transform your life for the better. It's all one and the same. I've done it and so can you, no matter what your level of play or your life situation. I guarantee that if you finish this book and put this plan into action you will once again be out on the course being calm, relaxed and confident with the understanding of how to perform to your excellence and your full potential more consistently than ever before. You already have the tools, understanding, and wisdom within you to this newfound freedom and joy within. Our objective together is to awaken and remind you, and draw those gifts and qualities out of you. When the student is ready the Master appears, everything unfolding in perfect harmony in this eternal process called life. One of the most compelling understandings in the universe is ask and it is given. The final piece of the secret is allowing it in, finding harmony between the energy of your desires and your feelings in allowing it to be.

Golf and life are intertwined. Create your best life on the inside and you'll play your best golf. It's all about awakening and becoming more aware of whom you really are. It's about releasing your inner champion and building a winner's image. I was once floundering, both on and off the golf course, but thankfully others helped me to "wake up" and recognize my magnificence that lies within. I am here to do the same for you. I was once lost and now I am found. I was asleep and now I am awake. You can then take this new awareness, this new perspective, and these new empowering life principles to all aspects of your life—including the golf course.

It sounds complicated but it's really pretty simple . . . I'm here to show you how to clear the blocks, fears, and obstacles that I struggled with on the golf course, forty years-worth to be exact! I'm still working through these issues. It's a never-ending process. Yet now I'm in the game. Now I have the tools or secrets that have been kept locked away. They say that great teachers teach what they need to learn and understand. And in the process of teaching others the teacher evolves as well. Jesus did not go around teaching to change the world. He changed the world because he went around teaching.

Everything and everyone is connected in the web of life. Everything is energy in motion, moving forward as leading edge extensions of Source Energy, responding to the Law of Attraction, that which we give our thoughts and our vibrationally energy upon. Perhaps the greatest discovery in the field of psychology lies in these five simple words: We become what we think. What are you thinking about? How come some seem to manifest the life of their dreams and some do not? Herein lies the roadmap. How do you choose to live your life?

> *"There are only two ways to live your life. One is as though nothing is a miracle. The other is as though everything is a miracle."*
> —Albert Einstein

Golf—and life— is supposed to be fun! But for many it is not. It appears to be such a constant struggle and a grind at best. Many people I observe appear to be working really, really hard with this game. It's like they feel great pride and honor by paddling really, really hard against the current. Soon to be starting my sixth decade of observing and playing golf I have noticed that many play the game, like I used to, with embarrassment, in fear, with frustration, worry, doubt, inconsistently, overly anxious and uptight at times, in a constant struggle, and nowhere near their full potential. But you don't need to despair or resign yourself to this form of mediocrity and disappointment. Just because it has been this way in the past doesn't mean it needs to be this way now. Yet in order to change this scenario you've got to change the way you think, because the definition of insanity is repeating the same behaviors over and over again expecting different results, another Einstein enlightened understanding. Change your thoughts and you will change your life.

Past faults, failures, and patterns of limited beliefs linger in our subconscious mind and affect our thoughts, words, feelings, and actions with what we are experiencing and manifesting now. What we allowed to filtrate into our subconscious mind years ago runs everything in our life, including the way we play golf. Some of these old patterns build within us a self-image that is often no longer what we want. Some of these less than desirable thoughts we hold about ourselves no longer serve our best interest and it's time we replace them with new more empowering beliefs and focus. We all suffer with some form of unhealthy self-image of ourselves, whether we admit it or not. But the good news is that we can, indeed, change and re-program our subconscious mind and replace old paradigms with new ones to reflect who we truly wish ourselves to be, instead of regurgitating the same ole story. Through commitment, courage, trust, and a belief in yourself you can live the life of your dreams and play your best golf ever.

We all have tasted the fruits our own brilliance, our own highest Self, our true authenticity. We all have our moments of brilliance on the golf course that keeps us coming back, yet wouldn't it be great if we could do that more often? Wouldn't it be great if we knew why we are getting what we are getting? Wouldn't it be great if we could simply adjust a dial within our own frequency and align with what we desire, and with our higher selves? Wouldn't it be great if we each unlocked the mystery to playing golf more often in The Zone and really understood how this game of golf and life really works—for our advantage and for those whose lives we touch by the clarity and power of our example? Guess what? The power lies within you. Let me show you how to unleash this extraordinary power within.

By the clarity and power of my example—and through other case studies of golfers including Tiger Woods and Lorena Ochoa—you will read how I went from a frustrated, misaligned 10-handicap golfer to a more confident, connected 1-handicap golfer in just one summer, and have stayed there four years running, simply by embracing and integrating the universal life principles to the game of golf. You will also read about how other golfers *just like you* made tremendous strides in performing to a level of freedom beyond their wildest dreams. The multiple benefits you will reap by doing this program are astounding. Once you find the relief and understanding within, you too will begin to play the best golf of your life. You will find more of your true authentic Self in this journey together and you will become more of the magnificent and wonderful person you were born to be.

This will be a great journey that needs to be savored, so slow down and relax as you process this book. Too often we take things too seriously, heaven forbid, I know I have! Relax into this and have fun with it. Life, after all, is supposed to be fun. Honor your own commitment to the betterment of yourself and your game. Treat this experience like a dance-with-life instead of boot camp. Learn to go with the flow. The moment you stop *trying so hard* will be the moment it all clicks into place. When you catch yourself getting too serious, I remind you to lighten up. Take off the edge and soften your righteous position. Stop paddling! In fact catching yourself, if you choose, from going down a path that no longer serves you will become a common theme throughout the rest of your life both on and off the golf course. And you won't have to beat yourself up anymore.

When you find yourself in one of those less than desirable places simply stop paddling, drop the oars so to speak, and find some relief. Reach for the best feeling thoughts you can. Perhaps not the best feeling thought you have ever thought, just the best feeling thought at this moment. As you progress things will get a little bit better. And the better it gets, the better it gets. Soon you will be accepting and embracing both the highs and the lows along your journey. You will come to understand the workings of your own emotional guidance system keeping you more aligned with who you really are. Instead of letting a score on the scorecard be your measure of success, let joy be your new measure of success. When you're enjoying, the score will take care of itself. I'm just reminding you. Simple Secret Reminders are scattered throughout this text to remind you to what your soul already knows.

Simple Secret Reminder # 1 – Catch Your Self
Catch yourself when you're feeling frustrated.
Catch yourself when you think you're not having any fun.
Reach for a better feeling thought.

You are here right now because you are drawn to hear this message and you are asking to become a better player and a better person. The universe always hears our asking, our calling within, and our desire to become better. Now it's up to you to get up to speed with yourself, to close the gap, to expect it, and to allow it to be. The first step in becoming a better player and a more authentic you, is you must first *ask to become one*. Once you ask, the universe answers; now it is up to us to allow that in. If you doubt that or say "but . . ." or "I can't ..." then the, "yeah but . . ." or the "I can't . . ." is what you get. That's your challenge. Your challenge is your own self-doubt, your own fear, your own limited belief, overcoming the illusion of obstacles, and your own shadow that is nudging you to evolve into who you really are. When we ask we begin the process. I also invite you to enjoy and embrace this process.

When I was out doing my Life Coaching and Life Education programs practicing being a spiritual being on the inside, I also was asking to become a better golfer. Isn't it amazing that I really never asked before in this most direct manner? It felt kind of weird, almost like it's something you're brought up not to do like, 'don't be too greedy in this life accept your fate. Don't you know you're not supposed to ask, God will provide you with the necessary tools.' So, I allowed this kind of thinking to filtrate into the depths of my subconscious mind, until I decided to change. I decided to ask. Gosh, it does say *ask and it is given, ask and ye shall receive* in the scriptures. What's up with this asking stuff? Can we ask for more than just God-like stuff? Can we ask to become a better golfer? Perhaps there really is something here?

> "Don't just sit there...ASK! *There is an ancient saying,*
> *'Ask and ye shall receive.' The biggest reason you don't get*
> *answers is that you haven't asked the questions."*
> — Richard Bach

> *"Ask wisely, with love, for everything you want."*
> —Mark Victor Hansen

Ask and it is given. Ask with kindness and respect, with love and compassion, with sincere heart and authentic desire. Ask to become your highest Self. Ask to become a better golfer. Ask to become more authentic, more loving, more of who you really are. Most likely our asking can be a bit challenging and often scary at first. What are we scared of? What we might be asked to do? What will happen if we fail?

We are scared of what we don't want to look at, scared to fail, fear of the unknown, afraid of our own shadow, which keeps us safe and playing small. Therefore, many of us simply don't ask – either because we're afraid of what might be asked of us, or afraid of what we might uncover once we "go there." We're also scared of our own brilliance—our light, which keeps us settling for mediocrity. I am here to remind you that nothing will be asked of you, lest what you are asking of your self. I know now how this works, because I too was afraid to find out – for many years. Now, I'm here to reassure you, everything you're asking for from the depths of your soul, is a most precious gift that awaits you.

Are you ready to make a quantum leap forward? Are you ready to play to your full potential with the freedom to more fully express yourself? If you nodding your head yes to these questions then you are being invited to change the way you are thinking. Now if you like what you are getting then please keep on. And to understand what you are getting all you have to do is look at the results you are getting. Look in the mirror so to speak. Trying to change our life on the outside is just as foolish as trying to change the reflection in the mirror. In order to make changes we have to change what's on the inside. Beating golf ball after golf ball without a purpose and understanding of the golf swing only ingrains potential bad habits. Beating golf ball after golf ball without an internal champion's self-image of our selves is just as foolish.

Like a classroom of life, you will be challenged within. There is no other substitute; you must experience it on your own. Should you choose to embark upon this mission of becoming the remarkable you, the benefits are no less than incredible. Should you fold, you wither back into the soil like a dying plant. The good news is you get as many chances and choices to nurture and cultivate, to tweak and refine, to announce and declare, to express and experience, to become and fulfill, and to create anew as you wish. Yes, like the magic genie, your wish is my command. You have an unlimited number of wishes or asking to come forth. You're never cut off, and it's never too late. You may start, stop, and start up again at any moment. You can grow and move at your own pace. There is no judgment either way. Your true self makes no judgments. There is nothing or no one to fear. For you are the master of your domain and creator of your reality. What are you asking to experience yourself to be next?

If you choose to become more of who you really are, your demeanor on and off the golf course will change dramatically for the better. You will begin the process of embracing every golf shot, the good, the bad, and the ugly, with open arms because you will know why you hit it there and you will accept everything as it is – much better than before. You will become more of an objective detective in your own process. You will acknowledge your negative emotions and release them in a healthy manner, allowing yourself to return to center and The Zone. You will live more often in the present moment, the only moment we ever have. You will focus more upon what you really, really want and so shall it be. You will laugh more often and smile a lot. You will shrug your shoulders with acceptance, take life and golf less serious, and you will keep on re-creating yourself anew when bounces don't necessarily go your way. You will beat yourself up less often, as you begin to embrace the agenda and wisdom of your soul. You will know how to pick yourself up when feeling down and why emotions exist. You will move through the full scale of emotions and you will understand how they work in your favor. You will find yourself residing more often in the upper scale of positive emotions more often than ever before. You will understand levels of human consciousness and how yours impact your life, and the life of others, in all aspects. Yes, what you do to yourself, you do to others. What you do to others, you do to yourself. You will understand the enormity of the concept that every act is one of self-definition. You're already feeling it now just simply a few pages into the Introduction. And none of this will diminish one ounce of the competitive juices within you. It will, however, deepen and enhance your desire to become your personal best.

Life and golf will take on a whole new meaning, and you will finally understand that you are the creator of your reality, and that the answer and wisdom lies within. You will understand that in ultimate reality nothing really matters, except for what you announce and declare and decide to make matter—literally and figuratively. You will come to understand that you really are making it all up—every bit of it. Yes, you will gain all of this wisdom, plus much, much more. The power, the answer, and the wisdom lie within you being and becoming your authentic (higher) Self, and the understanding of going with the flow.

Allow me, an awakened spiritual messenger and aspiring Master deliver to you a message about golf and life, and an action plan to get you to play golf with outrageous joy more often to the very best of your God-given talent. Allow me the opportunity to show you how to transcend your personal self into The Zone of your authentic and highest Self. The Zone is the ultimate experience. It's the flow of pure positive energy. The Zone is the breakthrough paradigm point where inner awe and gratitude meet the flow of Well-Being. The Zone is the place where transcendence of personal self moves from ego, personality, emotion, thoughts, and fears to effortless bliss, grace, ease, joy, peace, and oneness—a knowing and a flowing of life to you and through you. Allow me to show you how to tap into this more joyful and incredible place we have come to call The Zone.

How I Came to Be the Spiritual Messenger

Why am I the person to deliver this message? I was born with this gift. Just like you are born with yours! I remember being connected and in alignment as a young child. I have always been a seeker in understanding the meaning and purpose of life, constantly asking and pondering the big questions. I always knew life was a little different than the ways and teachings of the world. I always desired to remember, connect, and expand even more. As life and pressures from others often does to us, for a time I temporarily wandered off track from my true path. I became spiritually and emotionally disconnected while feeling the calling to return on a constant basis. I went in and out of alignment with my higher Self. Life simply does not *feel good* when you are disconnected from yourself. And that is why feelings are the internal guidance system to tap into too and allow them to guide us along our *True North*, our true path.

Yet in order to understand or "get" this principle, I needed to experience the opposite of who I really am *first* in order to more fully embrace my *true* authentic Self. How would you know hot without first experiencing cold? How would I know my authentic Self without first experiencing being out of integrity? The same goes for everything in life. Contrast exists for a reason. Once you understand that opposites exist for our own benefit, you can choose which direction and which path you wish to follow.

As I evolved in this personal growth arena I felt drawn to the mental, emotional, and spiritual aspects of sport, more specifically golf. Yet the same principles apply to all aspects of life. I became fascinated with the concepts of sport psychology and this idea of The Zone. I read about them, I listened to the tapes, I read articles, I studied them in school, and I sought intensely to apply them to my life on the golf course at first with very little success. I had the intellectual and analytical understanding; I lacked the emotional and spiritual connection to really listening to the language of my soul, my heart space and what it really means to be in alignment and go with the flow of life.

In all those years of *trying so hard*, I came up mostly empty handed. I intellectualized in my left-brain without dropping deeply into my heart space, where my feelings and connection with life really exists. There was something missing. I had some of the wisdom and only glimpse of what The Zone was all about. To play great golf you have to be out of your mind, and by that I definitely do not mean crazy! You have to turn off your analytical, conscious, thinking brain while you are performing. Why? Because zero thoughts exist in The Zone, only the purest of positive energy: no unhealthy egos either. The moment you spin confidence to arrogance or cockiness is the moment you turn birdie or par into bogey or worse sooner, rather then later, it's like God pinching us. I was trying so hard to think my way into becoming better that I avoided going inside. I avoided listening to my small, still voice within—the wisdom of my soul. Perhaps I was afraid of what I might find, or what I might be asked to do. When the going gets tough it's easy to go into a state of denial, suppression, hiding out, running away from, back to the ways of the world, or eventually just simply pleading ignorance. Perhaps back then I never thought of life like I do now. All I can tell you now is that life really is an incredible journey and there is no turning back. Once you venture down this road you've got to get yourself up to speed with who you have become, otherwise you just won't feel good.

Life's Purpose Through Inspiration and Divine Guidance

Debbie Ford, author, integrative life coach, and an emotional, spiritual teacher, told me her unique gift to offer humanity. Debbie stated that while Marianne Williamson got *A Return To Love* and she got *The Dark Side of Light Chasers* —she challenged all of us. Mine came to me one night during my stay in San Diego at one of her retreats in the still of my connection to God: <u>golf is supposed to be fun, create a message around that</u>. How simple and how profound! It's what I've struggled with my whole life.

I was imagining creating a theme around this called…<u>Play Golf For Fun Day</u>. The intention being is that millions of golfers get all worked up over a game that is supposed to be fun. Why not bring this intention to their attention…and on this day, or weekend, we set an intention to play golf for fun – no matter what. Why not make it over the July 4th weekend? Other countries can choose other weekends that fit their individual historical perspective. Perhaps there would be a wake up call and a carry over affect? Perhaps this simple reminder could awaken more people making this world a better place to live?

Before you know it, all of these other thoughts came swirling. It was so clear that night in my room. I could hardly sleep. I was tuned in, tapped in, and turned on. I was also hearing and feeling all the frustration, fear, anxiety, and worry that I see in others and myself of how we get all worked up over a game that is supposed to be fun. A game that sometimes we love to hate. Not too mention that I wanted to play better golf too! I noticed that my golf game was actually regressing. What's it going to take to play better? How can I play golf for fun? It's such a grind and a struggle. I get so nervous and scared; sometimes I can barely finish my swing. And to think about those dreaded yips…oh boy! I felt exposed, yet I was open to hearing this message and communication with God.

God was talking to me that night in San Diego to create a message around all of this…all the while I was working on becoming more of my authentic Self. First, I knew that I would have to be the one to experience this new change myself long before I could coach and tell others. Coaching others or writing a book wasn't even on my radar screen. I had a lot more processing, healing, transforming, and investing to do on myself. I knew that I would have to experience all of this stuff myself first. And I was reminded about this from my coaches.

Nevertheless, God was talking to me in the still of that night in San Diego on the eve before our closing ceremonies. And do you want to know the real reason…the deeper understanding why God was now talking to me? Underneath all of this new revelation, I've been asking to surrender to God for several years. Now here I am… as prepared as ever, ready to take that leap of faith into the unknown with both feet, yet still scared as can be. I wanted to surrender and like an orchestra building to a crescendo it happened the next day in the stillness of my connection with God. I surrendered to "him" fully that day at the retreat! Like I state in all my communication with everyone who is going through or wondering about this same experience: <u>Surrendering to God is the most scary and most liberating experience of my life!</u> This too is an area that I coach others in. It's really a calling about connecting with your authentic Self, with who you really are. It's a complete awareness and a calling within of becoming who you really are and what you really know. It was time to wake up and be this! Phew…

This leads us to our second Simple Secret Reminder, nuggets of acquired wisdom throughout this book that will provide a resource for you both on and off the course:

> **Simple Secret Reminder # 2 – Surrender To Your Authentic Self**
> **Connect with you authentic Self.**
> **Wake up!**
> **Become who you really are.**

Surrendering and connecting with our authentic Self means making peace with where we are and embracing the wholeness of our true self. In order to play our best golf its imperative we become our best self. Making peace with our story and our past allows us to move forward less arduously, without beating ourselves up. We're now free to express ourselves without resistance, which only drains our energy. One example of this sub-personality aspect of our selves that deserves our attention is people pleasing. Debbie Ford explains this insidious disease through her writings about the exhaustion of people pleasing. Just imagine what it's like trying to win or please the approval of others on the golf course versus simply being our best. If we are constantly seeking approval of others to be the good little boy or girl on the golf course, then we're not free to fully express ourselves.

The Exhaustion of People-Pleasing

There is an affliction quietly and insidiously affecting us that crosses all lines of age, gender and race. It began when we were young and learned that in order to fit in with our families we had to ignore our own needs, stay silent, follow along, and give away our power. As adults this syndrome continues to rob us of our ability to ask directly for what we need and want and drives us to violate ourselves, and our own integrity. When we're in its grips, we contort ourselves to fit in, to belong, and to ensure our status as a "good person". In a moment of desperation and powerlessness, we forsake ourselves in order to avoid confrontation and the mere possibility of rejection.

This is the disease of trying to be liked, being nice,

seeking acceptance, and trying to please others as a strategy - as a way to feel safe in the world and worthy in our own skin. What is even more important to recognize is that seeking the approval of others is a way to avoid how deeply we disapprove of ourselves. The feared rejection of another is actually an outward reflection of how we have already rejected certain aspects of ourselves.

In all of the books I write and the trainings I lead, I encourage people to acknowledge the cost of their limiting beliefs and behaviors. When it comes to people pleasing, the cost is so pervasive and damaging that I want to draw special attention to it this week. The moment we try to please another and abandon our own truth for theirs, we essentially hand our power to them, violate our own integrity, cut ourselves off from our inner wisdom, and - at least for a while - disconnect from our ability to love and nurture ourselves. [I know this so well, because I've done it a million times!] We may do this with our children, spouses, employers, friends and society at large. When being a "good girl" or a "good boy" becomes a way of life, we can be sure that exhaustion will accumulate, resentments will build, desperation and neediness will increase, and we'll travel deeper into the land of victim consciousness.

Deep within our story lie our gifts–awaken!
The answer lies within!
My way is merely one way, and there are plenty of paths!

"There are only two types of player—those who keep their nerves under control and win championships and those who do not."
—Harry Vardon

There are only two types of player—those who keep their nerves under control and play golf to their full potential and those who do not.

If your nerves are completely under control, if you are playing golf to your full potential, if you are fully aligned with Source Energy, if you are allowing the flow and Well-Being to infuse you, if all your thoughts, beliefs, and confidence resonate in complete harmony with positive expectation and feeling good every single moment, if you are always in The Zone, if your intentions match your manifestations, if you accept the simultaneous moment of cause and effect (everything is happening now), and if you are always getting better, then read no further. You have mastered the mental game of golf. Congratulations! You're one of a kind.

Tiger Woods comes as close to this excellence as any human being has, yet even Tiger can do better—and he knows it. He wants to be better tomorrow than he was today. It is my intention to inspire you to reach a stage of excellence you never thought possible. Mastering the mental, emotional, and spiritual game of golf is a never-ending process with each new, enlightened experience building upon the next. While this sounds like Sisyphus sweating and struggling and pushing the rock up the hill for eternity, this is actually a joyful experience. When Sisyphus chose to push the rock up the hill the curse was broken.

Coaches Notes: When you chose to celebrate the struggle the curse will be broken. Understanding struggle is a sign of higher evolved consciousness. We struggle because we are asking for more. We struggle therefore we grow. We grow and evolve from our struggles, unless we don't. What we resist; persists. And "whatever that is" will keep on getting our attention in new ways until we move through this experience. A Master understands and welcomes everything to his gate. Be like the Master. It is as simple and as complex as that!

The journey along the fairway of life begins exactly where you are now, and as you start telling yourself a better story, reaching for better feeling thoughts, remembering your worthiness, your subconscious mind begins gravitating to that new knowledge of Well-Being. That is why the better it gets, the better it gets. Before too long you have forgotten or let go of whatever wasn't serving your best interest, and you evolve into what *is* in your best interest.

You give more "air time" to what you do want. Again – we become what we think, recreating ourselves anew in this next grandest moment of now.

I became the messenger when I chose to move from journaling about my experiences to coaching others and then deciding to put them all into this book. Step-by-step and piece-by-piece I evolved into being a coach and messenger giving humanity my unique gift.

My Story: How I Got to This Stage

Getting up at first light, teeing off as the morning haze lifts, watching the sun rise slowly over the verdant rolling hills on the horizon, practically touching Lake Michigan in the near distance reminds me of why I love this game so much. I started playing golf frequently as a youngster when every day was filled with promise and adventure, before life with its responsibilities and expectations made me think otherwise. I was a good athlete and played all the seasonal sports in Northern Michigan, such as, golf, baseball, tennis, football, basketball, volleyball, skiing, and speed skating. I especially excelled at baseball and golf and soon discovered that, of all these sports, golf was my favorite and soon I wanted to play it all the time from early spring to late fall. I was always one of the first on the course always playing around patches of snow and one of the last to leave.

My dad introduced me to the game of golf when I was nine years old and soon thereafter I became old enough to caddy. It didn't take long to develop new friends who also caddied and played the game at our club. For fifty dollars a year Dad signed me up to play limited access golf as a junior member at the Petoskey Bay-View Country Club (PBVCC). We could play just about any time that it wasn't busy, though never on Wednesday's (Stag day or Men's day) or weekend mornings unless a member invited us to join them. As is the case with most kids, summer lasted forever. Back then we all lived in the present moment, totally focused on what was happening in the here and now. If I was a tad off, I believed I would eventually find my way. Most often I eventually found something that resembled a confident golf swing. There wasn't a whole lot of worry of what might happen next, mostly eager anticipation. By the age of 10, I was breaking 50 on a regular basis. My goal was always to make par or better.

Every once in a while my dad and I would get out and play together. We played 9 holes together when I was real young, and he even let me drive the golf cart. (Heck, I remember when I was thirteen or fourteen, and he let me drive his new Audi on scenic M-119 through the tunnel of trees between Cross Village and Harbor Springs!). As I grew a tad older my dad challenged me to beat him, although he never spoke the words, I knew what he meant. Never would he intentionally lie down. He wanted to teach me to play tough and win on my own.

My Papa (grandfather Otto Marquardt) did the same when we played a board game called caroms. I really did want to beat both of them badly. Papa and I would split winning, perhaps thanks to Nana telling Papa to go easy on me. When Nana wasn't nearby Papa also enjoyed playing full out being his best. He beat me more often than I beat him. I enjoyed watching his nimble knuckles fling the lead carom and watch the other caroms ricochet intentionally in to the net.

I remember a few close competitive encounters on the course with my dad before I eventually wilted down the stretch as well. He'd give me some sort of football—or basketball—coach speech to keep me from bowing my head. He'd tell me to come back stronger next time. I hated it when I didn't play golf to the level I knew I was capable of. I hated it whenever I would choke down the stretch. I hated not pulling off the shot. I hated missing the short putt.

Finally, as a young teenager, I prevailed. It felt great to have finally beaten my dad. He always felt that I would become better than him in more ways than just on the golf course. So, what he was really doing was encouraging me. But deep inside I was living in a new world paradigm of competition with thoughts of becoming better than another.

This model for competition carried over into the way I played everything, from monopoly to poker to football in the park with my friends. Most of my rounds in my early days were with my core group of golfing friends. We did play for the fun of it but we also wanted to win. We all knew pretty much where we stood with our score and with each other coming down the stretch. We didn't need a scorecard to tell us that. It was all calculated in the back of our heads. Beat the other guy and you where the best that day. Lose and you go home shaking your head with disappointment, in which I couldn't wait to play again as soon as possible to get that bad taste out of my head. I hated losing with a passion.

My dad always told me to "bull my neck", meaning to get tough and play my best. "You are a Marquardt and Marquardt's are better than 99 percent of the players out there," he'd implore. While his words sound arrogant when you say them out loud, in hindsight I know they were just a tool, or ploy to make me be my personal best. He knew I had game and good genes and just needed a nudge to keep me on track. However at the time I took him literally so the upshot is that I grew to believe that I *was* better than others, far into adulthood. I felt the pressure to perform well at all times—both on and off the course. Competition means you beat the other guy or the other team. You win the event. You get the girl.

Parents mean well with the tools and resources they have at any given moment of time. Yet parents did not always send forth the most positive message either. My mother was always supportive; she always encouraged me to be my best. So did my dad, however I always felt an intense pressure to live up to his expectations. I felt I had to win every time out. Most of my friends were brought up the same way I was– if you performed well you were acknowledged with praise, if you faltered and played badly, you felt like a choker, like you let them down or something. As kids we were always looking for recognition from our parents and older adults. In hindsight, all I ever have to be is exactly what I am being right now.

Now while my dad did offer his encouragement, this was often circumvented through unconstructive comments whenever I wasn't on my game. I recall a moment when I was playing golf with my dad when I wasn't playing very well. I was spraying the ball all over the place. Finally, by hole #6 I hit a great drive, and my dad said, "Now that's more like my son." I'm thinking, aren't I your son no matter what? Do I have to be great to be your son? I'm not faulting my dad, but kids take these subtle messages to heart and they get lodged in their subconscious minds. As adults, if we allow this kind of self-image to run our lives we keep getting more of the same.

When I was a freshman in high school my dad moved to Texas. My parents had been divorced for about five years prior to this and it stunned me to hear him tell me he was moving away. I'll never forget it. He told me just outside the golf pro shop at PBVCC. He was standing on the pavement below and I was on a grade about four feet higher. I was in total shock; my emotions were all over the board, from extreme sadness to bewilderment wondering how I was going to carry on. I was holding back the tears. It was one of the most difficult times of my life and forever changed my relationship with my father. Because of the distance I didn't have many more of those intimate father-son talks after my dad moved. Sadly, I felt that I never really knew him that well and don't know that I ever will, in this lifetime at least. My father passed away on December 10, 2008 just prior to this book going to print. Perhaps hearing about his turn around late in life may become an inspiration to you. Don't get me wrong my dad still struggled with his demons on the golf course. He was just becoming a little bit better than he used to be.

Just this past year during one phone conversation, discussing all those old memories my dad said, "Once you did beat me, you never looked back." I think now what my dad was really saying was I was becoming my best and he was proud of that. Who doesn't want what's best for their kids? I now believe that parents really do mean well and are doing the best they can with the tools and resources they have available. Perhaps kids pick up a different message?

Is it recognition, or becoming our best that we want, or both? I think recognition is a false sense of identity and security when we depend upon it for our survival and Well-Being. What's wrong with simply seeking to be our best, and certainly appreciating the admiration from another? Like the advice Arnold Palmer was told by his father, "Don't talk about your game; let your game speak for itself."

Perhaps other parents voiced their opinions about the play of their children's golf game in a detrimental fashion, or not?

Remember the interpretation of the event lies in the eyes of the beholder. Our real work is to break free from the same old stories we tell about ourselves. Like a broken record we keep on repeating the reasons why our life is so damn miserable, unless it is not? If you allow this kind of negative thinking to filter in then it absolute will affect you. "I hated to play golf with my dad and my older brother, Dick, because I wasn't as good as him," says my friend John Oelke, who rarely plays anymore. "It was too embarrassing to be constantly harassed. It was always . . . Dick, Dick, Dick. My dad didn't have the patience for me. I was younger and Dick was the better golfer. My dad would say, 'Now don't choke like you always do.' You get tensed up because of thinking like this. You can't make a putt unless you luck out. You can hardly draw the club back. 'Now this is for a buck, don't choke.' It's a little different when your friends are doing it than your parents."

In my own little way, there is a little bit of John in me. Even though I was a good player I wanted to perform so well that sometimes I avoided golf games altogether, other times I had to cheat in order to appear better in everyone else's mind. I wanted to perform so well that I often avoided certain golf games where I might be expected to play well or when others did not know my game. If I felt too much pressure, or if I felt I wasn't ready or prepared to play well, I simply avoided playing with other golfers.

The Big Lesson

As a youngster I cheated on occasion. I played balls that were not mine. I dropped balls where I felt the ball should be. I didn't always count all my strokes. I didn't always play stroke and distance on a lost ball. This kind of behavior carried over into young adulthood and I felt so awful about what I had done, that the guilt was literally eating away at me on the inside. I tried to put it out of my mind thinking I would take it to my grave. But, like holding a beach ball underwater, the guilt was always there, and it draining my energy. I didn't know how to deal with it, so I stuffed it deep inside trying to forget about it. Eventually, it all surfaced and I dealt with my transgressions, one-at-a-time, almost thirty years later.

As a teenage golfer, I was guilty of two major transgressions, one as a seventeen-year-old, the second as a nineteen-year-old, plus I had plenty of little out of integrity moments after that that kept me playing small until I decided to change and transform my life of quiet desperation. I'm a fraud, a liar, and a cheat. I'm guilty as charged, because I say I am. These are some of the worst things I could say about myself or would I want to be written about me in the local newspaper.

Because of one of these self-betrayals, I thought I would quit golf, perhaps forever. In high school, I was the number one player on our golf team my senior year. During the conference finals, on one hole, one of the players said he had gotten one less stroke than actual, so we all looked at each other and each shaved one stroke off our scores on that hole. I got my picture in the paper the next day for shooting a 38-36 for a 74, which was good enough to be the conference medalist. I really had shot 39-36 for a 75. So the honor was tainted. Although the outcome did not affect the match or me becoming the medalist, I had deceived and betrayed myself again, a pattern that showed up in other aspects of my life well into adulthood. I still ask myself to this day, "Did I really do that?" or am I just living an illusion? God, I must have. That hurts.

Allowing me to share with you some of my less-than-stellar experiences that kept me from evolving and progressing upward is important and I do so because it leads to one of the most powerful and essential Simple Secret Reminders that you will ever hear:

Simple Secret Reminder # 3 – Play Honest Golf
The truth shall set you free!

Tell the truth.

A Paradigm Shift

Are you beginning to see how we bring our life issues with us from years past to the golf course? My intention is to bring these kinds of issues to your awareness so perhaps you too will go through some kind of awakening, healing, or transformational

xxxiii

shift in your paradigm world as I did. Yes, I was very frustrated playing lousy golf and I even cheated some to combat my perceived failures. I was absolutely miserable and viciously mad at myself. I didn't know where or who to turn to. I didn't think there was any kind of help out there for these kinds of self-sabotaging behaviors, yet alone being blinded from my own self-deception, which I wasn't even fully aware of at the time. I just wasn't ready back then. When the student is ready, the Master will appear. It is up to each of us to take the next step. Nobody can do it for us.

My new understanding decades later is that you really can't get away with anything; it (these perceived demons) will keep coming at you. There's no fooling yourself. You may as well grow up and face the music. Deal with whatever comes to your gate. For what I resist, persists. If I don't face this problem or challenge or opportunity for growth now, then it will keep on getting my attention in new ways. So, I can ante up now, face my fears and challenges head—on, learn and remember what they have been trying to show me all along—or I can stay small, hide out, and keep pretending that everything is FINE (Freaked out, Insecure, Neurotic, and Emotional).

Tell Your Story As You Want It To Be

Our story is just that—our story. And in our story lies our gift. Our old story becomes the catalyst to tell a new story – we're constantly recreating ourselves anew. Our old story is also the primary reason that has kept us stuck and repeating the same behaviors over and over again. We live the story we have been told (by our culture, by others) and we end up believing it ourselves. It is possible to go back and make peace with all the incidents, circumstances, and events and give them new meaning.

In fact, one of the greatest healing measures and feel-good stories you can do for yourself is to create a new story. If you will let your dominant intention be to understand, revise, and improve the content of the story you tell every day of your life, I guarantee your life will become an ever-improving story. As I made peace with being rock bottom, I was able to see the gift this was showing me all along. The law of attraction feeds our story (whatever we tell ourselves about ourselves) and we have a choice in how we wish to perceive it. If you think that this is just the way it is, and then act the way it is, you'll experience it this way in spite of the fact it is *not*. Give your new focus and attention upon what you prefer. Now that you know what you know you can recreate yourself anew and it is my absolute promise to you that your life will become an ever-improving story, and perhaps you'll play better golf too! Yes, the better it gets, the better it gets. The message throughout this book is about telling ourselves a new story about ourselves – one that uplifts, inspires, and empowers us to be our personal best!

What This Book Will Do for You

The intention of this book is to get you to play golf to your fullest potential more consistently with more joy and appreciation. Yet I would be remiss if I didn't demonstrate how our personal life issues and our "story" influence our life on the golf course. Two examples of players on the PGA Tour at extremes ends of the spectrum come to mind.

It's well documented that Brad Faxon went through a most difficult divorce years ago. Faxon said it was a challenge for him to concentrate on his golf because of all the emotional issues and the new challenges that were now tied to him like a ball and chain. His game suffered because of it. In his mind he believed the distractions and emotional turmoil was just too great to deal with. Everyone who experiences these kinds of emotional roller coaster rides will deal with them in their own way, in their own time. What helped pave the way forward for me is a book by Debbie Ford called *Spiritual Divorce*. Ford gives us our gift and the tools to heal, forgive, and transform our lives.

Paul Casey from England became the world's #3 golfer in May of 2009. He attributes his recent success by feeling good and peaceful on the inside as a result of a happy marriage. His game rose to new heights. They say behind every successful person lies a wonderful and supportive soul mate. The message: it's absolutely essential to make peace with your internal world in order to play your best golf.

It is paramount to be at peace with our selves no matter what else is going on "out there." It's all a blessing in you becoming you… and *you* were born to win. This really is a book about winning, which is about feeling good, feeling joy, living the life of your dreams – creating a champions self-image that keeps growing even in the face of adversity, setbacks, challenges or extreme disappointments. It's what all great champions have attributed to their success. It's about keeping on…and it all starts with a dream.

Golf is a game but it is also a reflection of life. Golf is a microcosm of life. It's why they say you can learn an awful lot about a person after playing a round of golf with them. After reading this book I hope to give you a deeper understanding of this relationship. Everyone's story is different. My experiences may mirror yours or be completely different—but the end result, as far as golf goes, is the same for everybody – becoming our personal best, playing to our full potential, giving our maximum effort with joy, fun, and with a great attitude, a winner's demeanor, creating a champions self-image.

Ultimately, it is my goal to coach you through your own process. You are entering the process right where you are right now. I invite you to hop on the ever-evolving upward spiral to play better golf with more outrageous joy simply by following your bliss. We'll talk about the inner game of golf, your dreams, desire, and intentions, your commitment and trust, what it takes to be in The Zone, and I'll give you The Simple Secrets that will unleash the power within. I'll show you and coach you how to think, talk, play, and carry yourself like a champion. I'll show you how to build self-esteem and confidence and a belief in yourself and what you want. We'll explore what it means to be in the present moment, awaken to our magnificence, and how to be a champion and play great golf by creating a mental winner's image of your self. This is exciting stuff we're about to explore.

For now, I invite you to reflect upon your own personal life as it relates to your life on the golf course. I invite you to allow that next piece of wisdom come into *your* awareness. What I found is that the process to becoming a better you, a better golfer is really nothing more than a piece-by-piece process, one in which you enter at your own pace by just taking the next logical step down the fairway of life.

In the end I will remind again about your process more in line with a step-by-step program to keep you clear about what you really do want. This book will give you the tools to make those necessary changes one by one. There is no exact science or set way we each go about our own business; I just provide some tools and resources, some techniques and strategies, mental mindsets and new beliefs that have worked for me. Tools that have been passed down through the ages; tools that work for the greats like Jack Nicklaus, Tiger Woods, and Lorena Ochoa.

Follow this fascinating journey and you'll see how easy it can be when you remember to go with the flow and become one of those who awaken and become mindfully aware in this world. Your life will certainly never be the same. Always remember golf and life are supposed to be fun. Embrace the highs and lows along the fairway of life. Make peace with your past and forgive all you have trespassed against, and for all who have trespassed against us – no small step, but *absolutely essential* to living a joyful and peaceful life from here on out, otherwise the toxicity within will literally wreak havoc on our lives.

Life begins at both ends of our comfort zone: 1) Past – forgiveness and making peace with the people and those things that have challenged us in the past, our hurts and sorrows, our pain and suffering, 2) Now – courageously stepping more fully into our light, listening to the language of our soul, working through our own personal life issues in becoming who we really are. *The Fairway of Life* is another opportunity to gravitate towards living the life of your dreams, both on and off the golf course.

I invite you in kindness and respect to give service to all whose paths you cross and to give gratitude for all you've been given. Be grateful. Be both humble and hungry for more of the good stuff that life offers in never ending abundance.

Golf & Life is supposed to be fun…awaken, align, and connect with Life Force Energy (pure positive energy, otherwise known as

The Zone); reach for your best feeling thought you can; allow the Well-Being in; focus on what you want; dream; visualize; trust; Let go and let God; get out of your own way and simply…go with the flow ~

Be as you wish to seem,
"Coach"
Rand S. Marquardt, MA
Life & Mental Golf Performance Coach
coach@golfissuppposedtobefun.com
http://golfissupposedtobefun.com/
http://www.randmarquardt.com/
Inspiring Excellence Within!

Part I – The Inner Game of Golf ... and Life

Chapter 1

Awaken to Your Magnificence

"A Person asked Buddha, 'Are you a God?'
Buddha's reply 'No.'
'Are you an Angel?'
'No.'
'Then what are you?'
'I am Awake.'"

—Anonymous

Wake up!
You are either connected or disconnected with
the flow of life
You are either allowing or resisting the Well-Being

Awaken to your magnificence and embrace the wholeness of who you really are. Life & golf take on a whole new meaning and understanding once we surrender and connect with our authentic Self. Life & golf take on a whole new meaning once we accept ourselves exactly where we are while moving to what we prefer. Life & golf take on a whole new meaning once we shift from resisting to allowing the Well-Being in.

Life & golf are supposed to be fun, yet for many it is not. Most are never satisfied and would rather paddle really, really hard against the current. Many just never seem to get any better and resign themselves to lives of mediocrity. Few will appreciate and enjoy the journey down the fairway of life embracing both the highs and the lows. The paradox *is* embracing and celebrating the struggle, which leads to growth, which is usually messy all the while reaching for what you desire by going with the flow. It's about being with both of these. It's about being able to *be with* all of these life principles in the same breath: outrageous joy, being happy now, embracing the unacceptable, wanting to be better, having no clue, being disappointed, making it happen versus letting it happen, laughing at your obstacles or "bad breaks," taking the punch in the gut and still feeling good, etc.... all at once. This is the mindset I am inviting you to explore.

Most of us are raised with the idea that hard work and struggle is the key to a successful life. I'm certainly not going to deny that basic premise. However, when *we chose* to become that which we desire life takes on a whole new meaning. When *we chose* to enjoy playing golf, our game takes on a whole new meaning. All it takes is but a simple shift in focus and perspective.

In our society we teach that life is hard work, and the reward for that toil is a big prize. "To the victor go the spoils," is a common quote used to remind us that whoever fights the hardest will win the prize. Is hard work and struggle the cornerstone of what it takes to be successful on the golf course? Or is there a better, less arduous way? What about enjoying the journey, having fun, and going with the flow? Oh, that's too easy you say. Oh, I've seen those who go with the flow. While they appear to be thriving, you just wait they'll get theirs. Hmmm...it's working and they're thriving...and it's not working and you're frustrated...what's wrong with this picture?

Coaches Notes: We become so culturally conditioned and oriented to believe that hard work and struggle is the key to success. We think we must pay a price in order to get somewhere in life, and in this process we've come to believe that getting there is really important, therefore, it must be our purpose. However, if we're not getting to joy in this journey, then we've gotten nowhere. Joy in the journey with your golf is really where you are going. We did not come forth into this physical existence to struggle into joy...it's not possible. They're not on the same channel, the same wavelength, or the same frequency.

Struggle and joy cannot co-exist in the same space. Relax and find some relief. You joy your way to joy. You laugh your way to success. It is through joy that good things come, in life and on the course. Switch around your thinking. Literally and figuratively turn it upside down and let joy, fun, and laughter rise to the top. Let joy be your new measure of success…and then, watch your golf game soar and your demeanor improve. Hmmm…just another way to begin telling our selves a new more empowering story about our lives ☺. Yes, some golf professionals and amateurs are even putting smiley faces on their golf balls to remind them that golf is supposed to be fun!

Our old belief system extolling the virtues of hard work and struggle has been passed on from generation to generation and infiltrates all aspects of life in our society, from education to business, including leisure-time pursuits like golf. In the past I would beat golf balls until I was practically bloody thinking this is the only way to get better. At least half the time on the range I found myself getting extremely frustrated. I gripped the club so tight, and hit ball after ball that blisters formed and my only option was to wrap my fingers with athletic tape so I could swing some more. I was stubborn, willful, and refused to acknowledge that this way was not working for me. I must have been insane practicing the same things over and over again hoping for different results. I was bound and determined to grind it out. I would hit until I could barely stand, constantly wiping the sweat from my brow and hands. There were so many times that I literally had to lie down on the ground and close my eyes, just to find some kind of internal peace before I could hit again.

Chasing this elusive "pot of gold", struggling and still not succeeding left me angry and frustrated, year after pathetic year. Sure I found a bone now and then, but are golf and life supposed to be this much struggle and hard work? Are we supposed to be so "stressed out" playing this wonderful game even if it's a small part of our experience? The answer to both of these questions is a resounding, "NO!" Life is supposed to be fun and so is golf. Our lives, and our golf games, should fill us with outrageous joy. All it takes is but a simple shift in focus.

The moment I understood that struggle was for my own growth, everything changed. The moment I chose to practice with intent everything changed. The moment that I understood that life was supposed to be fun everything changed. I felt liberated once I embraced the perception of struggle and accepted life just exactly as it is keeping my sights upon what I now prefer. The moment I surrendered and really connected to my God Source and life within is the moment I started to really live again. I felt free, like a weight being lifted off my shoulders. The moment I could "be with" my fears and emotional demons is the moment everything changed. The moment I embraced life as it really is, without any false pretenses or self-deception, rather than how I thought it was *supposed to be* is the moment my golf game got better. And once I "got" this I began to tell myself a new story. I began to find relief, I dropped my paddle and pointed myself downstream towards a better feeling, and more enlightened space – where all the good stuff lies ahead.

Coaches Notes: The real trick is to embrace the concept of struggle while finding joy in our journey…you become aware they exist and both become part of your consciousness, yet on a deeper metaphysical level they no longer offer dueling points of interference.

Instead of beating balls insanely to a pulp, I began practicing with a new mindset. I started to slow down and breathe again. I dropped the paddle and found relief. I started to be more present, more open, and I embraced whatever did come to my gate. I loosened up and started to have more fun again. I started to ask the universe for guidance. I started to practice allowing the Well-Being in, versus struggling so hard to meet the demands. Immediately I began working on what we normally call my "weaknesses," paying attention to my thoughts, words, feelings, and actions. Soon I realized that weaknesses were simply areas in my golf game that I could improve upon. I was awakened to a new way, a more harmonious way to show up in life and on the golf course. I began observing myself and noticing what served my best interest and what did not. I began my journey of getting back into alignment with whom I really am. And once I surrendered into my authentic Self everything changed. I evolved into my natural state of higher consciousness within. Mahatma Gandhi had it and Jesus taught it.

We change our golf game by awakening to who we really are. The moment we stop the madness of opposing ourselves, and each other, is the moment we change our inner world by creating a better outer world for all those around us. It is the connection to Source Energy that is sought after by all. Esther Hicks, co-author of many books including *Ask and it is Given* describes this connection:

> "There are endless paths that lead to Source. And it is the connection to Source that is ultimately sought after by all. Everyone wants to believe that they have found the path. And, oh, it is glorious when you find that which you believe is your path. That is alignment with Source Energy. But when you say, "I have found my path, and you over there on that other path, you're not on the path," in that moment of judgment, you're not on your path either. Compliment them on their choices. Never push against their path. Never put them in a position where they must defend their path by condemning yours. Instead, appreciate their path. Appreciate it as their method of connecting with Source Energy. And we promise you, there is not one method better than the other."

When you awaken to who you really are and go with the current of life, everything else will fall into place—including your golf game. You already know this—I am just reminding you. All the other concepts and life principles are simply parts of the whole. One concept builds upon the other. That's growth and evolution.

In order to go with the flow and play golf to your full potential you must first awaken to your own brilliance and magnificence.

Here are the steps that will guide you on your path to golf enlightenment:

1) **Awaken to your magnificent, authentic Self.** Align and connect with your higher Self. Listen and feel your mind, body, and spirit being in the flow of the abundant stream of life energy. Observe yourself and practice non-attachment. It's all about the connection with life and Source energy. Awaken to your own magnificence, play inspired golf with outrageous joy!
2) **Live your dream; set an intention; follow your bliss.** We come forth to experience the splendor and grandeur that life has to offer. We are creators and our dreams give life purpose and meaning. Visualization is part of this imagination process. Follow your bliss, play inspired golf with outrageous joy!
3) **Become what you think.** The secret is the Law of Attraction. That which is likened unto itself is drawn. What we give our thoughts and attention to we become. What we give our thoughts to ... we give our energy to ... what we give our energy to ... we create. We create by our asking, receiving, and allowing the Well-Being in. Attract good feeling thoughts, play inspired golf with outrageous joy!
4) **Accept, trust, and embrace life.** Everything that comes to our gate is all a perfect plan evolving the agenda and growth of our soul. Our lives are divinely designed. See the gift, play inspired golf with outrageous joy!
5) **Let joy be your measure of success.** Allow the standard of our success to be the achievement of our joy, and everything else will effortlessly fall into place. Be joyful, play inspired golf with outrageous joy!
6) **Go with The Flow.** The Zone is The Flow. All the aspects and ingredients that are found in The Zone are all part of

the abundant flow of Well-Being. Go with the flow, play inspired golf with outrageous joy.

7) **Serve others, show up big, and remember love is all there ever is.** The greatest of these is love. Love is all there is. Love and believe in yourself by creating a champion's and winner's image. When you love yourself, you are able to love another. With love, appreciation and gratitude, play inspired golf with outrageous joy!

Awakening to your own brilliance and magnificence means embracing your dark and stepping fully into your light. And it is our light, our brilliance, and our magnificence that we fear the most. This famous quote through Marianne Williamson, spiritual leader paints a powerful picture in the game of life.

> *"Our deepest fear is not that we are inadequate. Our deepest fear is that we are powerful beyond measure. It is our light, not our darkness that most frightens us. We ask ourselves, who am I to be brilliant, gorgeous, talented, fabulous? Actually, who are you not to be? You are a child of God. Your playing small does not serve the world. There is nothing enlightened about shrinking so that other people won't feel secure around you. We are all meant to shine, as children do, we were born to make manifest the glory of God that is within us. It's just not in some of us; it's in everyone. And as we let our own light shine, we unconsciously give other people the permission to do the same. As we are liberated from our own fear, our presence automatically liberates others."*
> —Marianne Williamson

> **Simple Secret Reminder # 4 – Awaken To Your Magnificence**
> **Learn to love, honor, and cherish yourself.**
> **Let your own light shine.**

If you think but for a moment that it is selfish to love yourself, then I invite you to reflect upon this quote spoken by Esther Hicks through Abraham, "If we were standing in your physical shoes, that would be our dominant quest: entertaining Yourself, pleasing Yourself, connecting with Yourself, being Yourself, enjoying Yourself, loving Yourself. Some say, 'Well, Abraham you teach selfishness.' "And we say, yes we do, yes we do, yes we do, because unless you are selfish enough to reach for that connection, you don't have anything to give anyone, anyway. And when you are selfish enough to make that connection – you have an enormous gift that you give everywhere you are."

Therefore, let your own light shine and be true to yourself. It was the great Shakespeare who coined the phrase, "To thine own self be true." Be true to the brilliant and magnificent person you are born to be. Remember, life and golf are supposed to be fun. Embrace the highs and the lows along your journey. Be grateful and show up big wherever you go. Give service to others with your unique gift along the fairway of life. Be true to yourself and keep dreaming your dream as if it is so. And so shall it be.

Action steps:
1) **Awaken to your magnificence.**
2) **Wake up and allow the Well-Being in.**
3) **Go with the flow.**
4) **Let your own light shine.**
5) **Allow your self to feel the connection with life.**
6) **Play inspired golf with outrageous joy!**

Chapter 2
Dreams

"If you can imagine it, you can achieve it. If you can dream it, you can become it."
—William Arthur Ward

**Are you living the life of your dreams or...
Have you abandoned your dreams?
Are your dreams dying of neglect?
Perhaps it is time to revisit your dreams?**

Dreams evolve and unfold based on our will to either allow or repress them. Like water in a river they can either flow freely or slow down and pool up when rocks, boulders, fallen trees, or man-made obstacles block the way. Dreams are implanted into our brain, our psyche, and into the very fabric of our soul. The dreamer is at first thrilled—it feels good to dream. Soon the dreamer is terrified—worry, doubt, and fear appear. If he or she takes no action, terrifying thoughts turn into flesh-eating monsters. The dreamer considers the dream is unrealistic and too far out there. The dream withers back into the soil from which is sprang.

If the dreamer takes action terrifying thoughts turn into paper tigers. The universe conspires, providence moves, confidence soars, miracles unfold, and the dreamer begins to move and gravitate in that direction. Either way nothing remains the same. The ball is in your court: you can be, do, or have whatever you want. And if you don't know it, or don't believe it, then that's the problem.

All human creativity begins with a thought, imagination, a dream, and with a willingness to consider the possibility that something heretofore unimagined might actually come into being. Let go of limited beliefs and limiting assumptions and an infinite universe will instantly manifest and conspire with your desires – right before your very eyes.

It all starts with a thought, a dream. In order to become your very best as a golfer and as a human being you start with a dream. A dream gives us purpose, direction and a reason to wake up in the morning feeling eager, excited, and ready to take on the world. Dreams are the very essence of thought energy that stirs our soul and makes us each unique in our asking. When enhanced with the essential ingredients of desire, commitment, and trust, dreams enable us to be champions and winners both on and off the golf course. We feel joy about who we are and what we are becoming. Champions and winners persist in pursuing the life they've strived to achieve even as their dreams change. Your dream for your life when you were a child or young adult might change. Dreams evolve as we evolve. What is important is that you have a dream. What are your dreams? Are you living the life of your dreams?

> *"You never know what dream can become reality - unless you commit to it."*
> —Cary Adgate, Olympian Skier

Are dreams real? The truth is, dreams are simply dreams and they are what they are. If others think your dreams are foolish, are they right? Should you abandon them? No, it doesn't matter what others think. Your dreams are totally yours and all that matters is that your dreams have meaning to you. It's about living your dream, enjoying the journey, and holding to that vision. Our dreams are about something new, something better about ourselves. They are about standing up for our selves saying, "This is my life and this is my intention, this is what I'm going to do." Not only do we have the power to dream, we also have the power to express and live our dreams. But we must know exactly what we envision in our dreams, and what we want in order to fulfill our destiny.

I know what you are saying to yourself right now: I have a dream, but I also have responsibilities—a job, a mortgage, a pile of bills. I agree. If life were simple we would all realize our dreams with little effort. Instead life throws us many challenges, obstacles,

The Fairway of Life

and what feels like tests, often at unexpected or inopportune times. Unless we are a Master who is unfazed, these challenges can terrify us, make us lose sleep at night, make us want to run or retreat. But if we reconfigure our thoughts, we can instead view them for their true meaning: a golden opportunity for growth and evolution.

In this context the freedom to dream is being accountable and responsible to our selves. It's why we are here. Holding that vision keeps us on track through the numerous and varied obstacles, challenges, and adversity that all great champions have overcome:

- Ben Hogan was in a near fatal car crash in 1949. Not only did he recover, sixteen months later he became the 1950 U.S. Open Champion at Merion Golf Club after an 18-hole playoff over Lloyd Mangrum and George Fazio.
- Lee Trevino was still an unknown in 1968 when he won the U.S. Open by 4 strokes over defending champion Jack Nicklaus at Oak Hill, shooting all four rounds in the 60's.
- Two months after arthroscopic knee surgery, Tiger Woods suffered through excruciating pain during the 2008 U.S. Open at Torrey Pines. His leg buckled mid-swing, his face twisted in pain and he groaned audibly. After forcing a 19-hole playoff, Tiger prevailed over good-guy Rocco Mediate who said, "He's so hard to beat. He's unreal." All it takes is a simple shift in focus and perspective.

Dreaming doesn't restrict us or make us shirk our responsibilities. Instead it gives us the freedom to be authentic to our higher Self, while treating others with kindness and respect each step along the way. To allow your life to unfold naturally you must keep asking yourself these three questions in this order:

1) Who am I? Keep answering this question. *Hint – you are more than your name, body, and title. I embrace the wholeness of who I am while aligning with my authentic Self.

2) Where am I going? These are your dreams, desires, goals, and intentions.
3) With whom? Now who's coming with you on this incredible journey?

While everyone can dream, the act of pursuing our dreams is what separates the achievers from the pipe dreamers: those who say they have a dream about their life, but then engage in self-sabotage. These people often unknowingly practice the same self-destructive behaviors over and over again, effectively preventing themselves from ever realizing their dream, goal, or intention. Through the years their subconscious mind gets filled with these self-limiting beliefs, and like an airplane on automatic pilot their behaviors become fulfilled exactly as planned. Yes, we fall into our own safe, little comfort zone, unless we don't. So how do you get there, how do you realize your dreams and release that inner champion?

I am here to show you that you are able to be, do, or have whatever your heart desires. You are God's special creation and you are meant to win. So, let's get back in the game of life even more than ever before.

Our work is to enhance a new and more powerful self-image of ourselves while shrinking old self-defeating and limiting beliefs that eventually fade away. Before long a new more positive self-image of ourselves gets burned into our subconscious mind and takes root. Our old limited self-image becomes a distant memory all the while we reap the benefits of playing better golf and becoming a better human being.

What are your dreams? The first place to begin is to have one. Otherwise, just hearing about other feel good stories will only be that. Yes, you too must dream, and dream big. It takes passion to dream big, and courage to take action.

Living the Dream

Let's take a look at a few case examples of those who have a dream and are choosing to live it.

Lorena Ochoa, twenty-seven, grew up next door to the

Guadalajara Country Club in Mexico and took up golf at the age of five. She is the first Mexican golfer of any gender to be ranked the #1 player in the world—ala Tiger Woods in the PGA—of the Ladies Professional Golf Association (LPGA) Tour and being named the Associated Press (AP) 2007 Female Athlete of the Year.

Lorena grew up in Guadalajara, Mexico, without a role model in her country, but she had a dream. At age twelve, she admits that she didn't exactly look like anything that would resemble a world-class golfer. So, it was quite surprising when she told her coach that she wanted to be number one in the world. "At that time, with the way I was playing, and being in Guadalajara, it was a little bit crazy to think that way," Ochoa said toward the end of a historic season. "But I did it. It took me a long time, but I did it."

It took Lorena five years of playing golf on the LPGA Tour to establish her reign and replace Annika Sorenstam as the world's top female player. Maybe it wasn't such a crazy dream after all. "My main goal is to maintain myself as the number one. Therefore, I can promise to keep improving," said Lorena. Her commitment to stay number one is in her relentless practice routine. While I can only imagine her mental toughness, take a look at her winter workout schedule for 2007.

1) 7:00 – 10:00 AM: Short game 100 yards in
2) 11:00 – 1:00 PM: Putting
3) 2:00 – 5:00 PM: Long game afternoon
4) 5:30 – 7:30 PM: Meditation, yoga, and a gym workout

It is quite amazing, isn't it, when we follow our dreams, and speak our intentions out loud. We tend to get after it!

Pete Green, sixty-eight, a former four-time Michigan Amateur Champ in four decades (1969, '79, '86, '96), also had aspirations as a young golfer, inspired by attending PGA Tour events with his dad and watching the best players in the world.

Back in the 50's and early 60's professional golf had not quite yet become a big spectator sport until Arnold Palmer vaulted golf into our living rooms. "You couldn't watch golf on television in those days, so I watched the best players in person while attending several PGA Tour events including the 1953 PGA at Birmingham Country Club. Walter Burkemo won this event beating my idol Ben Hogan. I got a chance to watch Hogan's swing several times at events and on the practice tee. It's incredible to watch him practice," said Green, who continues to run his family construction business. "I thought that perhaps being a Country Club Golf Professional would be a great job; instead I opted to stay in the family business and become a top-notch amateur. Back then amateur golf was pretty big and many amateurs could compete with the professionals. Charlie Coe, Ken Venturi, and Frank Stranahan could all play with the professionals. Eventually, Stranahan turned pro and won an event." Venturi went on to win fourteen career PGA Tour events. Pete Green fulfilled his aspirations and dreams and will forever be recognized as one of the greatest champions Michigan amateur golf has ever seen.

Pete recalls the times when he would show up at the amateur events with Jack Nicklaus in the field and notice how Jack's dad spoke with Jack like Earl Woods did with Tiger. Pete enjoyed playing in Amateur and U.S. Open qualifiers and also with the likes of Ben Crenshaw, Julius Boros, and Sam Snead. When you're that good, you're that good.

Golf is a family affair for the Greens. Pete's daughter Suzy Green-Roebuck, an Ohio State University letter winner in golf (1986-89), ended up playing about eight years as a professional golfer on both the Futures Tour, winning four times, and latter competing on the LPGA Tour. Ochoa also played on the Futures Tour in 2002 winning three events out of ten topping the money list and an opportunity to play on the LPGA Tour. Pete's son, Mike plays to a 1-handicap and his children appear destined for greatness in golf as well.

When I asked Pete about how a champion thinks, he went on a roll and I sought out my best to keep up. "The biggest thing you can do is know your own game and have confidence in that and be able to repeat it. A lot of guys in my day did not have classic swings but they knew how to manage their game. Anybody can beat anybody on any given day. I had confidence in my short game because I practiced it a lot. I can hit all the shots around the green. I even played some with Dave Pelz (the short game guru) and I would say that I was pretty good. I had plenty of confidence to play all the shots around the greens. Champions like Tiger are efficient around the greens and often make the 5-6 footers. They hit the ball in the easiest spot to make them below the hole."

When I asked Pete about what is most challenging for him in the game of golf a couple things surfaced. "Winning is the hardest part of all. In match play your biggest opponent is yourself. Very often the other guy loses the match. Most of the time I felt I didn't really win; he lost it. All I had to do is control my self. In medal play it's like the song that Kenny Rogers sings: you've got to know when to hold them... Sometimes making a par or bogey is a good score versus ending up making triple. You play the kind of shots you can play."

When I asked Pete, "What about when it all comes down to a big putt? What are you thinking?" I proceed to tell him the story about how Mark O'Meara talks about his 4-foot putt on the 72nd hole at The Open Championship in 1998 after his first putt de-cel, and how Mark recalled his frame of mind thinking even if he misses he's not going to die. O'Meara made the putt and eventually went on to win The Open Championship over Brian Watts by two shots in a four-hole playoff. Pete recalls, "I remember that, it's huge, at least it's huge for the player, whether it's playing for the Club Championship, Michigan Amateur, Open Championship, or U.S. Open. You hope for success and to hit a solid putt. Sometimes I think, 'What is the worse thing that will happen (similar to O'Meara)?' My wife will kiss me and welcome me home. You've got to keep riding the rainbow instead of looking at the pot of gold. Just hit a solid putt. Once you hit it, it's up to God (but not really); it's going to be what it is. I tell myself, 'I'm not going to hit a lousy putt; I'm going to hit a solid putt.' And you know what? I've made my fair share of them." At sixty-seven years young, currently a 1-handicap, he's still pretty solid.

South African Trevor Immelman, twenty-nine, won The Masters in 2008. Trevor was the youngest of three children and by age five his "prodigy-like talents" became recognized by his parents and three-time Masters champion Gary Player. Before he even turned ten Trevor had a dream to one day play professional golf and be the best in the world. His parents sacrificed in order to get him to where he is. They knew he had special talents and now his dream came true. On this week in golf Trevor Immelman is the best golfer in the world!

Joey Garber, seventeen, from Petoskey, Michigan, has a dream to become one of the best professional golfers in the world, too. At age seven his won his first junior golf tournament. At age nine he won his first "major" junior golf tournament, The Meijer Junior Tour, at Michigan State University, Akers West Course, in East Lansing, Michigan. Joey shot a 78 and was even par through 13 holes. The heat index that day rose to 115 degrees and he literally collapsed climbing hole #18 carrying his own bag. Fortunately Joey's mother, Trish, was allowed by a course official to help him up. Remarkably, Joey went on to win by six shots.

Since his first victories in tournament golf, Joey has already put together quite a resume, shooting a 66 as a freshman in high school in the Michigan State Finals Golf Tournament. He qualified for the 2007 Michigan Open shooting 71 as a fifteen-year-old. He made the cut with rounds of 75, 69. He finished tied for 48th place. He currently ranks in the top 35 in the United States in his high school graduating class of 2010. In July 2008 Joey won the Michigan Junior Amateur with scores of 73-70-67=210 at Forest Akers West Course. He tied for 4th at the Coca-Cola Junior Championship in July 2008 at Boyne Highlands conducted by the American Junior Golf Association (AJGA) at Boyne Highlands Resorts with rounds of 73-72-69=214. Yet another amazing feat he can add to his resume is not only winning the Club Championship at his home course PBVCC, he also took medalist honors in the Golf Association of Michigan (GAM) Club Champions Great Lakes Regional at Indianwood Golf & Country Club in September 2008 shooting a 69.

Joey had dreams of playing professional golf as an eleven-year-old, but this really solidified when he turned thirteen. He just

The Fairway of Life

wasn't as passionate with all his other sports, skiing, soccer, and basketball, as he is with golf. Here are Joey's three major goals.

1) Play Division 1 golf for a major university that understands his ultimate intention to play professional golf.
2) Make the PGA Tour.
3) Be one of the best professional golfers in the world.

My suggestion to Joey is to keep holding his vision and to keep dreaming his dream. Joey is willing to endure many setbacks along the way. His dream is his guiding light. I invite Joey to feel what it is like to talk like a champion. To really feel what it is like to walk like a champion. To really feel what it is like to play and carry himself like a champion. My suggestion to Joey is also the same for you: act as if this is what you are right now and you become that. You gravitate toward becoming that. The universe has an amazing way of aligning with our thoughts, feelings, beliefs, intentions and intuition.

Tiger Woods, world's #1 professional golfer and an advocate for allowing kids to live the life of their dreams share's his story as well. It all starts with a dream and good family values to follow that dream. Tiger shares his dreams and visions to millions who watch him and attend his clinics and foundation activities inspiring us all to live healthier and happier lives. "From early childhood, I dreamed of being the world's best golfer. I worked hard and applied my family's values to everything I did. Integrity, honesty, discipline, responsibility, and fun: I learned these values at home and in school, each one pushing me further toward my dream…"

Tiger Woods

Notice how he applied his family values to *everything* he did, including his golf game! Tiger dreamed of being the world's best golfer. And he is. Enough said. Like Arnold Palmer, Tiger lets his golf do the talkin.' Sure helps to follow a practice routine like this on his days off from tournament golf.

1) 6:00 AM: Lifts Weights
2) 7:30 AM: Breakfast
3) 9:00 AM: Hits balls
4) 11:00 AM: Putting
5) 11:30 AM: Plays 9 holes
6) 12:30 AM: Lunch
7) 1:00 PM: Hits balls
8) 3:00 PM: Short game
9) 5:00 PM: Hits balls
10) 5:30 PM: Putting

Now I realize most of the readers here are everyday amateurs, just like I am, and have a life outside of golf. However, I do believe when you do see the discipline behind the scenes, then perhaps you too can find some more discipline in your life if you say you really want to become better. To say you don't have the time; means you don't really want to do it.

Another clever way to envision living the life of your dreams is how Nick Faldo, a past three-time Masters champion ('89, '90, '96) described it during a Friday broadcast of The 2008 Masters. Veteran sport broadcaster Jim Nantz and Faldo where talking about the dream that Fred Couples and Nantz shared with each other regarding The Masters back in the good old college days. Jim would tell Freddie how someday he would win The Masters, and Fred would tell Jim how someday he would announce The Masters, seeing him win. Faldo said, "Living your dream is like painting the picture and gravitating toward your goal." That's exactly what it is like! You paint the picture and you keep holding the vision, involving your senses, feelings, intuition, and sense of direction as the universe aligns with your asking and *you* gravitate toward that.

During the CBS broadcast of the 2009 Masters Nick Faldo offered even more wisdom and insight into his psyche and what

he believes it takes to become a champion in being one's best. He says, "You really got to believe you will make everything. Today I will hole everything. What it takes is to be totally in the moment." In order to pull off the shots you will need:
- Inner Courage
- Inner Knowing
- Inner Self-Belief
- Creative Visualization
- A Wonderfully Def Touch
- And from high above the Georgia pines the golfing gods on your side...

Faldo talks about meditating and "...how the new guys on tour look at him and say, what's that?" He talks about how he used to meditate twice a day, which allowed him to become more present, more peaceful, and helped to set the tone and clear intention for his day and his round.

Visualizing Like Dreaming is How To Play the Game

Visualizing upon your desires and taking action is one of the quickest ways to get you from where you are to where you want to be. Every golf shot is like having a mini dream. Every round of golf is like having a mini dream. You visualize and dream about your round before you play. You play it over mentally in your head. On the course you visualize each shot and you commit to your club and shot of choice. You see your target, you know what you want, and you visualize your shot. In order to calm yourself you go through a consistent repetitive practice routine to quiet and steady your mind, you commit, you get out of your own way, and you allow it to happen.

Coaches Notes: You trust your vision, your feel, your wisdom... and you simply allow your body to hit toward the target you have visualized. It's a feeling of letting go and trusting it versus trying to control and steer it. Great teachers like Jim Flick embrace this concept and that is how he likes to play as well. Sure he teaches sound fundamentals, yet when it's time to play you've got to let it happen versus trying so hard to make it happen. Remember: the shot produces the swing.

No one understands and implements these principles better than Tiger Woods. He's been practicing these understandings since he was a little tike and he keeps getting better. Tiger Woods' dad, the late Earl Woods, would tell then-youngster Tiger to putt to the picture. Trying to describe depth and distance to a child in adult language was a formidable task. Now watch him putt to the picture. His mission is to give it his best stroke, his best effort, head down, present moment, never attached to the outcome. And like Tiger, putting to a picture, I believe the shot or putt produces the swing, not the other way around. Perspective is everything.

Not to get off track, but when talking about Tiger anything goes. I would also imagine Tiger's mother, Kultilda, inspired her son by the clarity of her example as well. Her roots are grounded in Buddhism and deep spirituality. According to *Role Models on the Web* website, "Tiger says that his religion (spirituality) has given him self-awareness. He says his religion has taught him that he is here to work on flaws in his personality. The two things he has worked on most have been stubbornness and impatience—he used to want things to be perfect right away. Now he understands that he has to work on things in his life and that this takes time and discipline."

We each can live our dream to the very best of our individual effort and God-given talent as well: one moment, one shot, one vision that in the end becomes one round. Yes, each shot is like a mini dream and our big dream is taking us to where it is we desire to go next—to lower our handicap, to lower our comfort zone, to have a better demeanor, to have more fun, to play better golf, to play on the PGA or Senior Tour, to win The Masters, a Major, Member-Guest, or win your flight in the local Club Championship. We continue to have new desires even after that . . . never getting it all done because there will always be more. Our mission is to dream and enjoy each moment along the fairway of life. All it takes is simple shift in perspective.

The Fairway of Life

> **Simple Secret Reminder # 5 – Shift Your Perspective**
> **Give your attention to what inspires and uplifts you.**
> **Turn into the direction of your dreams and heart's desire.**

I am going to invite you to keep holding the vision of your dreams and involve all your senses and your feelings. Listed below are five helpful reminders to get you back on your path of living the life of your dreams:

1) Practice what it feels like when you are imagining and realizing your goals and dreams everyday for fifteen to twenty minutes. Involve all your senses and intuition. Imagine yourself being that. Imagine what it feels like and continue to hold that vision every day. For example Joey Garber practices feeling his feelings of what it feels like playing golf on the PGA Tour. If this is your dream, involve all your senses. Smell what it is like—the grass, spectators, crisp air. Taste what it is like— an apple, banana or snack during your round, a toast of champagne, or an Arnold Palmer drink after the tournament. Hear what it is like—clean golf shots, flag blowing, raging roars. See what it is like—supporting fans, excellent golf shots, fairways and greens, putts rolling in. Feel what it is like—love, appreciation, gratitude, humility, family.
2) Create a vision board. Cut out pictures of your ideal dream about what you want in your life. There's Tiger Woods, Lorena Ochoa, Jim Furyk, and Retief Goosen all on your vision board reminding you about mental qualities that also lie within you—focus, passion, perseverance, knowledge, trust, personal style, confidence.
3) Trust your instincts and intuition. Follow your bliss.
4) Be the person of your dreams. See your golf game unfolding and life through their eyes.
5) Act as if it is already done, as if it is already so. Here's

the real kicker: your dreams and what you want has no bearing on whether or not you will get it...none, nada, zilch, zippo. It's really a question of whether or not you can behave as if you already have it. Feel that shift and live your life as if it is already done.

Really feel those wonderful feelings as you dream, as you visualize, as you ask. Tune in and involve all your senses. Act and carry yourself like a champion, as if it is already so. Paint the picture. You are that! Within no time at all you'll be strutting down the fairway like Loren Roberts, Ernie Els, Tiger Woods, Lorena Ochoa, or Natalie Gulbis.

> **Simple Secret Reminder # 6 - Dream About What You Really Want**
> Involve all your senses.
> Feel your feelings.
> **Act as if it is already done. Paint the picture. You are that!**

As you go through this process you will, slowly but surely, become transformed and absolutely amazed by the fulfillment of what you really want. Repeat this process over and over and really focus on what you want—only on what you want, both on and off the golf course. Examples: You're teeing off...what do you want? You're hitting an approach...what do you want? You're putting from twenty feet...what do you want? Imagine performing the shot where you want it to go before you hit it. Imagine sinking the putt before you hit it. Keep holding the vision and begin carrying yourself as if it is so. You ask, you dream, you envision—the universe answers—you allow it in and you fully expect it to happen. That's how you play golf. It's how you play life, too. See what you want and just be it and do it.

When you are in the process of executing a shot you don't need to try (trying is an expression of fear and a crutch), and you don't need to think when you are in the process of executing (you've already done your thinking). You visualize...then let it go. You simply have fun and allow it to happen, regardless of what your swing looks like. Visions and visualizations on the course are like mini dreams. We always get what we hold in our vision unless we somehow resist it. We offer resistance because of incongruent vibrations, or mixed emotions, indecisions. These vibrations, emotions, or moments of indecision come in the form of judgments, fears, beliefs or other obstacles, like our own ego or being our own worst enemy. The ultimate intention is to clear these obstacles and open up a pathway and connection to our authentic Self, a place that golfers like to call The Zone.

Dreams can be scary because they are meant to move us beyond what is to what we prefer. Dreams take us outside our comfort zone. In truth, in order to attain dreams or inner peace, one must be willing to pass through what at first appears to be difficult to that place of peace and tranquility. This is the wisdom that lies within. And you know that!

If your dreams don't scare you, then they're not big enough and you haven't played full out. It's easy to be mediocre or play middle-of-the-road. That's playing it safe. If you do choose to play it safe versus getting after your dreams, some day you're going to wake up and look at yourself in the mirror and wonder where your life went. Just take the next step.

"Faith is taking the first step even when you don't see the whole staircase."
—Martin Luther King, Jr.

Setting Unreasonable Goals

"The greater disappointment is not that we set our goals too high, and may fail to reach them, but we set them too low and we do."
—Michelangelo

Parents often think that having too big of a dream sets up their child for disappointment and discouragement. They truly believe that this will hurt their child emotionally and scar them for years to come. The way I see it we have two choices: either we teach each other to keep dreaming our dream, acknowledging that perhaps we will have some setbacks and disappointments along the way (all meant for our own growth), or we settle for less, undersell ourselves, play small, and have disappoints later in life because we never went for it. We were too scared to think so big of ourselves.

Either way we have disappointments. At least in the first scenario we offer no regrets and we climb however high our desire, our will, our passion, and our talent allows. I am here to encourage your dreams, ignite the passion, and renew your desires, just as I am myself. I get to spread my message and my unique gift unto you. As I give away I also receive that which I desire myself. And it certainly helps to build up an empowering self-image and positive self-esteem in order to handle these inevitable temporary setbacks or disappointments along the fairway of life. Part of the journey is overcoming these challenges and disappointments. Embrace life's tests (adventures) when they come to your gate.

Here is an excerpt from *Soul Lessons and Soul Purpose: A Channeled Guide to Why You Are Here* by Sonia Choquette, a spiritual author, intuitive, and counselor. This is what is really happening and it's time that you too embrace life's tests the next time you feel challenged from living your dream. I also prefer the perspective to see life as an adventure versus a test; a journey, not a destination; a playground, not a laboratory; fun, not a struggle. Once again, a simple shift in perspective makes all the difference in the world. The major emphasis that Sonia points out is that life is all meant for our own growth.

Embrace Life's Tests

Your soul progresses toward mastery by facing tests. These help you temper your human reactions and develop your higher spiritual ones. They appear in the form of challenges, disappointments, betrayals, upsets, trials, losses, and even injuries and sickness. It is easy to believe that you are a Divine Immortal Soul when everything goes according to your wants and desires. It is more difficult to remember your Inner Being's purpose and power, and to remain connected to your Higher Self and centered, when life becomes demanding. It is only when you confront all situations with grace, patience, and love that you find your strength and ultimate freedom, and graduate to living in harmony with your Greater Consciousness.

Tests are not in place to harass you, but to move you toward soul mastery. They help you measure your spiritual understanding and mark your progress. In order to advance from one grade to the next in school, for example, you are given exams that you must pass. Similarly, to obtain a driver's license, your knowledge is evaluated, and you must demonstrate your competence on the road to ensure your safety, as well as that of others.

The same holds true for your sacred learning curve. As you move through the classroom of life, you encounter an endless stream of tests to expand your Inner Wisdom. Challenges do not arise to threaten you, although it certainly can feel that way when you are in the middle of one. These trials are only in place as a neutral aid to help ensure your spiritual progress and advance your purpose. You can then become aware of your soul's weaknesses and strengths and work to develop the areas that require further growth.

The intention of embracing life's tests is to give you the courage and willingness to hang in there when the going gets tough and to never give up. Life's challenges and tests are for our own good—embrace everything and, similarly, all golf shots that come to your gate. It's all meant for the growth and evolution of your own soul.

Perhaps now you will revisit your dreams with greater determination, passion, and persistence to become the very best of who you really are—no matter what! It doesn't matter what anyone else thinks…your dreams are yours. Perhaps now you will acquire the self-esteem to persevere when you encounter a disappointment. It's called courage and willingness to endure *no matter what.*

Perhaps now you will become more aware of your strengths and weaknesses (the things you know you can improve upon), and become more apt to make the necessary changes to develop the areas in your life and golf game that you desire to fulfill.

I have heard it said, that the best time to plant a tree was perhaps 10, 20, 30 years ago, and the second best time is always today. It's funny how planting trees and taking action on living the life of your dreams are the same. There's no reason to wait for Earth Day or New Years Eve…you'll celebrate them with even greater awareness. It's never too late for anything. Just start!

How To Know What You Want

Now let's get to specifics, you've got to get really clear about what it is you really, *really* want before you can get it. Here's a simple test about dreams and knowing what you are wanting. If holding the vision of your dreams makes your heart sing as you dance toward it, then keep on. If holding the vision makes you uneasy, tense or it doesn't feel good, then you will also know what to do. Take some time to dream over the next few days, and as you do so begin to set some powerful intentions that will lead you in the direction of living the life of your dreams. The power of intention is one of the most powerful forces in the universe. Our dreams and intention—what we think about, what we give our attention to— is our law of attraction. You don't need to know how; you just have to take the next step. The universe will conspire with your desires.

Here's the real kicker about dreams: the very best moment in any long journey comes not when you realize your dreams have come true but instead discovering or remembering that having the dream in the first place, and the journey you took in search of it, was its own reward. You see dreams and desire are the spice of life and what they inspire is the excitement that causes us to get going again and really enjoy life in the present moment, and there will always be more of that! Just when one dream or desire ends there will always be another and another and another . . . it never ends.

Coaches Notes: Dream plus action equals the how plus

manifestation. You'll gravitate towards the picture that you paint. You begin acting as if it is so. You become so good at what you want; pretty soon you're living your dream. You take on that aura, that feeling. Like Cary Grant in the movies, you literally become the vision of the picture you are painting.

All great athletes first dreamt about how they saw themselves being with an end result in mind first. They may have not known how, yet they took the first step and the how's were shown along their journey. And enjoying the journey is what it is all about. Tiger's dream has taken him to where he is today. The secret to life is enjoying the journey each step and each moment along the way, even embracing the highs and the lows, the great shots and the not so, being grateful to exactly what and where you are. Eventually, more of the good stuff comes into your life.

Dreams Light a Fire

1) Having a dream takes courage
2) Visualizing your dream takes persistence
3) Putting your dream into action takes guts
4) Gravitating toward your dream takes commitment
5) Allowing the how's to come through the understanding of providence, which is divine inspiration and guidance, takes wisdom
6) Manifesting your dream takes an unwavering eternal will
7) Keep dreaming your dream is life expressed

Here's one more perspective for you to ponder regarding living the life of your dreams. When you think of taking consistent and diligent action towards the general direction of your dreams, do you imagine hard work, discipline, stamina, monotony, and courage? Not to say that I must certainly muster up a bit of courage now and then myself. However, what about a new perspective...life is supposed to be fun! How about thinking adventure, and a glorious and spectacular journey? There is a renewed interest, there are new friends and eager excitement as you rise…there's magic, fun, laughter, surprises, and each moment really is a miracle?

You can visualize a life on the course in which you possess a fabulous golf game, or you can visualize your golf in which you are creatively fulfilled, dancing across the fairways and greens, and you possess a fabulous golf game.

And guess what? There is no dream that you now have that you will not manifest. Try these apples on for size. According to brothers Andy and Mike Dooley in their creation of Totally Unique Thoughts (TUT), "You needn't worry. There is time. You have all the time in the world. You preceded time and you will exist beyond it. Age is irrelevant, more meaningless than a number. Forever, you have FOREVER. There is no dream you now have that you will not manifest. There is no challenge you now face that you will not crush and dispose of. There is no point in spending one more second of your awesome, amazing life, thinking anything to the contrary." Good to be you! Now you have that going for you, which is nice.

> *A little known secret concerning life in the jungles of time and space is that however far you reach, you will go farther. However great your dream, it will be grander. And however much you love you will be loved much more. We call it the law of increasing returns.*
> —Mike and Andy Dooley, Totally Unique Thoughts

Live your life like a dream. Follow your bliss and be as you wish to seem. Live your golf like a dream. We gravitate towards the picture we are painting. We gravitate towards the picture we imagine and visualize. We gravitate towards the picture we are dreaming about.

Until you dream, there isn't a vision.
Until you speak, there isn't a commitment.
Until you take action, there isn't a path.
You are a powerful creator!
Remind yourself that I created this and I can change it just as fast.

Action Steps:

1) Dream big and hold that vision. Open yourself to unlimited possibilities.

2) Remain focused on your dream and move with unwavering faith. Through providence (divine inspiration and guidance) the how's will take care of themselves. Be the champion that you know yourself to be.

3) Spend more time focused upon your dream than upon the reality. Your reality has given birth to your dream – but the dream is where it is you want to put your focused attention as you gravitate towards that – feel the joy vibrate through your body. This is a never-ending process. *Hint – this also is one very natural way to stretch and expand your comfort zone. Embrace your imperfections along your journey.

4) Visualize the life of your dreams as if your dreams have already come true, every single day, even it's for just 5 minutes or so. Breathe into that!

Chapter 3
Desire

"Be as you wish to seem."
—Socrates

Be whatever your heart desires
Ask and it is given

Be as you wish to seem. Here we are with yet another inspired message about the power of becoming that which you desire to be. What is it that you desire to be as a golfer? Be as you wish to seem. What does that *being* that you wish to seem look like? Start being that and act as if it is so. Begin thinking, talking, playing, and carrying yourself like you wish to be. Engage all your senses, feelings, and emotions. Really involve your entire being.

Desire is the beginning of all new creation. Be intent and take the lead in being a deliberate creator focusing on being as you wish to seem. Do you want to be a better golfer? If you were to be that, what does that look like...what does that feel like...what are you being? Do you want the freedom to more fully express your true potential? What is it that you desire to be? Go straight into being that which you desire to be.

Having a desire for something is like expressing a wish, a dream, a craving, and a longing for—you ask and it is given. It is given when you are in alignment and allow it in. A dream is like a manifestation to be; just like what you are currently living is a manifestation from your thoughts, yet a dream is quicker and easier. Spend ten minutes a day imagining more, and the quicker and easier your dreams become.

We must ask ourselves, "What kind of golfer do I desire to be: better, more consistent, more relaxed, calmer, feeling confident? Better demeanor? Free from resistance? Free to express and play more to my full potential? Becoming the kind of champion we know ourselves to be. What would that look like? What do you desire yourself to be? Has it ever occurred to you that you could ask for more? And not just more than you now have with your golf game, but more than you are now asking for! Tiger keeps asking to become better than he used to be and he believes it. Why not you?

Your own desire in all aspects of golf and life is a direct match to what it is you are experiencing in your life lived. Your external world is a direct reflection of your internal world. What to change? Change your thoughts and you will change your life. Change your desire upon what it is that you truly do want and all things in your experience will gravitate to meet that match every time. Never mind what-is. Imagine it the way you want it be so that your new vibration is a match to your desire. Stop looking at what-is and start looking at what you prefer.

I observe that most golfers are stuck in the rut of accepting and thinking that this is "what is", thinking how frustrating this is, and thinking upon what they don't want, which only holds them in the constant space of what is. Most golfers are in a constant state of beating themselves up, or if you're Woody Austin beating yourself over the head. If we keep regurgitating the same ole story…we keep getting the same ole results. If we keep thinking what we've always thought, we'll keep getting what we've always gotten. And if you like what you're getting and seeing then keep on! If you'd like to change and become better tomorrow than you were today, then you've got to offer a new vibration of what you prefer. You've got to start telling yourself a new story and it all starts with what you are being.

You've got to offer a vibration that matches your desire rather than offering a vibration that keeps matching what is. You've got to get yourself into a mode of what you prefer and keep pointing yourself in this new and exciting direction. I hear so many people talk about how terribly things have gone; how they choke; how they get scared; how awful they played; and how this happens time after time. Like a broken record, this kind of thinking becomes a self-fulfilling prophecy. Thinking upon what you don't want only draws more of it into your life…and the vicious cycle repeats itself.

Coaches Notes: We end getting what we are getting based upon the energy we have allowed to come forth. What we really, really want we get. However, the universe is an all-inclusive universe, meaning that it is completely impartial to what we are asking for. Likewise, what we really, really don't want we get. Herein lies our work. What thoughts are we giving our attention too? Often when we simply relax and let go after the initial stress and worry we play better. It's almost as if the body says it's silly to get all worked up over this and the weight gets dropped like a lead balloon. Whew! We find relief. Why not be this more often?

The answer is we've got to change the way we think. We've got to imprint the kind of thoughts and feelings that serve us, those that we prefer and choose . . . to take root and deposit them into the treasury of our subconscious mind. We've got to train ourselves mentally, emotionally, and spiritually to be as we wish to seem. This is the ancient wisdom of the ages that you have been asking for. We keep getting what we're getting until . . . we don't, until we change our thoughts. Reach for what you prefer and you'll gravitate toward that. This is the law of attraction at its finest. Become a Master at creating your own new reality. What do you prefer? Break the cycle and *Go Be That!*

Soon you will begin gravitating toward your most preferred thoughts and dominant vibration, which is following your *True North,* your true path. At first it may seem rather profound thinking this way, you being a creator and all. At first it might seem rather profound, and soon you discover that ultimately you're responsible for everything in your life, including your golf game. No longer can you blame your life on outside circumstances. No longer can you resign yourself that life is just happening to you. In the beginning once you grasp this enlightened perspective, it can be a bit daunting because many are just not ready to be fully responsible for their entire lives. They'd rather live within the drama of everyday life.

One of my objectives here is to break you out of your drama,

The Fairway of Life

the old story about your self that has kept you safe and playing small...because you are so much bigger than that. What if you could create "you" the way you want to be, rather than the way you think you are? Everything here in this book is about telling yourself a new story...that which you prefer to be...and go straight into being that!

Do you find yourself shaking your head in agreement, or are you still a bit puzzled or bewildered? You have the ability to decipher what rings true for you in your own heart. Whatever it is that you resonate with will make you feel good inside. Let your feelings be your guide, your internal compass if you will. Soon you'll be on your way to feeling really, really good more often than ever before, all because you desire to experience yourself as such. You begin gravitating to what it is you prefer—you go beyond "what is." And then enters the illusion that everything opposite comes into your experience the moment you announce and declare yourself to be something new. In actuality, you're just becoming more aware. Don't give up when it appears challenging or scary—that's temporary. If you do, you settle back into mediocrity, which is the exact thing you wanted to break free from. Remember, what you resist, persists.

Coaches Notes: In the beginning of your new becoming or transformation you may very well feel like you are in a catch 22 in more ways then one. The old you and the new you will be both on display performing, experiencing, and playing. Simply notice and observe that. The more you move forward in becoming the new you, the more the new you will show up. Be patient in this process. You will catch yourself from time to time forgetting and you will remind yourself to get back on your true path. There's no reason to beat your self up, simply notice and get yourself back on track. Nobody is judging you, not even God. Now that you know that, there is no sense to judge yourself anymore. You're just evolving from some of your imperfections (of being perfectly imperfect just exactly as you are) into a more enhanced and expanded version of who you really are.

Another catch 22 is in the beginning of your becoming it may appear a bit challenging, a bit scary, and you may be unsure if you wish to travel down this path or turn back. The moment you announce a new revelation into your experience the exact opposite enters your experience immediately and you may at first appear to want to run away. It's a temporary catch 22. You're just becoming more aware. You're more aware of all the good stuff of life you want and more aware of the things that are holding you back. Once you start down a new more enlightened path you may want to turn back to where you have found safety or your comfort zone, but you know you can't because you do want to experience more of your full potential. You're asking for it and you've got to get yourself up to speed with that which you have become, otherwise you just won't feel good.

Another catch 22 is you'll want to act out like you have before with your anger and frustration; yet your new self is asking for accepting and embracing the moment – learning from the moment and *being with* that. You may feel that you want to scream *bloody murder* out loud only to catch the stillness *within* realizing it's all small stuff showing you a new way. You may feel as if you are damned if you do let your negative emotions get the best of you and you're damned if you don't handle yourself with internal peace. How you handle your own catch 22 is part of your journey along the fairway of life. Your job is to find out what is working for you on the golf course and what serves *your* best interest.

Perhaps your most mysterious catch 22 of all is the less you think about *how* you can get something, like money, love, laughter, or a better golf game…the faster it will come. The universe, God, hears your asking and always answers – your work is to find relief and allow it to be. The key is to ask, then let go of it, simply enjoying your journey, going with the flow, and just knowing it shall be. Letting it and yourself be is perhaps one of the most difficult understandings about life, and in the same breath the easiest. We like to be in control, yet life is best served by simply being joyful and allowing the Well-Being in. Practice the art of just being your self and letting it all be. Then watch your life and golf game soar effortlessly and less arduously. In the beginning, it may very well feel like, how did I do that? Soon you'll begin trusting yourself and life more and more realizing that everything *is* a miracle and this is how life is supposed to be after all. Therefore, give your attention upon your dream and follow your bliss, your intuition, your feelings, and listen to the language of your soul. Allow the Well-Being in. Yes, the most enlightening and most mysterious catch 22 of all –Let God, and let Go.

Coaches Notes: Perhaps some of you are thinking but I really want to become a better golfer…where's my stuff? You've got to get into alignment with it. Sometimes you've got to soften your angst to allow the flow. And here's the thing, most are using the word "want" as a yearning for something that is currently unfulfilled. I want you to use the word "want" as an object of undivided attention to your desire. In other words, allow the stream of energy that creates world's flow through you upon your desire – undiluted, pure, and natural. It's more of a feeling and a shift in focus.

The only reason to do anything is to announce and declare, express and experience, and become and fulfill who you really are. That's it! Our soul aches to experience the grandest version of the greatest vision ever we held about who we really are. Do you desire to experience the grandest version of who you are as a golfer? How committed are you? In your vibration lies the answer. It is as simple and as complex as that. We are always getting what we are asking for. And in our asking is our desire. Therefore, there should be no more surprises. No more excuses, no more blaming, and no more playing small.

The way you feel in every moment is what this enjoying the journey stuff is all about. The destination becomes the joy of each moment along the way. Life really is a series of continuous moments of now. In ultimate reality there is no final destination—for their will always be more. Destinations are like dreams; they keep us desiring to be. If you're going on a vacation and the itinerary calls for you to leave on a certain date, spend time at various sites, and return home on a certain date, the destination becomes your home. You're already there, so why leave? The journey, like a vacation, is here for us to enjoy, to experience new sights, and have fun along the way.

Life and golf are supposed to be fun. But for many it is not. We keep chasing the rainbow hoping someday we'll arrive. I used to get all hung up on the destination – when I arrive, or when I'm ready to begin. It's here NOW. It's about enjoying the journey right now, while gravitating toward the picture you're painting – eagerly anticipating where it is you are going next. Heaven or hell is here right now, depending upon your perspective and how you see the world. Author and spiritual leader Dr. Wayne Dyer said, "Heaven on Earth is a choice you must make, not a place you must find."

Competition and Desire

In ultimate reality on a deeper metaphysical level there is no competition. It is man who puts himself in a position where he declares there is only one prize, one winner, and one victor. And we are making it all up!

A better perspective while playing this wonderful game of golf might be one in which we see many opportunities and there is more than one prize. There is enough to go around for everybody. The one who wins on any given day, at that given moment of time, is simply the one who is clearest about her desire, her wanting, and is most expectant of it. It's why Tiger "wins" more often than others. He is clearest about his desire and expects to win. If competition gives us anything, it is when it stimulates our wanting or our desire to be something. Tiger expects to win, while most others simply are happy being there.

> **Simple Secret Reminder # 7 – The One Who Wins…**
> **Is "clearest" about his/her wanting and most expectant of it.**

Justin Leonard progressed through the ranks from being a very good player to desiring to play in all the majors, to contend in all the majors, to winning a major. It really is quite amazing how we grow through the process of believing in ourselves. It really does come right down to believing in our selves. Sometimes we can be full of confidence and we end up overwhelming ourselves, which means we are not ready to allow it all to be. We choke or throw up. Expectation can get too high too fast if we are not ready to be in a state of allowing it to be and really believing in ourselves. Match your own clarity of desire and fully expect it to happen. There are plenty of prizes to go around.

The Intent of Desire

"There is one quality that one must possess to win, and that is definiteness of purpose, the knowledge of what one wants, and a burning desire to possess it," Napoleon Hill, the father of personal growth.

The intent in this previous dialogue is to raise your level of awareness around the concept of ambition and desire and how ambition and desire really work. The intent is to see if you truly desire to become better than you used to be, or if you are just venting. Really, this is a book about life, yet we apply these life principles to the game of golf. You can apply these life principles to anything and it all works the same. I believe we all come forth to experience ourselves as such and growth and evolution of our soul is our mission. What else could it be, to glorify God? What better way to glorify God then to become the grandest version of the greatest vision ever you held about who you really are. We evolve by being appreciative, grateful, joyful, and rich in our abundance in becoming our personal best, inspiring and uplifting others along the way, giving humanity our own unique gift. We evolve when we overcome adversity and challenge. We evolve when we choose to evolve.

It is my belief that you are reading these words here because you have been drawn to hear them and you desire to become better than you used to be. Here are the bakers dozen. You desire to play:

1) Better golf

2) Less arduously, with more freedom
3) More consistently
4) To your full potential
5) More often in The Zone
6) With commitment, focus and trust
7) With acceptance
8) Being fully present
9) For fun
10) In alignment and connection going with the flow of life's energy
11) With a belief in your self
12) Eager and excited knowing you have the shot and you do
13) Like no one is watching

It is my belief that you already know all of these things and that I am just reminding you and inviting you to get back in the game of life.

This is a book about personal excellence; it's a place where desire meets joy. It's about playing golf and life in *The Zone* and going with the flow more often than ever before. *The Fairway of Life* is meant to be an enlightening and enjoyable journey awakening you to your true path, allowing you to play better golf. Yet understand this, life is perfectly imperfect just the way it is right now. It's all a perfect plan unfolding like a great sculpture chipping away leaving only the masterpiece of what lie in his vision along the way. There is joy in the journey. Therefore, why not eagerly anticipate instead of being afraid or worrying of what might happen next? Why not go with the flow instead of struggling so hard to figure it out? It is all a perfect plan unfolding right in front of your eyes. And you will not have to think but a moment of why this is so.

I still go in and out of my connection with God and Life just like everyone else. It's just that now I know why. Yes, I still forget to do the simple things that you would think you are supposed to remember. I often catch myself half way through my round before it dawns upon me that what I was doing wasn't serving my best interest, or I just forgot to remember something simple. Oops! It's okay and now I can once again connect with this ever-abundant flow of life's energy that golfers come to understand as The Zone – pure positive energy. Yes, we will talk much more about this mystery and the secret to being in The Zone.

The Zone is a place where pure positive energy, pure desire, and one's pure natural state of inspired being become one. It's all of those things described by professional athletes and sport psychologists. The Zone is pure positive energy: fun, present, relaxed, clear, confident, peaceful, being totally focused; it's in sync, in harmony, slow motion, blissful, and joyous. It's a place where you are completely connected to Source Energy flowing to you and through you, and you are allowing the Well-Being in – the floodgates are open. I think of Michael Jordan's spectacular and outrageous display of athletic performance on the basketball court as he gestured with his shoulders, arms, and hands. He was in The Zone. He was on fire. I see the focus and intensity in the eyes of Jack Nicklaus. I see Tom Watson licking his chops. Both were electrifying to watch. I see you being and doing the same. Do you?

By practicing these powerful tools of the trade in the chapters to follow you will find yourself in better feeling places more often than ever before, just like some of the greats you too admire. You will find yourself in gratitude by giving appreciation to these natural laws of the universe. Sometimes you may find yourself internally quiet about your joy in the company of another as you appreciate within, other times you might want to dance and sing like no one is watching. After all, you're on fire. Each of us has our own unique way we express ourselves: Michael shrugging of his shoulders; Jack raising his putter; Tiger's pumping his fist; O'Meara raising his arms; Crenshaw putting his hands to his face; Gretzky, the Great One's craft and humility; or Ali declaring "I am the greatest." These expressions are all examples manifesting from being in The Zone. They will be forever etched upon the memories of all of those who observed transcendence and excellence in sport. Soak it in and make it yours.

Like these great champions, our desires begin within our own thoughts and creative imagination. While some may caution you to desire not, because it leads to suffering either way, which may appear to some as a no win situation. Instead, simply shift your focus to a more "softer" form of desire and allow this powerful life force to create the life of your dreams. We are asking beings. We will always have desires. We will always have unfulfilled desires. Their will always be more. We will never get it all done. We are propelling forward. We are evolving. We are here to experience both the joy and our growth. The real trick is how we interpret this phenomenon.

Dream Coach Marcia Weider advises us to not confuse desire with need. She says, "...that desire is a powerful force that can be used to make things happen."

Desire has an entirely different quality to it. You can desire something without needing or requiring it, which is the trick in making it work. Therefore, desire, but do not require. Desire in this context propels life forward, whereas requiring compels. Instead of trying to compel or desire something you want so badly, simply fall back into the soft texture of desire and allow the river of life to carry you downstream where all the good things you are "desiring" or thinking about lie.

What you dream about with intense focus and burning desire within your belly is what you create.

As Socrates advised, be as you wish to seem.

Action Steps:

1) **Whew! Practice being happy now and be as you wish to seem. Soak in the joy you have for the game of golf and the game of life.**

2) **Create the life that you desire both on and off the golf course and make it yours.**

3) **Let it be.**

Chapter 4
The Power of Intentional Golf

"There's a vibratory action to your thoughts, your feelings and your body. I'm asking you to increase those frequencies so they're high enough to allow you to connect to the power of intention."

—Dr. Wayne Dyer

Setting an intention starts a most powerful process
Why positive thinking is admirable, yet there is more to the story...

What are your dreams? What kind of golfer do you desire to be? You are "knowing" what you are wanting? "There are no happier people on this planet than those who decide that they want something, define what they want, get hold of the feeling of it even before it's manifestation, and then joyously watch the unfolding, as piece by piece, by piece it begins to unfold. That's the feeling of your hands in the clay," Abraham through Esther Hicks. Therefore, just as I've done and just as Tiger has done, and millions of others in there own unique way, with definiteness of purpose and intention decide what you want.

Yeah, that's right Holy Cow you could have thought anything... and been anything, but what about your limits? What about pie in sky? You mean dreams really do come true and there is unlimited possibilities and infinite potential. Yes, and guess what, there's still time.

So, now that you know what you know, you are ready and eager to set new intentions. You are embracing your unfulfilled desires.

And you know that you will always have new desires and it never ends. You are ready for a change. You are ready to reach for more and step outside your current comfort zone. You know you have the potential within you. You know life is really about unlimited possibilities and infinite potential. I'm inviting you to stretch beyond your comfort zone and be unreasonable with yourself. It's time to let go of your limited belief system and create new beliefs taking you beyond what-is to what you really do prefer. Think and feel *yes I can*. Involve all your senses, emotions, feelings when thinking about living the life of your dreams, desires, and new intentions – we gravitate towards the picture we are painting.

Perhaps this wake up call is just what you needed or have been asking for even if the pain or discomfort is part of the trigger. You're invited to more openness and to see and experience new horizons, and of course play better golf!

Strap on your seatbelt because today some very amazing things are going to begin shifting. Perhaps they have already. While the mind thinks, the soul knows. Up to this point we were merely watering the seeds of desire and wisdom that lies within you— nurturing a sleeping giant. Now it is time to watch your desires grow into the purpose of why you are here.

In this chapter you are going to learn how to lock in your focus and clearly set your intention. As you read in the beginning chapters, the power of intention is born from your desire, from your dreams. All throughout our lives we arrive at forks in the road that make us choose one direction over another. Sometimes we're ready to handle the higher ground sometimes we are not. Yet know this: as we go back and connect the dots we find that life always unfolds perfectly in a metaphysical sense, and perfectly imperfect from a human perspective. Metaphysically, life unfolds exactly as to what we have given our thoughts and our energy upon. Golf shots unfold perfectly imperfect the same way. While it may appear that there is no such thing as perfection on the golf course, at least the kind of perfection that many of us have been brought up with to believe, perfectly well struck shots only happen every so often. Everything is always unfolding perfectly from this stream of energy, which is the law of attraction. We can practice and sharpen the art of allowing

The Fairway of Life

the stream of pure positive energy to flow. And the better it gets, the better it gets.

Ben Hogan is perhaps the best ball striker of all time. He only hit what he called a "perfect shot" perhaps once or twice in his round (if that), yet when he did he described the sensation of hitting the perfect golf shot as a feeling that goes, "Up the shaft, right into your hands – and in to your heart," as written on the plaque at Hogan's Alley, Carnoustie's signature hole # 6. So, while we can certainly reach for our own excellence while playing, let us avoid the trap that unless we hit the "perfect" shot we will some how have seemed to have failed. We're responsible for our effort in being the best we can be at any given moment.

Coaches Notes: Enjoying the process. When you're playing your best golf, it's surreal; you're in The Zone – no thoughts or emotions. There's a feeling of being able to let go and just hit it gracefully and naturally (almost like your hitting to nowhere, which means now here). There's zero tension in your swing or your thoughts, and you're not worrying about where the ball is going; yet you are visualizing allowing the shot to produce the swing. You just know where the ball is going. And the moment you "think" you do, you don't. It's more of a feeling that you are riding. There's an understanding of letting go of being result-oriented to being in The Zone, out of your head, being present-oriented. It's about enjoying the process, yet there is no process. We only think there is. It's embracing this feeling and this understanding without "thinking" about it. Sometimes we play these games of intermediate steps along the way to give us the feeling of becoming, and understanding of what it is we desire in the long run. That's called enjoying the process.

Nothing stops the forward march of artistic golf like the need to do it absolutely perfect, or to play when you think you are ready. Those demons crush more golf swings and forward progress than imaginable. It's perfect just the way it is and you've always been ready. Who is to judge what is "perfect" anyway? Perhaps the definition of "perfection" is something that actually gets *done*.

What really matters is your desire and intention to play to your personal best, which I like to call *Inspiring Excellence Within!* I like to think in terms of giving your best effort aspiring to excellence versus having to be "perfect" on each shot. Gravitating towards our own personal best, our own excellence just feels better. Then perhaps you will end up hitting more of those "perfect" shots once you let go of your need to control and hit the perfect shot. Let it be and go with the flow.

Targeting Your Future

In order to know where you are going you've got to have a plan. You have to have a target, a bull's-eye to shoot at, a canvas and a brush to paint your ideal future, something that you gravitate towards. How much will you make? Where will you travel? How much do you want to weigh? What kind of home will you live in? What kind of golfer will you become? You've got to ask these kinds of questions. You've got to ask for what you want, without a need to have it.

Coaches Notes: If you think you "need" something it will feel like you lack something. A feeling of lack keeps you stuck without having it. In essence, you're giving you attention to not having it… and we always get what we're asking for.

Once you decide the answers to your questions with firm conscious conviction, you set the power of intention into motion. I desire this. I intend that. I hold the vision of my dream and I am dancing toward it—and it feels great! This is who I am, and this is where I am going. You might not know how to do this right now, but you will be shown how. Once we commit providence moves to us and through us. New pathways will emerge. New momentum of thought will expand your universe. New rockets of desire will explode. The power of intention and the law of attraction set forth a chain of events and kicks in immediately once you commit.

Allow the wisdom of the following quote, widely attributed to

Johann Wolfgang von Goethe, to stir your soul and set you free upon your new desires and intention:

> Until one is committed, there is hesitancy, the chance to draw back. Concerning all acts of initiative (and creation), there is one elementary truth, the ignorance of which kills countless ideas and splendid plans: that the moment one definitely commits oneself, then Providence moves too. All sorts of things occur to help one that would never otherwise have occurred. A whole stream of events issues from the decision, raising in one's favor all manner of unforeseen incidents and meetings and material assistance, which no man could have dreamed would have come his way. Whatever you can do, or dream you can do, begin it. Boldness has genius, power, and magic in it. Begin it now.

All successful people know this to be true as they harness the power of intention and commitment to a goal to move forward—and you can do this too! We all have the ability to succeed. So, instead of just watching your heroes on television and saying, "I wish I had what they have," focus, lock onto the moment, become mentally strong, and do it yourself! We all are modeling something, we all can dream. Instead of thinking wistfully about the accomplishments of Tiger or Lorena or any other exemplary person or athlete, choose to model whom that they are and what they do. Or decide to become something entirely new, on your own, that you envision yourself. You have the power within you.

We accomplish much more and become more productive in the presence of others who guide and support us into living the life of our dreams. We push ourselves with goals or intentions along the way. We are accountable to ourselves and to others because we say we are going to do what we intend to do specifically and sometimes by a certain date, so many times a day or week, and we do it. Set a powerful and outrageous intention and watch the universe align with your energy. And so shall it be.

First, be specific with your intention: give details of how much, how often, by when. For instance, I will loose ten pounds in ninety days. Next the "how's" will start coming forth. I will exercise four days a week for at least thirty minutes a day raising my heart rate up to 130-140 beats per minute. I will eat healthy and eliminate foods that I do not need and only indulge in two snacks a week. Next thing you know more clarity and wisdom will be drawn to you. Your body will magically transform and you will be inspired to keep your goal in sight.

Other times it may not be a specific directive. It may not warrant how much, how often, and by when. It may be an overall goal and the how's simply present themselves. Listen to the wisdom and clarity of your body.

Setting an Intention

Here is how I set my intention. Once when I was attending a Life Education Program, I found myself daydreaming, wondering and wanting to know how to play better golf. I was really asking how to play golf to my full potential without all these fears, demons, and butterflies that seemed to get the best of me. In January 2005 I remember asking one of my life coaches, Jim Fritz, that I wanted to to play better golf and overcome my fears. He said, "What kind of golfer do you desire yourself to be? What seems to be holding you back?" I said mostly my fears. "Can you *be with* these fears, he said?" These reflections started me back on my true path to being a better golfer. Providence began to move as I continued to meditate upon my desire, my intention. I started to ask to become a better golfer and I wanted to know how.

Then one day out of the blue I just said it. Within a month of returning home from thirty-three straight days attending the Conversations with God Holiday Retreat followed by an intense Life Education Program in Ashland, Oregon, I set my new intention. I was having a conversation with a very good friend of mine—one of my frequent golfing partners whom I now coach—Chris Shepler, a.k.a. "Sheppy," from the Shepler's Mackinac Island Ferry Service. This conversation prompted me to begin my quest to play better golf. In 2003, my golf handicap

The Fairway of Life

soared to an all-time high, and this then carried over into the 2004 golf season. I had a hard time breaking 80 and sometimes 90.

Chris and I have this humorous and long-standing tradition. Whenever one of us says something out loud worth quoting, we get out a piece of paper and immediately write it down, repeat it to the other, then put it away and save it for a rainy day to share with each other. In this particular conversation, Chris quoted me talking about golf. I had just come off my worst playing year ever. I had broken 80 only a few times all year. I was in my mid-forties and beginning to think my good golf days were all behind me. My golf handicap had risen to an all-time high of a 10.6 index. As Bagger Vance told Rannulph Junuh, "You lost your swing, now we gotta go find it." I lost my swing, my confidence, and I was playing scared out of my wits. Not only was I not breaking 80, I was finding myself shooting in the 90's. Most of my adult life up until this point I played to around a six (6) handicap. My "overall" comfort zone was somewhere in the high upper 70's to the low to mid 80's. Shooting a 75 would be considered an outstanding score, and shooting an 84 would be considered acceptable. I was shooting between 76 and an 83 with a good outing in my heyday. I would say my hope in my prime was to break 80. A 79 just sounds better. All of sudden I'm shooting 85's and 88's, and on some nines I'm not even breaking 50 on one of the nines—ouch!

The following year, I played sparingly as I waited for our new golf course to open. True North Golf Club of Harbor Springs, Michigan, opened on Friday, August 13, 2004. Before the grand opening, I played a couple times a week, sometimes three, and I played with a competitive group of guys in the Boyne Highlands Golf League. My handicap in their league rose to over a ten (10) as well. Breaking eighty became a real challenge. I wondered if I would ever return to those glory days of shooting in the 70's again. I felt like a laughing stock as most everyone else had passed me in golf performance. Terrible to compare your self to others, isn't it?

So, what did I do? On February 19, 2005, at 10:45 a.m., in the dead nuts of winter in Northern Michigan, I tell Sheppy: "I'm gonna drop it (my handicap) down to a five or less by July fourth." He gets a big chuckle, and pulls out his pen and paper. He knows how badly I've been playing. So, while putting on my new golf shoes in the house, trying to break them in, I go on to say, "This is going to be the year of the Scout." (Scout is one of my longtime nicknames. Scout evolved from being the Boy, the younger kid who played sports and cards with the older kids, to Boy Scout, giving me some credit because I could play all the games and win, to Scout, a natural evolution I guess).

When I was saying this, I didn't actually believe it right away; I was kind of making it up. It was supposed to be somewhat funny. Yet within a few moments something magical began to happen. This intention began to penetrate deep into the very fabric of my soul. This intention longed to come out, and even though it's scary to set such an outrageous intention I did it anyway. Immediately the exact opposite entered my psyche – doubt and fear. I started thinking about all the negative thoughts. What happens if I can't do it? What happens if I fail? How will I deal with any disappointment? How will I do it? Yes, immediately the power of intention and conviction, as well as, the exact opposite, doubt and anxiety, started to come in to play. The moment you announce and declare yourself to be something, the exact opposite will enter your new experience first. However, now I was armed with new understanding.

Moments later, something else was triggered in me, something that says, "Yes, let's get after it. Yes, let's play better golf and return to what you're used to, and even beyond." Now, you've got to realize this, at the time a 5-handicap seemed like such a huge goal, something kind of far out there. I opened my mouth; I declared it, now I gotta go do it. I put myself "out there" on the line; now I gotta go do it and overcome or clear or make friends with my demons and obstacles that lie in the way. I didn't know how, I just decided to take the next step. I decided to trust the power of intention. It takes courage to begin taking the first step in any endeavor. Boldness has genius, power, and magic in it—begin it now! This leads us to our next Simple Secret Reminder:

> **Simple Secret Reminder # 8 – Set an Outrageous Intention**
> **Announce and declare your intention out loud in front of others.**
> **Trust the power of intention.**

Begin with a general statement of what it is that you want to be. For me, it began with, "I'm gonna drop my handicap down to a five or less by July 4th." I don't really prefer deadlines when setting intentions, yet I don't like to think I'll never start either. See what feels best for you. Go ahead and make your own general statement of what it is you would like to be. Here is a step-by-step plan to get you going.

The Power of Intentional Golf Statement
Begin keeping your new journal now!

Step 1. Create your overall general intention statement. See the vision and hold it. Bring your senses and feelings into play. Example: "I'm gonna drop my handicap down to a five or less by July 4th."

Go ahead and do it *now*. Otherwise, close the book and set it back on your shelf and go about your merry way, settle back into your life of quiet desperation, mediocrity, or wishful thinking. I am inviting you to step up to the plate and let responsibility become your new friend; it ends up turning into greater freedom, more peace of mind, and becoming better than you used to be. In order to break free from your comfort zone you've got to come out and play and find out what has been holding you back. Look adversity and your demons square in the eye. It's easy to hide out and stay small. Remember: if your goals and intentions don't scare you, then they are not big enough. Growth begins at the end of our comfort zone. Setting an intention is taking us beyond where it is we are now.

While it takes courage and willingness to achieve your goals and intentions the reality of it all, is that playing full out and being fully committed can be a most enjoyable experience. Thinking about getting started and taking the next step is your greatest challenge, everything else will take care of itself. Set the intention…then take inspired action. Get off the couch; listen to your mind, body, and spirit. For many goal setting is the challenge in itself. We say we want something but we don't write it down and get specific with what we actually do want. Nothing really manifests without getting after it and really seeing it on paper and in your mind and telling another about it. This is imperative! Providence moves the moment in which one definitely commits oneself with definiteness of purpose and conviction. The secret to step one is commitment and playing full out.

Okay, now you've got an inspired statement of intention. You've stretched your boundaries, and you may continue to tweak your new intention(s) as this evolves. I certainly have tweaked mine many times. I began by saying that *I am* a five-handicap golfer – something that certainly seemed pretty outrageous to me at the time. Once I saw how this was unfolding right in front of me after a few months, I then stretched the limit even more, extending my intention by saying that I am a two-handicap golfer, which would have seemed practically impossible not too many years ago. I've never been a two before. From there I said I am a scratch handicap golfer. Wow, powerful stuff. Now my statement reads that I am a positive (+2) plus two-handicap golfer. Egads, how far do I go? As far as I allow myself.

Can I live up to this expectation? What does this mean? How far will it go? What happens if I don't make it that far? So what, I'm enjoying the ride. It's nice to dream big. Look, I'm incredibly blessed to be able to play at this kind of level regardless of where I end up. It's about enjoying my journey. This is how it evolved for me. To attract new experiences and growth into your life, you have got to keep stretching the envelope. As you practice these concepts even more, you will be amazed by your own power and the power of intention, and what you are now becoming. You are a powerful creator.

Another important point to remember while you are setting intentions is to observe yourself while you play golf, take notes along the way, then when you are off the course, keep a journal about these observations: feelings, emotions, and any resistances

The Fairway of Life

or fears that come up. Also take note of any insights, intuition, and wisdom that comes through. Keep your notes and journaling organized. A voice recorder works well too! Write them down otherwise those insights are gone in a blink of an eye. I can't tell you how many times I would get a hit on some deeply inspiring thought only to see it fade back into our collective conscious la la land just moments later.

Okay back to intentions. Rather than assessing your total game first, which seems logical, set an intention and then clear away the resistances or obstacles as they surface, because you might not even know what they are until you begin to stretch and observe yourself. You might have a basic understanding of your own golf game, yet until you *really* push yourself you might not fully experience what has been holding you back.

Allow your fears, weaknesses, denials, and resistances to bubble up to the surface and make note of them. Instead of resisting or running from them, I'm asking you to acknowledge them fully. Also make note of your strengths, courage, confidence, insight, and joy. There is always a balance between the two. Eventually, you'll end up shoring up both ends of your weaknesses (areas you can improve upon) and your strengths by clearing away your obstacles and creating more of a champion's and winner's image within your subconscious mind.

For now, simply set an intention that is outside your normal comfort zone and experience the magic of the universe. Reflect here for a moment and give specific attention to your intention. This is where it all starts. This is the point of all creation, and it all begins with a thought. Listen to these words by James Allen in his treasured book, *As You Think*, a timeless classic published in 1904:

> You will become as great as your dominant aspiration… If you cherish a vision in your heart, you will realize it. You have everything you need: a miraculous body, a phenomenal brain, and a vast and powerful subconscious mind. Now it's just a matter of focusing them in the right direction.

Give yourself the gift of fully expressing your dominant aspiration as to what kind of golfer you desire to be. Let your thoughts and imagination run free. Think in terms of unlimited possibilities. Also, recognize what you've already got. Be grateful for all that you have been given, and more will be given to you. When you wake up in the morning and at night before you go to bed, write down the things in your life, no matter how seemingly insignificant, that you are grateful for. Keep a gratitude journal and find yourself giving thanks on a daily basis for all that you do have and for all that you eagerly anticipate while holding your vision. Those couple minutes here and there makes all the difference in the world. And you will enjoy it. So…Just Do It!

I Am

Step 2. Create a bunch of general "I am …" statements as to what you desire to be. Go ahead and let your imagination run free. Everything is an open menu, you can choose any ingredient from the cupboard or any form that you would like to be. You are the guest of honor in your own game of life. Create your own pie as to what kind of golfer you desire to be.

The two most powerful words in our human language are—I AM. And they are an important component in developing your Power of Intentional Golf Statement. Remember these are powerful words as you engage your feelings and vibrations, sending forth a new intention within you. Begin communicating with yourself like the champion that you are. Spoken words are only part of the process. How do champions think of themselves? How do champions carry themselves? How do wish to be on the golf course? Begin telling yourself what it is you desire to be, and so shall it be. You will gravitate toward being this.

I am an excellent golfer.
I am relaxed, confident, and focused.
I am present in the moment.
I am appreciative and grateful.
I commit to and trust every shot.

The Fairway of Life

I am a tremendous putter.
My short game is fantastic.
My demeanor on the golf course is exemplary.
I accept all my golf shots with gratitude.
I walk with confidence and vision. I see my shot, I trust my swing, and I execute exactly where I visualized.
I am grateful to play such a fantastic game.
I am loved and all is well.

Coaches Notes: One very important note before moving on—be very careful in doubting your self, Thomas. Two things here: 1) Reprogramming your subconscious brain takes some time. Whatever negative juju you put in there over the years takes a certain amount of time to be squeezed out and replaced with better feeling thoughts and new beliefs about yourself. Keep on with the *I Am* positive golf statements, and 2) If you find yourself saying to yourself, "I am a tremendous putter, but not really," or if you find yourself talking to yourself like, "I'm such an awful putter, I really suck." then that, too, is still an overriding negative belief. Even giving thought energy to negative vibration creates more of that. In other words, thinking what you have always thought will get you what you have always gotten. These are the exact issues that you and I will be working on.

The first example wanting to believe "I'm a tremendous putter," then underneath it all you're thinking, "but not really" is a subtle form of subliminal denial and lack of belief. The second example "I'm such an awful putter, I really suck" is simply a negative belief you have allowed to filter in to your subconscious brain. These kinds of scenarios will be fighting or conflicting with each other as you move toward your intended goal. The first one is why positive thinking simply doesn't work because *we* hold ourselves in that space, until we clear out the negative. The second belief is simply a negative belief that no longer serves our best interest. No wonder you end up getting what you are getting. The use of ending statements with a "but" or a belief that does not serve your best interest or thinking that you can't do it sabotages the whole deal. You can't have dueling points of perception and perspective, dueling points of thoughts and beliefs. Ultimately our objective is to give more "air time" to positive focus and beliefs reaching for the best feeling thoughts we can...eventually squeezing out the negative thoughts and beliefs that no longer serve our best interest – literally shrinking them or clearing them altogether. We tell ourselves a new story – we create ourselves anew! It's just that simple. Remember the human body is completely brand new after seven to nine years, and to think that your thoughts and new beliefs can change much quicker than that. Perhaps we can help facilitate this process by offering some intermediate steps and processes along the way, which in the end will perhaps allow you to see the bigger picture, as you become the new you.

What is Denial? What is Reality?

There are several ways to look at denial. Many have been told to deny themselves too much goodness, too much joy, too much of anything – that's bad. Better not ask for too much, God won't like it if I'm greedy. What do you think God wants for you? Your will for you is my will for you.

What is denial and what is reality anyway? The only thing that matters is what you are giving your attention upon. Abraham expressed through Esther Hicks explains this phenomenon with clarity and wisdom, "You've trained yourself to face reality. You've trained yourself to tell the truth. You've trained yourself to tell it like it is. So in the beginning, these fantasies feel a little inappropriate, because it's like you're fooling yourself. Sometimes people will say, "Well, isn't this just denial?" And we say, we hope so! We hope that you are denying the absence that you do not want. And we hope that you are embracing the presence of what you do. But somehow the idea of denial has become a dirty word to you, like it is virtuous to face the reality of the horror of your own lives. And we would be ignoring anything that did not please us. We would get our eyes on what feels good."

I invite you to deny yourself something that you don't want and begin giving focus upon what it is that you do want – then

The Fairway of Life

release it. No reason to dwell on it anymore – your wish has been heard and answered – your work is to get yourself up to speed and in alignment vibrationally with your asking and who you are now becoming. By telling yourself you're something that you feel you (currently) are not will eventually override past programming (of what you think you are), and by being diligent and keeping on (to what you do desire) we become our new thought. So activate more beneficial beliefs gradually drowning out less empowering ones. Therefore, give your focus and vision upon your intention, your dream, and upon your end result in your imagination of how you intend to see yourself, all the while enjoying this journey down the fairway of life as we gravitate towards our target. We see our vision and we paint the picture – we live this experience. We become what we think.

As we acknowledge and clear the negative or stuck energy that has been holding us back, we begin anchoring our new positive focus and belief. Sometimes deep-rooted shadow beliefs keep us stuck spinning in the muck. Dueling points of negative and positive energy cannot co-exist within the same space to give us our best effort and excellence. I invite you to find out what process works best for you. I simply provide the tools for you to choose. These tools are presented in the proceeding chapters. The simple version is to keep reaching for better feeling thoughts all the time – the better it gets, the better it gets…and on and on – keeping on!

What I find is that most people seem to be forever trying to figure it out *on their own* gaining some ground and then taking two steps back. Many are walking around in this land of limbo and don't really know what to do about it, thinking maybe next year? They want to be positive, *but* they are not. They keep perpetuating the same ole cycle year after year. Notice how they talk to themselves. Notice how afraid they are. Notice how frustrated they get. Notice that every once in while for a few holes or a round here and there they feel a bone has come their way. Finally, they have relaxed and stopped beating the drum of trying too hard to make it happen and simply allowed it to happen. Trying too hard is a form of fear and resistance. Allowing it to be breaks down resistance. You can't play your best golf and resist at the same time. Remind yourself about the lyrics of *Let it Be,* by *The Beatles.*

You are either allowing the Well-Being in or you are resisting. Whenever you feel a positive charge, good feeling thoughts, and a sense of eager anticipation you are allowing. You see your target and you allow your swing to be and the ball ends up there in harmony – the shot produces the swing.

Whenever you are feeling a negative emotional charge over an issue or aspect of your game; like putting, chipping, iron play, driving the ball, lack of distance; embarrassment; pleasing others; fear, doubt, demons, worry about your round; judgment over a bad lie; the water hazard; or the scared emotions of playing against another, you are resisting.

The Mental Edge Golf Technique, which you will soon be introduced, is one such intermediate technique to loosen up our resistance and get us back into the mode of allowing pure positive energy to flow. Or you can simply take the quantum leap forward by going with the flow right now. Why not do both as I have? Through my coaching and observing I find that some form of resistance (anger, frustration, anxiety, thinking I can't) is common to most golfers who may not be completely aware of how this process actually works. Now the mystery is solved. No one ever you told you so quite this way until now.

We can't clear the obstacle and begin telling ourselves a new story until we first become aware of what has been causing us all the problems. Once we become aware of our resistance or obstacle, instead of running from it, we acknowledge it. We open ourselves to our truth. And once we open ourselves to our truth we're able to face new issues and begin dealing with them one by one. What you will usually find is that very often the issue we think is the issue is really something else deeper yet. For instance, we show frustration with a shot because we have embarrassment or perfection issues or people pleasing tendencies. Our work is to uncover the hidden assassin, allow it to purge through our system, while planting new seeds of positive Well-Being. Our work lies within us. No one else is exactly like you, therefore, it's not a one-size fits all program, yet many of us struggle with the same similar issues. Our work begins exactly where *we* are.

With *your* new powerful golf statement, remain focused on what you truly desire yourself to be. Really keep holding that vision; you will gravitate more and more toward being that. Eventually, you'll replace all those negative thoughts with new more powerful beliefs. Trust the process. Trust yourself. Trust life and let life know that it can trust you. This is a common theme interwoven throughout the fabric of this book. All these techniques and strategies are meant to give you reflection upon your own life. You get to choose your own path and what strategy or technique works for you. It's all about keeping on…

All of these mental mindset principles, strategies, and techniques are all part of the bigger picture meant for you to keep on…to never give up…to tell yourself a new story in recreating yourself anew. Life and golf is like a circle and our new intention is to expand and spiral upwards as we evolve rather than remaining in status quo or its opposite, spiraling downward. Each one of us is exactly perfectly imperfect right where we are. Our next message is right here. Tiger Woods is exactly perfectly imperfect right where he is. Lorena Ochoa is exactly perfectly imperfect right where she is. Chris Shepler is exactly perfectly imperfect right where he is . . . and so are you! In ultimate reality everything is unfolding perfectly and life is perfectly fair just exactly how it is, how it was, and how it will always be. The magic formula, the secret, is right in front of your eyes. It's the law of attraction and you are its creator. Simply open your eyes and be a witness to the splendid perfection in this very moment. What you give thoughts to you become.

Step 3. Keep a separate list of all the things that you do not believe yourself to be from your power of intentional golf list. Call this list your denial list. This will bring to light certain aspects of your belief system that you have allowed to run your current programming. Go ahead and write them down. Soon you will be given the tools to work with through your denials or negative emotional energy causing you to stay stuck, or worse yet, paralyzed in fear.

Denial List

1) I am not a good putter. I miss way too many short putts. I get the yips.
2) My short game and bunker play is horrendous.
3) I do not have the guts to play in big tournament events.
4) I can't even tee up without being scared about what I might shoot and what others might think of me if I play scared and poorly.
5) I'm still nervous and scared. I choke horribly, especially when it counts the most.

Positive thinking is ultimately the way we wish to be, yet until we clear the denial and really acknowledge our fears, blocks, and obstacles – for many of us it just doesn't work! It's not working is it? Positive thinking isn't working like you desperately want it too. The negative juju is so strong that it continues to run our life. So, hang in there and listen to your own body. I wish things could be so cut and dry, black and white, easy, simple to explain, yet life is also full of lessons, challenges, adventure, subtleties, and complexities. Yes, it is as simple and as complex as that. Just take note about how you are feeling about the subject without fooling yourself thinking you are a positive player, when in truth you're as scared as a little white rat. The first step to begin is to acknowledge our current level of truth about ourselves. We clear the negative and stuck emotion in order to make room for the pure positive energy. We create a new champion's self-image giving our focus and attention to what we really do want.

Step 4. Create your own personal, empowering self-talk golf intention. As an example, here is my own. The intention is what you desire yourself to be. Take from mine anything you wish; be creative in your own way. Remember present tense form, holding the vision, and use I am in your statements. Your work is to piece together the string of statements you used in the preceding steps. Then fine-tune your intention as you go along.

Golf is a fun game and I am an excellent golfer

Golf is a fun game. I am in The Zone. I enjoy the game of golf. I look forward with eager anticipation, and I have a positive attitude every time I tee it up. I am psyched to play. I am relaxed, confident, and focused leading up to my round, in my practice, and throughout my day—from my very first tee shot and to my very last putt I am relaxed, confident and focused. I intend and allow only positive thoughts throughout my entire round and throughout my entire day. I give thanks and appreciation. I intend and allow only positive thoughts and vibrations prior to, during, and after every golf swing. I commit to, trust, and believe in every golf shot. I am centered and in the present moment on every shot. I trust every shot with joy and confidence. I visualize and feel every golf shot and I allow the flow of life's energy to flow through me. I am in The Zone. I love the game of golf. I love and embrace and accept every swing and every shot. I am learning from every shot, and I evolving into a higher expression of myself. I acknowledge every shot and see the understanding of what every swing and every thought is showing me. I am expanding my awareness and evolving into a much better golfer. I acknowledge a higher power flowing through me. I am in The Zone. Golf is a fun game.

I am an excellent golfer. I am in The Zone. I am a positive (+ 2) handicap golfer, and my game is steadily improving. I am consistently fine-tuning all my golf game shots. I have all the shots and I especially give attention and practice to the shots I desire to improve even better. I am an excellent driver of the ball; my iron play is solid; my putting is spectacular; I am a terrific bunker player; I have all the specialty shots. As a result of my dedicated practice, physically, emotionally, socially, mentally, and spiritually, my golf scoring is steadily improving as I reach and expand into my true inner potential as a golfer and as a spiritual being. I am in The Zone. My comfort zone area of scoring is moving lower and my mind, body, and spirit embraces this change. I am confident and completely at ease playing my best golf to my fullest potential. I am at peace playing golf, and I most grateful. I intend to play well, I allow it to be – and it is. I allow the Well-being in as life flows to and through me. I am in complete peace, harmony, and joy playing golf. I am in The Zone. I am an excellent golfer.

Golf is a fun game. I am in The Zone. I enjoy the present moment. I am relaxed, focused, and confident. I have all the golf shots and I am in complete control in the course management of my golf game. I choose the shot and the club that is best and most enjoyable at exactly the right moment. I ask, it is received, and I allow the flow of Well-being into my swing. I trust my intuition, and I choose good feeling and inspiring thoughts. I see the shot, I feel the shot, I commit to my shot at hand, and I stripe every shot with exactly the correct rhythm, tempo, lag, whip, sound, compression, and flow. I fully rotate and finish balanced in the slot. I hit down on all of my irons and I rip all of my drives. I give full effort to my performance in the moment. My trajectory and penetrating ball flight produces wonderful results. I finish every shot in complete balance exactly as I intend. My mind, body, and spirit are in blissful harmony playing golf. I am inspired to play the game of golf. I am in The Zone. Golf is a fun game.

I am an excellent golfer. I am in The Zone. I am an honest and authentic golfer. I play the game according to the rules of golf. I accept and embrace all my golf shots, all my golf breaks, and all my golf lies. Golf is a game of integrity and my personal conduct throughout my whole round is exemplary. As in golf, so in life, my personal integrity and my behavior within myself is impeccable. I am forever growing and evolving into the authentic person that I am. Golf is a wonderful tool for the evolution of my soul. I am grateful and appreciative to remember more of who I really am through this great game of golf. I am in The Zone. I am an excellent golfer.

Golf is fun game. I am in The Zone. I enjoy the company of all my golf partners. I am here to honor, respect, and perhaps uplift, inspire, and empower others in achieving the life of their own dreams—simply by the clarity of my example. I appreciate the opportunity to be ONE with nature, and I am grateful in the opportunity to play such a splendid game. I appreciate the God Force, the Source Energy that flows to me and through me in life and on the course. I am empowered to play the game of golf. I am joyful in perhaps causing another to enjoy golf and life even better. I am a messenger. I am in The Zone. Golf is a fun game.

Wow! That was inspiring for me once again. I read and embrace my intention to myself as often as I choose. I recommend that you set your own intention as to how often you read yours. In the beginning of your transformation, I am suggesting that you read yours at least three to six times a day for the next twenty-one days. After that perhaps a couple times a day for the next six weeks. Our intention is to create and integrate a new more powerful belief that will eventually override other less than desirable thoughts, beliefs, or denials you may have picked up in your subconscious along your journey. And if you find that you have any stuck energy or issues that seem to be getting the best of you, then we deal with them one by one. Start paying attention to your golf game by becoming an objective detective.

I suggest you read your statement as often as you feel inspired. It has been well over a few years, and I still go back and read my statement, and whenever I do, I always get uplifted and inspired even more. I suggest you read it slowly and allow it to start sinking in. Welcome your new creation into your life. Welcome your new reality. Before you know it, you become that!

Step 5. Next, read over your first rough draft copy and make any changes that immediately come up for you. Remember—present tense, positive intentions; using I AM statements. Okay, let it go, and come back to it later. Remember three to six times a day for the next twenty-one days, and continuing on thereafter.

Once again, the intent here is to create your personal empowering self-talk golf intention based upon your intention as to what you desire to be. I also invite you to immediately begin thinking, talking, and acting as if it were so, even though you may have tendencies to think otherwise. The secret is acting as if it is so.

The first thing I observed in myself after I began was that I was now more aware of certain weaknesses, the parts of my game I could improve upon. I was scared before I even teed it up. I noticed that I had the dreaded yips on occasion, usually in the very beginning of my round. I also learned how to *be with* my fears and nervous energy. Notice I say *be with* my fears and nervous energy. Allow yourself to be with what shows up. Most of us have been conditioned to deny or run and hide from these fears or act out in frustration, being just plain mad at ourselves. I am inviting you to be with whatever comes up for you on the golf course and simply notice. For instance: okay, here it is, this is what I am feeling. I'm feeling anxious before I tee off. I'm feeling embarrassed that I might miss this short putt. I'm feeling scared of this narrow fairway. I'm feeling afraid to play golf in this competitive group of golfers that I am not very familiar with.

First we observe then we begin to notice and become keenly aware of ourselves. The key is to acknowledge what we are experiencing versus running away from or denying our demons exist. In order to clear our resistances we first must acknowledge them. For now I am asking you to be with your demons and just notice and observe what you are feeling. I find it extremely beneficial to not take any of this too seriously. Practice observing your self as being completely open no matter what happens. When you find something unusual play along, like hmmm . . . isn't this interesting, or hmmm . . . isn't this funny that I'm feeling this or I did that? Lighten up on yourself as you play along. Our goal is to gather information about our selves. While we're playing this little game of observing ourselves...and *being with* our fears or demons, in that instant, we actually begin to improve. This experience is actually one of the most beneficial techniques of all. Have fun with it... lighten up, laugh at your self...and smile at your obstacles. Yes, you will begin to trust yourself even more...allowing the shot to produce the swing.

One very powerful benefit when we observe ourselves in this non-judgmental way is we can now actually experience our fears and demons without feeling ashamed of them, or overly anxious when they do arise. What you are able to be with, acknowledge, and look at often disappears.

> **Simple Secret Reminder # 9 –** *Be With* **Your Demons & Fears**
> **Observe yourself non-judgmentally.**
> **Become an objective detective.**

Remember: what you look at disappears.

Coaches Notes: Being with our emotions, demons and fears is an actual technique in itself. What you look at—what you embrace, what you integrate, what you love, what has been seeking to get your attention—disappears when we are able to be with it. When it no longer gives us a charge we heal our wounded aspect within.

After I observed myself, I noticed that I began welcoming in more of the universal Well-Being. I refer to the pure positive flow of universal life energy as Well-Being. I was welcoming The Flow and connecting with this energy. I was literally talking to myself quietly under my breath about allowing the Well-Being in, and letting go of my resistances. I trusted my full swing much better. My putting stroke became more confident. My demeanor and attitude immediately changed for the better. No reason to get upset—I caused it. I began embracing all my shots, even the errant ones much better. And yes, my scores lowered dramatically. I found that even being 5 over par after 3 holes of golf was not about to do me in. I had new resilience, often still shooting in the 70's after a horrendous start. * For the purpose of this book, I acknowledge using the word "horrendous" to make a point in context, otherwise, it would be a judgment to think that. It is my observation that I had some resistance in the beginning of my round.

In the beginning I still had fears of being nervous, but it began to get better. I kept telling myself: be with this, accept this, trust this, give my attention to what I desire, give my attention to what kind of shot I want to hit (too often we give our attention to what we don't want, give our attention to the lack of, or aren't specific enough about what we do want), visualize on where I want it to go. And of course I kept track of my feelings and how I was showing up. Life began changing for the better.

> **Simple Secret Reminder # 10 – Focus On What You Want**
> **Where do you want the ball to go?**
> **The shot produces the swing…not the other way around.**

Begin observing yourself and notice how you are showing up on the golf course. It's all a process. Trust in the process. One understanding builds upon another. You may become Superman or Wonder Woman overnight, or it may take you a little time. It's about keeping on piece-by-piece, layer-by-layer.

The Fairway of Life is an invitation to explore the depths of life's most amazing universal laws, and yes, like life, golf is supposed to be fun! The messages will empower you to play much better golf, and to play less arduously than ever before. We tend make the game so complicated; yet in reality it is as simple as that. We tend to shy away from certain things for fear of failure in what we perceive another may think of us. Do you think a baby thinks that others perceived her as being a failure before she first began to take her first awkward steps? Of course not! That's why the baby keeps at it until she is cruising independently all over the room. It is our inner critic that passes judgment on us when we stumble as an adult. It is our job now to embrace the message and love our selves exactly as we are and tell our inner critic to take a hike. Trust your intuition, listen to it, and let it be.

An Outrageous Intention

You might ask, "How far should I reach—for the stars?" I say, stretch your comfort zone to an outrageous goal and push the outer edges. Growth begins at both ends of the continuum.

Part of the message of these simple secrets is that you embrace your less-than-desirable golf shots *and* your entire rounds of golf as well—it's not always going to be all "hunky dory." How would you recognize what it's like to play great golf if you didn't first experience yourself as the exact opposite? This will happen at times. There is a gift in the crisis moments, and yes, sometimes growth can be messy. In order to know ourselves as champions we experience what it's like to not be a champion first. How would you know what a champion is otherwise? We've come here to experience what our soul already knows. It's why we breathe, skip, swim, and enjoy all that life has to offer. The moment you embrace the opposite of who you are . . . will be the moment you evolve in quantum leaps.

Overcoming challenge and adversity is what all champions have embraced, which propelled them through to the other side. I invite you to embrace this quote from the late, great basketball coach Jim Valvano, "Don't give up; don't ever give up. No one can take away your mind." You have a brilliant mind. I invite you to use it more to its fuller capacities. See life from a brand new perspective and let go of those old beliefs that no longer serve you. Recreate yourself anew in each splendid moment of now.

"My heroes are the ones who survived doing it wrong, who made mistakes, but recovered from them."
— Bono, lead singer of U2

In ultimate reality there really is nothing *right* or *wrong*—only what works, and serves our best interest or doesn't work and doesn't serve our best interest, however, I can certainly relate to the self-forgiving nature in Bono's message.

Observing Your Self-Talk

Ever notice how awful people talk of themselves? You would never say such harsh comments to others, why do we do it to ourselves? I have observed so many people, myself included, talking to themselves in such a negative, downgrading, and destructive manner. It's no wonder we're getting what we're getting. Things like, "I'm such a jackass . . . I'm such an idiot . . . dumb ass . . . dummy . . . I'm an awful putter. Sheppy you jackass," and "I can't ever seem to get it up and down." And then there's the classic, "Dammit, John!

What the *&^% was that?" Be very careful in what you ask for. The universe only hears and matches our own vibrational energy, and it never lies.

Now that I know better, when I feel it is appropriate, I might ask another—and I did this with my own father—He's John in the above example, "Who hit the shot" or "What happened?" Let's take a look inside. As in the case with my own dad, it took a little courage on my behalf to begin meddling in his affairs. However, once we got to the source, he seemed to be more open. I asked him these questions and he answered both of them honestly. He said, "I didn't finish my swing because I don't like these downhill lies. I thinned the shot." Well, at least we have a new perspective from which to begin anew. I'll share with you a little bit later more about my dad.

Trusting Life—Letting Life Trust You

You will create what you want and intend from your burning desire within. Find what most inspires you and yearns to express itself. Give it permission. And then, almost without effort, it will manifest. You will look back and say, "How did this all happen?" almost in amazement. Trust in the creation and process of life, and let the energy flow to you and through you. Trust life and let life know that it can trust you. This is very powerful stuff you are playing with.

The power lies in your ability to move through three levels of awareness:

1) Hope – I hope to make a thing happen, but it might not. I sure hope it does.
2) Faith – I have faith a thing will happen. I feel certain it will. I have faith in the outcome.
3) Knowing – I know a thing will happen. Knowing is a statement of fact. The energy of knowing is more powerful than any other energy in the universe.

I chose to apply these incredible life principles to the game of golf having hope and faith in trusting the process. I allowed myself to believe it would be so even though I had no idea how. I allowed myself enough trust in the laws of the universe that somehow I just knew it had to be; otherwise perhaps it's all for naught – some kind of hokey witch-hunt. And I can tell you that goal setting has never been big on my list of things to do; it's always felt like too much work or it wasn't fun enough. However, trusting in this process was much more intriguing, to say the least. This is how the universe really works!

Giving Attention to What You Desire

Setting your intention on what you desire will eventually override your current subconscious programming by activating more beneficial beliefs. Before you know it, your old way becomes a distant memory. Something as simple as giving your attention to and focus upon what you desire versus what you don't want is the subtle message that keeps many stuck. I once asked a friend of mine what he was thinking about when he was hitting a wedge shot from a hundred yards out. He came up with all sorts of thoughts from not chunking it, to just making contact, to hopefully hitting it on the green. I simply asked him what do you want? Why not give your attention to what you really do want? The light bulb clicked and he, being a former college football player, said, "God that's so simple how come I never thought like that before on the golf course?"

Our work is to give our attention to what we really, really *do* want versus what we really, really *don't* want. Wherever your vibrational energy lies is what you get – a perfect match every single time.

Reasons Why You Desire to Play Better Golf

Write down all the reasons why you desire yourself to be this kind of golfer. The purpose of this exercise is to enhance the power of your intentions. Example: I am an excellent golfer. Why do you want to be an excellent golfer? Get out your journal and spend some time writing. Just thinking it in your head is a half-ass approach and will only give you half-ass results. Believe me, I've been guilty of being a half-ass most of my life. Do you wish to be half-ass or play full out?

I am an excellent golfer – Because I truly desire to experience myself playing to my fullest potential. I know what I am capable of and life is too short. There is no reason to settle for anything less than me being my absolute best. I want to play to my full potential so that I can appreciate golf and my life even more. I want to play full out and become my best. I want to play golf to my full expression. I desire to be my absolute best.

I am relaxed, confident, and focused – Because this is how I desire to experience myself. I enjoy being a relaxed and confident golfer. I love it when I am focused and in the moment of now. I am in The Zone and play my best golf when I am relaxed, confident, and focused. I play my best golf because it makes me feel good inside when I am being relaxed, confident, and focused. I love this feeling.

I am present in the moment – Because I enjoy being fully present and fully aware in the present. I know I play my best golf when I am present and fully engaged in the task and effort at hand. I am in The Zone when I am present in the now, because that is when I am going to play my best golf. I feel my best when I am living in the present moment of now. I know that playing my best golf is simply one shot at a time. The present moment is all I ever have and I wish to enjoy it.

I am appreciative and grateful – Because I understand that life really does flow to me and through me. I am appreciative to experience myself playing golf in The Zone and to my fullest potential. I am grateful to All That Is in allowing me to experience the joy of golf. I acknowledge a higher source, the essence of All That Is flowing to and through me. I feel a tremendous love when I am appreciating. I desire that feeling of love, of oneness and

The Fairway of Life

connection. I truly am grateful to be alive and experiencing life saying yes to the things I love.

I commit to and trust every shot – Because it is essential to commit and trust. Because committing and trusting is such a significant and instrumental part of playing golf to my full potential. Trusting builds confidence, and confident breeds trust. I desire to being fully committed because it keeps me grounded, centered, confident, and focused in the present moment. I love the feeling of trust and knowing believing in myself.

I am tremendous putter – Because putting is such a huge and significant part of the game. I enjoy making putts, being mentally focused, stroking the ball with confidence. I desire to be a tremendous putter because every stroke counts as an effort and as a skill. The more skilled I am at putting the lower my score at the end of the day. I desire to be a tremendously skilled and confident putter. I enjoy making putts from every distance and from every angle. It feels good to make putts. I desire to be a mentally tough putter so I can relax, feel confident, and stroke each putt to my full potential.

My short game is fantastic – Because I desire a delicate touch. I enjoy hitting the golf ball into the golf hole or getting it really, really close. It feels good to hit such a wonderful golf shot. Getting the ball close or in the hole is the object of the game. I desire to play golf to my full potential and the short game of golf is certainly a significant part of playing golf to my full potential. It pleases me to have a great short game. I score much better and enjoy being my personal best.

My demeanor on the golf course is exemplary – Because I desire to carry myself like a champion. In order to be the change I wish to see in the world, I must be it myself. I live by the clarity of my example and every act is an act of self-definition. My demeanor defines who I am. I desire to carry myself like a champion. Exemplary behavior allows me to be my best.

I accept all my golf shots with gratitude – Because life and golf just is. I understand the spiritual law of acceptance and being the messenger that I am – I live my life accordingly. I accept all my golf shots because I embrace life. Acceptance is the way of being a peaceful warrior and Master. I desire to experience myself as such.

I walk with confidence and vision – Because I am a champion. I desire to experience myself as a champion. I play my best golf when I am confident and when I have a vision. I am in The Zone. I desire to be in The Zone. I love the feeling of being confident and visualizing upon what I desire and allowing that to be – and so shall it be.

Thank you for allowing me to play such a fantastic game – Once again, I am grateful to have the opportunity to play such a fantastic game. I have the desire to play with joy and eager anticipation. I am grateful.

Smile – I am loved, and all is well – Because life and golf is fun. Because this is a loving universe we live in. Love is all there is.

Reasons Why You Believe You Will Have What You Want

Write down all the reasons why you believe you will have what you desire. The purpose of this exercise is to enhance your beliefs.

I am an excellent golfer – Because I am. I love playing golf to my full potential. I love having all the golf shots and performing to my full potential in The Zone.

I am relaxed, confident, and focused – Because this makes me become a better golfer. It allows me to set an intention to be relaxed, confident, and focused on every shot. Because this is the way I desire to play.

I am present in the moment – Because this is the way. I believe I will play golf in the present moment because that is when I play my best golf.

I am appreciative and grateful – Because I believe that is how life really is. I believe being appreciative and grateful is who I am.

I commit to and trust every shot – Because I believe in playing golf this way. Because I believe I will become a better golfer. Because I believe it is essential to playing golf in The Zone – to my fullest potential.

I am tremendous putter – Because I am. I fully believe that by believing in myself, by appreciating my God-given abilities that I am a tremendous putter. I have all the tools, knowledge, wisdom, and physical talents within me. I believe I am a tremendous putter because I know I have it in me.

My short game is fantastic – Because I am blessed with talent and touch. Because this energy, this belief in myself, this gift flows to me and through me. Because I believe I have been given a wonderful gift.

My demeanor on the golf course is exemplary – Because it is. Because I believe that God has called upon me and I am awakened to become the grandest version of the greatest vision ever I held about who I am. Because I believe I am becoming more of who I really am. Because I believe I am full of authenticity, character, and integrity.

I accept all my golf shots with gratitude – Because I fully believe and embrace the spiritual law of acceptance. I accept everything that comes to my gate. I am appreciative.

I walk with confidence and vision – Because I believe there is only one way to be in playing my best golf.

Thank you for allowing me to play such a fantastic game – Because I believe I have a desire to experience myself as such.

Smile – I am loved, and all is well – Because I believe smiling and being happy is the key to a healthy life. Because I believe that the universe is a joyful and loving place to be. Because I believe that is how it is intended to be.

Intentional Golf Exercise: Setting powerful intentions work in so many magnificent ways. In the overall big picture we set an intention (we paint the picture) and we gravitate towards that. We can set overall intentions as to the kind of golfer we desire to be, why we want this, and why we believe it to be so. We can also set intentions on this very day or on this very round of golf. We can get very clear as to the kind of person we desire to be for a particular part of the day. Let's say at work you are presenting a very important message in front of your peers and leaders. This could make you feel a bit anxious, or not? Take a moment to sit still, take a couple of deep breaths and imagine how you wish to be in your presentation. Is it calm, clear, wise, articulate, and to the point? Then set that intention. Today in my presentation I am choosing to be calm, clear, wise, articulate, and to the point. My intention is to be calm and clear. My intention is to be wise, concise, and articulate. I set this intention and so shall it be. What this does is that it brings together mind, body, and spirit. You're setting an intention, bringing into conscious awareness that state of being that you prefer. You simply notice that this is a part of who you choose to be. If you find yourself drifting away some, simply draw yourself back repeating in the stillness of your mind calm and clear.

The same principle applies to the golf course as well. Start out with simple segments of intention. On the putting green I am practicing to be focused and present on the process for one hour. You allow yourself one hour to be this. Everyone can stay fairly focused and present for one hour when you keep on reminding yourself. Tell yourself focused and present in the process. On the driving range I am practicing with purpose and clarity. Tell yourself you are practicing with purpose and clarity, otherwise our mind begins to wander and we can even become agitated and upset. Keep drawing yourself back to the intention you set – whatever that intention is. On the golf course I am choosing to be calm and relaxed for my entire round. Keep reminding yourself of being calm and relaxed. Very soon whatever intention you desire becomes a more natural way to be. You are for all intense purposes gradually training your mind to optimal states of being, which allows you to play as a peak performer to your full potential, expressing yourself freely going with the flow.

Coaches Notes: Everything we say and do and give our attention upon reflects that which we value and that which we are committed too. What is it that you are giving your attention too, dedicating your energy upon, and how you spend your time? It starts by setting an intention upon what you desire. Here's another one I just set on my walk connecting with nature, "I'm gonna express myself more freely on the golf course this year!"

Power Shazam

One final thought to brighten your spirits and lighten the mood. Use the power of Shazam to bring a little more magic or bling to the course.

Pardon me to even ask about your golf game, however, and since the universe knows it like the back of your hand, wouldn't it be great to have a little more bling on the course. You think you could stand for that? No, I haven't fallen off my rocker just yet, but I am laughing with you. Yeah, a little more laughter, some high-fives, some slow knuckles, a fist pump here and there, and for good measure throw in a few oh my's and oh yeah's.........woo hoo I'm on fire! Now that's what I'm talkin' about. I wasn't kiddin' when I said that golf is supposed to be fun.

Visualize these feelings and allow them to become your dominant vibration in the power of your intention. See and feel the joy. Hear the cheers and laughter. Imagine and visualize amazing shots. Smell the fresh-cut grass and the sounds of nature in between your golf shots. All of these images will literally summon the resources, ideas, concepts, circumstances, contacts, understandings and *how to* live the life of your dreams, and by the way, play much better golf. Not only that, you'll find yourself more grounded, more centered, more present, and happier. Hmmm... all of these are the wonderful qualities of playing golf in The Zone. Power Shazam!

Why, because the usual mundane just plain ole trudging around just ain't going to hack it anymore. Cymbals and Shazam!

Did you do it? Did you bring your hands together like you were holding on to a pair of cymbals or simply imagining it in your mind? C'mon you're smiling some and the mood is a little lighter, correct? Isn't this how you'd rather play? And even is you're a tad off so what? Shrug your shoulders and give that facial expression like the great Walter Hagen would. So what? Moving on...

While you go through any of these processes please remember to lighten up. There's nothing too serious here, just you reaching for better feeling thoughts. Little by little the better it gets, the better it gets. Relax into this and go with the flow. Let it be easy.

Action steps:

1) Set a powerful intention for which you desire to be as a golfer. Trust in the process that the universe will conspire with your desires. As this process unfolds become aware of what emotions and thoughts come up for you that feel like denial, or resistance.

2) Keep a journal about your feelings. Take your journal to the golf course and write down whatever specifically is coming up for you that feels like resistance or denial. Resistance and denial is all part of the process. Soon you will be given the tools to clear them. It's your work to recognize them and become aware of yourself.

3) Take little baby steps towards realizing living the life of your dreams. What little, mortal, baby steps can I take today that will express and demonstrate expectancy, prepare and pave the way for my dream, and place me within reach of life's magic coming attractions, even if the steps are similar to what you took yesterday?

4) Set powerful intentions as to what state of being you desire to be today!

Chapter 5

The Power of Present Golf

> *"Neither the past or future has any reality separate from the present moment, and yet we act as if both are real. Look into the heart of your own immediate experience, and you will see without a doubt, that only the NOW is real, all else is an illusion in your mind. This is the only path to enlightenment."*
>
> —Joe Anthony

A reminder to play present golf – one stroke at a time
Deeper understanding of the power of NOW
How becoming mindfully aware and meditation helps ground the present moment

The present moment of now has so many subtle and deeper meanings, and even more yet. Begin to notice and observe that now is all there ever is. Begin it now. Play golf in the now. There is only now. There is nothing else. Only now is real. Life is our experience of awakening into this awareness. Awareness only exists in the present moment. The moment to begin is now, and there is only this shot. The present moment is all that counts. Make each moment of now better and the future will take care of itself, while the past will not matter. Enjoy your now…the scoring will take care of itself.

In case you are still waiting for whatever it is—begin it *now*. In case you are waiting to be ready—begin it *now*. In case you are wondering when you will be ready to commit—begin it *now*. As you ponder the above quote by Joe Anthony allow the depth of it to permeate your soul. Allow the wisdom to filter into your psyche. Allow the courage, commitment, and trust it inspires to be with you now and forever. Fortune favors the bold, right here and right now.

The most important shot there is in golf is *this* shot, right here and right now. It is the only one there is. If it is our desire to play golf in The Zone we must be in the Now. We must be fully present. Being in present moment is an absolutely essential ingredient to playing golf in The Zone. You cannot be in The Zone if you are not present in your Now. Life takes on a whole new meaning when you center and ground yourself by being and enjoying your present moment. It is the only moment you will ever have. Capture it! And when you capture that moment remember that memories are simply fragmentary mental images, a sliver of the full Essence of who you really are and what it is you are becoming.

> *"It is nothing new or original to say that golf is played one stroke at a time. But it took me many years to realize it."*
> —Bobby Jones

Sometimes I remind myself that this shot, this space right here where I am swinging, is the only thing that matters. After I visualize my shot I am responsible for this effort right here and right now—in this little space where I am executing this one particular rotation and swing of the club. When I am finished executing (holding the finish), then I look up at where I *intended* the ball to go in my mind's eye.

Simple Secret Reminder # 11 – This Shot is the Most Important
Life is simply a series of continuous moments of now.
And now is all you will ever have!

Coaches Notes: This golf shot right here, and right now is the most important. It truly is the only shot you have. Imagine playing golf by giving your wholehearted attention to this one particular golf shot right here, and right now. What would become available to you?

> *"You must live in the present, launch yourself on every wave, find your eternity in each moment."*
> —Henry David Thoreau

For most of my adult life, I did not understand this concept of being happy now, let alone the idea of being fully present now. I heard about it, thought about it, but I didn't fully embrace it or practice it. I brushed it off thinking I could figure it out. In retrospect I see that I was always in a hurry: scurrying to get that next degree, to meet that next girl, to get that next job, to have that next moment of fun, to play that next round—all in order to, hopefully, be happy, someday. Sure I had my many delightful moments along the way. Still I was always searching. I thought that someday—when I finally arrived here or there, at that next station or mountaintop—then I would be happy, and my life would be full. Year after year I thought that's how it worked. But it didn't happen that way. That is not how life works. I was whittling against the grain, I was paddling against the current, and I was getting nowhere fast.

By this point my inner world was aching to wake up. I knew there was something else. I felt the void and I heard the voice calling. It was a voice summoning me. It repeated the words: "The secret to your happiness and success is surrendering . . . and going within." I now understand that surrendering to that small, still voice within is exactly what it means to return to who I really am. In practically the same breath it is the most terrifying and most liberating experience and feeling in the world.

Surrendering within allowed me to ground myself and become more fully present, and at peace with my inner world. As I make peace with my inner world, my outer world becomes more peaceful as well. As I calm my mind, I calm my body. Being calm is an essential ingredient to being present. Being present allows us to focus on the task at hand. Being focused is a key to being present.

Being calm, focused, and present are all essential aspects to being in The Zone.

The Key to Playing Better Golf

Being in THE NOW is not only the key to a happy life; it is also the key to playing better golf. While you might think to yourself that by being alive and conscious we are naturally always in the present moment—after all, we are living right now—yet many of us live "out" of "The Now" on a regular basis. If your mind has wandered from the shot at hand throughout your round, you know what I mean.

When I see another player's golf shot go astray, I often ask, "What happened?" Why, because I'm curious as to his or her thought process. Was it nerves, emotions, mind noise, negative thoughts, mixed vibes, or did they simply lose focus? Often I discover that the player is thinking about the shots ahead of him or her, or something entirely irrelevant to golf, instead of the one he or she is playing right now.

Many golfers tell me they simply lose focus at various moments, which ends up costing them usually a shot or two, and for some, many more shots than that. Sometimes when I'm feeling it's okay, I might ask my playing companion, "Where were you? What happened? What were you thinking?"

Coaches Notes: How much time does it actually take to play a round of golf? The actual gathering information, visualization, pre-shot routine and execution only takes about a minute or less per shot or stroke max. That's approximately a good hour or less from the total four hours plus you spend on the course. One-fourth of your actual time is really involved in playing the game and even a lot less in actually executing the shot. Keep your focus when it's time to play. Enjoy your complete experience.

Last week, I was playing golf with Chris Shepler and with a new friend and member at our club, Bill Anton. Bill hit a second shot on the 9th hole that went off his mark. He proceeded to hurry his next couple of shots before he walked off the green with a 6, or most likely a 7 on the par 4, before we even got to the green. He'd been playing pretty well up to this point hummin' right along. I asked Bill, "What happened? What were you thinking about?"

Bill's response, "I don't know. Nothing really. I just lost my concentration for a moment." I reminded him to bring himself back to center, back to being present. You see this kind of thing happens all the time. We lose concentration and focus and then end up spiraling further out of control—out of the present moment. We get mad and waste a few more shots because, well, you fill in the blanks. We allow the drama of our own saga take us down, unless we don't. We've all been there. And if you just give up and *let* things spiral out of control, you end up getting what you get.

The point is that even though people understand the *idea* of being present, they easily lose the *experience* of their NOW. Sure, daydream on occasion away from the golf course and eagerly anticipate your future when it is healthy to do so. Visualize it in quiet and still moments at home. When it's time to play golf be in your golf mode, give your focus on the present and be here now. Like Tiger, Faldo, and Azinger, and practically every other top-notch professional, turn on your "present moment" switch. Not only will your golf game soar, your relationships, and your appreciation for life will take on a whole new meaning. Connect with your NOW. Become more consciously aware of being more fully present NOW. When I play golf and live life in the NOW, I am much more fully connected to whom I really am. If I find myself daydreaming about the past, worrying about what went wrong, or what should be, then I keep getting the same results over and over again. There is only now.

On the flip side, when I get too far ahead of myself, I am living in the future, which has yet to arrive. Many golfers spend too much time living in the future, thinking that they *have to* make par or birdie, or worse yet, scared about their entire round before they even tee off. A better attitude is an understanding that there are many more pars and birdies to be had, all the while enjoying your present moment.

When we get ahead of ourselves we begin to focus on outcome

or the fear of the unknown, obstacles that take us out of our current moment and out of The Zone. Our ego likes to be in control. We desire stability, security, and some form of predictability. Our ego fears it will not survive or be safe without some level of comfort as we are constantly on guard. This fear of the unknown future paralyzes many golf swings and ruins many rounds of golf. In fact, many golfers stop playing altogether because of this dread of perceived future failure.

Giving your attention to fear of the unknown amplifies the fear. Conversely, giving your attention to trust in the present moment produces more trust. When you realize that by working to achieve a feeling of Well-Being in the present moment, it is impossible to dance with anything other than Well-Being. Ultimate freedom lies in the power of NOW through your thoughts, words and actions.

> *"There is surely nothing other than the single purpose of the present moment. A man's whole life is a succession of moment after moment. If one fully understands the present moment, there will be nothing else to do, and nothing else to pursue."*
>
> —Hagakure

Playing Golf in the Present Moment of Now

In the summer of 2006 I was playing very good golf. In July of that year I played in a golf pro-am tournament event at the Treetops Tradition course. On that particular day my thoughts were in the present moment, and I gave myself some simple reminders. I told myself to focus in on what I wanted. My pre-swing thought queues for the day was to set the club, align it to my target and let it happen. My anchor thought was to compress the golf ball and simply get out of my way. I proceeded to play very well throughout most of my round without too much swing thought noise.

Coaches Notes: An anchor and swing thought is a subtle

reminder about what you are doing on the course today. Swing thoughts can, and usually do change, which I believe is healthy. While I would prefer zero swing thoughts to be ideal (just zinging and zoning along), sometimes one natural swing thought in the beginning, without much thought, keeps me somewhat stabilized allowing this thought to gradually shift and melt away from barely anything anymore into nothingness. Ultimately, I prefer a feeling of knowing that all is well with my golf. I'm *licking my chops* ... eagerly anticipating, tuned in, tapped in, turned on – a one-minded focus, clicking along loving it!

* Carrying too many conscious swing thoughts in your backswing can distract you even more than a person talking out loud. Remember zero swing thoughts or turn your one swing thought into a natural part of your routine involving your feelings; unconsciously allowing it to happen.

Engaging in these simple steps helped me override my previous mental programming, training my mind more and more into becoming what I wanted to be, which is a more confident golfer playing the game to my full potential. My focus stayed present—for *most* of my round. Like any other experience in life, it's a process. By giving attention to the process in the present moment we stay more confident and focused. When we let joy be the measure of our success we're also being present, confident, and focused.

There I was playing great present golf for 17 ½ holes. I was aware of where I stood throughout my round, yet, when I approached the eighteenth green, I allowed my focus to shift. I had just hit two great shots to get me pin high left (there was a long trap guarding the front of the green), perhaps ten to fifteen yards off the green on this particular par five finishing hole. Then I started to think about what all this meant. I started to guard and protect myself from letting it happen. I started to think about my score. I knew if I made par, I would shoot 68. I also knew if I got up and down I would shoot 67. And not even once was I thinking *make it for a 66*. The thought of shooting a score in the 60's is a delightful thought, and it is also a scary thought. It doesn't happen that often for us mere mortals.

The Fairway of Life

Well, in the over-excitement of it all I decided to *putt* my ball from well off the green. It seemed like the safest play. I did have a very thin lie, and I wanted to prevent myself from chilly dipping it or thinning it badly. The negative thoughts were swirling and multiplying in my head and I was totally out of the present moment. A big, red flag went up. I had shifted my attention to what I did *not* want. I thought birdie would be too much to ask. I had shifted my attention to the future—the bigness of what accomplishing this would mean. I was guarding against myself. I was now being self-consciously un-Tiger like.

Champion golfers who know this concept face these self-sabotaging demons, or one-eyed giants, all the time. Ernie Els talked about his demons openly in plenty of interviews. They are nothing more than imaginary monsters lurking in our own mind. While they are not real, I invite you to welcome their perception. Trying to push them out of your head will only make them come back stronger. Conversely, walking with your demons and fears will cause them to melt away.

After I let my one-eyed monster hold my confidence hostage, I ran my putt from off the green some thirty feet past the hole. I gave it too much steam and it flew across the thin cut of the beautifully manicured fairway. In that instant my whole mind-set changed. Now I was thinking, just get in within a two putt and finish this sixty-eight thing off. I was starting to play scared again and being way too conservative. I'd gotten out of The Now, most definitely out of The Zone, and my mind swirled with past thoughts and future hopes. I wasn't thinking make this thirty-foot putt for birdie; I was thinking, just get it close enough to have a gimme tap-in…nervous and practically shaking in my boots. I stroked the putt tentatively and left it right and just short of the hole, a brutal deceleration like O'Meara on the 72nd hole of The Open Championship at Royal Birkdale in 1998.

Now I was faced with a three-and-a-half footer, definitely well over "normal" gimme range, and in this case playing in a tournament where there are no gimmies. I was literally trembling as all three of my playing partners watched. I could sense their interest from the panning of the play as I took the stage…they knew what kind of round I had going. I did manage to make a par on that last hole, but it was way too much work and pressure. It was way too much resistance against playing fully expressed golf. God, I would have kicked myself if I'd missed that putt and ended up with a bogey six posting 69. You can see my point, can't you? Everyone has been there before. What can we do in these kinds of moments? Phew!!!

In my case on that particular day, thinking about the grandiosity of it all, it opened the door to understand what fear feels like when you let it overwhelm you. It wasn't quite like Jean Van de Velde's famous 1999 British Open collapse at Carnoustie, called "Car Nasty" by many, yet I felt a similar pressure creep in because I had stepped outside of my present moment thinking too much about the bigness of what this might all mean. I got ahead of myself in the end just a smidgen.

I experienced the same kinds of thoughts on route to shooting a back nine 29 on July 24, 2008 at True North Golf Club. On the last putt I become tentative and scared seeking to "protect" my 29 instead of allowing the Well-Being in on a simple 10-foot slightly uphill putt. I was scared again.

Even as I write this, I know that thinking ahead of myself about being scared that I might play poorly is my biggest stumbling block, even though I usually end up playing well most of the time. Crazy, isn't it? Perhaps next time when the one-eyed monster grabs you or me, we will finish the entire round right up and through that very last putt. Then, like Ben Crenshaw or Zach Johnson, we will end our round with tears of joy!

Being in the Present

Live your life more in the present. Make peace with your past. Be happy with where you are. Look forward with eager anticipation to where you are going. Last night, I played some twilight golf, and I thanked my lucky stars. I actually gave appreciation to God for allowing me to connect with her in such a wonderful and deeply inspiring way. I was grateful to be able to play this splendid game on such a beautiful and challenging golf course. I was grateful to be more conscious and more awakened in the moment.

I invite you to become more conscious of the world around you. What's the hurry, and where are you going? You are moving through time; enjoy your present moment. As soon as you arrive at one station, there will always be another. Relax and enjoy the place where you are right here and right now. This concept is reiterated throughout this text because reminders and repetition reinforce our conscious awareness, and eventually become ingrained in our subconscious mind. It is meant to remind you even more, for you will soon be venturing *out there,* away from this book. What you set in motion days, months, and years ago, you are living now. Likewise, what you think about now you will become next. In simple terms, that is the law of karma. You are creating your own reality. It is all cause and effect. Like a photograph, begin capturing more moments of now in your own mind's eye. Live in the present.

How many moments in the past year did you capture in snapshot form? What can you remember? Were you being fully present or not? How many conversations do you have in which you are really listening? What kind of appreciation do you have of birds, trees, flowers, landscapes, people, and playing golf? How many snapshots of life will you place in your subconscious mind this year?

Eckhardt Tolle wrote an entire book on the subject called, *The Power of NOW*. I invite you to read this deeply inspiring book for a greater and more in-depth look at the power of Now. Ram Dass wrote a book called, *Be Here Now*. This new awakening of being in The Now is making its way back into the schools around the land. There is a shift, an awakening going on as more and more beings find the secret within. Critical mass is creating a new way of life on this planet. I feel the energy shifting, and I observe the transformation unfolding. You are part of this movement by being here *now*.

So how do we live life and play golf in the present? Are there techniques? Is there more to it than just the understanding of it? Yes, and they will help to bring you back to center.

The Power of Meditation

So what is meditation? What are the benefits? What does meditation have to do with The Now?

Meditation helps calm and clear the mind, and allows us to pay attention and become more fully present. Since I started meditating it has helped me to connect with my core inner being and to learn, or better yet, remember my self. Moreover, it has helped me to become clear, to connect with my higher Self, my Inner Being, and set clear intentions.

The more I practice meditation, the more I understand the present moment and how to calm myself. Meditation allows me to be still from the constant mind noise of the day. If we never take time to be still, our minds will forever be racing, thinking about all that we have to do. I invite you to practice the art of meditation and more mindful awareness.

What does meditation do? This quote from Wayne Muller, founder of Bread for the Journey, who is also an author, therapist and ordained minister, sums it up beautifully:

> "Meditation calms our minds and makes it easier for us to pay attention to the reality around and within us. Meditation breaks through the masks that have built up as our identity. It helps us see through our defenses and connect with unacknowledged and unloved aspects of ourselves. It opens us to higher mind and the voice of intuition. We can consciously choose meditation as a way to become more aware of who we truly are. If we don't take the initiative to open to our authentic selves, we can be certain that deep challenge and pain from life experience will push us to awaken. Meditation helps me feel the shape, the texture of my inner life. Here, in the quiet, I can begin to taste what Buddhists would call my true nature, what Jews call the still, small voice, what Christians call the holy-spirit."

Meditation is the power to still your self and go within. I

have found that daily meditation supports me in being more consciously aware of my present moment, not to mention the other tremendous benefits it gives. Meditation will help you center yourself and align yourself more with who you are. As you become more grounded, you become more conscious. As you become more conscious, you become more present. As you become more present, you become wiser. Meditation is the path to wisdom.

"Meditation brings wisdom; lack of meditation leaves ignorance. Know well what leads you forward and what holds you back, and choose the path that leads to wisdom."
—Buddha

Play the Meditation Game

Meditation can take on so many different forms. There is still meditation. There is guided meditation. There is walking meditation. There is a workout meditation. I become more connected communicating with God and life when I go for a run; it helps calm my soul allowing the clarity and wisdom to flow to me and through me. You can even meditate with plants and animals. There is meditation in simply watching your kids play, or even meditation at a stoplight. There are many forms of meditation; I'm simply inviting you to use it as one more tool.

Inner Meditation is a tool to bring you back to fuller awareness and greater understanding. I began practicing meditation by asking another how she meditates. I was told to close my eyes, take some deep breaths, pay attention to my breath, allow thoughts to pass through, be present, be still, etc. What am I supposed to notice or find out? Am I doing this right? It's all a process that I evolved with, and how you go about your meditation practice will be totally unique to you. I do invite you to give it a go.

When I first decided to give this meditation thing a go, I had no idea what I was doing. All I know is that I decided to get in the game and see what it was all about. A voice within me was calling. In my past I would not have had the *time* to spend, as I was always in a hurry to nowhere. Even now, my meditation practice can still do better. I recommend about fifteen to twenty minutes of daily morning meditation. And I recommend the same in the evening. You end up sleeping with those good feeling-thoughts, and you awake inspired. Daily morning and evening meditation will soothe your soul and awaken your being.

In the beginning of my mediation practice, I experienced what the Buddhists call "monkey mind." I was all over the board. Sugarplums were dancing in my head. Thoughts raced across my imagination, and I found I had a difficult time slowing down, or I would just fall asleep. I didn't give up, and I kept at it. I got better. I continued on, and now I am reaping the tremendous benefits.

Our lives become so hectic that we never slow down to smell the roses. I might say, "I'm going to smell the roses," yet I'm in such a hurry to go there and do this, that when I finally do get to the flowers, I only sniff briefly because I am in such a hurry to go on to my next stop to nowhere. That's the point. What's the hurry and where are we going? Gotta do this—gotta do that. There's not enough time? Hmmm, time to do what? You always have enough time; however, some times we have conflicting priorities. And I can just hear the rationalizing going on, so spare me. If you don't have the time, you don't really want to do it.

We don't go on vacation or play golf just to get in done. Why would we leave if our ultimate destination eventually becomes our home? We go on vacation to enjoy ourselves, to enjoy new moments along the way, to experience new sights, and to relax and have fun. It's why we play golf as well. We don't go to the golf course to get it done; otherwise we would never leave our house. We play golf for the fun and joy along the way. It's called an experience…something many of us just take for granted.

Coaches Notes: In his hey day, Nick Faldo used to meditate twice a day to calm his mind and set clear intentions. He said it allowed him to be fully present with his thought processes, which ultimately benefited him on the golf course. He believed he could make the shots, and he did. When we meditate we connect with our higher Self. We get really clear about who we are, and what we desire. Remember: We Become What We Think.

The Fairway of Life

Meditation Exercise: Here is a technique recommended by Dr. Teri Daunter, Psychologist, Author and International lecturer who has trained people in meditation on 5 continents.

Mind is ever restless and psychological conflicts produce distortions. If you have opposing impulses that are simultaneously demanding expression, you will create significant mental tension, i.e. 'I want to par this hole, but I am a lousy golfer.' Therefore, meditation will aid you in producing changes in the electrical activity of your nervous system in order to create coherence and synthesis allowing you to experience mastery over your golf game. It will aid you to be in the NOW allowing your true potential to unfold each and every time and allowing you to enjoy your game more fully. You will learn to have more fun with the game. So for those of you who have never had an experience of meditation, let me recommend Primordial Sound Meditation which will help you to live mindfully in the moment and restore mental and physiological balance. Meditation is easy and effortless. The less you do, the greater the rewards you shall experience. So don't make it an intellectual process because it isn't. Just BE. Meditation is about the art of being.

Sit quietly and comfortably on a chair in a warm room or warm space with your spine straight and with your feet flat on the floor. Let your arms hang loosely in your lap. Now gently close your eyes. At this moment, just begin to follow your breath. Become aware of the rise and fall of your abdomen. Breath is your life force. Put your entire awareness on your breath and follow your breath for about five minutes. As you continue to follow your breath, begin to chant mentally the Sanskrit word SO – HUM ...chant "SO" with your inhalation and chant "HUM" with your exhalation.

SOOOOO...HUMMMMM
SOOOOO...HUMMMMM

Now slow down that breath, ease your breath, follow it and direct it. Expand your abdomen like a helium balloon on the inhalation as you mentally chant "SO", and push that belly button all the way to your spine with the exhalation as you continue to chant "HUM". That is all. Now you are meditating.

Dr. Daunter recommends that we do this twice a day for twenty minutes. Best time is 5:30 a.m. and 5:30 p.m. BEFORE meals for 20 minutes. But if these times are not convenient for you, find a time that works and meditate. It is important that you meditate before eating; otherwise your body is busy digesting food and you will not gain the clarity you could achieve on a full stomach. Do this meditation every day the same way each time and the transformation will be remarkable.

If chanting is too weird for you then simply be still, and be present. Let go of all thoughts and concerns of the day and simply be. Just slow down and connect with your Inner Being, with wisdom, with clarity and with peace within. You end up taking that energy out into the world with your work, your relationships, and your golf game. Meditation presents the opportunity to be at ease and at peace with oneself guiding the way to what your soul already knows. Ohm…

Mindful Awareness Exercise: Mindful Awareness is a present state moment of being that simply notices. Being mindful is becoming fully aware without judgment or criticism. Begin by becoming mindful on the simple things in daily life. Be mindful and fully aware while brushing your teeth, preparing meals, eating meals, washing dishes, folding clothes, or any kind of daily activity. Take the time to enjoy the task at hand. Simply notice. The more we practice a more mindful awareness way of life in our daily activities the more we train our minds to practice mindful awareness on the golf course as well.

Many great golfers have practiced some form of ancient eastern Zen philosophy, Buddhist middle way of life, or more modern western versions of being more mindful and keenly aware in the NOW. Ben Hogan used to practice his version of being mindfully aware the moment he got up in the morning. He would intentional move in the same way he would play throughout his day. He would go about his business with the same rhythm and tempo as he would on the golf course. He would tie his shoes with keen awareness, stretch and warm-up in perfect harmony, and walk with purpose and understanding. He practiced "mindful awareness" intuitively because this kept his attention upon his intention in the here and now. He set the tone for his day by paying attention and keeping himself focused and present. Tiger does the same with similar clarity, focus, and purpose.

*It is important to note that being more mindfully aware is simply a process of noticing, paying attention, and becoming acutely aware of being present, noticing and observing ourselves without judgment or self-criticism. The mind becomes aware of our thoughts and feelings, which drift in and out like waves crashing the beach and receding back under. Yet the ocean remains intact. It is important to note the difference between "mindful" observation and self-critical conscious behavior. One allows us to go with the flow and the other restricts us from playing our very best. Having a critical eye that judges our performance on how well we are doing or not only brings with it a sense worry and fear in which we get caught up in the game of result playing. Trying to play a certain or particular way, trying to make things come out right, and worrying about whether we are succeeding or not is playing the self-critical conscious behavior game. We get caught up in the process of result thinking, which takes us away from enjoying the process in the present moment where we are free to fully express ourselves. Ideally, we want to be mindful in the process of swinging the club or stroking the putt. We want to be fully present and aware of what we are doing without the self-conscious critic tapping us on the shoulder. When we apply the strategy and technique of being mindfully aware to our golf game we begin to recognize and reinforce positive and successful behavior and even learn from our mistakes. We train our mind to greater awareness keeping on to continual improvement.

The Story of a Buddhist Monk

There once was a very wise monk who lived in sixteenth century Japan whose name was Stichiri. He was sitting one day in meditation in his austere little home when a thief broke in. The monk was so quiet that the thief didn't even realize that he was there. As the thief was busy sneaking around the room, looting, he suddenly heard a sound.

"Excuse me, sir, but could you be a little quieter? I am meditating here."

Though unnerved at this, the thief drew a sword, "If you make a move, I am going to cut your head off."

The monk raised his hand calmly and said, "Please, take whatever you like; don't be afraid; just be a little more quiet; I am meditating." Then off he went right back into his meditation.

Totally off-centered by this, the thief looted the entire house, keeping one eye warily on this strange monk. Just as the thief was opening the door to leave, he heard, "Excuse me. But I do have some rent to pay this week. Could you please leave a little for that? Thank you."

Disarmed, the thief reached into his own pocket and pulled out some money. Just as he was about to go out the door, the monk spoke: "Don't you think that when someone gives you something, you should thank him for it?"

Nervously, the thief mumbled, "Thank you," slammed the door, and ran.

The thief was caught a couple of weeks later robbing another house. When he was brought to trial, the monk was asked to testify. The judge told the monk, "Please explain how this man robbed you."

The monk looked up at the judge and at the man lovingly, "This man didn't rob me. I gave him everything, and he thanked me for it."

With that the monk left the courtroom.

The thief was convicted, however, because of other testimony, and spent two years in prison. The day he was released, he went directly to the monk and became one of his devoted disciples.

The moral of this story has to do with accepting and embracing all that comes into your life. It's about a calm demeanor and compassionate understanding. Meditation helps pave the way. The monk gave the thief's life back to him. The key is in understanding how he did it. Now what do you draw from the story?

> **Simple Secret Reminder # 12 – Meditate, Smile, Laugh, Enjoy**
> **Being present really does mean smelling the flowers along the journey.**
> **What's the hurry, and where are you going?**

Smile

Thich Nhat Hanh, the second leading Buddhist monk just behind the Dalai Lama, has said that if you smile five times a day for no good reason your life will change. By golly, he's right! Smiling and laughter are wonderful ways to connect with who you are. My God…is it good for the soul! Smiling also brings us back to being present. Go ahead and smile ☺. What do you think Patch Adams did with all his patients? He loved them and made them laugh and smile. It's good for the soul. It's good for our golf game.

So, smile for no good reason, and laugh like no one is watching. As I write this I am reminded of a song I heard not too long ago, a song that brings me back to center and warms my heart. The lyrics are forever ingrained in my psyche. The song is entitled, *Come from the Heart*, written by S. Clark/R. Leigh and sung by Cathy Bolton at the Conversations with God Annual Recreating Yourself Holiday Retreat:

> "When I was a young girl, my daddy told me a lesson he learned. It was a long time ago. He said, 'If you want to have something to hold onto, you're gonna have to learn to let go.' You gotta sing—like you don't need the money—love like you'll never get hurt. You gotta dance like nobody's watchin'. It's gotta come from the heart—if you want it to work. Now here is the one thing I keep forgetting. When everything is falling apart, in life as in love, you need to remember, there's such a thing as trying too hard."

So play golf like no one is watching. Ground yourself in the present. If you played like no one is watching, would you take it seriously or have more fun with it? Would you stay in the present moment more often than not? Would you roll with the changes and not take them too seriously?

> **Simple Secret Reminder # 13 – Play Golf *like* No One Is Watching**
> **Be free to express your self.**
> **Lighten up and have fun.**

Yoga for Golfers

Yoga is yet one more form of meditation and a golf-specific practice that can be most helpful to grounding golfers back to the present. This ancient practice provides an additional tool to connect the mind, body, and spirit in the present moment. I practice a form of yoga on my own and it helps in numerous ways. I am calmer, more relaxed, more connected. I am more flexible, and I am in better shape, more fit.

Find a yoga program that works for you. You can make yoga golf specific or simply enjoy the complete workout. You will find that yoga teachers are compassionate about the individual strengths and flexibility of all their students. You perform and progress at your own pace. A place to start might be with Katherine Roberts, and her Yoga for Golfers programs. Lorena Ochoa practices yoga and I would be shocked if Tiger Woods didn't practice some form of yoga as well. Hank Haney, Woods' instructor says, "My students have improved their game with Katherine's unique and effective program." It only makes sense to be better fit, more flexible, and more connected to life. Yoga helps to pave the way. It's an excellent form of exercise in so many ways.

Being Aware Living Moment to Moment

The power of NOW is well understood by those who practice

it. The intention of this chapter is to bring greater awareness to the present moment on so many levels. By being mindful of the present moment we are more apt to open to new levels of awareness. As we nurture this moment-to-moment non-judgmental awareness we will cultivate and sustain that attention over greater periods of time.

Becoming more mindfully aware in the moment may very well be the secret to break the spell of repeating the same behaviors over and over again. Our angst on the golf course repeats itself time and time again, year after year, until it doesn't. Without awareness and presence we live superficial lives, often one-dimensional thinking that life is happening to us rather than through us. Becoming awakened, aware, and present changes our lives both on and off the golf course on so many new and inspiring facets. With awareness we approach each moment as being brand new, letting go of past limiting beliefs while reinforcing clear mind, clear body. We become open and attentive.

"If moment by moment you can keep your mind clear then nothing will confuse you."
—Sheng Yen

Golfers who live in the moment are able to keep their mind clear. Being in the moment is a key component to playing golf in The Zone—one shot at a time.

> **Action Steps:**
> 1) **Practice being here now.**
> 2) **Practice meditation.**
> 3) **Practice any exercise to calm your mind, body and spirit.**

Chapter 6

Embrace All Your Golf Shots

"For when I can love all of me, I will love all of you."
—Debbie Ford

Can you embrace *all* of your golf shots?

As soon as I can learn to embrace and love *all* of my golf shots, I can begin to embrace, and love *all* of the game of golf. Did you just hear that? As soon as I can learn to embrace and love *all* of my golf shots, I can begin to embrace and love *all* of the game of golf. Once I *really* understood and *practiced* this concept it not only became a huge revelation, it took my game to another level. And this practice will take your game there as well!

Embracing everything allows us to accept those shots that we may have previously thought as undesirable, the "bad" shots. By not attaching qualifying labels to shots—a shot is just a shot—we can focus on acceptance, and learning from this experience – becoming once again, an objective detective. Our thinking can shift from being all pissed off, which takes us further out of our zone, to how we can improve next time? Our thinking, once we allow ourselves to purge and understand what just happened, can move into what can we do better next time? The shots that don't necessarily go our way are actually providing us a gift to become better paving the way forward.

Accepting all of our golf shots is also a subtle way of forgiving ourselves in the moment. There's a feeling of forgiving ourselves when things are slightly out of sync. It's okay. The more we practice this concept…the better we end up playing in the long run. This simple embrace-all-of-it formula is essential to our happiness and

The Fairway of Life

success. After all, judgment, irritation, and frustration simply draw us further away from our center and away from The Zone.

> **Simple Secret Reminder # 14 – Accept Every Golf Shot**
> **Practice a "pre-accepting" type of attitude in your mind.**
> **Embrace this moment for exactly what it is.**
> **Learn from this experience and become even better next time.**

A Morning Run and More Conservation with God

Meditation helps to set the tone for the rest of our day when we allow this connection with our Inner Being become our dominant vibration. Meditation helps us to embrace all that life has to offer. Meditation calms our soul and aligns us with our higher Self. Playing golf and playing life with this kind of mindset and connection creates miracles. We're literally transforming ourselves through our thoughts, words, feelings, and actions. Imagine living your life like a dream, a prayer, a meditation.

Meditation helps to inspire us to what it is we desire and what it is we know what is best for ourselves. All we really have to do is get still, connect, and be. Upon *coming back* from my morning meditation I felt inspired to go for a run and do some yoga. Listening to the wisdom of our body paves the way forward. Our lives become much less hectic and more in harmony with our own deepest desires.

Because of my meditation I felt connected on my morning run. The carryover effect went directly into my run, which set the tone for the rest of my day. I began having more conversations with God as I felt uplifted and very light on my feet. I felt inspired to keep on keeping on. I felt like Jimmy Stewart in *It's a Wonderful Life*! I had many questions about life. My questions are just like your questions. And just as I ask them, so can you. Sure I have a desire to play my best golf, yet I also have a desire to enjoy my life's work and experience the joy of an intimate relationship. God informed me to stay on my true path and keep on being whom I really am.

My run was filled with excited anticipation as each stride carried the feeling of empowerment. I felt as if I was jogging along effortlessly, God and I connected as ONE, talking to each other. Yes, there were words, feelings, and understandings. All of it meant to serve me and I am most grateful. I was also reminded and inspired to keep on, to follow this wisdom within, and take action. There is nothing to fear.

As I finished my run at the top of the downstairs walkway into Harbor Springs (the platform where the noon siren rings), I began seeing the beauty in everything. "Hello, beautiful tree. Hello, you wonderful cedar hedge. Hello, telephone pole. Hello there, garbage can. Hello, you wonderful bark," I expressed as I felt the crevasses within maple tree. "Hello, fire hydrant." Yes, I felt like Jimmy Stewart must have felt—I had renewed vigor and interest in life. I am having my own conversations with God, and, right now, I am deeply connected to this wisdom. Everything seems so clear. It's like I'd better keep on writing while I have this connection, for who knows how long this will last and remain so clear?

God was talking to me on my run, and I was talking back. It was great! The timing could not be more perfect. I have been given an enhanced and expanded awareness. I am grateful. Yet, understand this, the truth is, God talks to each of us all the time. Not just in times of difficulty or challenge. This communication is all around us, all the time. God is always communicating with us; it's just a matter of who's listening?

The opposite of not listening to this communication and heeding the wisdom of our own soul is what causes us the most suffering. I know I have lived and experienced that. The opposite of embracing leads to frustration. I know I have lived and experienced that. Frustration and anxiety comes from not listening to ones soul.

The Opposite of Embracing

In the past, I've had my fair share of issues on the golf course: anger, frustration, irritation, and dishonesty. Back then my awareness was not as sharp and as clear as it is now. I didn't understand what I do now. I thought life was just happening to me, and I was responding in a less than desirable way whenever bounces didn't go my way. Golf was a game I loved, but these issues led me to become frustrated and disillusioned. I felt like quitting many times over, yet I knew I couldn't do that. The frustration lead me to keep beating more golf balls forever in search for a swing that would hold up without feeling like I was *always* starting over. I was *always* scared to play again the next day even when I ended up playing well the day before. I didn't know how to deal with being so scared.

I now see it was all laying the groundwork for showing me who I really am. In my earlier days, I threw my share of clubs. I've even flung a few in my *later* days. I've witnessed friends flinging whirlybirds and helicopters in classic fashion. I've gotten so damn mad that I once wrapped a club around the nearest and biggest tree.

The incident I remember most clearly happened during the Ferris State College Professional Golf Management Program back in 1978. I was playing an early spring round with a group of new friends. I made an awful late round shot and out of sheer frustration I flew into an absolute rage. I threw my club so far and with so much angry and so much force, that one of my wide-eyed playing partners turned to me and said, "I hope I never have to play golf with you again."

Ouch! Well, he hasn't, and that embarrassing, out-of-control moment has stuck with me decades later. I didn't understand why I'd get so damn mad. I am grateful that it played out the way it did, because it served as a wake-up call.

Two Quick Frustration Stories

A few summers ago at the Petoskey Bay-View Country Club, Dick Oelke, Dan Anderson, Jack Zlotow, and I had a game going. Dick and I play even; both of us have had around a six handicap most of our lives. Dan is a relative newcomer to the game of golf. He doesn't play that often (about once every two weeks), yet has a terrific mindset no matter what. His handicap would be around an

18 or bogey golf. Jack plays to about an eight. And he hates it when he doesn't play within the comfort zone of his handicap.

Well, Jack got into a funk on the upper nine. I forget his score exactly—probably around a 43 or 44, and he was pissed. Jack was my partner. On hole #10, the elevated par three, I asked Jack if he could let go of what just happened, embrace it, and focus in on the bottom nine. I know he heard me, but I didn't hear a response. I could see him seething inside, like there was invisible smoke coming out his ears. He was so angry from that earlier nine, that he let the whole rest of his round go to hell as well.

This is the kind of thing I'm talking about. And I've been there—many times—so I'm not pointing fingers. Although Jack apologized for being a disappointment and no fun to be around, it still didn't help when I had to ante up for our team bet. But the money is trivial. One's state of being is the essential component. We do have a choice: to be angry or not.

Heck, once a long time ago, in the late seventies, playing the same course, our foursome included Tom Oelke, Mark Page, Jack and me. We played quite a few rounds together and got to know each other's game pretty well. I recall a moment when my emotions got the best of me. We were playing hole #12, an easy par five, which is a hole I want to birdie. See I was getting ahead of myself focusing on outcome. Well, I was the last to play, and somehow or another, I missed a short par putt. Everyone was walking off the green and on to the next tee when Jack, the official scorekeeper, asked me what I had on the hole. He knew; he just wanted confirmation. I was steaming and pretty soon the whole emotional kettle boiled over. I screamed at the top of my lungs, "Sixxxxxxxxxxxx!" I am sure my outburst woke up the entire Bay View neighborhood. I was obviously not embracing my shot or the outcome. Often, that is just how it is. I experienced the opposite of embracing for most of my life.

We went on to finish our round, and there I was again on hole #18, faced with a similar four-and-a-half foot putt for par and a make-or-break money situation. I missed the damn putt and lost the game. Mark Page walked off the green and up the pathway and called me, "Missster Clutch." That taunt made me feel awful, like a looser, a choker. I hated losing whenever I let my nerves get the best of me.

I've recalled that day on several occasions. What I resist; persists. And it is all for my own good, for it brings me to where I am in the present day. I resisted this for thirty-six years of my golfing life. See how I can relate to Freddy Couples? At least Freddy simply shrugged his shoulders. Very rarely did Freddy get too visibly upset on national TV, although I have seen him kick his putter blade in disgust. Like Freddy, I have also made my share of clutch putts over the years too. There's always a balance.

By the way, as Jack recalled this memory in a recent phone conversation we had, he reminded me of how Mark Page is also known for his swinging big from the heels. He was a big, strapping guy who worked his ass off on the grounds crew under the leadership of Leo Peterson, about a four to five handicap golfer himself. Page could really knock the snot out of the ball and hit it a long ways, however, he'd sometimes top it or drive it so far out bounds that he'd just smile and say, "Give me a double." The most we could post on a scorecard was double bogey. We call them pocket doubles. They help with the ego thing.

Jack has confirmed with me today how all these principles have worked in his life—both for and against him. He reminded me of the time he first broke eighty. Jack was playing golf with Mike Davies, an old local sports star from the past, and he told me how he was six over par after six holes, obviously beside himself. He went on to shoot seventy-eight. He said that it was key for him to remain as positive and as focused as could be. Well, Jack, that was then and this is now. How do you want to show up next, especially in the face of adversity? That is the other side of the growth continuum. We grow at both ends of the comfort zone spectrum. Embrace it all, and step fully into the light.

In my new awakened understanding, *being in* the moment more often, I am much more conscious of how I respond. I would like to say that I will never toss a club again, or became scared over a putt, but I can't. I might get all caught up in the heat of some future moment. Sometimes I, too, like to vent. But now that I am known as Mr. *Spiritual Golf*, my friends will be the first to point out any little frustration or anger they see in me. *"Embrace it,"* they say with a grin. It comes with the territory. Please, do not place me on a pedestal. I am a human being living with human challenges, and believe it or not, I don't always get it right either…just becoming a little better than I used to be. The real trick is in embracing the moment, learning from the moment no matter how pissed off you are. It's not necessarily expressing your frustration with yourself that's the problem; the aim is to be able to center and ground yourself in being your very best on your next shot. Incidentally, Tiger does that better than most. And even he can still do even better.

The Meaning of It All

My goal is to get to the root of the frustration itself and be with that before it escalates. The more I am able to be with whatever comes up, the less often it will. How beautiful is that?

Like you, I have witnessed my fair share of classic club-throwing moments. How many times have you seen a club break or land in the trees? What's up with that anyway? Is it good? Is it bad? Good, bad…who knows? Is it healthy? What's it showing you? How do you wish to express yourself?

Each situation is unique. Whenever I've witnessed another golfer throwing his club, I've felt sorry for the dumb bastard, or I've given a little snicker, sometimes under my breath. Other times I couldn't resist laughing out loud. Now, for the most part, I simply observe. I also observe how another will respond with their next golf shot, as I also observe myself. How does a champion respond?

What I do find myself doing is playing more often with a more enlightened group of golfers who are now embracing playing this form of spiritual golf themselves. Even if I am in the company of those that may not understand, I can still set a tone of acceptance and peace and offer inspiring messages whenever I sense an opportunity. Remember we teach by the clarity of *our* example not our words.

I have used my share of foul language on the golf course as well. Actually, swear words by themselves are not a problem for me.

The Fairway of Life

However, when they're used offensively, against yourself or another, they can be very damaging. I mean, even Tiger Woods says his fair share of expletives. I've heard he's fined a healthy sum, year in and year out, for dropping the "f-bomb" on the PGA Tour. Is this kind of behavior healthy? Is this kind of behavior setting a clear and empowering example for others to follow? My answer is that each person answers that question for himself. A little muttering or a quiet gentle reminder to yourself—hey, it's your call. As long as you can immediately regroup, see it for what it's showing you, and move on to the present moment of NOW. Tiger does that better than most. And even the best can become better.

Making the Best Better

Even the number one golfer in the world can do better, and perhaps he could score better too with just a little bit more of the acceptance and embracing concepts. If Tiger has room for improvement, imagine what lies in store for the rest of us! Over the years, I have observed Tiger recreating himself anew. He has worked diligently at it. He carries himself differently. He's more mature. He manages his game and his emotions much better. In interviews on television, Tiger talks about cooling his jets. He says—paraphrasing—I used to be way up, too high (ecstatic) or way down, too low (upset). Now you might not see me smile as much or be as angry as much; I've learned you just can't do that. He's saying he is more in control of his emotions. What I'm asking is, is controlling or managing your emotions the key, or is the key *being with them* and seeing what they are showing you about yourself? Regardless of the semantics, I believe the latter has more depth.

Yes, Tiger is learning to *control* his emotions better. He decided that being way up or way down did not benefit his overall game. Too many highs and lows either way amount to self-sabotage. Just coming off a disastrous hole or a string of birdies can play havoc with your mind and emotions—if you let them. It's more about staying in the present, not about thinking about the past, not jumping too far ahead into the future. And it's not about "the not," it's about focusing on this exact moment and executing this exact shot with what you do want. It's about tapping into the job at hand. It's about getting out of your own way. It's about focusing on what you are doing right now. It's about thinking downstream thoughts. And that is what Tiger does better than most! There's a difference between *"being with"* your emotions, releasing them in a healthy way versus trying to control them.

What is it, exactly, that makes Tiger tick? Is there anything magical or mystical? Is there something different in Tiger's DNA? Are there secrets that lie within his psyche? The only one able to fully answer these questions is Tiger himself. I believe he's blessed with a gift, believes in himself, and fully expects to win. That is the power of his psyche. He has no fear in being the best. Study what Tiger does and make it your own. It takes great courage to summon the strength of perseverance, drive, energy, sacrifice and responsibility. Yes, it takes responsibility to assume the role of being a Tiger.

If you fall prey to the "intimidation factor," then what you get is intimidation. If you allow the tiger to intimidate you, it will. The tiger is any opponent in which you *feel* inferior too. It is your own vibrational energy that gives you your own results. I am inviting you to focus on your own task at hand and believe in yourself. It isn't how Tiger does it; it's how *you* do it, and it's how *you* wish to show up. Now, if you like what you see in Tiger, take back your power and make it your own. I believe Tiger embraces it all to the very best of his ability today; and he continues on in his quest and mission to get even better tomorrow. Tiger is chasing down holding the number of majors won by Nicklaus at eighteen. Tiger's goal is nineteen majors, and beyond – perhaps leaving his legacy as the world's best golfer…ever. Tiger currently stands with 14 majors on his mantle through 2008.

Embracing it All, Right Here, Right Now

Playing spiritual golf in The Zone is about embracing all of it. Once you begin to embrace all of it, you will play golf with renewed interest and vigor. There's really no reason to get upset. Once you start accepting, embracing, and being with your emotions, you begin to play golf more consistently and on a more even keel. You begin to go with the flow. You begin to see more clearly. You begin to find that the things that were not desirable, like your bad golf shots, begin to melt away. You actually have less of them by embracing them. Yes, it sounds implausible, but it is true. Because what we resist, persists. If your game is actually falling apart, let it; it just may be falling back together. Don't hang on so tenaciously to things that may not be working. The nice thing about falling apart is that you get to pick up only the pieces that you *want*.

You can call it controlling or managing your emotions or *being with* your emotions. How you go about your business of semantics is your business. These are just words. Simply ask yourself, "Is what I am being and doing with my emotions working?" For me, it is my new understanding that my emotions are nothing that I *want* to try and control. Emotions exist as a wonderful gift. Your feelings are the language of your soul. This intuition, this knowing, is your sixth sense. Open up and experience your feelings on a much grander scale. You *want* to be with them. You want to gain the wisdom that lies within them. It's God communicating with us.

Examine your emotions; see what they are all about. Then regroup and focus once again on what you want. The more you are able to *be with* your bad feelings, the less likely they are to return. The more you understand this, the less you will get off center in the first place. Remember, your feelings are your internal guidance system. Whenever you feel a tad off, simply focus on a better feeling-thought, and bring yourself back to center.

Being Calm and Conscious

The best players don't like some of their bad golf shots. Who does? I know that I don't like them either. But I can embrace them. The best players let them go, regroup, and refocus on the task at hand more often than most. I can't say for sure that the world's best players embrace all their golf shots. I observe many that don't. But every golfer can learn instantaneously what it was that caused the mishap, or what brought about the great shot. What it takes is feedback in the NOW, and the only way to get that feedback is to be calm, conscious, and present after the shot. You take this immediate feedback and continue with your intention for your next shot.

I believe that this is what the best golfers are doing. It's just that some folks process this kind of information more quickly than others do. The quicker you can close the gap from your knowing to your experiencing the quicker you will be on the road to mastery. The quicker you can close the gap between what just happened now and how you learn to accept, embrace, and *be with* your shots and emotions, the quicker you can get on with what you really want. And what you want is more and more of those better feeling thoughts and great golf shots, which comes from being in The Zone. The more often you hit the better golf shot, usually, the lower your score. Lower scores equal lower handicaps. Lower scores equal more fun. Lower scores equal a bigger paycheck. Embracing these concepts produces a better demeanor, more fun, more consistent, and as a side benefit, perhaps better scoring. What you're really asking for is the freedom to play golf less arduously; calm, clear, connected, focused, present, shots flying freely where you want them to go.

The more I embrace the moment and consciously understand why I did what I did, the more completely I will take this understanding into my next shot. If I am all pissed off and frustrated and let it bother me, I am only setting myself up for more frustration, and this means that I did not reap the gift in the moment. Ever notice others getting all pissed off at their golf game? So what? Is that what *you* want? It takes a lot more internal fortitude to *embrace* all of it. The gift is in knowing what you did correctly and what you didn't. If I fail to finish my swing and release the club, and the ball ends up weak right, my gift is to calmly integrate finishing my swing and releasing the club next time. I quietly embrace this and simply see it for what it is. There is no reason to fight it. There is nothing to be afraid of; there is no one to please; you have nothing to prove. Get out of your ego. Let go of your *need* to win. There is a huge difference between your needs and your wants. Allow your true burning desire that comes from pureness of your heart be your calling.

The Fairway of Life

The ego loves to divide us up into winners and losers. Remember who you really are. You are not your winnings, you are not your victories, and you are not your score. You're not even your name. You're much more than that. The surefire way to disconnect from yourself is to let the ego in and think you *are* these things. You may play competitively, but you don't have to be there in your thoughts. This concept of ego may be too difficult for many to embrace; yet in order to play well, you have to let go. Let it happen naturally and effortlessly with joy and with a burning desire within. It's not about the scoring; it's about the enjoying. The scoring will take care of it self.

Regroup and Refocus in THE NOW

The intention here is to understand how important it is to regroup and refocus, to center yourself and get back into the present moment of NOW. Yes, Nick Faldo and Paul Azinger, your commentary at The Open Championship in 2007 on being in THE NOW is spot on. The more often you are in THE NOW, the less arduous the play. And when there is a distraction, for the one who embraces it, regroups, and realigns him self has a much better chance. Within this margin lies the difference between an early exit and perhaps an opportunity to play on the weekend. It is the difference between your hoisting the Claret Jug and watching someone else "just do it." Imagine how many strokes we amateurs could shave off if we just regrouped and embraced even just a little bit better? Our handicaps would drop simply by embracing this concept alone.

The one who lets irritation fester has much less chance. More often than not, that person will have the same problem time and time again, not only on the golf course, but also in other aspects of their life. Therefore, playing spiritual golf can be therapeutic once you begin to embrace it all. For, as we say, what you resist; persists. Let irritation get the best of you, and you may end up getting so pissed off that you simply give up on the rest of your round, or worse yet, quit altogether.

You say I don't give a shit. I don't care anymore.

Okay. If it makes you feel good to wallow in your sorry self, then go ahead and be my guest. Is that how you want to spend the next few hours? Of course not! You *do* care. I'm calling you out, and I'm calling your bluff. If I'm making you angry, then that's just fine too. Go ahead, get in your car without saying good-bye and hit the accelerator while you're speeding off in anger. Does golf cause you all this emotional chaos? Is that who you are? Is that what you want? I've done it, so I know. Does this serve a purpose for you? It takes a strong-willed person to embrace it all and shrug your shoulders as to what just happened out there. See the gift, and there will be fewer and fewer of those situations. It's just a game.

The Process That Ends in Poof

Golf is a fun game, right? Or is it only fun when you are playing well? Part of the reason for this dialogue is to help you embrace, accept, and honor every shot—the good, the bad, and the ugly. I mean *you're* the one who hit it. Nobody else hit your shot, did they? Are you going to focus on your next shot or whistle Dixie? I don't know. Let's ask Clint, or better yet, Fuzzy. I'm sure his whistling is all meant to keep him calm, to keep him in his element.

I invite you to see the wisdom that each of your golf shots is seeking to show you. Listening, being calm and conscious of what just happened may lessen the likelihood that what you don't want to do will happen again. Likewise, when you hit the great shot, embrace that too.

The Real Benefits

Now that we've chatted a bit about embracing and accepting all our golf shots, let me tell you about the real benefits of actually being it and doing it:

1) You will learn to enjoy, appreciate, honor, and respect the game of golf that much more.
2) As you begin to accept and embrace all your golf shots, your frustration level will begin to disappear. You'll hit

less of those so-called bad golf shots, and when you do, you'll take it with a grain of salt more often than ever before.
3) You will recover much faster and quicker, and save more shots, more holes, and more rounds of golf then ever before. The quicker you recover, the quicker you will be back on your path to mastery.
4) You will like yourself much better, and so will your playing partners.
5) You will play golf in the present more often then ever before.
6) You will play golf to your full potential more often then ever before.
7) You will play spiritual golf in The Zone more often then ever before.

Greater conscious awareness means greater clarity and wisdom—signs that you are on the road to mastery. Close the gap from where you are to what you are becoming. Keep holding the vision of who you really are and what you really, really want. This is a mantra that I keep telling myself. I see the shot . . . I feel the shot . . . I trust the shot.

This too is a spiritual law. The quicker you understand embracing and accepting, the quicker the irritation will go away. I am not saying you have to necessarily *like* the awful shots, I'm saying *embrace* them, and as you embrace them, there will be fewer of them—the bad shots, that is. Soon, even the "bad" shots won't get you so down. It just is.

I have come to accept that even after a horrendous start, by choosing to accept where I am—five over after three—by keeping my cool, and by believing that my alignment will return, I will ultimately score better in the long run and enjoy my round that much more. In the past, seeing I was on my way to a very high number would affect my demeanor and my enjoyment—not only for the next few hours, but sometimes well into the evening and sometimes even longer. The benefits of embracing it all are astounding!

I cannot begin to tell you how many rounds of golf I have *saved* recently because I accepted and embraced my poor play in the beginning of my round, and kept my composure and demeanor under control through to the end. I have been five, six, seven over par early going, and most of the time I still ended up breaking eighty. In the past—forget it, I'm done. I'm mad as hell, and I'm not going to take it any more. Understanding how to accept and embrace is, in itself alone, another one of those worth-its-weight-in-gold concepts.

Embrace every single bit of it. Accept everything as it is. Welcome whatever comes to your gate. Recreate yourself anew in your next moment of NOW. For life is nothing more than continuous moments of NOW.

The intention is to embrace being perfectly imperfect. Embrace the observation, and be mindful to not judge. Judgment says that was a *shitty* shot. Observation says *I* hit it there; it's just a shot. Judgment blinds; observation witnesses. Judgment hinders; observation is an opportunity for growth. Judgment is often a negative. Observation is non-bias. Judgment narrows; observation widens. Judgment pushes away and rejects; observation welcomes. Judgment hinders; observation enhances. Judgment justifies, observation accepts. Judgment blames, observation embraces. Judgment is a righteous opinion; observation either resonates with something, or not. Quick judgments often are based on false assumptions. Judgments are based in FEAR. Observations are based in LOVE.

Acceptance and Patience Is a Beautiful Thing

Acceptance and patience on the golf course is a beautiful thing. The more patience you have, the less irritated you get. The more patience you have, the more accepting you are. The more accepting you are, the more joy you experience. The more joy you experience, the better you play. Playing patient golf, complete and utter acceptance in the moment, is a sure sign that you have found your path. Take what the course is offering, play within yourself, and when the time is right, when you are feeling it, go for it, and color outside the lines. You will know when to rein it in, and when to let it go. Acceptance in the moment is freedom. Acceptance is a key ingredient on your road to mastery. Relax and let it be.

> *"Don't hurry, don't worry. You're only here for a short visit. So be sure to stop and smell the flowers."*
> —Walter Hagen

Don't take anything too seriously. The highs and the lows—they all pass. Trust your golf and let your golf know it can trust you. You are on a wonderful journey that is beyond what words can express.

Action Steps:

1) **Practice embracing all of your golf shots, and learn from them.**
2) **Practice new perspectives in how you wish to see the world that feels good.**
3) **Practice acceptance and playing patient golf.**

Chapter 7

Thoughts Create Swings

> *"The thoughts you choose to think and believe right now are creating your future. These thoughts form your experiences tomorrow, next week, and next year!"*
> —Louise Hay

I can and I will

I prefer I can and I will over I'm trying. I prefer I can and I will by keeping on. One of the biggest mistakes we make is "trying" to do something. Trying is a crutch word that not only expresses our underlying fear, but also gives us an easy out when what we say we will try to do does not work out. "I'll try to do it," we say. Can't you just hear the trepidation? Or, "I'm trying my best!" May I suggest we replace this word *trying* with belief of eager anticipation, having fun, believing that *I can and I will!* What sounds better, to keep *trying* or to keep *on*? I invite you to use this new mindset reminder wherever you go, both on and off the golf course and watch your life change for the better!

> *"It is essential to think strongly and forcefully, I can do it, without boasting or fretting."*
> —The Dalai Lama

The word "trying" by itself is not necessarily the culprit that will derail our dreams; it is our interpretation of it and the resultant creation of self-limiting beliefs or state of mind that is the real culprit. "We have met the enemy, and he is us," said Pogo. I was brought up with the attitude that trying something meant I was willing to take a chance and give it the ole' college try, to give it my best. I still believe that my work is to give my best effort. However, I have also come to understand, that "trying too hard" to make something happen or "trying too hard" because of fear or "trying too hard" when used as a crutch to give up or give less than your best effort, can actually inhibit or block peak performance. What is your mindset around the concept of *trying*? It's not in the word itself, it's in the vibrational energy that we create within our own thoughts. Instead of trying to do something, simply be it and let it happen.

Here are some examples to which I refer from various sports to give you a better perspective. A baseball pitcher wishes to pitch to a certain location. He is best served by unconsciously letting it happen trusting his natural instinct and going with the flow. Trying to aim at a target with conscious thoughts takes us into a place of fear. A person throwing darts at a target is best served by letting it happen versus aiming and trying so hard to make it happen, which often paralyzes the thrower. A basketball free throw shooter tries to make the shot and often "short arms" it. A golfer seeking to hit the left side of the fairway is best served not by steering or trying to control it, but by getting out of their way and …letting it happen.

There is a fine line we transcend in seeking to make something happen versus getting out of our own way and letting it happen. And you know what that feels like. One is awkward another is flowing. Drop the thought of trying, and simply let it be. Think about what it would be like if you thought too much about driving your car, hands tensed on the wheel seeking to keep it perfectly straight. Think about the little things that you just do: walking, talking with your best friends; taking a drink of water; riding your bike. Let it be natural. Let it happen.

Coaches Notes: There are two phenomenon's going on here. One is our interpretation of the word *trying*. This really has more to do with our vibration and internal fortitude than it does with the actual word itself. We just have to be honest with ourselves. The second understanding is a deeper metaphysical concept regarding our limited belief system we have created and allowed to take root, which is only a small, yet significant aspect within the concept of "trying." The reason we don't think we can is because we have allowed ourselves to think that way. This goes deep and even deeper still. *Trying* to explain the vastness of your full potential is like *trying to* explain life itself. Everyone has been given the gift of tapping into their full potential; however, it is our beliefs that stop us from unlimited possibilities, infinite potential, and ever-evolving wisdom and intelligence. A Buddhist monk can literally connect with the air and open up the space to another dimension. The only thing holding us back is our self!

Now, there are plenty of tricks we can play on ourselves that just may give us more freedom to self-express ourselves on the golf course, but ultimately, it is best to be free and fully self-expressed, a 10 if you will, on a scale from 1-10, with 10 being the highest. How do you rank your self? Where are you on this scale? How self-expressed are you on the golf course? The good news is that we can change. We can change all aspects of our lives, including our golf game. Our work lies in making peace with our past, clearing away limited beliefs, obstacles, or resistances we've allowed to exist within the confines of our subconscious mind. Our work is to tell ourselves a new more empowering story, opening up to unlimited expansive knowledge and wisdom, and to think thoughts that allow us to thrive in harmony by living the life of our dreams.

Putting Exercise: Dr. Joe Parent in his book, Zen Putting, discusses a mindset that may help with short putts that he describes turning knee-knockers into tap-ins. Ideally what we desire is confidence and belief. Perhaps when we take extra stress out of the equation then this will open up a new pathway in allowing it to be. Parent suggests we putt to a spot 6, 8, 10 inches in front of our ball on line with the path to the hole. The idea is that everyone can knock in a very short tap in. Once the ball rolls over our "tap in" mark it keeps going into the hole. We eliminate fear-based thoughts and just do it. The idea is you don't need to try and hit an eight-inch putt it's easy, this mindset eliminates the variable of trying, which is an expression of fear. Another concept to consider is that when you do hit a tap in putt from eight to twelve inches away and stroke it firmly in the hole that putt will generally roll out to a length of three to four feet if the hole wasn't in the way, often the exact measurement of those knee-knockers in the first place.

I also love Parent's concept of putting to nowhere while practicing (more freedom in your stroke) and imagining a path to the hole instead of a narrow line.

I highly recommend you read his books to gain even more mental training and more mindful awareness understanding. Dr. Parent does a great job explaining his coaching techniques and exercises. He guides his readers along focusing on the process and the mental image getting a feel for optimal performance. I highly recommend you add his books and philosophy into the library of your mind.

> *"I never stroked a putt that I hadn't already made in my mind."*
> —Jack Nicklaus

The Zone happens naturally when we get out of our own way. So stop trying so hard to manufacture something; and start allowing it to be. Just become your most inspired natural state. The moment you stop trying so hard and simply let it be by going with the flow everything changes.

Simple Secret Reminder # 15 – Let It Be
Stop trying so hard and let it be.
Let it be—The Beatles

Listen to the words from Barbara Rose, spiritual author and retreat leader:

"Trying too hard is an expression of fear. If you can replace the fear with faith that everything always serves our highest good, your confidence and peace of mind will serve your aspirations. So many people work so hard, to achieve, attain, accumulate, and cherish their fortunes. How many of us blissfully fill our days and nights being the Divine expression we are? This is the meaning of life. It is to be. As a result, all of your creations are a natural outflow from the Divine within your being. This is the joy of life."

A big obstacle for many golfers is *trying too hard.* This happens with golf professionals, and amateurs alike, whenever their minds perceive the event, or the shot as bigger than it really is, or when they want to do so well that the lack of not having it overwhelms them. Wanting something so bad in this way only pushes it further away. I understand there is a lot on the line…however; golf is still simply a game…a game of chasing a little white ball down the fairway getting it into the hole with the fewest strokes. You must ask yourself, "What does it take to play my best golf?" Is it trying to make something happen because of the "bigness" of the event or being calm, focused, centered, and allowing your best golf to come forward one stroke at a time…ohm…? Do we play our best golf with a "trying" type of attitude, which sounds like we have to work really, really hard, or do we play our best golf when we simply feel, trust, allow, let go, and go with the flow? You already know the answer. Some will have a hard time letting go of the struggle and the grind, which they perceive is the answer.

The Ryder Cup would be prime example where *trying too hard* may filter into one's psyche, along with *trying* to manufacture camaraderie. While both teams are playing for country, what I have observed is that in the last couple Ryder Cups before 2008, the Americans appeared to be trying too hard to play their best versus simply playing for the fun, *genuine* camaraderie, and love of the game. I have observed it in their body language, how they addressed the media, and the short time they have in really getting to know each other. Whereas, the Europeans travel together, hang out together, toast and encourage each other year round, versus

The Fairway of Life

just a week or two every other year. Why is that? Perhaps it's a part of tradition in Europe, whereas Americans charter jets, stay at separate locations and rarely see each other, other than at the course. With talent being even, I would give the edge to the team offering the least amount of resistance in their energy, and the team with more of the genuine camaraderie…having fun allowing it to happen.

The 2008 Ryder Cup is a prime example of turning the tables on one's own medicine. In this years' event U.S. Captain Paul Azinger brought in Life Coach Ron Braund to bring individual personalities together in pods, or groups of four based upon similar personalities and where leadership might take root bringing out the best in the overall team concept. It worked. The team was focused in the present moment as evidenced by some incredible shot making, *and* they had fun. Boo Weekly made sure of that with his "down home" Happy Gilmore expressions to loosen the edge. After the win when asked by reporters, 'What does the victory taste like,' in his southern draw and simple small town demeanor he says, "Chicken."

Amateurs fight the dreaded *trying too hard* to make something happen whenever they allow the perceived bigness of the event or shot get the best of them as well. Sometimes it lasts a shot or two, sometimes a few holes, sometimes the entire round. *Trying* literally screams out: RESIGNATION, FEAR, AVOIDANCE, FAILURE! I can clearly see the difference between someone who is trying too hard to make it happen versus someone eagerly anticipating and allowing it to happen, can't you? One swing is rushed, awkward, and tensed. The other swing is smooth, in tempo, effortless, rhythmic, and free flowing. It's the subtle difference of working really hard to make something happen versus enjoying yourself and letting it happen. And you know this.

Instead of having a "trying" type of mindset, I like to think of myself as keeping on, all the while eagerly anticipating where it is I am going, allowing it to be. I like to reach for the best feeling thoughts I can. My dream, my goals, and my intention help pave the way. I like to think thoughts of following my bliss. I like to think in terms of keeping on. Keeping on feels like an eternal process, whereas keep trying feels like I'm spinning my wheels. My new perspective feels really, really good.

Seek to align yourself with pure intentions of what you desire with thoughts of joy, feeling good, believing that, I can and I will. Connect and align with Source Energy. And here's to keeping on!

> **Simple Secret Reminder # 16 – Keep on!**
> **Live your life like a dream, a meditation, or a prayer.**
> **Eagerly anticipate where it is you are going.**

Mental & Emotional Golf Exercise: When anxiety, frustration, or anger enters the equation this is an indicator that you're not thinking in alignment with who you really are and what you really know. Left unchecked, other thoughts similar to these come about. The solution is to willingly acknowledge to your self at that moment that you want to feel better.

What you think about with your life on and off the golf course you become. It is essential to think in such a way that will support your highest calling. Over time each successive moment of thought *is* who you become. If you like what you are seeing and getting in your life on or off the golf course, then by all means keep on. If you don't like what you are seeing and getting in your life on or off the golf course, then by all means change. I have found that most of us have settled for less than we are and stay stuck because of our old story. To see the results of what we have settled for all we have to do is look in the mirror. Our outer world is a direct reflection of our inner world. Therefore, in order to change the results we get we have to change our thoughts. We have to change the perspective of our inner world. Change your thoughts and you change your world.

We become what we think about ourselves, and how we view our world. We become conditioned, ignorant, boxed in. Left unchecked, we enter a hypnotic state, this limited belief comfort zone. To some degree or another we have all done this. Broken down to the nth degree, each of those short little thoughts, eventually create things. You literally become what you think about.

Since thoughts create things, therefore, thoughts also create swings. What you are thinking about as a golfer you will get. If your mind is racing with all kinds of thoughts prior to your swing or putt it will show in your results. If you think negatively, you will get that. If you worry about what might happen or what might go wrong, you will get that. If you are pressing to make par or birdie you are too far ahead of yourself and prone to a let down. Just prior to executing your swing be present, feel it, and let it happen because zero thoughts are found when you are in The Zone.

So, there are really two concepts here regarding thoughts. One is when we are actually in the process of performing or executing, in which case we would rather have zero thoughts residing in our left-brain, our conscious analytical side. We would rather be operating out of our right brain, our unconscious, artistic side letting it happen. The other kinds of thoughts are those we allow to sink deeply into our subconscious mind on a moment-to-moment daily basis, which forms of self-image. Thoughts that serve our best interest are the kind of thoughts champions allow to be part of their belief system.

I'm inviting you to think like a champion. If you can really *see* and become really *aware*, you will realize that your thoughts, words, feelings, and actions become who you are both on and off the golf course. If you think clearly and powerfully, you will keep getting that. If you think your golf game is getting better, then it will. If you believe in yourself your golf game becomes better than it used to be. How does a champion think? How does a champion talk? What does a champion allow to filtrate from his or her conscious mind into his or her subconscious mind? What we are today changes tomorrow. Do you wish to become better tomorrow while enjoying your today? Think and talk I can and I will.

Tiger Woods was recently quoted in a story in *Golf Digest* as saying, "The greatest thing about tomorrow is I will be better than I am today. I will be better as a golfer, and I will be better as a person. That's the beauty of tomorrow. The lessons I learn today I will apply tomorrow, and I will be better."

Tiger's "I will" statements are paving the way forward and drawing even more momentum on his quest to become his personal best. Allow his desires, thoughts, words, feelings, and actions to become our inspiration. Tiger is a champion. Tiger thinks like a champion, talks like a champion, plays like a champion, and carries himself like a champion—and so can you!

Think, Talk, and Play Like A Champion—*Today!*

If it is your desire to think, talk, and play like a champion, then act like it starting right now and those positive attributes will be drawn toward you. How does a champion think, talk, and carry them selves? The more often you find yourself thinking, talking, playing, and carrying yourself like a champion, the quicker you actually become one. And now more of these kinds of thoughts are drawn. Imagine and act as if it is so. No one started out being a champion. Everyone starts out with hopes and dreams. Champions persevere because they have one-dimensional focus to be their best.

Steven Spielberg imagined himself being a big-time film director and producer long before he was one. He presented himself as if it was already so. Having been rejected three times for admission into the University of Southern California's School of Theatre, Film and Television, legend has it that he got his first big break, an internship and guest in the editing department at Universal Studios, after sneaking away while on a tour there. Wearing a business suit, as though he were a studio executive, he found an old abandoned janitor's trailer and attached a shingle with his name on the outside: Steven Spielberg – Director. He continued to show up for work seven days a week, without pay, striding purposefully through the studio gate as though he belonged there. The rest is history.

Steve Stricker learned what it takes to be a champion from playing golf with Lee Janzen, in the final round of the 1998 U.S. Open at Olympic Club in San Francisco. From the 5th to the 18th hole Janzen had been amazingly calm, making four birdies and no bogeys, an unbelievable stretch for a final round of the U.S. Open.

The Fairway of Life

He had shot 68. Janzen was in The Zone for those last 13 holes. Steve Stricker was so impressed with Janzen's shot-making, and his dialed-in look, that he had to remind himself that he was still playing in the golf tournament as well. "If nothing else, watching Lee that day is going to help me down the line," he said. "I got a close-up view of what a champion looks like when the pressure is the greatest." Indeed, Stricker got a birds-eye view of what a champion looks like when playing golf in The Zone, and when the pressure is the greatest. Steve Stricker took back his own power and decided to become a champion himself.

> *"Imagine your ideal future. Your imagination is your preview to life's coming attractions."*
> —Albert Einstein

Mark O'Meara became the 1998 Open Champion in the same year he won The Masters. Yes, he did it to Tiger, again, this time by one stroke. O'Meara beat a feisty Brian Watts in a four-hole playoff at Royal Birkdale. Mark O'Meara looked as cool as a cucumber coming down the stretch. He's as good as anyone controlling his emotions. However, O'Meara is human too, imagine that…just like you and me. Coming down the 72nd hole O'Meara knew that a par would close Woods out by one and force Watts to birdie to tie. O'Meara started to take it all in: the crowd, the grandstands, the notion that he was on the verge of claiming his second Major of the year in what he calls, "…the most special championship there is." Watts birdie's hole 17 and there is huge roar. Now O'Meara was faced with a 20-foot birdie putt that ended up right of the flag. Normally his magic putting stroke is like money in the bank. Not this time. "Absolute de-cel," he calls it. A "de-cel" in putting is a cousin to the yips and it comes from nerves. His putt came up slightly more than four feet short. After that first putt O'Meara said he gave himself a good talking to—something we all do from time to time.

As O'Meara walked up to his ball he said he felt an amazing calm. "For some reason, it occurred to me that making this putt wasn't life and death," he said. "Obviously, I wanted to make it, but

I said to myself, 'If you miss this, you aren't going to die; just go through your routine and knock it in.'" And that's what he did.

Amazing, isn't it? Simply thinking that it's not life or death can help calm you down even when you find yourself on the biggest stage of your life. Thinking that, yes, *you can*, will bring you calmness and confidence. Believing in your self is powerful stuff.

The Middle Way

The middle way is often described by Zen Buddhists as being in balance, being in harmony not too high not too low, just right. It's the balance between risk and reward, focus and relaxed, intense and calm. To get a sense of the ideal state of mind to achieve this ideal foundation for everything you think, say, feel, and do practice a technique that Dr. Parent teaches in the final stage of his mind training session called Panoramic Awareness. The intention is to gradually expand the scope of what your awareness includes. Parent describes it this way in *Zen Putting*, "With a very soft gaze, looking straight ahead at eye level, imagine that your awareness is extending in all directions. Start (your awareness) with the room you are in and gradually expand farther and farther, being open in all directions to the surrounding area, to the horizon, beyond the horizon to the sky, beyond the sky into space, and beyond the farthest star you can imagine. It is not that your awareness goes out in one or another direction at a time; rather, it is truly panoramic and open to all directions at once. Rest for a minute or two in that vast spaciousness. In that state you are completely open and your mind is limitless. You are as open and expansive as you can be. Paradoxically, you are also as centered as you can be. That is the state of mind that is the ideal foundation for everything you think, say, or do."

I Think I Can

One of my favorite childhood books is *The Little Engine That Could*. Originally published in 1906, this classic tale imparts the value of believing in yourself and "stick-to-it-tive-ness." A long train must be pulled over a high mountain and all the big engines refuse to do it. Then, the littlest engine of all decides to give it a go. Huffing and puffing, he says, "I think I can, I think I can, I think I can." As the journey becomes more challenging the little engine puffs a slower tune, "I–think–I–can, I–think–I can, I–think–I can." The story ends when the little engine achieves what the bigger engines thought was impossible, by telling itself, "I thought I could, I thought I could, I thought I could."

What this story drives home is that it all big dreams and achievements start with a thought. The message within this tale parallels life for many of us. We are all born with value, worth, and in complete connection to life's pure positive energy. Somewhere along the line many of us start doubting our abilities and question whether we could do it. Not wanting to fail and face ridicule from others because of it, we often give up before we have even started. It sounds crazy but we are often afraid of our own greatness.

Here is a new message, there is no such thing as failure and you cannot get it wrong. There is enough of everything for everyone and you can be, do, or have whatever your heart desires. Like the innocence of our young childhood, return to the land of your soul, where dreams are fresh, and visions echo, I can do it.

The One Who Thinks He Can

"Whether you think you can or think you can't, either way you are right."
—Henry Ford

It is essential to think strongly and powerfully about what you want with an "I can do it" attitude. The one who thinks she can or the one who thinks she can't are both right. It is law, and it never fails. And you know what, just like the little engine that could, you understood this concept a long time ago. Giving too much attention to what you don't want, or too much attention upon the lack of not having it, or too much attention to thinking you can't, produces just that.

One of the most tragic examples of giving your attention to what you don't want is the story of Karl Wallenda, the world's greatest trapeze artist. Karl began having nightmares of falling. He created in his own mind what ultimately got the best of him. Instead of giving his focus and attention to what he wanted, Karl started thinking about *not falling*, which lead to his ultimate demise. In Karl's case he created a tragic result that took his own life. On the golf course we're talking about the swing of a golf club producing a golf shot. We're also talking about the quality of your life lived both on and off the golf course. Over a lifetime of moments, each shot is the culmination of your life's work.

Reflecting back, think about how these principles show up in your own life. Contemplate how these universal laws of creation really work. Think back upon how you have created everything in your life based upon your thoughts. The Law of Attraction says, "That which is likened unto it self is drawn," Esther and Jerry Hicks said in their wonderful book, *Ask and It Is Given*. "Every thought vibrates, every thought radiates a signal, and every thought attracts a matching signal back. Whatever you are giving your attention to causes you to emit a vibration, and the vibrations that you offer equal your asking, which equals your point of attraction. In Essence you draw into your experience whatever you are predominantly thinking about."

Wow! Why not create the life of your dreams with your thoughts! There is nothing more exhilarating, more exciting, more enjoyable than to play a round of golf understanding that the universe is always there to yield to you whatever you want – what you give your attention too! There is always an abundant flow of Well-Being; all you have to do is allow it in. Your objective is to tap into it. Go with the soul and go with the flow. If you get so fixated on the golf shot you want; you literally drown out any other vibration except that to which you give your attention and focus. That's why golf professionals are golf professionals…and we can do this a little bit better than we used to.

> **Simple Secret Reminder # 17 – Focus on the Shot at Hand**
> **Give your attention and focus upon what kind of golf shot you want.**

Upstream Thoughts vs. Downstream Thoughts

All the good stuff in life is downstream. Imagine the analogy of paddling your kayak upstream against the current or paddling downstream with the current. Which is more fun, more enjoyable?

Some may believe that paddling really, really hard against the current is the key to success. Why, probably because someone told you so. All it really does is tire you out. The moment you stop paddling and relax into yourself you will understand. Stop, pause, sigh, breathe, and relax. There is nothing upstream that resembles anything to do with being in The Zone and going with the flow. In fact, upstream thoughts only block and hinder peak performance.

Once you've stopped paddling for a moment, now allow the flow of the river of life to carry you downstream less arduously. All life force moves through you the same way as the river. Everything is happening now as each new moment unfolds downstream. All the new good stuff is downstream. Once you understand going with the flow you can begin to paddle with the stream enjoying being exactly where you are. Sure there will be rapids to navigate, obstacles to maneuver, adversities to embrace, and most likely some challenges and setbacks along the stream. Yet once you understand that everything that comes into your life is meant for your own growth, you can then begin to appreciate what life has to offer. As we evolve downstream new levels of awareness and understanding enhance and expand our experience. Life is an eternal process and there will always be more unfulfilled desires, more good stuff downstream. Embrace that!

Reflect upon these thoughts and choose better feeling thoughts whenever you catch yourself, or find yourself thinking upstream thoughts. Allow your golf game to reflect your new more empowering thoughts. Remember, thoughts create swings.

Here are some examples that show you the differences between an upstream thought and a downstream one:

- I never seem to get any better – upstream thought
- I can't get myself out of this funk – upstream thought
- I'm such an awful putter – upstream thought
- I'm not having any fun – upstream thought
- I'm visualizing where I see my ball landing – downstream thought
- I feel this shot, this putt – downstream thought
- I've missed this kind of shot before – upstream thought
- I've made this kind of shot before – downstream thought
- I don't want to hit the ball there – upstream thought
- I want to hit the ball here – downstream thought
- I've got this shot – downstream thought
- I'm feeling good – downstream thought
- I'm on fire – downstream thought
- I blame God for my misfortune – upstream thought
- I appreciate playing this wonderful game – downstream thought
- I'm choosing to commit and trust myself – downstream thought
- I can't do this – upstream thought
- I can do this – downstream thought
- I'm scared to play – upstream thought
- I'm eagerly looking forward to playing – downstream thought
- I have no idea what I am doing – upstream thought
- I know exactly what I am doing – downstream thought
- I've got to make par or better so badly – upstream thought
- I give my best effort on this shot right here, and right now – downstream thought
- I'm afraid I'll embarrass myself – upstream thought

- I'm confident in who I am – downstream thought
- I'm doubting myself – upstream thought
- I believe in me – downstream thought
- I've buckled and choked before coming down the stretch – upstream thought
- I've prevailed before coming down the stretch – downstream thought
- I'm taking a licking – upstream thought
- I'm licking my chops – downstream thought

If you let upstream thoughts flood your mind and you fixate on things you do not want you will not experience abundance and richness in your golf game. Incongruous thoughts bring disharmonious results. Conversely, there is this mantra that my editor Christine wishes to pass along. I invite you to use it the next time you are meditating or preparing to play. *My thoughts are the basis for the attraction of all things that I consider to be good, which includes enough positive feeling thoughts, belief in myself, and visualizing what I want, for my comfort, joy, and happiness.*

Journaling Exercise: If this quote resonates with you then write it down, pull it out and remind yourself of why you come to play. Use this mantra three times a day and watch your life change for the better. Bask in the magnificence of you. Remember, we become what we think. Keep on imprinting more of these downstream thoughts into your subconscious mind as you literally squeeze out the less than desirable thoughts that have held you back from experiencing more of your full potential. Give more airtime to better feeling thoughts.

Practicing Positive Alignment with Source Energy

There's really nothing magical that is happening, yet everything is a miracle manifesting from your thoughts (vibration). Either you are aligning and connecting with Source Energy Well-Being, giving your attention to what you want, or you are not. The Law of

Attraction is always responding to your thoughts and how you are feeling about everything. You have a choice to align with Source Energy, which is the dominant factor of the universe, or you can continue with your trained thoughts to look at what could go wrong.

Most of us, if not all, have trained ourselves to look down the road for disaster. Doubt, fear, and worry are not designed into golf courses; our brains put these hazards in for us. We don't see the green ahead; we see what could go wrong, instead. We focus on what we don't want or the lack of what we don't have. We give our attention to worry and we fret over the simplest things, from a 4-foot putt to a 90-yard wedge shot. It's no wonder that we get less than desirable results. Our dominant vibration, our thoughts, and our feelings are on what could go wrong or what we don't want or what we don't have. This creates a feeling of lack, which only draws more of that experience into our golf game. Like Karl Wallenda we've taken ourselves out of alignment with our own Source Energy.

Source Energy is an ever-flowing stream from the Universe. Its power is available to all of us anytime we desire. We can choose to become angry, or go with the flow and move on. We can focus on what we don't want, or what we do want. We can see the worst of something, or the best. We can complain or reach for solutions. We can worry or look for reasons to feel good. There's nothing magical happening here, when you choose to see the good, the positive and the optimistic, you will…and that is nothing short of a miracle.

What have you been practicing? What kinds of thoughts have dominated your focus and attention? What kinds of feelings have you allowed to persist? What kinds of practiced thoughts have lead to your belief about playing golf? How do you talk to yourself?

You see, when we are all caught up in the illusion of practiced thoughts and feelings that don't support us we can't break the cycle because we don't know how we got there. If we try and think positively when our vibration says we can't or we are afraid, we end up in quagmire of mixed emotions, diluted focus, or denial.

The reason I played scared is because I allowed myself to think scared. I allowed my thoughts to wander and worry about what

The Fairway of Life

I didn't want or the nightmare of what might happen. All those negative thoughts ran over me like a freight train in the night. I was unaware of these new more empowering tools that I have now. Like the big engines in the childhood story, I assumed that I couldn't do it when faced with a challenge. I didn't trust myself. I didn't believe in myself. I allowed thoughts of self-doubt to filter into my psyche. I sabotaged and cheated myself. I played small and I settled for less.

I hit the ball out of bounds, into the trees, over the fence, into the pond. Sure—there were times when I saw in my mind's eye a good shot and I allowed the Well-Being in and, as a result, I hit some pretty good golf shots. There were also plenty of times when the hole just didn't set up well for me either, and I hit some pretty disgusting shots. I resisted the Well-Being. I am now narrowing the gap and focusing more on what I want, even on the most challenging of golf holes. I see in my mind's eye the picture of Bobby Jones narrowing the field, as he gets so fixated on what he wants. Better than most, he successfully drowned out reverberations that did not serve him well. So, I see in him that I, too, can make it my own. And so can you! So let's keep on shall we…just becoming better than we used to be.

When you become better than you used to be you gravitate to better feeling thoughts. When you gravitate to better feeling thoughts this eventually becomes your new dominant vibration. As you become your new dominant vibration you evolve into being a powerful creator. As you evolve into being a powerful creator you stop looking at what was or what is and move to what you prefer. And the momentum of this process keeps growing as that which is likened unto itself is drawn. With your newfound freedom and perspective, things will keep on getting a little bit better, that is, if you allow yourself to get up to speed with who you are now becoming. Before you know it you have recreated yourself anew and you are now living your new creation. You're simply telling yourself a new more empowering story about your self. And like Einstein, you become a champion because you have allowed yourself to imagine your ideal future.

Coaches Notes: As you evolve you open yourself to a higher form of being. With a higher form of being comes greater personal responsibility. You have got to get yourself up to speed with who you have become otherwise you just don't feel good. You will feel bad when you dip into being less than what you have become from an impeccable behavior and authenticity perspective. With evolution comes responsibility. Being responsible allows us to evolve. Therefore, make responsibility your friend. Life once again is like a circle and you get to choose what it is you desire to be. Your only other alternative is to stay stuck and "comfortable" with where you are?

Creative Anchoring

Sports psychologists and life coaches talk about creative anchoring all the time. Pick a golf hole you have played that feels good to you and place that vision into your vibration, into your thoughts, into your mind's eye. Do it whenever you're faced with an especially challenging shot. Do it all the time. Drown out any negative energy causing a stir inside. Get so fixated and focused on what you want that you literally override any other thought. Activate more beneficial beliefs.

Coaches Notes: The shot produces the swing. By narrowing your vision of your intended target the chances for hitting an entirely acceptable shot increases. Start with your vision of playing to a particular point on the fairway. If you miss it by a few yards or more you're still in good position. However, if your target is the fairway and you miss that then you're off in the rough or worse yet. The same goes for putting. Picking out a path with a more specific target allows for more wiggle room. The hole is 4 and ½ wide and the ball has better chances to enter even is you miss your exact target. Get dialed into to what you want and your body will take you there. Thoughts create swings.

The best way to play is by being completely dialed in to what you want. You see the field, visualize it, hold the vision, call out the shot, allow the Well-Being in, expect it to happen, and you let it be—and so shall it be. It's fun to be creative and call your own shot, and let your brilliant and miraculous mind, body, and spirit allow it to be. It's a great feeling to have confidence and just know that you are going to hit a great shot. There are plenty of techniques you can use to bring yourself back into better harmony, back to center. It could be any kind of anchor that works for you. It could be a thought, a rhythm, a picture, a feeling, an experience, or drawing upon another golf hole that looks good in your mind's eye. Let go and let God. Have fun with it; it's only a game. "A game that cannot be won, only played", Bagger Vance.

Dancing in my head are memories of Phil Mickelson winning the 2004 Masters. Did you notice how he smiled after missing a short putt or making a bogey? Now, fast-forward two years. Did you notice how wonderfully a new Phil played by winning the 2006 Masters? Did you notice how joyfully he carried himself and how much exuberant confidence emanated from him? Did you also observe how wonderfully Fred Couples played as well? From tee to green, he was spectacular. His iron shots were phenomenal. However, if it not for missing a few short putts here and there, it would have been Freddy donning the Green Jacket for a second time.

It is my observation that Freddy is slightly challenged by the four to eight-foot putt, just like I am. I wonder if Freddy's thought process is one of giving attention to what he wants, giving his best effort at the moment (like Tiger), or if his thoughts are scattered? God, I've missed these before. What is more empowering, "I'm putting forth my best effort here and now", or "Gosh, I better not miss this putt because it means I'll make a par or bogey"? Then out of nowhere I watch Freddy make a "tougher" twenty-footer with some break. He appears more relaxed and confident. He feels it. What's the difference? By now you're starting to be able to answer your own questions.

Perhaps Freddy is like Sergio, thinking too much? I really don't know unless I was to be privileged to coach them. I do however notice and sense the doubt and not fully expecting to make it. They look scared. Tee to green, awesome. Putting, sometimes horrendous. Everyone wants to make the putt, it's just we have this contradictory energy going on.

My intention is to get you to think more clearly upon what it is you want, believe it to be so, and *fully* expect it to happen, drown out any other thoughts, and then allow it to happen—no thoughts. Through time and with practice and applying the principles that work for you, you will actually become a new person. You can become a better player and a better putter than you used to be.

Let It Be Easy

What about when the doubts and demons start creeping in? Is there anything else you can do immediately? In order to solve a problem you first have to detach from it. You have to observe it outside of your experience. What you really want is to keep on activating more and more beneficial beliefs. Our visualization and pre-shot routine helps to pave the way, it helps to keep us centered and grounded in the present moment on the task at hand. Here are a few other techniques I might suggest:

1) Shift your attention to what you *do* want. Focus on the solution. Then let it go.
2) Practice affirmations like "let it be easy."
3) Ground yourself in the present moment (involve your senses, feel your feet touch the ground, see the beauty all around you).
4) Notice your breath. Take a couple of deep breaths.
5) Reach for a better feeling thought, the best feeling thought you can.
6) Like Mark O'Meara and Pete Green remind yourself that you are going to live and someone loves you. Sometimes we just need to loosen the resistance to allow the flow.

The first step in getting rid of your problem is to switch your thinking away from it. It is as simple and as complex as that! Golf just *is* . . . *you* get to choose how you want to create and respond. Keep on reaching for better feeling thoughts. The better you practice these techniques the more natural and less arduously will you play. Before too long you won't have to even think about these techniques—which is the ideal way to simply be.

Mental Golf & Life Exercise: The first step in getting rid of the problem is to switch your thinking away from it. Unless the process is simple there is a tendency to avoid it. There is a tendency to analyze and over analyze our golf problems, which only draws more of it. Before you know it the problem seems too big to solve. "Nothing is simple; nothing is complex," as told by Master Nathaniel Carlisle Rishian to John Harricharan in his wonderful and inspiring short story book called *Power Pause*. "It's how we look at a problem that determines how hard or easy it would be to solve. It's not the problem itself that causes us most of the stress, but what we think about the problem."

1) For the next sixty seconds be quiet and still and do not think about *elephants*. Do not read any further than the end of the next sentence—no peeking! A *full* sixty seconds – do not think about *elephants*. Look away from the book. Begin now.
2) What happened? What kind of elephants came into your experience, the kind in Africa roaming the plains or circus elephants? Any peanuts, water, or stunts come into your experience as well? Because I said *not* to think about elephants *of course* you thought about them!
3) Okay, let's take it one more step. Think about the greatest golf vacation or trip you have ever taken. Go ahead recall those wonderful memories. Imagine where you were, whom you were with, some of your best rounds, awesome meals, the nightlife, and just all around good times. Got it? Do not read any further, just take a minute and think about all those good times. Don't peek.
4) So what ever happened to your elephants? *Poof*—they were gone! You see how quickly we can change our thoughts? So, whatever we don't want to think about we get. We've got to shift our focus away from the problem

and onto what we prefer. Thinking of not hitting it someplace, only draws more of those kinds of thoughts. Shift your focus upon what you prefer. Think about how you wish to be, where you want the ball to go and let *that* happen. It just takes a simple shift in focus and perspective. Change your thoughts and you'll change your golf game.

5) Sometimes we get so caught up and attached to our problem it seems hard to let go of it. When we're attached to our problem or negative thought it is difficult to solve and shift our attention. It's like rowing a boat that is still attached to the dock. I invite you to disconnect from the "perceived" problem. In other words, seek to get the problem or negative thought "out side" of you. Detach from it. Now think of something more desirable, a more pleasant experience.

6) With an open mind and honest effort we can actively challenge our fears and face our doubts with new simple solutions. Look at your problem, examine it, see what you can do about it, and if it feels right, take action and do something about it. If you're feeling powerless to do anything at this time, then disconnect from it and go do something else – watch an inspiring movie, read a book, go for a walk, talk to a kind, compassionate friend who will be open to letting you share without judgment. Don't eat, drink, and sleep with your problem…find something to distract you for the time being. Perhaps you just need a little bit more time…just let it be for a while. In this whole process, be careful with using the word *try*. You must have the *intent* to disconnect, just a little prod and redirection. You are not your thoughts; you only think your thoughts. Like the sun, which is always shining, above our problems there is always a light. Simply turn your thoughts to times when things were bright and sunny. Often the solution will come to us when we have finally let go of being attached to the problem.

7) I also invite you to use affirmations that will help break

The Fairway of Life

the spell of fear and remind you to keep on your true path and in alignment with who you really are and what you really know. It is fear that is our greatest enemy on the golf course. Fear is always the greatest enemy of our success and happiness. Conquer your fear and you're well on your way to victory over stress, resistance, and imbalance. Use affirmations to help break away from fear and doubt. As you do so, you'll be breaking focus with your problem. And as you break focus, in some mystical way, in some glorious form, the problem starts resolving itself. And then do the heavens rejoice.

I looked "fear" in the eye and said, you come to me with confusion and darkness and failure…but I come to you in the light and strength of my being. I am in alignment with myself and you cannot stand against me.

"I refuse to give into fear, real or imagined, or to be afraid either consciously or unconsciously of anything or anyone. I smile at my obstacles."
—Tiger Woods

In summary, it is your job to ask for what you desire to come forth. Give your attention to your intention. Next, the universe responds to your asking. Finally, it is your job once again to allow it in and expect it to happen. Your work is to continually give your attention to more of the good stuff of life. Your work is to continuously work on allowing it in and fully expecting it to happen. The last part of the equation is where most people give up too soon. Most people really don't believe it can happen. That's why the secret appears to be a far-away dream. Boldness has genius, power, and magic in it. Begin it now.

As you focus in on what you intend, as you feed your subconscious mind more positive focus and belief, as you activate more and more better feeling thoughts and beliefs you will hit better golf shots. Expect it to be so and it will. Hitting better golf shots will create more confidence. More confidence increases your chances for greater joy and playing better golf, having more fun. Life is like a circle. Allow the spiral to move upward as your life expands and evolves. The better it gets, the better it gets.

What else? I suggest you give appreciation and gratitude by thanking God and The Universe...all of life for hearing you and responding to your desire.

Remember it's just a game. Laugh more; shrug your shoulders. Don't take anything too seriously, the best rounds or the worst, for they too shall pass. Embrace it all.

Action Steps:

1) **Practice focusing on positive feeling thoughts.**
2) **Practice thinking "I can and I will".**
3) **Carry yourself like a champion.**
4) **Be thankful and appreciative to all that you are and to all that you are becoming.**

Chapter 8

Golfer's State of Inspired Being

"Your emotion controls your motion."
—Nick Faldo

How to find and be your most inspired state of being

Nick Faldo says your emotion controls your motion. Agreed, now it's a matter of what kind, or form of emotion, are you experiencing playing golf? And do you have a choice? Here are several examples from the bottom up: fear; rage; anger; worry; doubt; disappointment; boredom; contentment; hopefulness; enthusiasm; passion; and joy. Each one of these emotions you express will become an exact match to your motion. The Universe is responding to your vibration, and your vibration is about the way you feel. You have a choice in the way that you feel.

In general terms, a fearful emotion controls your motion, most often producing an undesirable result. Body language coming from internal state of being does not lie. A look in a person's eye does not lie. Your swing motion does not lie. A motion filled with worry or doubt, will most likely lead way to hesitation producing a less than desirable result as well. As we move up the scale we tend to feel better about our swing, more willing to grind it out, more hope and light at the end of the tunnel. If I'm feeling hopeful then that's what I will get: a lot of hope. Not too bad a place to be, just not great. When our emotions are experiencing joy our motion tends to be more flowing, more rhythmic. We're feeling it. It's The Zone.

When we are in The Zone we've transcended emotion to a place practically ineffable to describe – a surreal pure positive energy. The Zone is our highest state of being where the floodgates of Well-Being are raining pure H_2O. We'll talk in depth about The Zone in the next chapter paving the way forward. I mention The Zone throughout this text because ultimately that state of being is our highest vibration; it's what we're all seeking to be. In this chapter we are laying the groundwork to understanding how our emotions really do work and how this all plays into us becoming a peak performer.

Once you understand how emotions actually work, that they are temporary, and it is our job to reach for better feeling thoughts, we begin moving back up the emotional scale more quickly. Once you understand how this process *actually* works, instead of how you may have *thought* it works (either by default, chance, ignorance, or that life was just happening to you), it becomes much easier to be in a better feeling place (since you created this feeling and these emotions in the first place). As an example it is much more difficult to move from rage to gratitude in a matter of moments. However, you can move from rage to doubt and feel better. Before too long you can move from doubt to contentment, which again feels better, and so on and so forth. You do have a choice in how you are choosing to feel and your emotions help guide the way.

In fact one of the biggest and most simple secrets to better thoughts is a concept called pivoting. In the game of basketball you're taught the idea of pivoting on your planted foot and you're able to switch and rotate directions. The same idea can work with our thoughts. Anytime you feel a negative emotion, stop and think: something is here, what is it? What is it that I want? And then simply turn your attention to what you *do* want. In the moment you turn your attention to what you do want, the negative attraction will stop, and the positive attraction begins. You'll start feeling good again simply by pivoting or changing your thoughts. Shift your attention from the negative thought (the problem) to a better feeling thought (the solution).

> **Simple Secret Reminder # 18 – Pivot or Change Your Thoughts**
> Whenever you're feeling negative emotion, notice it, and simply turn your attention to positive feelings and to what you *do* want and the positive attraction begins.
> Give your attention to the solution.

As we shift our attention to what we do want little by little we start changing the way we feel. We get a little bit better and it feels pretty good. We get a little bit better and it feels pretty good. Before you know it we are changing our beliefs creating more of a champion's self-image of ourselves. We feel better we play better golf. Feeling better and playing better 50 percent of the time is better than 25 percent of the time. Feeling better and playing better 80 percent of the time is better then 50 percent of the time. We end up having a better life and playing better golf. It's just that simple. The goal is to close the gap and eliminate the variables causing the resistance or limited beliefs we hold about ourselves. The more we understand resistances the quicker we can move up the scale of emotions, the closer we get to being back in The Zone, our most natural state of being.

When we play golf in The Zone emotions of joy, freedom, knowing, appreciation, empowerment, and love have the potential to be transformed and transcended into pure positive energy giving way to an effortless and confident swing producing amazing results, without you really knowing how you did it, or thinking one iota about results or outcome. The feeling of The Zone is difficult to put into words but I'll attempt it. You are lost in the moment without emotion or thought or resistance. You are in a complete state of allowing and all the Well-Being is coming through you. You get out of your own way and out of your own mind, and just allow it to be and you let it happen. Trust your golf swing and let your golf swing trust you. This is our natural state of being or way to be in life—going with the flow enjoying the moment. You do it all the time in life from walking to talking and from hiking to biking. Now it's time to be it on the golf course.

I believe that only pure positive energy exists when we are playing golf in The Zone. It's the ultimate state of being. It's the ultimate feeling. It's the ultimate expression of life. Think of it as making love with life, fully connected and fully aligned. No thoughts, no emotions (only pure positive energy), no ego, no mind noise, just a complete alignment with Source Energy and Well-Being. It is pure positive energy flowing to you and through you. It's a feeling of oneness with All That Is. There is a transcendence of personal self into higher Self, a shift from not knowing to knowing, from hesitation and hope, to inner awe and gratitude. The feeling of outrageous joy is practically indescribable; one simply experiences it.

When pure positive energy aligns with our own state of inspired being (clear, connected, wise, creative, artistic, knowing, etc.) by focusing on exactly what we want (visualization), and when we fully expect it to happen (a belief in ourselves), and when we allow it in (Well-Being) we can literally move mountains. Golf becomes surreal.

When we are actually playing golf and swinging the club in The Zone there is no emotion. We are free, and we have transcended our personal self into a place of our natural most inspired state of being. We are at peace. There is a knowingness within that ultimately produces an effortless and graceful motion. The feeling or state of being is blissful and harmonious, and we are in alignment with Source Energy. You just know with joy and appreciation that you are about to hit a great shot because you are calm, relaxed, and feeling confident. When we are in The Zone we are just being. Before our shot we think, we visualize, when performing our shot we just are, after our shot we may think again, and perhaps show some emotion, or not.

If you want it, it can happen, when you get out of your own way.

Being in The Zone is a complete letting go of any thought or any emotion other then pure positive energy. You are just being, and life just is. Yes, you have to be out of your mind to be in The Zone. Only when we get out of our head can we naturally allow it to happen. You've got to allow it to happen. You can't think too much or try too hard. It just is. You just have to be. It as if you are letting go of your need to control and just allowing it to happen. It's the

The Fairway of Life

ego's need to control that gives us the rough edges. When we let go we soften and align with the aura of who we really are.

The purest form of being is when life is simply flowing to you and through you. There is no thought or any emotion, other than pure joy. Experience your joy and follow your bliss. Play golf with outrageous joy. See it, feel it, trust it. Make this your natural way to be. Be your natural, most inspired state of being.

Your best golf is played with pure positive energy flowing to you and through you. Your best golf is played when you are *being* your most inspired state, which is, when you are being in The Zone, effortless, in awe, in alignment and connected. The Zone is our purest state of being. When you are being your most inspired state of being, you just are. You've transcended into pure positive energy, your highest state of being. If our highest state of being is when we are in The Zone, why not go straight into being that?

We each have our own unique state of inspired being. Our goal is to find out what state of being most inspires us and go straight into being that. When we are being our most inspired state of being we are in The Zone. Most people find themselves going in and out of The Zone because they never really understood how it works. The Zone is always present, always shining; it is us who cloud it over. We are our own worst enemy. The Zone is not some place we seek to find, The Zone is a place that is always flowing right here and right now. The Zone is not a place we seek to find or get into, it's place where we clear or remove the obstacles that have kept us from experiencing what has always been, always was, and always will be.

The Be-Do-Have Paradigm

The Be-Do-Have Paradigm is another universal and spiritual law of creation. Most people get it backwards; they think that when they finally *have* this, then they will be able to *do* that, and then they can *be* this. In his book, *Conversations with God, Book 3*, Neale Donald Walsch discusses this principle with greater clarity. And you can substitute your own descriptions as they relate to your life on and off the golf course. I use Neale's template and add golf specific examples to it. I find this very interesting as all of life operates the same way.

Most people believe if they have a thing (more time, more money, more love, a better golf game), then they can finally do a thing (write a book, go on vacation, buy a home, take up a hobby, undertake a relationship, really play better golf), which will allow them to be a thing (happy, peaceful, content, in love, or a calm, confident golfer).

In actuality, they are reversing the Be-Do-Have Paradigm. In the universe as it really is (as opposed to how you think it is), "havingness" does not produce "beingness," but the other way around. First you "be" a thing called "happy" (or "knowing," or "wise," or "compassionate," "calm," "clear," or whatever), then you start "doing" things from this place of beingness—and soon you discover that what you are doing winds up bringing you the things you've always wanted to "have."

The way to set this creative process (and that's what this is . . . the process of creation) into motion is to look at what it is you want to "have," ask yourself what you think you would "be" if you "had" that, then go right straight to being. In this way you reverse the way you've been using the Be-Do-Have Paradigm—in actuality, set it right—and work with, rather than against, the creative power of the universe. Here is the short way of stating this principle: In life, you do not have to do anything. It is all a question of what you are being.

As in golf, so in life it is a matter of what you are *being*. Your state of beingness sets the stage for what you are doing, what you will have, and for how you will play. Your state of being (focused, clear, creative, artistic, poetic, confident, relaxed, calm, present, machine-like) produces your doing (your takeaway, back swing, rhythm, tempo, lag, whip, strike, follow through) which allows you to have (scoring, enjoyment, fun, prize money). It is the order of life's paradigm that matters. You are a human being *first*. So stop trying to find the right and perfect thing to *do* and start creating the right and perfect thing to *be*. *Be* your most inspired state of being on the golf course and allow yourself to *do* it. Then you will be *having* fun and the results, scoring, or prize money will take care of itself.

The formula for success on and off the golf course is BE, DO, HAVE. If we seek abundance and joy, we must be abundant and joyful in spirit. We cultivate riches and spiritual abundance by opening our hearts and spirit in gratitude—giving thanks. Think of all the things you are grateful for, and give thanks to all of that. Start a gratitude journal if you haven't already, and keep filling its pages with all that you are grateful for. The more we practice gratitude, the more we open up and tap into the ever-flowing stream of abundance. Begin thanking the universe for what little you are grateful for, because, as the old Estonian proverb says, "Who does not thank for little will not thank for much." Develop an attitude of gratitude and more will be given.

> *"Often people attempt to live their lives backwards: they try to have more things, or more money, in order to do more of what they want so they will be happier. The way it actually works is the reverse. You must first be who you really are, then do what you love to do, in order to have what you want."*
> —Margaret Young

Our state of being determines our doing and having. This is the missing link that many are clearly not seeing. The law of attractive works in harmony with what you are vibrating in your beingness, not your havingness. You say you want to have a great golf game or how can I have what I want? With respect having something is kindergarten stuff. I want to have that toy – either you get it or you don't. Having something is what children want. Being something is the road to mastery, to graduate school if you will. Being is what students of mastery seek. Everyone is so concerned about "having" everything in there life. Why not be concerned about being everything you always wanted to be?

So, according to Neale Donald Walsch, "The first step in having everything that you want is to not want it, not need it, not search for it or reach for it or strive for it or yearn for it. First of all, I said, your life has nothing to do with your body. It has to do with your soul. The body is something you have; it is not something you are. As I've said, it is a tool. A device. A mechanism. It is a physical machine, and a marvelous one, impeccably designed to facilitate the creation of the soul's desire. And what is the soul's desire? To experience itself as some aspect of what it knows itself to be."

Therefore, try first to be what you came here to be, exhibiting all the qualities in your daily life of the identity that is truly yours. Then you will find yourself having all the things you were previously stressing and straining to have, without your doing anything. Give your focus on being, and you will have all that your heart desires. Focus on the states of being that you enjoy while playing golf and go straight into being that. The heck with all the stress, strain, anxiety, fear, doubt, and worry. Go be aware, clear, compassionate, understanding, wise, love, abundant or any number of divine aspects that it pleases you to be.

How to Find Your Most Inspired State of Being

What is your most inspired state of being? Imagine yourself playing extremely well. What is that state of being that has caused you to play well? Is it being focused, relaxed, calm, wise, artistic, creative, powerful, or clear? Are you being inspired or connected? Are you being sensual, comical, or a risky renegade? Are you best playing golf like Freddy Couples or John Daly? Are you best playing golf like Lee Trevino or Loren Roberts? Are you best playing golf like Annika Sorenstam or Lorena Ochoa?

Ask yourself what you would *be* if you *had* that? What would you be if you had the golf game you most desire? "Well," you say, "I would be confident, relaxed, focused, present, creative, wise, clear, and happy. I would execute with precision and finish every round in style. Boy, I would be all of those things! I'd be on top of the world!"

Okay. Find out which state of being most resonates with you. I invite you to go right straight to being the one or two states that most inspire and resonate within you. How? First, find that state of

The Fairway of Life

being, and then look at it closely and become very clear as to what it is and what being in it involves.

The one that most inspires me is being fully connected to Source Energy and being very clear in this moment. I am joyful when I am being appreciative and actually communicating with this essence, this Source Energy. I am clear and fully present, focused on this particular shot. My state of being is my authenticity. When I am in alignment with myself I play my best golf. I am in awe of this connection with life. I am connected and clear because I am being authentic and most appreciative to the splendor and joy of life. Stop and think about that a moment—fully connected, clear, and authentic. I'm being focused, clear, and artistic (a certain form of excellence in execution).

So *being* connected, clear, focused, artistic, and authentic—is when I play my best golf, that's my trump card. Whenever I lose my connection, or whenever I am unclear, have doubts, become scared, or whenever I am out of integrity—that's when I play my worst golf. Now you have another tool in your bag of tricks. Go straight into being your most inspired state of being. Get yourself up to speed with who you really are!

When I'm connected, clear, artistic, and authentic I *enjoy* playing. I feel inspired, in awe, in alignment, and very wise and very clear. I feel I am being confident and I see what I want, I believe it to be so, and I most fully *expect* it. I'm feeling a calm, yet powerful energy through my body. I just know I'm going to hit a great shot. I love that feeling and state of being. Sometimes I'm so wonderfully connected, it's as if there's no effort involved. I'm just being creative and letting it happen. When I lose my connection, I fight against the grain and begin to struggle. I especially struggle in life whenever I find myself not being my authentic self, (your greatest gift can be your greatest betrayal). I know that first hand because I have experienced that already, and I've had enough of that experience.

I am a *feel* type of player, and I like what I call *knowing*. It's wonderful to *feel* and call my shot, *knowing* where my ball is going. Knowing is knowledge. When I'm in this state, golf becomes poetry in motion. I'm being artistic. I am actually in my own little world. I feel as if I am licking my chops eagerly looking forward to playing this shot right here and right now. I just recalled a shot like this moments ago pacing my house feeling really, really good. Yes anchor that! An anchor is a reminder. We do it through feelings, visualizations, and vibration.

I invite you to play golf from your most inspired state of *being* and stay out of your place of *doing*. Doing, like scoring, will take care of it self. When you come from a place of being, there really is no agenda—you just are. When you come from a state of beingness it is the most authentic experience of you in the moment. Your beingness always comes from desire. It is spontaneous and it is created in the moment, that's the brilliance of it. All you are really being is experiencing outrageous joy. It's like Robin Williams delivering a stand-up comedy routine. He's being creative and extremely funny allowing the flow in and through him—it's his unique gift. John Denver did it with his guitar, music, and singing. I wonder what is Tiger's "trump card" state of inspired being?

Find the state(s) of being that stirs your soul and allows you to enjoy the moment beyond your wildest dreams, and tap in to that. Here are some words that describe those states again: wise, clear, artistic, creative, fun, sensual, relaxed, focused, present, analytical, mechanical, appreciative, compassionate, wild, powerful, fearless, easy going, confident, feeling, and knowing. Or make up the state of being that works for you. Generally, you will have one or two personal states of being that you enjoy most.

If you've got it the other way around, and you're in the opposite state of inspired being (confused, scared, fearful, frustrated), it produces your doing (out of rhythm, rushed, unfinished, erratic, chunked, topped, thinned, sliced, hooked) which brings you to have substandard results (very little fun, pay out, quitting).

At least you will recognize what it is you are being, what it is that is causing your doing, and why it is you are having and getting what you are getting.

There is *power* in your state of being and what you desire to be. The universe delivers a perfect match to your own vibrational energy on how you are being and the desire of your intention. Choose wisely that which you desire to be.

The Power of Role Models: Life is a Mirror

Now, let's look at the power of role models and how their states of being and character traits that lie within them also lie within us. All of the elements and minerals of the universe exist everywhere. We are all connected in this web of life. Every life lived offers tremendous wisdom. What lie within others lies within all of us.

"Everything that irritates us about others can lead us to an understanding of ourselves."
—C.G. Jung

"We discover in ourselves what others hide from us and we recognize in others what we hide from ourselves."
—Vauvenargues

Our world mirrors who we are back to us. All of the substances of life are present in each of us. What lies within you, lies within me. Therefore, what lies within Tiger and Lorena lies within you. We all come from the same source. We all have the same chemical makeup. Like Jesus stated, "You too can do all of these things and more." He just wasn't referring to himself. You see we all possess the same character traits. We all have unlimited potential and possibility. You might perceive that one person possesses more or less than another, yet that simply is not true, no one is more or less valuable than another. Yet we each possess our own unique gifts and we each call forth our own unique experiences. We each possess our own unique dreams. The substances of life like mental toughness, lies within each of us. Our work is to harness that energy and take back our power.

Empowerment exercise: Go ahead and pick the three people you most admire. Make sure at least one of them is a golfer. Go ahead and search your memory bank. Who in this world do you admire the most? It could be a living legend or someone who lived long ago. It could be a president, a king, a poet, a philosopher, an activist, a humanitarian, someone wealthy or someone poor—it matters not. We can take from them whatever qualities we want. Just make sure at least one of them has ties to the game of golf.

Now, once you have found your three people, pick three qualities or aspects in each of them that inspire you. Obviously, if you cannot narrow the field, you can have more than three. And, like before, you can tweak this along the way. Remember, there are no right or wrong answers.

Here are my some of the role models that I admire: Tiger Woods, Jack Nicklaus, and Johnny Miller. Ben Hogan and Bobby Jones also possess unique character qualities I most admire, it's just that they were a little ahead of my time. I think of the miraculous recovery of Ben Hogan, his perseverance, his strive for excellence and his mental state of focused concentration that I watch in clips and documentaries. I think of how Bobby Jones brought integrity to the game of golf. I stand in awe at how Tiger Woods executes with consistent excellence. He not only wants to win, he wants to win *big*! Tiger says, "It's a lifelong ambition to get better." In my mind's eye, I see Jack Nicklaus staring down a putt that he absolutely must make. Raymond Floyd has his own unique stare. Their focus is on this very putt, this very shot right here and right now. Ian Poulter has that same intense look in his eye. I embrace the confidence that Johnny Miller eloquently displayed in his pursuit of one dominant golf shot after another. I loved his grace and his charm and how he acknowledged his fans. I also acknowledge what he described as having "the yips" that kept him from continuing from playing competitive golf. These things I too am working through as well.

Here are the three who most inspire me, and the qualities they represent to me:

1) Tiger Woods—The greatest golfer of all time
   Qualities:
   - State of Being – A fierce competitor with an intense focus and will
   - Skillful at all levels in golf

> - Dedicated to making this a better world, spiritually connected

2) Jack Nicklaus—A winner, a champion
   Qualities:
   - State of Being – Mental focus, ability to remain calm and present
   - Strength & Internal fortitude to be his best
   - Family Man – a balance between golf and family

3) Johnny Miller—Vibrant personality, honest and solid character
   Qualities:
   - State of Being – Charismatically confident
   - A genuinely honest and compassionate human being
   - Most gracious at winning and loosing

Obviously, I have many more role models whose qualities I also choose to integrate into my life. Pictures of Mahatma Gandhi are hung in my room. I am constantly reminded about "being the change I wish to see in the world." There are also the wonderful qualities of Mother Teresa, MLK, JFK, Susan B. Anthony, Patty Berg, Babe Didrikson Zaharias, and Annika Sorenstam. I'm also embracing the Champion's Image that Lorena Ochoa carries with her. I take a little from each one of them and make them mine. Their qualities lie within each of us. Take back your power. Espavo means thank you for taking back your power.

Allow me to add one more name to the list. When I think of the greatest athlete of all time, one who really defines the concept of being who they are, loving what they do, and becoming their intention, and being a champion, without a doubt, I think of Muhammad Ali. He, more than any other athlete, has taken this spiritual and natural law of attraction, deliberate creation, and art of allowing to the peak of ultimate performance. Regardless of whether you think he crossed the line of arrogance (complete confidence) or not, Ali believed in himself and became the greatest of all time. His *I am* statements of himself rang throughout the world. As a kid, I remember Ali as being the most recognized figure on the planet. He announced and declared who he was, and because of the law of attraction, he was that! Muhammad Ali, the greatest of all time embellishes and represents what you can achieve by applying the law of attraction, deliberate creation, and fully expecting it to happen.

So, as challenging as it may seem, those qualities of believing in him self are the most profound declaration of this principle that I know of, while Tiger just declares he wants nineteen majors. I also resonate with Ali's humanitarian efforts and his stance on peace. Muhammad you are the greatest!

The most challenging part of integrating these qualities are the embracing of self, and the idea of being selfish, which really means taking care of oneself. As Ali took care of himself, he was that much more able to be there for another and our world. He made this world a much better place.

Next, put all of the qualities you've written down into a list. The qualities you listed from another lie within you. How else would you recognize that quality in another? Then accept those qualities as your own. See them in yourself and take back your own power.

How do you go about integrating these qualities and accepting your own power? Use your imagination. You might build a collage or put up pictures of those you admire: Gandhi's compassionate eyes and peaceful smile are on me everyday, reminding me to persevere. Learn about them: read their biographies or autobiographies, and get copies of movies that portray their lives to watch now and again. If possible, make pilgrimages to their birthplaces and add recordings of their speeches to your library. Post their sayings on your wall and make them your personal mottos. If you are an artist, draw their portrait and frame it. And think—think about what your icon has said and done. Be that, and act as if it is already so—carry yourself like a champion.

For instance, in April, 1913, from the book *The Greatest Game Ever Played* by Mark Frost, Francis Ouimet found his inspiration while attending an opera, a local production of a Verdi melodrama when a young singer took the stage, Good Lord, thought Francis, will you look at that woman? She had committed herself to this song so completely; she appeared to be in a kind of trance. Then the source of it came clear to him; a clean, concentrated light in her eyes that Francis intuitively understood to mean she'd given up her very soul to let this music come through her, nothing stood in the way of it, he could see she wasn't even aware anyone else was watching her, and at that moment, the tumblers in the lock he'd been trying to open to reach the heart of his own talent all clicked into place.

This is just what I want for golf, Francis said to himself.

Skill guided by belief, practiced without fear and with absolute commitment. Believe shots could fly on line and they did. He slowly gave up his fear of being judged, his fear of failing. His distance increased dramatically. Putts dropped.

The power of role models is around us all the time. Like Tiger Woods closing the deal, you too have all of this in you. Go with flow. Play like nobody is watching.

Next you must not only accept that those qualities are a part of you, but that they *are* you—you as a person, and you as a golfer. Now write down what you are in terms of those qualities.

For example, as I integrate the qualities I listed and make them my own, I might write something like: I am a peaceful, connected, and a mentally tough golfer. I am a fierce competitor who is confident and skilled at all levels. I play the game of golf with integrity, and with a spirit to be my best. I give my full attention to every shot, and I rise to the occasion when I absolutely must. I have overcome hardship, and I am a compassionate teacher who is dedicated to making this world a better place to be. I am dedicated to helping you play life and golf to the very best of your ability, and all the while, I play mine. My personal character and demeanor reflect my peaceful nature.

Coaches Notes: Notice, I say with a spirit to be my best (I have not used the thoughts or words as Ali would, which is, *I am* the greatest <u>of all time</u>). This is my work. How far do you, how far do I wish to take this? The only limits are the self-imposed limits we place upon ourselves. Tiger Woods, Babe Zaharias, Jim Thorpe, Jim Brown, Michael Jordan, Wayne Gretzky, Lance Armstrong, and Muhammad Ali all wanted to be the best at what they did. Each of them are considered not only the greatest at their sport, but are thought of as, along with Babe Ruth, as perhaps the greatest athlete(s) of all time.

It is my humble observation that Tiger Woods is vastly approaching the status as *the* greatest athlete of all time. I also observe in him other larger and more purposeful legacies that he will give to humanity when the time is right—for he already is being this. Like Ali, Tiger is becoming the most recognized athlete and perhaps someday individual on the planet. As he evolves he will change our world for the better. His dad has seen this gift, and now Tiger is awakening to this even more. His mother will leave Tiger with even more insight. Yet know this, inside each of us lies our own unique gift to offer humanity. It is my intention to draw it out of you, and awaken the magnificent sleeping giant within you, just as I am being this myself by allowing the flow. That's how critical mass wakes up our planet, one magnificent being at a time. That's how we change our world—in our own hearts.

Finally, take the qualities of those people you admire with you throughout your day and into the night; sleep with those thoughts, and live them as your own. If you do, I guarantee that your mind-set and state of being will begin to change. Your whole paradigm will begin to shift. What was once dormant will become full of life. New avenues will open up to you and will play more often like the champion that you are. Yes, you will practice more, you will work on your weaknesses, you will observe yourself, your demeanor will get better, you will think more clearly, you will talk to yourself like a champion does, act like a champion does, and yes you too will experience yourself as a champion. You will become more of who you really are. You will come to understand, that the only thing stopping you, is you. And this too shall change. You are becoming a champion.

Zen and the Road to Enlightenment

From a parable passed down through the ages, the anxious

student asked the Zen Master how long to enlightenment. The Zen Master answered a long time, at least ten years. The student said, "Well I will work twice as hard." The Zen Master said, "Then it will take twenty years." "No!" said the committed student, "I will work three times as hard." "Well then," said the Zen Master, "it will take thirty years."

Do you need to work at being spiritual? No. You already are spiritual. Do you need to work at being human? No. That's just who you are. The spiritual path doesn't require us to get anything. It's a process of opening to new dimensions of who we already are. It's a process of awakening to our own truth. It's a process of allowing ourselves to be authentic, "It is not by your actions that you will be saved, but by your being," said Meister Eckhart. The way to enlightenment is being who you really are and when you say you are enlightened – then you are. Meditation helps to pave the way in calming the mind and connecting with this awareness, this Inner Being.

The spiritual path doesn't require us to get anything. There's nothing you have to do. It's a process of opening to new dimensions of who we already are. It's a process of awakening to our own truth. It's a process of allowing ourselves to be authentic. The spiritual path doesn't require us trying too hard to make something happen. The spiritual path is one in which we intend and allow it to be. Through our inspired state of being we allow whatever we desire to happen. Intention is a seed in consciousness and has within it the power to fulfill and orchestrate countless details to its own fulfillment when opportunity meets with our calling to take action. There is such a thing as trying too hard. Learn to let go, and let God flow to you and through you. You are the leading edge divinity aspect of this Source. Be like the Zen Master and open up new dimensions to who you already are. Play Zen golf with authenticity.

Action Steps:

1) **Practice your own alignment as being an extension of Source Energy.**

2) **Practice being your most inspired state of being.**

3) **Practice taking back your own power.**

4) **Practice eagerly anticipating, feeling good.**

Chapter 9

The Zone

"The privilege of a lifetime is being who you are. Follow your bliss."
—Joseph Campbell

What is The Zone...
How does one get into The Zone?

Golf is the perfectly imperfect game. The challenge it brings, along with its imperfections; paradoxes; and divine dichotomies make it practically perfect in every sense of the way. It is an equal blend of physical stamina, emotional acceptance, personal desire, mental endurance, and spiritual alignment—an inner game that challenges you to go deep within yourself to drive a small little white ball long distances, but then deftly maneuver it into equally small targets, called holes, spread out over acres of land, where even a slight ripple in the contour of the ground can throw you off.

Golf is the perfect metaphor for life, asking you to endure the adversity and roll with the punches as you aim toward your desired target, all the while avoiding the out-of-bounds, sand traps, water hazards, trees, and the tall rough, or other assorted obstructions along the way. Sometimes the journey along the fairway works out great, just like you envisioned it. But when you inevitably find yourself in one of these less-than-desirable spots, or even when you are playing absolutely spectacular golf, it is how you respond to the situation that ultimately matters. And when you come to understand that *you* have created your reality and each golf shot, the way you respond becomes an even more enlightened perspective. A warrior athlete creates first and chooses to respond in harmony with this energy.

In life and in golf—it is how you first create, and then respond to each situation, to each moment of "now" that matters most. As you train yourself to respond in ways that support you, you become that vibrational match. You become more trusting, more responsible, and more in harmony with the universe and with yourself. Nothing really matters except what *you* decide to *make* matter. A Master accepts and welcomes all that comes to his gate. *You* have caused and created the golf shot, no one else. How you respond and learn from *all* your golf shots on the golf course is what really matters. If you find yourself losing your cool, giving in to frustration and anger, and ready to give up on your game and yourself...now there is hope. You can change. Little by little you can replace the way you used to respond, ways that no longer serve you, with a new way that empowers you. All it takes is a simple shift in perspective. Golf and life begin to make sense once again.

It is only when *we* keep on beating up on *ourselves* because we'd rather choose that for now – we get what we get. And sometimes we don't care because we just want to scream bloody murder. And that's okay too! There's no right or wrong way to go about your business...instead, think what works and what doesn't.

The first step to change is self-observation. By beginning to observe yourself you will find the wisdom that lie within the experience. Gradually you will become more of these new more empowering ways through feeding your subconscious a new more empowering perspective, one that serves your higher Self and best interest. The buy-in must come from within. Will this make me a better golfer, a better me? You get to choose. For me, the answer is a resounding, YES!

A player to watch on the PGA Tour is Robert Karlsson from Sweden. Why, because his new mindset is one of awakening and awareness. He is choosing a new way in how he chooses to respond to his golf shots. His emotions are more even keel and he carries himself more like a champion. Having watched Tiger Woods open with a double bogey on the first hole in the 2008 U.S. Open and how Tiger handles it, Karlsson has taken his own game to a whole new level by keeping his emotions more in check. Watch him; it's just a matter of time before he wins something very big. Karlsson's simple shift in focus is awakening a sleeping giant into becoming a warrior champion. Where he takes the level of his game is always an internal challenge, which we get to witness as his outward expression of how he plays.

> **Simple Secret Reminder # 19 – Choose Your Response**
> **Remember you have created your golf shot.**
> **It is how you *choose* to respond to your golf shot that ultimately matters.**
> **Learn to *be with* adversity, keep emotions in check, and how to handle success.**

Golf is the perfectly imperfect game because there is no such thing as perfection like we may have previously perceived it. And there is no such thing as a perfect round of golf like we may have hoped to perceive it. To think otherwise only sets us up for more frustration and a perceived belief in failure. Ben Hogan would hit what he would call a "practically perfect" shot only on rare occasions, sometimes only one shot in his entire round would come close to what he deemed as a "perfect" shot. The problem is that many people, myself included, grow up thinking we have to be perfect; after all, our parents, our schools, and our society tells us to strive for perfection. When we take the misplaced desire for perfection to the golf course, the inevitable feelings of disappointment and frustration that well up when we don't perform perfectly results in a cycle of self-loathing, which again takes us further out of The Zone. In school, at work, or at home we may have gotten straight A's, had a successful presentation, made a lot of money, or cut the grass just right. We were perfect! Then we hit the links and find we can't perform perfectly. Anything less than being perfect or at least close to perfect, becomes a big let down. We are forever chasing the Holy Grail.

We're trying to please everybody, including ourselves because many of us have been raised with a perfectionist type of attitude, which will only set us up for perceived failure and constant frustration. We wanted to please our parents, teachers, and coaches so badly that we've crossed the line of what being our personal best really means. We're always fighting in this space that we think we can figure it out. And when you think you can figure it out, that's exactly what you'll keep getting in life – thinking you can figure it out, never really happy. Being perfect from this kind of perspective, that we have to be "perfect", only sets us up for failure, which by the way, does not exist either. Let go of the ego's need to be perfect. We are perfectly imperfect just the way we are. Life is unfolding perfectly. Think excellence in being your personal best and everything *will* evolve just "perfectly." A simple, yet profound shift in perspective, and never, not once, losing any competitive spirit whatsoever!

So if things are "perfect" just the way they are and there is no such thing as failure what is there? There are just results and outcome. How many times did it take Thomas Edison to invent the light bulb? What was his mindset? He was shown thousands of ways of how not to invent a light bulb—nothing had to do with failure. He didn't believe in the concept of failure; he saw through the illusion. He kept on creating new ways to invent the light bulb, and he responded in harmony with the universe. It is how we respond to our results, to our golf shots; that *we* have caused that ultimately matters. And in ultimately reality nothing really matters because we are making it all up. Life is meant to be fun – lighten up! Golf is a game to be played and enjoyed.

In a deeper spiritual sense, golf is a game that is practically perfect in every way to show us the way along our *True North*. The lessons in golf are but opportunities to become more of who we really are. So, instead of fighting against yourself out there on the course, welcome the gift this exact experience within the experience is showing you about your self.

The champion golfer becomes aware of what is causing the results she is getting, because she is aware of herself. The champion golfer becomes a champion because she has a winner's self-image of herself. The champion golfer is fully connected to who he really is

The Fairway of Life

and believes in himself. The champion golfer becomes a champion because of how he thinks and what he believes, which will produce how he chooses to respond and react to each situation along the fairway of life.

The true champion understands that frustration takes him further away from his own Zone. The true champion accepts and acknowledges her disappointment quickly in the moment where cause and effect become one, learns from that experience, clears her disappointment, and immediately, or within a few short moments centers herself – often with little muttering, like Tiger, or without any form of emotion. The true champion finds a way to clear and move through a negative experience and back into center. The true champion understands that the golf shot simply is. Acceptance in the moment can be a challenging thing to do—but, yes, it is possible. Remember, it is *you* who have created it.

Most feel obligated to react negatively to show others their displeasure for their performance; they are better than what they have shown. Like Pavlov's dogs, it's a trained behavioral response over many years of socialization to feed the ego's appetite. They simply cannot let go of showing displeasure to a perceived bad golf shot because of a conditioned or trained hypnotic trance. Ironically, this is this very reason they continue to flounder shot after shot, round after round, and year after year. What we do about our results and how we respond to them are ultimately what matters which ultimately leads to our net result – our score. In order to get better, it's as if we must de-hypnotize ourselves from society's stranglehold, and the influence we have allowed to enter our own psyche. Instead of being lead around like trained pouting rats, empower yourself and rise above the status quo to a new level of excellence.

Golf is a game to be played, not won. Winning and playing well will take care of itself as a result of giving our attention and focus to our present moment and playing our personal best. The true champion focuses upon what he wants in this moment, plays with the best he's got at this moment, and simply allows it to happen. The true champion understands that winning and losing are not the only options; that simply being his personal best is what really matters—and there are plenty of prizes to go around. The true champion understands that whoever wins on any given day was the best on that day—the one whom was clearest about his wanting and most expectant of it. The true champion gentleman, like Harry Vardon to Francis Ouimet in the 1913 U.S. Open, congratulates the winner graciously and accepts his position on any given day graciously as well, always eager to play another round. Therefore, become a gratuitous winner and a gracious competitor.

Realizing that life is unfolding *perfectly* just the way it is, wouldn't it be better to think in terms of excellence instead of being a perfectionist? Which one empowers you more? Excellence is when we are being our personal best; giving our best effort, and playing this wonderful game we love to the best we can be right now. That's all anyone can ever ask of anyone else, and it is all you ever have to ask of yourself. And the more you accept, embrace, and enjoy being your personal best, the better player you will become. No better than anyone else, just becoming better than *you* used to be.

The challenge is on both ends of your golfing ability. If you are playing extremely well how come you end up choking or making double bogey? There really is no reason to sabotage your success on this particular golf shot right now, unless you are thinking ahead about what it might mean. Fearing-the-result thinking sabotages more shots than you can imagine. Thinking ahead about results draws us out of the present moment. Feeling anxious or being too hyped up also takes us out of The Zone.

Likewise, learn to accept what many will call their "bad" golf shots and look adversity straight in the eye. Calling something a "bad" shot is a judgment in itself and that takes you further away from The Zone. You may not like what you are getting or seeing on any particular golf shot here and there, however, what that moment is showing you, *is* your connector, a wonderful opportunity to change. Can you simply be with it, after all, you created it? All you have to do is embrace it, see the gift, observe why, and become better next time. Ask yourself, "Why is this showing up for me?" When you can ask the question instead of reacting, and finally answer back, you will be on your way. Before too long you will

The Fairway of Life

become better simply because you have embraced what is and chose to feel the experience instead of wearing your emotions on your shirtsleeve.

Coaches Notes: Frustrations, irritations, the uggghs, and anything that pushes our buttons or gives us a charge, show up in our life to get our attention. When in ultimate reality these irritations are actually a gift nudging us to higher ground, which is growth within. Yes, that is why spiritual Masters will say the growth can be, and usually is messy. Once we begin to show up big with them, and see the gift, then they melt away. Once again, what you resist persists. And it is the experience within the experience where this wisdom lies. Life will keep throwing us these curve balls until we see the gift in the experience.

Here's a simple exercise that has nothing to do with golf that may perhaps allow you to see more clearly this concept. Do you ever get irritated driving your car in traffic? Do you ever feel you are in such a hurry that cars in front of you are going too slow? Do you experience some form of road rage? This is form of irritation, correct? You're irritated by traffic, being in a hurry, before you know it a large truck or semi or worse yet, a garbage truck is in front of you. Your thinking how stupid *they* are and it's their fault. No, it's not! You're the stupid one. What you see in another lies within you. You're stupid for acting like your acting. Here's the solution: allow yourself a moment to be calm before flying off the handle. Allow yourself the opportunity to embrace the moment. What happens is that the more you remain calm in a more meditative state the less times you will find yourself in these situations and the more you will allow yourself the time to get to where you are going. The reason you experience road rage is an opportunity to heal yourself. Don't believe me – go experience it for yourself. The same goes for everything in life including the golf course. Plus, it may very well be a calling for you to leave a tad bit earlier for your appointments ☺, or move to a less congested area.

The challenge for most people is that they do not embrace, and cannot accept their bad golf shots and end up hanging on to their negative energy, which once again draws them back out of The Zone. If you cannot accept what you do not like, you will keep repeating those same behaviors over and over and over again. What you resist; persists. It's a Catch 22 where you want to get mad at your bad golf shots or what you might consider bad breaks, yet the more angry or frustrated you get, the slower the process to change and get better. Anger and frustration only keeps us stuck in a never-ending repetitive cycle. Anger and frustration do not exist in The Zone . . . you won't either. The challenge is acceptance of "what is" so you can move into what you prefer. And once you begin to accept what just happened, you will evolve much quicker to what you prefer. Once you stop beating up on yourself and relax you start playing better. Works every time and you know that! The challenge is the discipline in the moment. All you have is this moment. You *do* have a choice.

Simple Secret Reminder # 20 - You Have a Choice To Be Angry, or Not
What you resist persists.

Interview excerpts with Geoff Ogilvy – 2006 US Open Champion
By John Huggan, *Golf Digest* June 10, 2007

Q: As a young player, were you impatient on the golf course?

A: Oh, yeah. I was horrendous. I could hit five good shots in a row, then one bad one, but remember only the bad one. I'm sure I was a nightmare when I was 16 or 17, as many at that age are.

Q: What sort of stuff did you do?

A: I'd throw clubs around. I broke a few. I used a

The Fairway of Life

lot of four-letter words. The temper stuff is easy to fix psychologically. You either get angry or you don't get angry; you have a choice.

I realize now that I was getting angry for everyone else around me, not for me. When you get that, that's the day you fix it. When you play by yourself, you never smack the bag with the club, or get angry…ever… because there's no audience. That's my theory, anyway. After you hit a shot you get angry because you want the person you're trying to impress to think that you're better than this. I think that's the root of it for nine out of 10 people. The other one is purely psycho.

Geoff Ogilvy is in the process of mastering his own mental toughness, and it shows by his outward expression of being calm more often than before. Does he still kick his putter and want to scream bloody murder? Sure, who doesn't? The key is to be able to ground yourself and find a way to either accept or allow this negative emotion to pass through you. If we truly seek to obtain optimal results it begins with a calm heart and self-control.

"A calm heart and self-control are necessary if one is to obtain good results. If we are not in control of ourselves but instead let our impatience or anger interfere, then our work is no longer of any value. Keeping your attention focused, alert, ready to handle ably and intelligently any situation which may arise—this is mindfulness."
—Thich Nhat Hanh, *The Miracle of Mindfulness*

Eventually you will arrive at the destination on the beautifully landscaped and manicured green. You will now be faced with yet another stroke, or what is called a putt, and you will once again either allow the power and Well-Being in (focusing on what you really, really want) going with the flow, or resist it (what you really, really don't want) because of some level of perceived fear, judgment, belief, thoughts, ego or outcome-based mentality. Soon you find yourself once again playing each new hole that comes before you as best you can so that, in the end, it all amounts to a score you can be proud of, (proud in a sense of sheer joy of giving maximum effort for the sake of personal excellence). Each of those shots along the journey is the sum that will eventually yield your total score. The game of golf is simply one shot or one moment at a time.

How you think, create, respond, and react along your path in each moment of now is what life and golf is all about. Our thoughts and how we respond can either make us go weak or make us go strong. When we play golf, is it not in our best interest to be strong? Any thoughts of consciousness operating below the level of courage will make us go weak. Things like shame, guilt, apathy, worry, doubt, or fear make us go weak. Any form of consciousness operating at or above the courage level will make us strong. Things like courage, willingness, acceptance, joy, and love makes us strong.

What we really want is the ability to be free from the obstacles that are holding us back. It's not so much our actual score or result that we're after, we know scoring will take care of itself; it's feeling good about who we are – free to express ourselves and our talents without being held in bondage, without the heavy weight of baggage, without the fear of these perceived demons. What we all desire is the ability to be calm, relaxed, and free to play to our full potential. What we really want is to have peace of mind knowing that we are living our fullest expression—our authentic Self. The place we find this is called The Zone.

The Zone

"Obviously I was in The Zone and hopefully I can be in The Zone more often."
– Anthony Kim

Coaches Notes: Guess what Anthony Kim wasn't thinking when describing his lapse not realizing he just won his 2008 singles Ryder Cup match over Sergio Garcia. Anthony Kim was in The Zone, lost in this very moment of NOW – out of his mind. The truth is when we are in The Zone we really aren't thinking. Thinking while swinging is like trying to give your self a lesson while executing – it just doesn't work too well. Too many thoughts impede your natural life experience and rhythm. Often we get into an "I have to, need to, or am supposed to do this correctly mode for a multitude of reasons." Mindsets like these causes us to think we have to sink this putt, or need to hit it close, or am supposed to win this match, par this hole, or make this 3-footer carries with it a message of all kinds of unwanted baggage, which unconsciously tells us if we don't live up to "this kind of expectation" something undesirable will happen, not only on the course but very often with the subtle message that our own self-worth is on the line as well. We often avoid any kind of embarrassment this may lead to which only keeps us stuck in this cycle of fear-based fantasy appearing real. Left unchecked this lie can spiral wildly out of control, all because of the perception we feed our minds.

> *"Being in The Zone is like an out of body experience. I can't really explain it."*
> – Dwayne Wade, Miami Heat

As stated before, it's tough to explain The Zone. It's more of a feeling than anything else. The Zone is a place of complete stillness and pure positive energy where transcendence of personal self moves beyond the normal performance barrier into our higher authentic Self where the activity becomes an effortless, joyful, and peaceful experience. Personal self sets limits of the mind (more of a comfort zone), whereas authentic Self connects with infinite potential of the soul (unlimited possibilities). Yes, you have gone beyond the confines of your mind into the Inner Being of your soul. In The Zone you are lost and fully present in the moment, thoughts and emotions fade into oblivion and you become one with all that is.

The challenge within is to keep connecting to this ever-abundant flow of pure positive energy right through the entire performance. The true champion waits until the contest is completely over before honoring his or her challenger(s) first, then personal achievement. Too much early celebration or too much excitement can get the best of even the greatest golfer. Better to ride the wave of humility then being too high or too low.

There is a tremendous difference between being grateful, humble, and virtuous than being pompous, diffident, and celebratory. One keeps you humbled and in The Zone, the other reeks of personal pride and ego, which pushes you out of The Zone. The form of pride in honoring human achievement is a much higher level of consciousness behavior than one of personal pride and boasting. Observe the true champion's speech after her victory. Most often there is humility and gratitude honoring the performances of others and being thankful to God or Source that flows to them and through them. Most often others that experience playing golf in The Zone acknowledge a higher power that was somehow miraculously part of their experience either verbally or within and they are just a channel receiving the signal and going with the flow. Athletes often describe this feeling as being surreal; like they don't know how it actually happened once it was over.

This similar form of flow or being in The Zone happens all over the world in so many professions where excellence abounds. It is the key to unlock the tumbler within. Observing someone in The Zone is powerful and inspiring as well. It doesn't have to be an athlete. It's the toll booth collector who cheerfully takes your change with one hand and waves you on to a great day with the other, the waitress at your favorite restaurant who anticipates all her customers' needs with grace and ease, or the compassionate teacher who knows the precise line between discipline and leniency to get the best from his students. Being in The Zone is an awesome experience, and you know that!

Our mission here is to provide you with tools, mindsets, universal laws, reflections, and simple secrets that will allow you to maximize your opportunity to experience being in your Zone more often than ever before – all the while playing better golf, having more fun, enjoying your experience, and carrying yourself like a champion. All of which translates into a winner's image of your highest self. How does a champion think, walk, talk, act, and play? Removing whatever blocks, fears, or resistances you have that lie in the way of your true winner's image of yourself is your

The Fairway of Life

mission if you so chose. Your own self-imposed limited belief and set comfort zone is one of your biggest blocks from playing to your full potential. It's the hidden assassin that lies deeply entrenched within. It runs everything in our lives—including our golf game.

Coaches Notes: The Masters Tournament is a prime example that shows us just how important it is to stay fully present right up through the 72nd putt. All you have to do is remember Crenshaw (sobbing hands in face), O'Meara (arms raised), or Mickelson (jump for joy) as all three allowed their emotions to come pouring out after just winning The Masters on the 72nd green at Augusta National. Perhaps the next greatest shot in Master's lore, aside from Gene Sarazen's rare double eagle, the shot heard 'round the world, holing 4-wood from 235 yards for a double-eagle two on the 15th at Augusta National in 1935, was in 2005 – Tiger's chip-in for birdie on hole # 16, the par 3. Many remember the incredible ball hanging on the lip for a full two seconds, the Nike logo spinning, and then watching it disappear. It certainly was an incredible moment. Tiger celebrated as all playing partner Chris Dimarco could muster up was "nice shot."

Yet what many fail to understand is what happened next. Tiger hit his tee shot into the pines on hole #17, which lead to bogey. On 18 he missed the fairway again, pushed his second shot into the bunker and failed to get up and down which lead to a playoff. Although he beat a feisty Dimarco on the first playoff hole – too much early celebration took him out his Zone for a short spell. It could have cost him the tournament. Remember Dimarco's chip shot on 18 that hit the lip, which would have won him the tournament? Imagine what it is like for us mere mortals playing a $5.00 nassau? Our demons and emotions are the obstacles and resistances to us playing to our full potential, playing golf more often in The Zone. Even Tiger admitted later that he "threw up" all over himself finishing bogey, bogey in the 2005 Masters having taken himself out of The Zone.

Practically any display of positive or negative emotions, too much early celebrating or too much frustration, are blocks to playing golf in The Zone. The Zone is a place where there are no thoughts, concerns, emotions, or worries—it is pure, positive energy flowing. What appears is that you cannot do any wrong. In actuality, you are being your natural most inspired state all along. It's what we are born with. The Zone is a place of natural flow and Well-Being. It is just plain fun—exactly what golf and life are supposed to be. The Zone is when you experience yourself in absolute outrageous joy. In The Zone you will experience feelings of humility and gratitude. And your *feelings* are subtly different from your *emotions*.

Feeling peace, harmony, and joy is in alignment with our Inner Being. Feelings of joy can be found in the emotion of tears. Emotion of tears can be a happy or sad experience, where feelings tell more of an accurate story. Have you ever noticed a person crying and you can't tell if it is a happy tear or a sad one? That's exactly how Ben Crenshaw reacted upon winning the green jacket, tears of joy. Emotions describe the tears, whereas feelings describe what is underneath them, and emotions are the release—the reaction to our feelings.

When one is in The Zone we transcend ourselves where bliss and joy becomes a grateful experience that goes deep into our heart and into the very fabric of our soul. The joy and oneness we experience while being in The Zone is unmatched by any other state of being. It is our natural and most inspired state of being.

Coaches Notes: Feelings exist for a reason: to guide us into the direction of our heart's desire. Feelings are the language of your soul. Feelings transcend emotions, just like love transcends sex. Personal excellence is transcendence into a connection with All That Is that flows to us and through us.

The breakthrough point is when you begin to experience and feel inner awe and unwavering gratitude. The breakthrough occurs when we get out of our own way and allow personal excellence to be our new standard. The Zone occurs when we experience ourselves performing beyond our normal functioning capacity or apparent limit of ability. It is our highest state of bliss consciousness and pure positive energy. This phenomenon is commonly described in terms of allowing oneself to the point where one suddenly breaks through a normal self-imposed performance barrier and the activity or skill becomes an effortless and joyful experience. What we observe in another is effortless grace in motion. The state of joy transcends even the success of the event. The Zone is a connection and Oneness with All That Is.

The Zone Is Every Golfer's Pure Desire

Whether they realize it or not The Zone is every golfer's pure desire. Everyone wants to play golf to there full potential. Everyone wants to play golf in The Zone. Everyone wants to become a better golfer with a better demeanor, even Tiger Woods. It's the spice of life. Desire in its purest form keeps us going forward and evolving. It's a natural evolution to want more and become better all the while being happy exactly where we are.

In its weakest form, desire for more with the sake of accumulation and greed can be an unhealthy experience. Simply put, playing golf for greed of solely wanting to win the prize money will make a golfer go weak and he will play golf nowhere near his full potential. "We play for the sheer bloody pride in being the best, that's why we do this," Harry Vardon once said – still hallowed as the greatest British champion golfer of all time. That's all this really ever is, it's about being your personal best, that's why we play. The chips fall as they may after it is all said and done. And if I receive an honor, trophy with my name on it, or a paycheck because of my excellence, then I am extremely grateful. We play to be our best.

Make your burning desire within come from the pureness of your own heart—and so shall it be. Allow your desire to play better golf in The Zone come with humility and gratitude thanking the source from where it all came, humbly accepting what has been given, being grateful for what just happened. Being in The Zone is really pretty simple. It's our natural most inspired state of being. You're feeling gratitude and appreciation, pure positive energy connected with All That Is. Being out of The Zone is really pretty simple, it's our resistance to our natural most inspired state of being, which is allowing the Well-Being in. Our work is to get into alignment with our asking and allow this natural flow. Anything else is simply our resistance. Resistance comes in the form of feeling doubt, worry, judgment, and fear. Resistance is any form of stuck or blocked energy that we have allowed to exist. Like kinks in a garden hose our work is to one-by-one open the channels or remove the blocks.

The Zone Is Always Shining

"Removing the clouds does not cause the sun to shine, but merely reveals that which was hidden all along."
—Dr. David R. Hawkins

The Zone, like the sun, is always shining. Our resistances are like the clouds covering the sun. Rather than seeking to *discover* this feeling and wondering how to *get in* to The Zone, the true process is in removing or releasing the blocks and resistances so that you naturally tap into The Zone.

In order to understand what The Zone is, we often experience what it is not. When we are not in The Zone we are not allowing the Well-Being in. If we are not allowing the Well-Being in, then we are standing in a place of resistance; it's just that simple. Resistances are all the things that cloud our natural state of being. When we are not in The Zone why is that? The Zone is a place free from any control or judgments, thoughts and concerns, ego and personality, limited beliefs, fears and mind noise. The Zone is a place that only occurs when we remove the obstacles that lie in the way. Our mission is to take the necessary steps clearing one obstacle at a time. Eventually we see light at the end of the tunnel. That's the growth process in this eternal dance-with-life. And the better it gets, the better it gets. The intention is to get to the core of your being, your authentic and higher Self. Once you align yourself with your higher Self the blocks disappear. Jesus said it best, "Once I was lost, now I am found," which has nothing to do with religion and everything to do with who you are being.

The further I go in the process the better I like my chances, the better I feel about playing. Any removal of obstacle blockage (resistance) is a healthy experience, like a weight being lifted off your shoulders or clearing a pathway. This negative energy can get stuck in the body as well. Once we clear it, the mindset is one of hope and eager anticipation to keep on keeping on. Eventually we start seeing light at the end of the tunnel. We now understand our work is to clear or remove one obstacle at a time; whatever is unique for us. All the while implanting positive visualizations, feelings, desires, dreams, and what we prefer – all the downstream thoughts upon our subconscious mind. As I have said before, eventually we just give more "air time" to the things that feel good.

Golf evolution occurs as a result of removing obstacles and not actually acquiring anything new. Once we remove or clear the obstacles voilá. We've known, and are now experiencing what we have wanted all along. We just forget how to be in it. Sometimes we get into The Zone because we simply temporarily forget about our obstacles. We fall back into the present moment. It's like, "I don't how I played so great; I wasn't really thinking about it." It's like hit or miss. All of sudden *you are* in The Zone and it's like you don't remember what exactly just happened: "I did what, go 3 under the last 5 holes?" Then you pop out of it, or something pops you out of it, unless it doesn't? Now you are being reminded once again about what seems so surreal when in actuality it is as real as it gets. The Zone is as simple and as complex as that!

Golf Is Just a Game

Golf is just a game, a game that cannot be won only played, like building sandcastles or skipping stones at the beach. When we are in The Zone the game is fun. It's effortless. It's now. We're focused, relaxed, confident, in no hurry, and full of joy as we gracefully move in slow motion through time—the only moment we ever have. In that present moment of pure joy and single-minded focus, without thought, just being and playing, we are in The Zone. The Zone is always present. The Zone never goes away; people have a tendency to cloud it over with all their negative thoughts, limited beliefs, judgments, and fears.

We tend to create this image that golf is hard, a struggle, and it is most often a grind. While I certainly can agree that golf can sometimes be a grind, it is because we have allowed our fears, blocks, or resistances to enter in. Yes, sometimes we have to manage our game with what we have at the moment. Sometimes we are caught up in a spiral of negative energy, personal issues, or mind noise for one reason or another. Maybe our conscious thoughts are focused on our body position? Or maybe we're thinking too far ahead of ourselves? Maybe we're trying too hard? Maybe we're thinking about the argument we had at work or home? Maybe our biorhythms are just a little off. Maybe we're just a tad out of sync with whatever it is? Golf professionals come to the golf course and simply manage with what they have on *this* particular day. Like them, learn to go with the flow with what you have today. Not to rationalize or justify anything here. It just is what it is, unless it is not?

During times of struggle and grind perhaps there is a bigger lesson presenting itself to us and for us. Ask yourself what is the message this is telling me? What is the broader perspective? Your mind, body, and spirit are all miraculously intelligent as one. The answer and wisdom lies within you. Once you answer, you'll find relief. Once you find relief, you'll begin playing better. And the circle of life continues…

Adversity and contrast can be our greatest teacher if we are open to the gifts. Golf provides us an amazing opportunity to evolve the agenda of our soul. According to acclaimed golf instructor Jim Flick, "Golf is a lifetime pursuit of problem-solving. You've got to be honest with yourself. You've got to be able to identify your problems and fix them when they happen on the course. That's why guys who are champions can make adjustments. They know how to handle the challenges they are faced with." Golf really is a great game that allows us to not only work on being a better golfer in times of challenge and adversity; it allows us the opportunity to become a better person. My invitation to you is to pay attention, become aware, and see the broader and bigger perspective. Align with the connection to Source Energy and with your own Self.

Make peace with yourself and allow the Well-Being to flow to you and through you. Allow what you are asking for in.

The Grind & The Zone

Which comes first, the chicken or the egg? In golf I liken the analogy of which comes first, The Grind or The Zone? Which comes first…The Grind so that we can find The Zone or relief so that we can avoid the struggle? How would we know what The Zone is unless we first experienced being out of The Zone and being in a struggle? Perhaps by working through these understandings we can choose to have better control over our own self.

We tend to create this image that golf is hard and it is a grind. While it is certainly an admirable trait to grind it out versus giving up, our aim is to find relief and align ourselves with feeling good, which gives us confidence and a belief in ourselves, otherwise known as being in The Zone. Whereas, The Grind is often thought of as a buckling-down approach—whatever it takes to scrape out our best. Admirable: yet not ideal.

Many of us have a tendency to make things out to be such a struggle, such a grind; most of us end up paddling real hard against the current because we think that is how golf and life is supposed to be: a constant challenge, a hard-fought battle, a grind. Who told you so? Some people even get so good at it, that they actually embrace the grind every time out, perhaps it's a self-defense concept they created to allow them to make sense of it all. It's like we hear them saying, "Hey look at me! I'm struggling really hard over here." Or, after the round, "It was a real grind out there." Sometimes we give them a pat on the back, "That's my chip off the old block. Keep up the good work." However, the truth be told, in those moments of the struggle we end up taking ourselves out of The Zone once again. The Grind is some sort of resistance or rationalization that is blocking the flow of Well-Being, which is where The Zone exists. What is causing you to grind it out? And I know sometimes it just feels that way. I'm inviting you to relax into this game, find some relief and learn to go with the flow. Remember golf is supposed to be fun. Many think the answer is to keep on paddling really,

really hard–beating more golf balls than ever before. This kind of repetitive vicious cycle keeps repeating itself over and over again. Like Einstein reminds us about the definition of insanity. You can't solve a problem with the same energy that created it.

I hear you when thinking about how Tiger often talks about how much of a grind it was "out there." I'm not saying this feeling doesn't exist. I'm just saying we all can do a little bit better than we used too…even Tiger. And when we do a little bit better than we used too – we end up playing a little better. The spiral moves upward versus the other way around. The better it gets…the better it gets.

Tiger's grind on the other hand may be slightly different from the rest of us mere mortals, wouldn't you say? He misses three or four fairways or the pin by 25 feet on a couple occasions and he's missed the shot. We end up in the blackberry bushes or tall weeds 30 yards from the green. His desires and expectations are a tad higher. Plus, he aligns his vibrational energy to match what he intends and expects. He executes and performs to what he visualizes more often than not. In other words, Tigers allows his intention to be. He's in alignment with his asking. That's what makes Tiger tick. What a mindset and focus. Imagine Tiger's view of the field and that narrow window or rectangle of where he intends to play the shot giving his best effort in this moment on this particular shot or putt. Go be something similar to this mindset yourself. Begin visualizing and narrowing your field. The shot produces the swing, not the other way around. With a mindset like Tiger's we too can become better tomorrow than we are today.

What you don't hear is how often Tiger is actually clicking along and playing pretty well. He does play in the now. However, his mindset is always wanting to be better tomorrow than today. That's his inspiration and motivation. Tiger appears to be never satisfied; yet he is still the greatest ever. He's hungry and he's humble. I'd be surprised if he isn't absolutely ecstatic on the inside for everything he has accomplished and absolutely thrilled with how he plays when he's on. What I see is that he doesn't want to lose his edge. He just doesn't want to be or get complacent. He's on a mission.

It's called 19 majors – then perhaps more. To be the world's best means you hold the most majors on your mantle.

Tiger really does play pretty damn good golf after it is all said and done; wouldn't you say? When Tiger is on – which is often – he is pointing his kayak downstream and going with the flow. It's just that simple. He's in alignment with his Source and desire to be his absolute best...world's best. What more is there? Tiger has set the bar and keeps breaking it. Tiger keeps imprinting even more of a champion's self-image upon the inner workings of his subconscious mind...and so can you and I.

Wouldn't it be easier to point your kayak in the direction of the current and simply go with the flow of the stream? Wouldn't it be easier to allow yourself the freedom to build the sandcastle, skip the stone, or swing the club with your natural most inspired state of being and simply go with the flow? Wouldn't it be easier to play like you practice, like no one is watching, or execute like it was your practice swing: effortless and less arduous? Wouldn't it be easier to make your first putt more often than when you drop a second ball in its place? Second putts made. Wouldn't it be easier if you really knew what you are doing when you are practicing and you were practicing mentally in The Zone? The Flow is The Zone. The Zone is always present. There is only The Zone, a source of Well-Being—which you are either allowing, or not. Everything else is resistance or a block or an obstacle to The Zone that is *always* flowing.

It's really pretty simple; remove the resistance, block, or obstacle and allow the Well-Being in. Your Well-Being is The Zone. The Zone is always present. The Zone is going with the flow.

> **Simple Secret Reminder # 21 – The Zone Is Always Present**
> **The Zone is going with the flow.**

The best analogy I could give you is watching young children play. They're in The Zone practically all the time. They don't know any better or any different, they haven't been socialized or conditioned to our cultural story yet. There is no fear of failure or fear of success they are just being themselves. They're not being judged or think they are being judged. They don't think about results, they just do it. Problems arise when "well-meaning" adults begin meddling in their affairs…and you can fill in the blanks. Just remember: everyone is doing the best they can with the awareness and understanding they have at that particular moment in time.

Coaches Notes: A deeper lesson in this whole process is how we encourage, support, and guide another. While our intentions may mean well there is a fine line between critiquing and judging performance and giving advice versus offering positive feedback and offering support and guidance. Asking what questions at the "right" time allows the student to reflect and perhaps make the changes themselves. Invite the student to ask the questions themselves. Invite the student to explore the understanding that the answer and wisdom lies within them. Pointing out body positions through a camera film perhaps allows the student to see potential opportunity for growth.

Another analogy of being in The Zone is when Tiger is throwing darts and sinking putts. Tiger focuses on the moment putting forth his very best effort on this drive, on this swing, and on this putt – and he's not concerned about his result or outcome until after it happens, which in Tiger's case most often *is* a great result. He's tuned in, turned on, tapped in – he's locked in on this very moment. Plus he's like a kid having fun. Where did Tiger get his mental toughness? Was it from Mom and Pop, or within? Is it nurture or nature? Perhaps it's a little bit of both exposures; whatever he allows to filter into his subconscious mind.

Tiger is constantly changing and evolving and so are you. He used to get too high or too low with his emotions, and he now understands that he just can't do that—the season is too long and each event is like running a marathon. You've got to pace yourself and be present one shot at a time. It's more of an even keel type of performance. Tiger has learned a more healthy form of expression. The fist pump comes less often than before. It comes after a huge moment. A simple clenching of his fist or knuckling Stevie is his

The Fairway of Life

way of being thrilled and appreciative with his performance. His anger is less often than before. It comes when he is intense about his disappointment with himself. He learns immediately from the experience. The quicker Tiger grounds and centers himself after his celebration or disappointment, the quicker he will find himself back into his Zone.

A more healthy form of positive expression after an awesome shot is when you are in alignment with gratitude, joy, and inner awe. You simply resonate with inner joy. In this form of expression you are in alignment with your gift and you are in The Zone. A negative form of expression when you are playing well is when you are out to beat another or seeking to puff up your own ego. It's you against them. So you both get what you get. The one who ends up winning becomes the one who is least resistant. Whenever ego enters the equation after a great shot or a great hole, you can bet your boots that you're soon about to hit a disappointing golf shot and make bogey or worse. You are out of The Zone.

Likewise, expressing our disappointment or anger about a particular golf shot takes us further away from our Zone as well. That's called judgment. Is this healthy? Perhaps, depending upon what you are about to learn, or not. When Tiger honestly expresses and acknowledges his disappointment he moves quickly through the process, experiencing it, recognizing his error (his resistance), and then almost immediately bringing himself back to center—back to The Zone. Tiger does it better than most, yet it is my observation that even Tiger can still become better, and *he* knows it. Scary thought isn't it? The greatest in the world can still become better.

The quicker you can move through your disappointment and anger, the quicker your capacity to be back in The Zone. Understand what caused you to do what you did and move on—back to being grounded and centered in the present moment. Hanging on to disappointment serves no one. The Master judges not, and is appreciative in recognizing what caused her disappointment and she moves quickly through her process. The Fool judges harshly, and is ungrateful, blaming everything but himself and often stays stuck in repetitive forms of anger and frustration. It is all a matter of perspective.

For many this form of mental mindset and spiritual paradigm perspective is an extremely challenging concept to accept and embrace, many may even think of it as a bunch of hogwash, or worse yet, blasphemy. What do you think, and where did our beliefs come from? Can you laugh at your "bad" golf shots and smile at the obstacles? Can you resonate with success and stay present with more of that? When you can, you will be basking and resonating with joy shining your own light more often in The Zone for others to see. And when we let our own light shine we give permission to let others do the same.

Honor the Champion

Arnold Palmer, Jack Nicklaus, and Babe Didrikson Zaharias shine because their quest for excellence inspires humanity. Their gifts to mankind create and transcend our consciousness to an even higher awareness of what we can accomplish and become. Tiger Woods inspires millions of golfers to become their personal best and his influence on children will be heard around the world far into the future. Arthur Ashe did the same in tennis. Mother Teresa's love for the poor and downtrodden continues to inspire countless others to help their fellow man. Gandhi's *Be the Change* is in the heart of all those open to hearing his message. John F. Kennedy's "Ask not what your country can do for you – ask what you can do for your country," is a powerful reminder to be our personal best. There is great power in role models, and all of those attributes lie within each of us, while our own unique gift is what truly inspires humanity.

> "True athletic power is characterized by grace,
> sensitivity, inner quiet, and paradoxically, gentleness
> in the noncompetitive lives of even fierce competitors.
> We celebrate the champion because we recognize that
> he has overcome personal ambition through sacrifice
> and dedication to higher principles. The great become

legendary when they teach by example. It isn't what they have, nor what they do, but what they have become that inspires all of mankind, and that's what we honor in them. We should seek to protect their humility from the forces of exploitation that accompany acclaim in the everyday world. We need to educate the public that the abilities of these athletes and their great performances are gifts to mankind to be respected and defended from the abuse of the media and corporate commerce."
—Dr. David R. Hawkins,
From the Power and Sports section in POWER VS FORCE

The benefits of playing golf like a champion in The Zone are astounding and no less than remarkable. The breakthrough point is when you experience inner awe and gratitude. This is the highest state of consciousness, and bliss beyond imagination. Certainly, you will enjoy watching your scores plummet. But you will also end up detaching from a score per se, and end up engaging in the sheer joy of the moment. The score ends up taking care of itself. It really is amazing! Great champions are grateful and humble, honoring their inner awe with humility and appreciation that talent is a gift that flows through them. The Zone is a place of complete stillness where transcendence of personal self becomes an effortless, joyful, and peaceful experience. The breakthrough occurs when we get out of our own way and allow excellence to be our new standard. Commit to excellence and success will find you.

Coaches Notes: Excellence is dedication to the highest standards by being the best you can be (your alignment, character, demeanor, and skill) at any given moment, playing full out, 100 percent, transcending any self-imposed limits, open to unlimited possibilities, going with the flow, and being in The Zone. Every golf shot can then be held as an opportunity to glorify God by sheer purity of endeavor.

Remember, *you* are responsible for the effort and desire, not the outcome or results. Focusing and giving attention to outcome draws you out of The Zone. It's why many crumble on their way to the finish line – they begin thinking ahead about results and what it might all mean. Watch and observe Tiger Woods, better than most, he stays present, focused, and in The Zone right until the last putt drops after the full 72 holes. Then, if you so desire, allow your emotions of gratitude to naturally flow. For professionals and amateurs alike, the feelings are the same. It's all a matter of perspective.

The Swing Reflects The Soul

Another enlightening perspective of playing golf in The Zone comes to life through the book *Golf in the Kingdom* by Micheal Murphy. This magical tale delves deeply into the depths of ones own soul as we vicariously seek to live and actually reenact this experience. It's so seductive and desiring that like many, we tap into this higher consciousness and end up living the experience on the golf course ourselves.

Golf in the Kingdom is about a young man en route to India who stops in Scotland to play at the legendary Burningbush Golf Club, and suddenly his life is transformed. Paired with a mysterious teacher named Shivas Irons, he is led through a round of phenomenal golf, swept into a world where extraordinary powers are unleashed in a backswing governed by "true gravity." A night of adventure and revelation follows, and leads to a glimpse of Seamus MacDuff, the holy man who haunts a ravine off Burningbush's thirteenth fairway - the one they call Lucifer's Rug.

Esalen Institute founder Michael Murphy's divine meditation on the royal and ancient game defied categorization when it was first published in 1972, and it still does. Instantly hailed as a classic, *Golf in the Kingdom* is an altogether unique confluence of fiction, philosophy, myth, mysticism, enchantment, and golf instruction. The central character is a wily Scotsman named Shivas Irons, a Scottish golf professional by vocation and a Shaman by design, whom Murphy, as participant in his own novel, meets in 1956 on the links of Burningbush, in Fife. The story of their round of golf together culminates in a wild night of whiskey and wisdom where, as Shivas demonstrates how the swing reflects the soul, their golf quite literally takes on a metaphysical glow. The events alter not only Murphy's game, but they also radically alter his mind and inner vision; it's truly unforgettable. For a golfer, Murphy's masterpiece is as essential as a set of clubs.

Once awakened Murphy understands the feeling of playing golf that he understands, yet practically ineffable once again to define. There is a mystic connection to all that is, all that ever was, and all that will ever be. You lose yourself in the moment – the only moment you ever have, nothing else matters. Golf and life blend in as ONE, as with Murphy and Irons in their mystical round of golf.

Mystical Rounds

As kids and young adults we used to go out at night with the light of the moon and play these kinds of mystical rounds ourselves. We played at night, in the dark, cross-country style, cutting across and over trees and fairways to our make believe hole. We'd all get started near the clubhouse teeing off from the tee box of holes # 1 or # 10. Our spiritual leader Dick Oelke, graduated high school in 1971 was the first to read *Golf in the Kingdom* and more "in tune" with this type of thought process would make up the first hole, and never did we play it like it was designed by the architect. The winner on that hole would call the next hole. Because it was dark, we had to *feel* our shot in our bodies, and then we all listened quietly for the ball to land.

There was an eerie feeling of mysticism within our group. It was midnight, and the frogs were chirping in nearby ponds, while the crickets were singing carols to each other. The cool air settled in with an anticipatory excitement. In the breeze, you could sense that this was a magic moment. We were all becoming young adults, footloose and fancy-free. Nothing else mattered except for this very shot and these precious moments became forever etched into the memory of our soul.

Everyone was quiet, each wanting to know where our golf balls fell to Earth. Nine times out of ten, we walked almost directly to our balls, trusting our sense of space and intuition. If you were the unlucky one and didn't find your ball, you had to wait until the next hole. Tough luck lad because Dick, John, TO, Jim, Mark, Tommy, Jack—or whoever was playing—was sure to come up with his own ball. After all, quarter skins were on the line. The prize was the sheer delight of performing like Shivas Irons, the Scottish golf pro/philosopher with whom Michael Murphy played that mythic round in Scotland—a round that probably altered his game and his vision forever.

There is a lot of trust in playing golf at night. First you had to overcome the challenge of addressing your ball, getting a sense of posture, space, and feel – this made us pay attention and to trust even more. Without even realizing it, we were operating in high frequency vibration. That's what this spiritual golf, connecting with life, going with the flow, and playing in The Zone stuff really is all about.

I'd witness Dick (REO) hit a great shot, and he'd get all happy, shouting out loud, "My mother loves me!" REO was older, and he inspired me. I, too, wanted to hit a good shot and finish the hole. In order to play well you let go of all sense of what the world thinks. You tapped into this higher consciousness connection that this moment was bringing. You simply let go and let God. The only thing you are being is exactly what you are being right now.

The other day, I was having this mystical, spiritual golf talk with Dick. REO and I have played quite a bit of golf these past thirty-five years. He was one that seemed to master the demons better than most. So the other day, REO said to me, "It's about relaxing and not letting the shit get into your mind." And I said, "Dick that is precisely why I'm writing the book!" The trick is to keep your mind noise off it, all the while keeping your present moment focus and attention on it. And if you don't want the shit in your mind it's like the elephant example. You've got to focus someplace else. That's why a pre-shot routine, meditation, and quieting the mind is so important. Ohm…

REO is a Shivas Irons kind of guy, a spiritual type of golfer who experiences himself playing golf in The Zone most often every time out for some portion of his round, plus he's a lot of fun to be around. The other day when we were playing together I witnessed him talking to his golf shaft, giving it his appreciation and asking for good things, and—lo and behold—he hit a great second shot into hole # 12 at PBVCC. He's the Mark, the bird, Fidrych of golf. Bird talked to baseballs; what's wrong with that? It worked. REO talks to his golf shaft and putter blade.

REO is now 56 years young and still invites us to play "Shivas Irons" golf at night. We did it again summer of 2008. Last night, July 23, 2008, I played PBVCC with Dick, John, and Tommy. I was happy to shoot 72 on my home course from years ago and win a few chits. In the Clubhouse during dinner after our round REO told about his recent Chivas Irons round where he played across the fairway and ended up chipping in for a deuce in the dark as he heard the ball hit the pin. He said his first thoughts were of me.

Allow the metaphysical to flow and you too will be forever transformed in how you perceive and play this wonderful game. Be who you really are – aligned, connected, humble, brilliant, and magnificent. Open your imagination and allow a "Shivas Irons" to show you the way.

So, let me tell you more about how I went from a struggling, frustrated 10-handicap golfer and out-of-integrity being to a more authentic, aligned 1-handicap golfer in just one summer. I have held steady four years running simply by embracing these principles and by intentionally removing the obstacles to The Zone. And you can too! Skill, ability, and God-given talent are all relative to each of us. My swing didn't necessarily change too much; I simply changed my thoughts and my beliefs. I experienced a quantum leap in my performance in life and on the golf course simply by changing my thoughts, perceptions, and perspectives about life. It really is quite simple, yet so profound. For all of this, I am extremely grateful!

> *"A quantum leap is a change in status from one set of circumstances to another set of circumstances that takes place immediately, without passing through the circumstances in between."*
> —Deepak Chopra

Quantum leaps are those *ah-ha* moments that Oprah speaks of. They are moments when we *just know*. There is an intuitive hit, like a deep communication with Life. It's like when the light bulb goes on, we instantly get it. Confidence abounds, and everything becomes a miracle. The way to the quantum leap is like the way to The Zone. There is no way to The Zone; The Zone is the way. The secret lies in removing the obstacles that lie in the way. Once we begin removing obstacles, we begin to play golf and life in our most inspired state of being more often then ever before. Consistency returns to our life both on and off the course. Everything begins to feel like it's the next logical step as we uncover the obstacles that cloud the way. You will become blown away as you clear away all those obstacles of perception, real or imagined that are holding you back. And guess what, it WORKS!

Your objective is to become an objective detective about yourself on the golf course. Simply notice and become aware of your thoughts and where you are feeling negative and positive emotion. Any negative aspect is an opportunity to clear and replace with new focus. Any positive aspect is an opportunity to build upon.

We cloud our own soul by covering it up with our perceived fear of failure, fear of success, and fear of being judged. The golf course provides us the perfect opportunity to take a closer look at both our fears and our brilliance. The game of golf gives us a tremendous opportunity to transform our lives and take off our masks. Golf is the perfectly imperfect game. It's the greatest game ever in so many ways.

Actions Steps:

1) The next time you go out and play get even more specific about what you are feeling and observing about yourself on the golf course. Take notice of both your negative and positive emotions and experiences. Journal about your experiences. Your objective is to recognize the blocks or obstacles that lie in your way and to...

2) Honor your gifts and build upon those. Be appreciative for everything you have and for everything you have become. Being grateful is yet another way to connect with your higher Self and relax into this game with joy and eager anticipation.

3) Give your focus upon what you prefer. Remember the better it gets...the better it gets.

Part II – The Inner Game of Golf ... and Change

Chapter 10

A Game of Integrity

"If we are to preserve the integrity of golf as left to use by our forefathers, it is up to all of us to carry on the true spirit of the game."
—Ben Crenshaw

**Being an authentic person will make you
a more honest golfer
And playing honest golf will make you a better golfer**

The game of golf has always been known as a game of integrity. Golfers call their own penalties and keep their own score. It's as much as a mental game as any game there is. And we often have to remind our selves it's just a game…

Whenever our focus becomes our competition, whether it becomes our opponent, the prize, or the money, we've drawn our attention away from our true intention in playing this wonderful game. We're worried about playing against another or the bragging rights over a few dollars, or a championship.

Golf handicaps increase the temptation to cheat so that we can *look better* than we actually are, so that we can *keep up* with the other cheaters. Ouch!

Compromising our own personal integrity to win is also a form of lower level consciousness, which will make a golfer go weak. In this chapter we'll look at some of these common golf vices, how they take your focus away from your game, and how to get back on track.

The Real Cost of Wagering

Let's face it betting a dollar or two can make the game more interesting. It may even strengthen your internal fortitude and prepare you for the pressure cooker of competition. A friendly wager in small amounts can't possibly be harmful or—can it? You get to decide...no one is forcing you to play for money are they? It doesn't matter whether you wager one dollar or one thousand dollars, if you allow the money to take over as the primary reason you are playing, then you've fallen prey to playing the money game versus playing the game of golf. It's not the money that is evil (money is simply another form of energy), it's the amount of focus and attention we give to it instead of our true intention – to play golf and have fun, more often in The Zone, more often to our full potential. The money, like the scoring, will take care of itself. And don't get me wrong I play to win. Now it's just a matter of how I do it now versus getting all caught up in the mind games as before.

Lee Trevino once said something like, 'real pressure is having a golf bet without having any money in your pocket to cover your bet if you lose.' How you handle your own personal issues, pressure, and the money part of it is up to you. I'm just bringing it to your awareness. I will tell you that if you set out to play against another person—playing with an unhealthy ego—versus playing the course and against or within yourself, you'll end up paying for it both financially and emotionally. I've witnessed, observed, and done it myself too many times. Instead, choose a more enlightened path. Encourage another to be their best and you too will become your best, even if you've got a few bucks on the line. You'll end up having more fun playing better golf and sometimes paying out to another versus winning a couple bucks and playing less than desirable golf. Most often the one who wins wants it the most, is most expectant of it, and is in alignment with playing the course having fun. You get to decide on how you wish to show up.

Phil Mickelson was interviewed this past weekend during his fine play in the 2009 CA Championship at Doral – The Blue Monster in Miami. Phil was describing the Infallible Formula in his words of how he understood that you teach what you want to be yourself.

"Simplifying my techniques and to articulate and translate it so everybody can do it has forced me to simplify my own game and, consequently, I've never chipped or hit bunker shots as well," said Mickelson, who added that he has never felt so good standing over a shot in his career as he does these days. Not too mention the way he's freewheeling his Galloway FT-9 driver as well.

Mickelson recently put out a short-game video for the masses and said that has helped his own precision game get to be "as good as it's ever been." Gosh, here I thought he was already pretty dang good – one of the best in world. Now, he's even better than he used to be!

Coaches Notes: Encourage others that you play with to be their best and this will make you a better golfer. * In 2009 this formula is making Phil Mickelson a better short game player because he's causing others to be better with their short game. Plus he articulates and practices the simplicity of his message at the same time. Isn't it a lot more fun when the both of you are playing well? And if the other plays well enough to win the prize congratulate them on their fine play. Never root against another, never hope another misses, and never play for the money. Phil truly desires that Tiger will get back to being his best. The thrill of competition stimulates our desire to be our best. Play your game to the best of your God-given talent and perhaps you'll inspire another to be their best as well. Remember: life is like a circle. What you do for another, you also do for yourself. And what you do for yourself, you also do for another. Do it with pureness of heart, with kind spirit, and genuine compassion, and your life will be blessed even more. And so shall it be.

How many times have you found yourself getting all caught up playing against another, focusing on the cash you are going to collect or shell out, and either being all cocky about your play, or letting your opponent's cockiness about the way he is playing against you, get the best of you? How many times have you let the fear of losing a couple bucks get the best of your own golf game? Left unchecked the golf game takes a back seat to trying to beat the other person, to collect on the bet, or to avoid paying out. The real opponent is not the other person or their wallet—it is you playing the course. You already know this. It can be challenging to detach from the experience of playing against another holding that thought of a $5.00 nassau over your head, winter bragging rights on the line, yet I invite you to let go of that thought and give yourself permission to focus upon your golf in the present, and simply play your best golf. What you've wanted all along will come to you much easier when you get in alignment with yourself and simply go with the flow.

Coaches Notes: Once again the trick is to get out of the mindset of *not thinking about what you don't want* and more in harmony with what you do. Not thinking about something only draws more of that into your experience. You've got to train your mind to focus on *what you do want*, without wanting it so badly that you feel you cannot live without it, which is a lack mentality, which only produces more lack. Vision upon your hearts desires and dreams and let it be. Point yourself downstream into the direction of your vision of what you are asking for and have called forth and simply allow it to be. Eventually, you just give more *airtime* to positive focus and belief. Keep on activating more beneficial and positive beliefs. Over time you gravitate more and more towards your new beliefs. You are feeding your subconscious mind new more conscious empowering thoughts – make them the best feeling thoughts you can!

If you keep thinking I can't or what happens if I miss it or if I par or birdie this hole or make this putt I'll shoot 39 or break 80…or c'mon dummy this is for a buck or two, or don't choke… then guess what? Instead, focus vibrations and visualizations that support you. See the line, see the path, feel the shot, reach for the best feeling thoughts you can. Be present, see the field, and use your practice pre-shot routine to keep you honed in. Here's where I visualize the ball flying toward, I see the ball landing here, this is the path I can clearly see where I wish the ball to travel, and I just know I am going to hit a great shot. Yes, all of this is clearly creating

The Fairway of Life

and recreating a mindset that will support you in being your best. Remember all you have is now, this shot right here, right now. All it takes is a simply shift in perspective.

Now on the other hand if both of you get all caught up in the ego game of winning or losing the bet, then the person who is clearest about his wanting, is present and focused, having fun, and is most expectant of it wins – the one with the *least* amount of resistance. What I observe is that golf becomes a game of ego; someone wins and someone loses. Wherein actuality nobody is in The Zone. Neither player is playing their best golf. Like Pete Green stated earlier, most often someone else loses the match. Nobody really wins…the one who wins the money on this particular day may get a brief false sense of security, all because of a buck or two. Who's fooling whom? Your mindset and your emphasis are not serving you to your fullest potential. My intention is to refocus your mindset to being present, focused, calm, confident, visualizing and enjoying your golf all the way through the 18th or 72nd hole, and then let the dollars settle themselves *after* the game is over. And you already know this. Once again, I'm just reminding you. And you will not have to think but a second to know exactly why you received this message today.

And when all, or most of the players in the field grasp this understanding, then game on dude.

Simple Secret Reminder # 22 – Refocus Your Present Mindset
The dollars and the scoring will take care of themselves *after* the game is over.

To play in The Zone you need to get out of a mindset of winners and losers and play your own game to the very best of your ability. In the long run over time, you will come out ahead in the black numbers (unlike golf where you want to go low in the red numbers – below par) with more money in your pocket, providing that everyone is playing to an honest and fair handicap. When you dance like no one is watching, you end up with more money in your pocket. Abundance flows naturally and effortlessly when you show up big in life. The qualifier becomes, it's not *"the not thinking about the cash"* it's the focusing, visualizing, and dancing with your game. It's creating in the moment. It's the vibration and energy in this very moment of now, which paints the picture to where we will gravitate. It's the law of attraction in perfect harmony with our thoughts…no coincidences, no chance circumstances, no random chance. And if you are lucky, it's because you are so tuned in, turned on, and tapped in with your own internal alignment that it just flows naturally. And it is this connection to Source that makes all the difference. Then, after all is said and done let the chips fall as they may.

Nowadays, I play plenty of rounds with friends just for fun, without the money. Sometimes there's no reason to *exchange* money, sometimes there is. Just remember the *real* reason you're out there playing golf—to have fun! Golf is supposed to be fun and how soon we forget by attaching pressure that needn't be there. If we allow ourselves to get all hell bent for election over a few dollars, how dumb is that? The cost of the golf, the cart, your time, etc., is worth what, a couple dollars from a friend's pocket, or bragging rights to wave in their face over the next year? There should be a taunting rule in golf. Be a good sport. Graciously accept your winning and competitive spirit regardless which end of the winner's circle you end up on like a gentlemen or a lady, and remember, when you do bet and lose, to always pay up!

Handicaps and Honest Scores

First, allow me to go on record that the purest form of golf is straight up golf, no handicaps, no strokes, low score wins – period! Having and keeping a completely legitimate golf handicap, like paying taxes within our current system, is a temptation to cheat. And any form of righteous rationalization or justification that comprises ones own personal internal integrity is cheating nonetheless. And guess what, the only one that may ever know if we cheat is us, or in Rannulph Junuh's situation in *Bagger Vance*, Hardy Greaves as well. The ball moved.

The one thing that bothers me most when playing for money is honest handicaps. Why? Because in the past I did not always keep a completely 100% legit handicap myself. I know I did not always post *all* my scores honestly. It was only in the last 4 years that I can attest to being as close to being 100% full of integrity as humanly possible. And that was because of my awakening and investment into my self. It was because I had to constantly remind myself that if I wanted a completely legitimate handicap, then I had to stay on top of it and post every score, honestly. It's not the system that needs an overhaul, it's everyone involved in the system. The system can be easily manipulated to benefit those who ever so slightly compromise their own integrity. And I now know that even being a little bit out of integrity is *still* being out of integrity.

In the purest sense of the concept, handicaps are an awesome way to level the playing field. There are not too many sports in which everyone has a *fair* opportunity to compete with all ability levels. So the issue we're talking about here is not the handicap system itself; it's about those who fiddle with the system to give themselves an unfair advantage. It's all about playing honest golf. Many people simply do not keep an honest handicap, and that is part of a huge and growing epidemic. It's a personal integrity issue. It's because of unhealthy ego issues, money, or ignorance—or all three. I know I have walked in those shoes. Like I said earlier, keeping an honest handicap is similar to paying honest taxes, it's a rare feat. There's so much internal rationalization going on. Look, I'm not that good; this score will *kill* my handicap. You fill in the blanks with Uncle Sam.

Sometimes people cannot shoot their handicap, so they make one up. They fudge, they sandbag. They don't post all their scores. Why? Because most people figure they can't play to their true handicap. Guess what? You're not supposed to be able to. Your handicap is when you play golf to your full potential. It's supposed to be very difficult to shoot your handicap. Since a golf handicap is intended as a measure of your true potential, it is very difficult to always play to it. In fact, by definition it is practically impossible. You only play your very, very best, a handful of times. If half your scores are thrown out, leaving only your best scores, the top ten of your last twenty, and out of those ten scores half of those are better than the other half, and then there's the differential computation, my math tells me that you play to your true potential perhaps 25 percent of the time, or even less. Your very best potential is your very best scores for the year—only a handful. That's my take on why people fudge. They can't play to their handicap and don't want to look bad. Better not post this great score; it's an anomaly and it will kill my handicap.

I also find that people don't like the handicap system...they think it's not fair. They think it's not a fair representation of the way they play. Guess what you are right about one of these aspects: golf handicaps are a measure of your potential, not your average. The system is as close to fair as fair can be, unless you eliminated it altogether. The system is a temptation to cheat if you compromise it.

Posting all your scores is a challenge in itself. Intentionally or unintentionally, it just doesn't happen. The golf shop is closed, you forget, you let it slide, you rationalize, you post some scores, you played another course, you don't count this round, you don't deduct your high scores on certain holes, or you make something up. I know how difficult it is to post *all* your scores, but it can be done. I did it so that I could find out exactly where I *did* stand, and I found out it took a lot of work. I am now constantly reminding myself to play honest golf and post all my scores.

Here's a quick story about handicaps before we move on. It is my belief that some handicaps are more battle-tested than others. Tommy Winquist, who has a solid four handicap, brought this to my attention while playing a practice round of golf recently before a Member-Guest golf outing at True North Golf Club.

On this particular day, Tom is a guest of Chris Shepler's, who himself comes in as a seven. While walking to the black tees on the first hole, we start talking handicaps. It comes up every time, doesn't it? Tom says he posts every score and his handicap is legit. I believe him. Tom also informs me that whenever he plays, he plays the back tees—some courses well over seven thousand yards plus, and he plays in tournaments by the rules, with officials, and all. I understand there is an adjustment factor with course rating and slope, tournament play, etc. However, Tommy's handicap is battle-tested. If he were to play courses from up tees more often, I believe he would be down near scratch-golfer status.

In fact, Tommy and I did have a talk recently about handicaps. What he was doing is taking this handicap thing into his own hands and posting all of his scores without deducting shots. His belief is that: this is what I shot; if I make a 6 or 7 on a par 3, I post that score. His belief is that's how the professionals do it. "Professionals don't deduct a score when they make a triple or worse," says Tommy. Well, that's all fine and dandy, yet if you post the score you're supposed to post, your handicap will drop. You can only take a 5 on a par 3 if you're a single-digit handicap. If you shoot a 76 and take a 6 on a par 3, you post 75, not 76. While the margin of error is minor, it still begs to be honored. The system is the system and in order for it to work it must be fair, understood, and followed by *everybody*. Perhaps more education by the golf professional and the Club handicap chairperson to their members in learning the new rules for posting, encouraging honest posting is a topic for all clubs to revisit every year, instead of brushing it off on the back burner. It takes commitment and effort – just like everything else in life. However, the real challenge is the challenge within itself.

Golf handicaps becomes the number one topic for local golf professionals every year, yet many are reluctant to call foul play on the same people who pay their wage, or sit on the board of directors. It's a touchy issue. No one wants to piss off the members. So, now what do we do? It's no fault of the USGA or the PGA. Some golf pros will take the inflated handicap golfer with them to tournaments in hopes of winning, others will not. We again have met the enemy, and he is, us. No wonder we have a problem again Houston. What's the solution? Just post an honest score. Perhaps you'll inspire another to do the same. Perhaps a larger message will present itself to a larger audience in the new future…like what *The First Tee* and *The Tiger Woods Foundation* is doing for kids and adults – teaching integrity.

Coaches Notes: When I began teaching the concept of character education and integrity to children in our Sports CLUB program is the moment I started to really "get it" and become aware of my own being out of integrity. It's the moment I started to heal and invest into my own self. Otherwise, I would be just another two-faced liar. I had a lot of internal work to do myself – and I'm still processing. It's why I can walk my talk to where I am and evolve to such a level to even be able to write this book.

Some handicaps are battle-tested, and some fall into the category of comfortable home-course status. Others are made up to favor the riverboat gambler. I used to be a pretty streaky player, where once in a while I get hot; so my handicap doesn't tell the full story either. A handicap is a general rule of thumb. I am not as battle-tested as Tommy Boy, and I don't always play the back tees.

I could ramble on and on about handicaps, playing honest golf, money, ego, cocktail parties, crystal trophies, Las Vegas tournaments, more education, leading by the clarity of example, checking the validity of a handicap, how each individual Club handles its' policies, etc., but what this really comes down to is how do you and I wish to show up? How does playing honest golf and posting all our scores affect us both *on* and *off* the golf course? Remember once again, you can learn an awful lot about a person playing 18 holes of golf with them, especially the kinds of things you may not see. What's your truth?

What I found over the years is one very simple concept: "The truth shall set you free." Being truthful is the most liberating experience I know. If you are brutally honest with yourself, you will never again have to feel guilty on the first tee. Just tell the truth. Plus, telling your truth will radically transform your life. So I'm making the change one shot, one moment at a time, eternally challenged "receiving total consciousness on my deathbed" and like Carl Spackler from *Caddyshack*, "I've got that going for me—which is nice."

> **Simple Secret Reminder # 23 – Tell the Truth**
> The most important three words you may ever here.
> The most important three words that changes everything
> for the better.

Learn to Play Honest Golf

*"And ye shall know the truth, and the truth
shall make you free."*
—John 8:32

Life is a series of choices. You get to choose how you want to play the game of golf. If you want to play by dropping a ball here and there without much concern for your *real* score, that is entirely your prerogative. Remember there really are no rules in life except the ones we make up and choose to follow or not. We often make up rules that serve our best interests, because they make us feel good—at least temporarily. Yet know this: if you decide to play golf by the rules, then it's important to play *honest* golf by the rules of the game. How else can you gauge or measure yourself with other golfers?

Don't Forget to Laugh

I subscribe to the belief that a little humor here and there is good for the soul. I'm really a laid back, easy-going guy. So once in while I like to lighten it up. I can't recall too many rounds in which no one quoted something from *Caddyshack*. The humor certainly breaks up the energy of too much seriousness. Life is supposed to be fun. Playing golf is supposed to be fun. Returning to the land of fun is the subtle difference that makes all the difference, and how quickly many us forget sometimes. You do like the game of golf, correct? Have fun!

So here is some more *Caddyshack* humor:
Judge Smails: Ty, what did you shoot today?"

Ty Webb: "Oh, Judge, I don't keep score."

Judge: "Then how do you measure yourself with other golfers?"

Ty Webb: "By heighth."

Integrity and the Rules

Okay, back to the rules of the game. In golf, there is a governing body of officials to make sure the game is kept in its purest form. It is a game of integrity—one in which the participants call their own penalties and indiscretions. We keep our own score. In this respect, golf is like no other game. You can choose to follow these rules or make up your own. Likewise, any benefit you may receive from this book is totally your call. I just know that in order to understand where I am, I decided to play by the rules of the game. How would I know where I stood if I didn't keep accurate records and weren't brutally honest with myself? You do understand, that you have to be brutally honest, don't you?

Pause with me as I connect again with God on a deeper level. God, what do think about this statement of being brutally honest and playing by the rules?

> Playing golf is a metaphor for life. Every act is one of self-definition. You get to choose and decide how you wish to play, how you wish to show up, according to what you say you want to experience your self as. If you say you want to experience yourself as an honest person, or more present, or more patient, more accepting, more harmonious, then what better way then to find that through playing the game along the fairway of life, as you have so eloquently described. Playing golf provides a lens through which you can really see yourself. You know the old saying about how much you can learn about another playing a round of golf with them. Really, this is an opportunity to learn even more about your self. Every game and life situation along

this fairway is an opportunity to become more of who you really are according to what you say you wish to be.

Wow...deep stuff here. Golf is the venue to learn so much about our selves. It's another way to look at our life. Everything that happens on the golf course is an opportunity for us to become that which we say we wish to be.

Hmmm . . . so, if you are going to be playing golf by the rules, you may just as well begin to really play honest golf, and be of impeccable behavior. Otherwise, you are only fooling yourself, and you will always be behind the eight ball, so to speak. Now, if you wish to play entirely for fun and have no desire to keep track of your score that's entirely your prerogative.

The only way to truly monitor your progress is to be brutally honest with yourself by keeping an accurate scorecard. The only way you'll get better is by playing one ball and become very conscious and very observant in how you show up on each and every shot. If you find yourself doing something that you didn't like or that didn't work, then simply choose to do something different with your next swing, or when you are in that situation again. That's the real game of golf. Now if playing one ball or by the rules is not for you, then fine. You will just keep on getting what you're getting. Life is all about choices. But maybe it is time to do something different, or not?

> **Simple Secret Reminder # 24 – Play By the Rules of Golf**
> **Observe your self and become an objective detective**

Personally, I am choosing to play the game, for the most part, by the rules. Occasionally, I play for practice and hit three, four, five balls or more from one particular location. I'm practicing. Sometimes when I'm by myself I'll play two balls for the entire hole. I'm sure golf course maintenance and superintendents would grimace at that. I am conscious of all the extra divots and ball marks I cause. I do fix and repair any damage to the course within my power, and very often, on practically every hole I assist in helping to repair the damage left by others. Another subtle message and reminder—take care of every course you play, and leave it in better condition than before you arrived. This, too, is good for the soul.

> **Simple Secret Reminder # 25 – Honor the Course**
> **Show up BIG wherever you go!**
> **Ask yourself what do I want here?**

Honesty and Courage

Remember the old saying—you can learn an awful lot about a person by playing a round of golf with him or her. Boy is that true! Yet, let's not be so quick to judge either, for we all are changing and evolving even as you read this right now. Pointing fingers at another means you have three coming right back at you. What you recognize in another lies within you. Our work lies within us. We have enough to take care of right here. And when we take care of ourselves, we're much more able to guide and support another. It's an amazing game of life that God has created.

Playing honest golf is essential and dishonesty is a hurdle that you must climb over on your road to mastery—a hurdle that you must clear in order to more fully experience, and become your authentic Self. Dishonesty is a lower realm of consciousness, and you cannot experience your higher Self when you are experiencing your lower self. Embrace and accept life as it is; be happy with where you are, and set forth your new intentions with eager anticipation—what do you intend to be next? From someone who has experienced both ends of the spectrum, the end that feels better to me is the honest end. To move forward in your mastery of becoming a champion, you must be radically honest and truthful about and with yourself.

The tools and understandings that brought you to this place were the tools you had at the time. As you evolve you will have more tools to work with and more understandings to contemplate, reflect upon, and perhaps integrate into your life. Be gentle with yourself, choose to recreate yourself anew—or not. Nothing stays the same; change is inevitable. Doing nothing is still doing something. As you change, grow, and evolve it is imperative that you get yourself up to speed with who you have now become, otherwise you just won't feel good. With growth comes responsibility. You get to choose if you wish to grow. It all starts by telling the truth and getting real.

I invite you to start living your truth. Start by telling the truth to yourself about yourself. Tell the truth to another about who you are. Tell the truth to another about the other. Tell your truth about everything. Telling the truth and playing honest golf will transform your life. The truth shall set you free.

Adversity Is Our Teacher

> *"The period of greatest gain in knowledge and experience is the most difficult period in one's life."*
> —The Dalai Lama

Just think of that. "The period of greatest gain in knowledge and experience is the most difficult period in one's life." Boy, do I know that! I have experienced a tremendous amount of adversity in my present round on this earth, and now I know why.

While adversity often appears to be a tragedy, perhaps it is blessing in brilliant disguise. Barbara Rose, a spirituality retreat leader, discusses this challenging concept:

> Even the most daring and accomplished people have undergone tremendous difficulty. In fact, the more successful they became, the more they attributed their success to the lessons learned during their most difficult times. Adversity is our teacher. When we view adversity as a guide towards greater inner growth, we will then learn to accept the wisdom our soul came into this life to learn. No matter what difficulty you are facing, it is coming from Divine Light to bring you to a higher place within. Write down every conceivable reason that this situation can contribute towards your growth. Write down every way

this experience can possibly set the stage for serving to uplift others. When you are complete, and have come to the other side of this experience, you will then know "why" it happened.

Integrity Exercise: Write down every conceivable reason why your challenges and adversity has contributed to your growth.

Examples:
1) My cheating on the golf course was really seeking to get my attention to play honest golf and become a person of impeccable behavior and integrity, so that I can also tell others that they too can prevail and overcome.
2) Fudging my handicap and overcoming this issue has allowed me to become a messenger for a new way.
3) My divorce was a catalyst to become more authentic, more of who I really am. I was afraid to tell my truth. I was uncertain and scared of my truth and what I might find. I am learning to be in my truth, to stand in my truth, and tell my truth. I am drawn to my ex-wife because of who she is. We came together at the perfect moment for the perfect reason and so it is.
4) My failures and my many jobs where really laying the groundwork to advance the agenda of my soul, which when I go back and connect the dots have lead me to where I am today. It's all a perfect plan.
5) I learned dishonesty so I could learn what honesty is all about.
6) I experienced frustration on the golf course so that I could find acceptance.
7) I beat myself up, so I could find peace within.
8) I was a sleepwalker, so I could awaken.
9) I was lost, so I could find.
10) I tried and struggled to do it my way so I could take the leap of faith, and surrender into the unknown, so I could become more of who I really am, and get back into this game of life and this wonderful game of golf.

11) My lack of feeling secure financially has lead to my feelings of emotional insecurity. I'm working through these issues.
12) My immaturity has held me back. I am learning to become more mature, and a more responsible human being growing into more impeccable behavior.
13) All of this investment into myself has inspired me to write this book and bring this message and awareness to a new mainstream venue—golf.

Yes, yes, yes, and a more resounding YES! I have come full circle. Now I understand why. Adversity is our teacher. We learn from our past in order to remember more of who we are, and to retrieve those parts of ourselves that we have lost sight of. I have taken my past experiences, both good and bad, and drawn from them for my own growth and benefit. I no longer have to beat myself up and judge myself so harshly. I now know *why* those things came, and can go back into my past and attach a new label and a new meaning to each of my most challenging moments. This new understanding changes everything! The truth shall make you free. Play honest golf, and let life know that it can trust you.

Drinking, Smoking and Carrying On

It is not my place to judge another about their vices. I've had plenty of my own. I can tell you that like many warm-blooded golfers, I've enjoyed myself on the golf course. I certainly have had my fair share of social beers on the course. I've also intentionally used them as a crutch to loosen me up, to get some aiming fluid in me. I've used alcohol to calm (more like deaden) my overly excited nerve cells. I also have kept under control and have been much more focused without any beers.

My definition of addiction is anything that you *think you "need"* in order to make you feel good, besides the simple highs of life. You think you need something outside of yourself to get a feeling that makes you feel good, or feel better. If you think you need something so badly that you can't stop it or live without it, it's an addiction.

Addictions come in many forms. For the sake of this book, the most common addictions on the golf course are booze, gambling, and smoking (marijuana, cigarettes, or cigars). I've done them all. I can say that I have a very strong dislike for cigarettes and I no longer use marijuana. My cigar days are few and far between. I occasionally do enjoy a cold beer or two on the course, just not every time out like I used too.

I used to drink quite a bit on the golf course. It was my pacifier to deaden my overly anxious nerves. I remember telling my golf teacher at the time, Rick Smith, that I drank beers on the golf course so I could play better. He thought I was nuts. He said there is no way you play better golf under the influence of alcohol. He's right. Alcohol was my crutch because I did not understand how my emotions worked.

I also enjoyed drinking beer in the presence of my friends. It was a social experience, and I have many fond memories. Drinking beer on the golf course is a habit, like drinking beer and going to the beach or watching football.

Salute to the Captain

Many of my better rounds have been under the influence of "a couple beers", as my buddy, Tom, or TO, likes to call it. We both picked up the "couple beers" phrase from Tom's Uncle Dick. I would be remiss not to mention Uncle Dick and all those Pabst Blue Ribbon (PBR) Opens we had. You could always count on Uncle Dick, aka "The Captain", for a stashed beer or two as backup if you were getting low. I can just see Mrs. Oelke (Clara) now, smiling and shaking her head at her loving soul mate.

Hmmm . . . seems like we all consumed "a couple beers" in those good ole' days. I'll never forget the time playing the annual PBR Open, when John Oelke made the rare double eagle—an "albatross"—on the par five eleventh hole at PBVCC. Their team went 1 - 2 - 3 on holes #10, 11, and 12 (a par 3, 5, 5). Tommy Fairbairn made birdie on the par 3 with a stroke. Our team was one hole in front of their team, and went 2 - 3 - 3. We thought we were doing pretty well until we witnessed all of their amazing feats. To

The Fairway of Life

this day, I have never seen another double eagle—before or since. John told me the story about the time, when after twelve holes, he was seven under and started to think and get ahead of himself. He started to shake thinking about what it all means. He finished the day at two under, shooting a seventy—his best ever.

Mr. Oelke is no longer with us in body, yet his spirit remains. I hear the family will be planting a tree on the golf course as a tribute to his many wonderful memories.

We salute *The Old Man* often as we tip a cold one in his honor. He liked nothing more than playing a round of golf with his children and their friends, him being The Captain and telling us what to do, and how or where to hit it. He would read our putts and tell us what to do—and acknowledge us when we made the putt. You didn't want to let The Captain down.

"God damner—just like I taught ya. Way to go. Now, we're gonna . . . go . . . kick . . . their . . . ass."

We'll never forget the time when Robert Lawson spilled the beer cooler on the course, and all the ice came pouring out all over the fairway. You could definitely count on The Captain calling a spade a spade. "Robert, you dumb bastard. Now clean that God damn ice up!" There's nothing worse than not having cold beer iced down on the course.

Mr. Oelke co-owned a party store for a good portion of his life—a place called Tom & Dick's in Petoskey, Michigan. The slogan remains: For cold beer quick see Tom or Dick.

Perspective Is Everything

Another friend of mine, Keith Fitzpatrick (I call him Fitz), has a pretty darn good outlook on this golf game stuff. Fitz's perspective is amazing. He hits one into a bunker, and he says to him self, "I need this practice." He triples a hole, and he humors himself, saying he's padding his score, triple double; meaning he can only post a double. Don't get me wrong, Fitz is highly competitive but he has this easygoing attitude. He also plays *sneaky good*, and he is *sneaky long*. A new nickname of his is sneaky long pants.

Another positive thing I like about Keith is that we don't really compete. We encourage and support each other. My toughest opponent is myself, and he knows he is his own toughest opponent as well. We are playing against the course and encouraging each other. Now that's the kind of person I enjoy playing golf with. I'm here to play the game, enjoy the course, be part of nature, and enjoy all the camaraderie, am I not? Plus I'm here to encourage Keith, just like he encourages me. I'm also finding the balance between playing with proficiency and playing with a lighter heart than before. When I let go and let God, I end up playing a lot better. I am now seeing the bigger picture; golf is such a trivial thing. Like Tiger Woods said as he contemplated his father Earl's life and health, "It's just a golf shot."

"I'm writing a book …"

On Tuesday, June 28, 2005, I shot a 42–34 for a 76, post 75. It's here, on the fourteenth hole at True North that I discuss with my playing partners, Keith and Chris that I am observing life as it relates to golf. I explain to them that I'm journaling what I observe, and that perhaps I might be putting it all together in some kind of book, and that I intend to use real life and real time examples—like right now. Of course, what I'm doing is politely asking them if they want to play along and let me write them into the book. It seems only fair to ask. Both Chris and Keith agree and are excited to play along.

My Little Experiment: Putting Positive Thoughts into Practice

On the fourteenth tee, I offer Chris the opportunity to earn five dollars for a birdie and ten dollars for an eagle, no questions asked. No attachments. I'll simply give him the money right out of my pocket. I ask him if that will change anything in the way he plays. Chris says, "Absolutely, I'll be more focused and I'll care more." I wonder and ask out loud why a couple of dollars would change the way one plays golf.

The Fairway of Life

When Keith asks me the same question I answer, "I'm playing the course."

He says, "Good answer," as we drive away in our golf carts.

I can see by the way we approach our next shots that something has changed. It's like there's a new awareness in the air and a renewed sense of interest. Chris is first to hit, and he hits a great second shot to within ten feet on this par four. Keith hits next to within eight feet. Now, I'm thinking, "Gosh...how can I top this?" Here we go, and I ask myself, "Am I not playing the course, instead of playing against my friends? Isn't that what I just said no more than two minutes ago?" Yes, it is. I've caught myself again. I back off from my shot, shaking my head as I turn to my playing partners, and reiterate the very thought that's running through my brain. I refocus and can see peripherally that they're both eagerly anticipating my shot. Isn't it amazing how many thoughts can swirl around in your head in a few seconds? Isn't it amazing how quickly we forget some things we want to remember as well?

So I regroup and refocus once again. I'm looking to put these life principles I'm writing about into action. Am I over-analyzing and too focused on being focused? Do I have too many thoughts runnin' around my brain? How can I eliminate them and really give my focus and attention to what I want? This time my shot ends up within five feet of the hole. Unbelievable! How are you, this book's readers, going to understand this? I knew I would be writing about it before I hit the shot—and all of *these* thoughts swirled through my head too.

As we drive up to the green, here we are; we've got it surrounded. I get out of the cart to check out the cash in my money clip. I am ready to pay Sheppy (Chris), as he has an easy-looking birdie putt. The money is dangling in my hand. I'm thinking, "How dumb am I?" Oops, he misses. I am somewhat relieved, and I fold the five-dollar bill back into its slot.

Fitz (Keith) putts next; he, too, misses. Now I am a little giddy. It's my turn, and I'm still thinking that I am going to be writing about one of two scenarios; either I make the putt for birdie, or I don't. What do you think is going through my head? I'm thinking, "Make the putt because you are going to write about it. But is this fair to myself? Aren't I supposed to be playing just the golf course in this present moment of NOW—with no consideration of anything else? Don't I have just two opponents—the golf course and myself? Well, I am happy to say that I make the putt, and off we go to the next tee box.

While sitting on our golf carts parked by the fifteenth tee box, Chris comments that this kind of bet is more focused on playing against the course instead of another player. He says, "It just adds a little more fun and excitement to the equation." In other words, Chris is now experiencing himself playing more against the course than against us—as in most normal nassau-type betting.

We so often find ourselves getting into the mindset that we're playing against another person, and all that really matters is if we beat the other guy. If we win, our ego gets quenched—because the winner goes home and tells everybody how great they are, and the looser says nothing, pouts in the parking lot and drives away all angry and miserable for the rest of the day. That's how people keep track—through bragging rights. But there is a much better way and playing spiritual golf is meant to map that course.

Before we tee off from the fifteenth tee box, both Shep and Fitz congratulate me on my birdie, and dialogue begins about what we do next. My original intention was to see what would happen for one hole if I entice my playing partner. I tell Fitz that I will run my experiment on him as well. You see Fitz is a low single digit handicap, while Chris is still a low double-digit handicap at the time of this experiment. Fitz is more apt to make birdie than Chris. Fitz fires back, "Only if I can do it to you." Next thing you know, we are all offering the challenge to each other. As Judge Smales said to his playing partner, Dr. Beeper, in *Caddyshack* when the bet gets doubled at the turn, "You're in for half of eighty thousand."

I say to Chris that it is not my intention to hurt or take money from another. *"Yeah, yeah, yeah, okay,"* says Chris so the game's on again. All three of our tee shots are perfect. I lay up with a long iron and hit first, and I land within twelve feet on another par four. Sheppy chunks his second shot well short, and Fitzee hits it tight, five feet or so. Shep walks away with bogey and is looking forward to the next hole. I rim my birdie putt out—gallant effort—but it is a par. Fitzee rams his home for a solid birdie. I ask him if this format elevates his game. He says, "Not really, but after the three-putt for bogey on twelve and a poor start on ten and eleven, I've got to hunker down." With Fitzee, when he gets off to a so-so start, you can count on him either hunkering down or tightening up—his belt, so to speak. So, here we are, Fitz up one on both Shep and me.

Hole number sixteen is a par three over the road from high above. The tee box is slightly elevated. Fitz hits his a tad short off the ridge, and it falls back to the lower tier. The pin is located just above the crest of the second tier. It's a big green, and the hole is playing about a hundred seventy yards. I'm debating between a seven and an eight iron. I choose the eight and hit the ball poorly, ending up on the lower tier as well. Sheppy gets his ball up on the top level, yet we all two putt for par and move on. Life is good.

The seventeenth hole is a short par four from the blue tees, and my only intention here is to get it in play to within a hundred and fifty yards out. Fitz hits driver and is absolutely perfect. I hit three-iron and I am a hundred forty yards out. Shep loses it to the right and is out of the birdie chase. Fitzee and I have long birdie attempts, and I think he's going to drain his. Fitz pars, while Sheppy bogeys. I make a solid four, and we move on. My observation is that we are now all focusing on making birdies. Is that such a bad thing? Now I am focusing on what I want: an opportunity to make birdie and stay in the hole. I have narrowed my focus. What's the difference? Why should it matter? What's my motivation for being out here in the first place? Amazing how we talk to ourselves.

Eighteen is a par five finishing hole with two ways to play it—the upper level fairway with a tunnel window to go for it in two, or the lower level fairway to play it in regulation; although, in the past, I have gotten home in two before taking the low road. Fitz is screwed because he hits it in the trap right in front of the upper level fairway; all he can do is punch out with his sand wedge. Shep is in great shape up top and goes for it. He lands in the greenside bunker and makes par. I am on the lower level about a hundred seventy-five yards out, but it's a steep climb with tall trees right in front of me. There's really little chance of hitting a seven iron over these trees to an elevated green. It's more like a five or a six iron, and there's no chance to hit it over the trees. The safe shot is to play down the fairway and hit up from there.

Like Phil Mickelson, I decide to go for it and hit the seven-iron. I end up over-swinging and literally shank it into perfect position down the fairway; I was playing to go over the trees. *Wow*! Sometimes the golf gods are with you. My next shot, I almost hole out from eighty yards away, hitting up a steep incline, three inches within the hole and a kick-in birdie. Now, I have one and Fitz has one. We're having so much fun we decide to play four more holes, numbers one, two, eight, and nine, game on. Sheppy and I birdie number one. I miss an eight-foot birdie putt on hole number two, my nemesis, and the number one handicap hole out there. We all miss our birdies on eight and nine. The game has shifted to making birdies. Yet, we're still playing golf and having fun. We're playing the course with a renewed sense of interest. Like kids, we are making it all up as we go along. It's fun and it's our game of the day. It's a day I will always remember.

* * *

Anything that causes us to disconnect from the essence of who we really are, including the major golf "vices" of gambling (where money becomes the primary object), substance abuses, dishonesty and bragging, inherently has a negative affect on your game—and your Well-Being and eventually in the end will make a golfer go weak. As you work through your own process, begin to recognize and become aware of whatever addiction or vice that is causing you to disconnect within. When looking at your thoughts, words, and actions, continue to ask yourself, will this make me a better me? How does this make me feel?

Action Steps:

1) **Play honest golf and post honest scores.**

2) **Play a few rounds of golf without any drinking, smoking, or gambling.**

3) **Keep on observing yourself.**

4) **Ask your self...is this making me a better me?**

5) **Remember to play golf for the fun of it!**

Chapter 11

Conquering Self

"The first and the best victory is to conquer self."
—Plato

**A quick take for your own self-reflection…
Is your ego a healthy one?**

Ego and personality are practically synonymous; they co-exist within us, at least in this lifetime. Along with our fingerprints, they make us unique. A healthy, mature ego allows us to enjoy life and play our best golf, and allows us to be happy now. A healthy, mature ego is best served by being in harmony with our authentic or our highest Self. We learn to roll with the changes and accept everything and everybody…no if's, and's or but's.

However, an unhealthy, immature ego will cause us more misery on the golf course, than we can possible imagine. An unhealthy ego would rather be right than happy. It is also a major obstacle to playing golf in The Zone. All you have to do is observe yourself or others whenever the unhealthy ego rears its ugly head. Your thoughts, feelings, behavior, actions will tell you so.

While I'm certainly no expert in a doctor of psychology, I do observe how a healthy, mature ego can make a golfer play strong, and likewise how an unhealthy ego run amok can make a golfer play weak. A healthy mature ego operates on a higher level of consciousness in alignment with spirit, self, and soul. It is genuine and sees life as a gift flowing to and through us. The golfer who is dedicated to the sheer joy of giving maximum effort to the game he loves, holding in mind the honor of his country or sport, will play strong. We play the game of golf because we love it. Whereas, an unhealthy ego operates on a lower level of consciousness, disconnected from spirit, and will go weak. Just observe the one who brags, boasts, or roots against his opponent. Any golfer who seeks to defeat his opponent, become a star, or make a lot of money off his game is setting him self up for a big fall. All of that comes as a result of conquering Self.

All it takes is to listen to those voicing their opinions on television or other media outlets. Anybody who has challenged and called out Tiger to a match because they wanted to defeat him most likely got waxed and sent home, tail between their legs, i.e., Rory Sabbatini, Ian Poulter, Stephen Ames. According to Dr. David R. Hawkins in his book *Power vs. Force*, there is physical evidence and in depth studies to back up this claim.

Personally, I have never felt good whenever I have bragged, or rooted against another opponent, or tried to show someone how proud I was of my accomplishment. Self-centered pride will make an athlete go weak. Pride of nation and moving into selflessness will make an athlete go strong. Feeling good about who you are will make an athlete go strong. One doesn't have to look too far back into the archives of Olympic figure skating to see how low an athlete will go to achieve their dreams with an unhealthy ego or dark side of their shadow run amok. Fortunately, there are not many of these kinds of extreme stories that have taken place in the golf world, at least to my knowledge. It's mostly wars of the tongue that cut like a sword into the heart of our own lower level consciousness that could use some refinement. Notice how you feel whenever your ego gets the best of you when you seek to beat your opponent versus playing against the course and yourself. Notice how you play or show up the next time that happens.

Yet understand this, we all have our own unique ego or personality and in my view the term "ego" generally gets a bad rap. We tend to think that the ego is something negative. Why? Often because when we see someone with an overly inflated sense of self—the braggart, the bully—and immediately pronounce the problem as, "he's got an ego." Everyone goes around pointing fingers at others, when in actuality they have three coming right back at themselves. We therefore lump the term "ego" into a category as things that go astray and are evil or bad. The only thing that is evil in this world is the possibility of the twin living inside us seeking to get our attention, otherwise known as our shadow.

Debbie Ford has devoted much of her life work to this vaguely understood aspect of our selves known as the shadow, which was first coined by psychologists Carl Jung. Ford talks about our shadow as sub-personalities seeking to get our attention to be loved, healed, and integrated into the wholeness of who we really are. When left to be abandoned, suppressed, hidden, or locked away these sub-personalities or shadows eventually make themselves known. According to Ford our work is to heal them, transforming our lives into the grandest version of our true and authentic Self. In her book *The Dark Side of the Light Chasers* Ford describes the shadow this way:

> "It (our shadow) contains all the parts of ourselves that we have tried to hide or deny. It contains those dark aspects that we believe are not acceptable to our family, friends, and most importantly, ourselves. The dark side is stuffed deeply within our consciousness, hidden from our selves and others. The message we get from this hidden place is simple: there is something wrong with me. I'm not okay. I'm not lovable. I'm not deserving. I'm not worthy."

Okay so what does the shadow have to do with ego and personality? What does the shadow have to do with me playing better golf...nothing and everything...depending upon with where you are standing, with your perception, your perspective, and your understanding in the stream or flow of life. It is my understanding that the shadow is always seeking to get our attention, to bring us a gift, or a wake up call – so that perhaps we will align with our unique and wonderful personality and authentic Self. It's all about becoming the wholeness of all of who we really are. It's about us becoming a better person on the inside. A better person on the inside translates into a better golfer on the outside. That's the primary message of this book. Now it's a matter of how are we going to get from where we are to where we desire to go? Sometimes it means breaking down the resistances, judgments, fears, limited beliefs, or our shadow (the hidden sub-personality that lies deep within). Once we acknowledge and break these things down, like Humpty Dumpty we can put ourselves back together again.

The shadow is really seeking to get our attention and to guide us onto higher ground. It's the unhealed aspects of ourselves that we have not come to terms with as of yet, and the ego sits back waiting for this to happen so it too can evolve and *catch up* into what the soul already knows. In essence life becomes our mirror. This process is called growth or evolving forward. And when dealing with these issues we can either ignore them, pretend they don't exist, rationalize, justify, blame, plead ignorance, tell the poor me story, or we can deal with them head on and begin telling a new story and yes sometimes growth can be messy. However, would you rather be more free to fully express yourself or kept in bondage? Would you rather be right or be happy? Would you rather make peace with yourself or be at war? Would you rather make an investment in your life or let life keep draining away your energy?

Those that are first to point out that another has a big ego usually do so because it is a reflection of them selves, a look in the mirror if you will. It's how we recognize both the light and the dark that exists within us. The way in which we come to know ourselves is through others. We see and project the light in Tiger, and we anguish and relate over the dark side that sometimes comes out when our ego gets the best of us, like in the case where Stephen Ames challenged Tiger. Ames made this comment just before the 2006 Accenture Match Play Championship, in which he said, "Anything can happen especially where (Woods) is hitting it." Woods went on to humiliate Ames 10 and 8. That's 10 up with 8 holes to go – closed out big time. Perhaps to his credit, his (Ames) quote was taken out of context. However, when Tiger wants to make a point, enough said. He lets his golf do his talking, and we are best served by this example as well.

Rand S. Marquardt

Is Your Ego Getting The Best of You?

A sure telltale sign that your own ego is acting out is when you get a big charge by the perceived "bigness" of someone else's ego. It's really an internal cry for help. Yet, those with the biggest egos are the last to ask for help. Instead they will keep hiding out or only ask their closest and most confidential friends about their own misguided behaviors because deep down inside they are hurting from their own lack of security or low self-esteem; they just don't know how to fix it right now. They have not invested fully in themselves by going inside and connecting with their authentic Self. So, they have to talk a big game, and show others how worthy they really are, often at the expense of talking bad about another just to puff them selves up. Not to sound confusing or get off track, but that's generally how it goes. I have been this myself and I observe it in others. It's our shadow. We wear masks to hide the unloved aspects of ourselves. Usually, the ones with an unhealthy ego put on a pretty good show because they are making up for their own lack of self-confidence or self-worth, the exact opposite of what we would expect, often because of earlier childhood experiences, wherein most likely lies the root of the issue.

When the unhealthy ego rears its ugly head on the golf course, you can bet dollars to doughnuts that a big fall is about to happen. All you have to do is notice and observe. There is tremendous inconsistency from making birdie to double bogey, whenever we cross the line from being confident to being cocky. We may play decent golf with an inflated ego, but sooner or later there will be a crash. This kind of ego is the weak form of pride and will make an athlete go weak. Any competitor who is motivated by pride or greed, or who is primarily interested in defeating or beating another opponent will simply go weak. This form of lower level energy consciousness is a sign of an immature ego.

Whenever someone on the Tour verbally challenges Tiger we know that ego has gone astray. We notice it as soon as he trounces his opponent soon after. Whenever someone on Tour gets inspired by Tiger and desires to be their best we know that the ego is healthy and maturing. Tiger responds exactly how Arnold Palmer did; he let his golf game do the talking. That's how a champion carries himself. Period!

Coaches Notes: "Pride" can have a duel meaning and often gets taken out of context. Pride as in the form of "defeating an opponent", "becoming a star", or "making a lot of money" is a lower-level form of consciousness, residing just beneath the courage level, and makes an athlete go weak. It's the ego run amok. You can feel it in your body. It's a false sense of security.

Pride in playing for honor of country or sport, dedication of performance to another, or the sheer joy of giving maximum effort for the sake of excellence makes an athlete go strong, which is a higher form of consciousness. Likewise, you can feel this in your body. Which one feels best? With gratefulness, humility, and appreciation you go strong. When your heart is singing as you dance toward it, you are allowing Well-Being, and in essence you will feel strong.

As Dr. David R. Hawkins said, "America's Cup, and the Olympics [and to that I would gratefully and humbly add The Ryder Cup and The President's Cup] are all forms of personal excellence that transcends personal pride—honoring one's opponents for their dedication to the same lofty principles." Dr. Hawkins, a trained medical doctor, internationally renowned psychiatrist, researcher, and pioneer in the field of human consciousness is one of the most fascinating and enlightened individuals on the face of this Earth. In Power vs. Force, Dr. Hawkins encompasses particle physics, nonlinear dynamics, chaos theory, and his own discoveries about the nature and accessibility of truth.

The healthy ego like our higher consciousness is centered, grounded, and fully connected with life. It learns to Let God and Let Go. It would rather be happy than right. It would rather be at peace with it self than at war. In a sense ego is like emotions, you play your best golf when you are in alignment, connected, and centered, nothing too high or too low – your natural and authentic state of being – wise, clear, connected, joyful, happy, focused, aligned, flowing, artistic, creative, knowing, etc.

Nourish the Ego and Nourish Your Soul

So, what are we supposed to do? There is a fine line between cautiously challenging ourselves and shrinking back. How do we know the difference? How do we heal and nurture our egos in a positive way? It is my intention to give ego new hope and build it up in a positive light. You can begin this by reflecting upon your own life and deciding what serves your best interests and desires based upon your unique ego and personality. I think that "ego" gets a bad rap because we give our selves and others a bad rap. So stop it! Let's stop beating up on ourselves. Stop thinking you're being judged (by God or anyone else), stop judging and beating up on others, and in that moment, you will stop judging yourself so harshly. Instead, humble yourself and return to who you really are. Who you really are is a healthy ego that desires to inspire and uplift another. An unhealthy ego will attempt to belittle and crush another; get another's goat if you will, sometimes blatantly or other times subtly behind that person's back. When we hurt we tend to hurt others. A better question to ask our selves is what would love do now? Sometimes I even ask others what hurts you so much that you feel you have to hurt another? Then it's time to heal and get healthy again. When we're healthy we open the connection to allow others to be healthy.

A healthy ego can stand some fun poked at it. An unhealthy ego can be way too serious and crumble with the slightest sarcasm thrown at it. Why would something outside of you cause you such a stir? Because whatever that *is*, is seeking to get your attention. Heal yourself internally, and then you can begin to live more fully again.

Therefore, I suggest that we don't reject, or let go of the ego completely, but rather nurture it and allow it to mature and align with divine guidance. Keep on watering the seeds of compassion allowing our ego to blossom into our own unique magnificence.

The Fairway of Life

> **Simple Secret Reminder # 26 – Nurture Your Ego & Unique Personality**
> **Allow your ego and personality to mature and align with divine guidance.**

As we begin the process of nourishing our ego and one's soul, we start coming back into alignment with our true authentic and highest Self. We embrace the wholeness of our total experience, the good, the bad, and the ugly: painful and joyful; boring and exciting; depressed and empowered; doubtful and hopeful. We are whole and we are all of these things. Ego and personality are essential players on life's stage. Personality is the vehicle that allows our spirit to evolve. The path of our personality is to build a healthy, mature, and skillful ego. And only a strong, healthy, mature ego can take on the responsibility of carrying the consciousness of our soul. Begin to nourish, honor, and cherish your ego, your soul, your uniqueness, and learn to conquer yourself.

We nurture our ego and soul by honoring our own life, loving ourselves, and becoming the grandest vision we hold about ourselves, reaching for the highest within ourselves. We learn to love all of who we really are—the pains and struggles, and the joys and victories. A healthy, thriving, mature ego is essential to us playing our best golf. We accept and embrace everything that shows up on the golf course with gratitude and humility. We accept and embrace all our golf shots and golf lies exactly as they are. Through acceptance and embracing a light will shine by which a path to success may be recognized. Develop your ego and allow it to work for you. Keep on asking yourself, will this make me a better me? You must first learn to love, honor, and cherish yourself.

And once you remember to awaken and to love, honor, and cherish yourself you begin to see through the illusion and false sense of a disconnected and separate self and open up to the bright and brilliant Essence of whom you really are – vibrant, radiant, clear, and pure. That's how a healthy ego wishes to express itself. Understanding that we are all one and we come from the same source. Let your own light shine and you'll invite others to do the same. Remember you are a spiritual being living a physical life. Your ego is your limited identity allowing you to navigate time and space and does serve a useful function. Yet, *you* are so much more.

> **Action steps:**
>
> 1) **Nourish your ego / personality and allow them to blossom.**
>
> 2) **Ask yourself, will this choice right here and right now make me a better me?**
>
> 3) **Cause another to experience that which you desire yourself.**

Chapter 12

The Secret to Change

The Serenity Prayer

"God, grant me the serenity to accept the things I cannot change; the courage to change the things I can; and the wisdom to know the difference."
—Dr. Reinhold Niebuhr

How do I clear the mind noise, fear, or negative emotions from my experience?
How do I fill my mind with good vibrations?
How do I lower my Comfort Zone score?
What's the secret to change?

In this chapter we explore where we are; we welcome the serenity to accept the things we cannot change, we muster the courage to change the things we can, we connect with the wisdom to know the difference, we allow our humility to forgive, and we offer additional insights of how we can go about becoming this change, becoming better than we used to be. We assess ourselves objectively and honestly, with both compassion and love. We acknowledge and honor ourselves exactly where we are right now.

First, we must assess exactly where we are *and* in the same breath be happy exactly where we are. This is the paradox we must embrace before we evolve at a pace we've been asking for. Many people are unwilling to take a close look inside them selves afraid of what they might find. Most people are constantly chasing this elusive Holy Grail and are never satisfied or happy right where they are. A better mindset is one that Rafael Nadal, the 22 year-old Spanish tennis star embraces: be hungry and humble at the same time. The moment you embrace this understanding will be the moment you move forward in your ever-evolving understanding and appreciation for life. These points are reiterated throughout this text as constant reminders.

Growth and change happens in three stages:

1) Frustration arises when we long for our experience to be something other than what it is. We're *supposed* to be a better golfer.
2) Contentment and being satisfied arises when we savor the richness of our experience as it is. We're happy playing golf and being out in nature.
3) Full acceptance of whatever is arising in this moment is pure joy and absolute freedom. We're one with all that is.

> **Simple Secret Reminder # 27 – Be Happy Right Where You Are**
> **There is pure joy in this moment**

The first step on our journey to playing consistent golf in The Zone is to assess exactly where we are right now. The secret to change is that in order to get better and improve we have to get very clear and honest about where we are right now. We have to become honest with ourselves. The clearer we become, the greater the opportunity for change. The more real we become, the greater the opportunity. The less resistance we offer, the greater the opportunity. The more open we are to exploring what's really going on, the greater the opportunity. The truth is that we're either afraid to face our demons head on or we don't know what to do about them?

Emotions are meant to guide us along our path to better feeling thoughts and better feeling places. Positive and joyful emotions tell us we're in alignment with who we are. Negative and fearful emotions are indicators that we're not in alignment with our selves. Emotions are our internal guidance system. Negative emotions are indicators that we've strayed from our true path.

Coaches Notes: It is not our negative emotions that cause the problem. It is our resistance to feeling these emotions. Left unchecked these emotions are stored in the body in the form of stagnant or stuck energy, which can lead to physical symptoms like dis-ease. In order for the body to heal itself, which it does remarkably well, it needs to allow the flow of energy through all spaces efficiently and easily. Society may tell us that it is not appropriate to experience negative emotions so most of us suppress them, hence blocking free-flowing energy. We're told, 'It's not okay to feel your anger or anxiety. It's not okay to be feeling these feelings, it's not safe.'

My suggestion is to feel all your emotions, acknowledge them, and simply notice them – for in most cases emotions are gentle reminders to get us back on track, they are short lived, and you will soon once again move back up the emotional scale to better feeling places because you are willing to acknowledge that you want to feel better. If you don't feel or show these emotions your unconscious mind prompts the body to clamp down on these emotions, which only holds them in the body, preventing them from conscious awareness. Eventually, these stored emotions become tricky to uncover and release. That is our work. One must be committed to get messy when it involves growth.

Become an observer of yourself. In fact, become an observer who is observing yourself, and take this as far as you can through the hall of mirrors. A side benefit of observing or witnessing yourself is that you will develop the ability to step outside of yourself (detachment) and witness your thoughts and emotions rather than being all caught up in them. Imagine the differences when we are caught up in our emotions versus observing ourselves experiencing them? It's as if you will be having a conversation (silently or out loud) with yourself witnessing your own thoughts and feeling your emotions as an outside observer. It really is fascinating, this enlightened perspective. Observe your thoughts and emotions. As you do, the illusions melt away.

In order to assess exactly where we are in our golf game we must take a realistic inventory, and assess all ingredients to our chemistry makeup: our emotions, feelings, strengths, weaknesses (areas we can improve), blocks, resistances, and yes, especially our fears. By acknowledging exactly where we are, we are more apt to have a better understanding of the obstacles that lie in the way. If we understand and recognize these obstacles, we can take the necessary steps to remove or clear them from blocking the way to The Zone, which is always flowing. If you desire to play golf to your full potential, we start with assessing ourselves exactly where we are right now. Once we do assess ourselves and acknowledge what it is that is causing us to stay stuck we can begin recreating ourselves anew telling a new story of what we prefer. Little by little we soften the blow that has kept us feeling unworthy, undeserving, believing we can't, or we're not good enough. It's kind of like hitting rock bottom before we begin climbing out.

Want to play better golf? Let go of the ego's need to control and spill the beans. Because the more honest your assessment, the better the opportunity to address the issues. The better the opportunity to address the issues, the better golfer and human being you become. Think of it like the military, instead here *you* break yourself down and build yourself back up, perhaps with the support of a life coach. All of which is your choice. The coach is like the drill sergeant guiding you along to become better than you used to be. Except in this case *you* make your own call because only *you* know what is better for you.

While there is nothing we have to do, I might suggest it may be in our best interest to forget, dump, shrink, remove, clear most of what we were taught (whatever is not working and serving our best interest) and replace it, build it back up again, with new more empowering perceptions, thoughts, beliefs, focus, experiences (that will serve our best interest)—burning those new vibrations that enter our conscious mind into our subconscious mind, where our self-image and comfort zone lies. Keep asking will this make me a better me?

The Fairway of Life

The Mental Edge Golf Assessment Form is your opportunity to get real with yourself. All of those golf thoughts that have bubbled up are opportunities to become better. My intention up to now is to draw out of you exactly what is in you. I needed to stir your soul a tad and wake you up. Now it's time to get them all out there on paper. The more descriptive you can be, the more you will reap. Describe your answers with great clarity and make them as specific as you can. The more specific you can get, the better we can apply the solution. The more specific you can be, the quicker your journey in returning to The Zone. You are about to become much more aware of yourself – both your strengths and weaknesses. Have no fear Underdog is here. I just had to say it.

Embrace this challenge for it is yet another blessing in disguise. And if you are still with us here I know how much you are up for the challenge. It means you are awakening and becoming keenly aware of your actual condition, and perhaps self-defeating attitudes and beliefs that are holding you back. For others, like Tiger Woods, it is simply a fine-tuning and daily re-commitment to what you already believe. The key is keeping on . . . being hungry and humble. Even professionals must play this game of life recommitting them selves on a yearly basis.

If you are all pissed off and frustrated simply be with these emotions and become an observer of yourself. In order to become better we have to find out why we are all pissed off. The other day at True North Golf Club where I play, the golf pro's son, Jeffrey, whom I coach, was going on about his business at work, loading clubs and cleaning them, and in kindness and respect asked one of our members how he played that day. The response was a harsh, "I played like fuckin' shit." Caught completely off guard, Jeff could only grimace, feeling sorry he even asked. These are the kinds of issues I am speaking of. What is it that causes us to feel so frustrated over the wonderful game of golf that we love to play? And who hasn't felt like this at one time or another after a disappointing golf round? I know I have on numerous occasions. We can use that kind of information to delve deeper into what is causing all the resistance and frustration in the first place. We can ask ourselves, why am I feeling that way and what can I do about it? What happened to me on the course that caused all this irritation? How did I show up on the golf course?

There are three kinds of people I have found when doing this kind of work with golfers. One type, the majority, seems to be always pissed off when things don't go their way. They're all caught up within the frustration. They've allowed their anger to keep on spiraling out of control. They are only happy when they play well—otherwise they are decidedly unhappy. Another type, a very small minority, accepts everything joyfully and is open to bettering themselves. Things bother them very little. The last type of individual is the one who likes to pretend that everything is fine, when in truth everything isn't. That's denial. And denial only suppresses and keeps our energy stuck. So, instead of hiding out and not knowing what to do, like myself, I suggest that we deal with it, before it deals us.

It is my belief that 99.99 percent of us have some sort of underlying issue, sponsoring thought, denial, or self-righteous position that keeps us stuck from playing golf to our full expression, our full potential more often in The Zone. Which type are you? If you aren't sure here's another way to find out. The one who says that he is not something really is that. And the one who says he is something isn't. WHAT? It's a metaphysical thing. Try it on yourself. If ever you find yourself saying, "I'm not that," I'll bet you dollars to doughnuts you are, even if it is only a miniscule amount. That, too, is a sure sign of our shadow, any emotion that gives us a charge, or that we seek to hide from. For in essence all of these things lie within each of us. Whenever I find myself thinking I am something (all of that and a bag of chips) or I know something, the less I do. The closer you get to understanding, the more difficult it is to describe. The more I think I know, the less I do. What an amazing paradox. All that I really know is that I am what I am. I am that I am. I have a desire to appreciate and become more of what and who I am.

It is a great blessing to find out what kind of a player you are emotionally by being aware of what kinds of issues push your buttons or gives you a charge. For instance, I get pissed when I wimp out and I don't finish my swing and follow through. I hate it when I get scared playing with new people. I can't stand it when I give away so many shots around the green. I get angry. I'm pissed whenever I don't play well and score shitty, especially when it seems to count the most. Damn it I get pissed off whenever I choke. Damn it that was a bad lie that caused me to make double, then just to show how pissed off I am; I also doubled the next hole. And, just so you know it, I'm not pissed off anymore, and I have let go of that last hole that pissed me off. What causes us to be so pissed off, so self-loathing, so scared, and so angry?

Coaches Notes: Do you realize these unhealed aspects of ourselves are seeking to get our attention and are really the gift to guiding us back to our whole authentic Self? This is how God works in mysterious ways. We get to experience what it is we don't like in order to understand who it is we really are. It's kind of like passing a test, but not really. Rather than suppress this unhealed wound, love it, integrate it into your heart, and thank it for showing you the way. This doesn't mean frustration and irritation runs your life because you have allowed it to be part of you. It means we all carry all these ingredients and now we have control over them, they no longer control us. Love all aspects as a gift in showing you the wholeness of whom you really are.

Our goal is to acknowledge our emotions, see the gift, clear this energy, replace it with a new more positive focus, and evolve forward to living the life of our dreams. Being a life and mental golf performance coach is not meant to be all cheery and bright all the time; it means telling the truth and sometimes calling someone's bluff on occasion. It means telling someone to stop telling the same sorry ass story to your self over and over again. It means getting juicy with all the dark sides of our personality aspects as well as working on our light.

People who live in self-images of being positive, wise, pleasant, and everything is fine see no need to work on themselves, so they remain in the suffering and mediocrity of their own dreamland. The worse we see ourselves in true form, the more encouraged we should be. True growth begins in the dark. And there is gold in the dark. The best place to begin is exactly where you are right now. That is where the next message is—right here, right now. That theme will continue throughout this book and throughout our lives. Ram Dass said, "The next message you need is right where you are," Be open to whatever is coming up for you now. Be open, and once you get the message, don't object to it. Hold the voracity of where the source came from. Many want to reject the message if it is something they feel is either too grandiose or something they may not want to hear regarding themselves. The message keeps coming. It's all for our own benefit. Be open to your intuition, your Inner Being and walk with roar of the lion—and you shall find the deeper truth within.

> *"My messages will come in a hundred forms, at a thousand moments, across a million years. You cannot miss them if you truly listen. You cannot ignore them once truly heard. Thus will our communication begin in earnest. For in the past you have only talked to Me, praying to Me, interceding with Me, beseeching Me. Yet now can I talk back to you, even as I am doing here."*
> —Neale Donald Walsch,
> *Conversations with God* – Book 1

What I found when I decided to get real with myself is I became much more acutely aware of myself. I started to become aware of my intuition and aware of the messages I was given. I started to observe myself, observe my feelings, and observe any physical conditions going on in my body—like a racing heartbeat, nervous tension, shallow breathing, or sweaty palms. I started to notice if I felt confident and thought good feeling thoughts or if I felt scared with negative feeling thoughts. I started to notice what was going on within me. I simply observed and accepted whatever it was. This is the place that I intentionally decided to begin with—observing myself. That alone is worth its weight in gold.

Many of my weaknesses (the things I can improve upon) became more fully exposed. The universe has a marvelous way of painting that picture. It is also has a marvelous way to present encouraging solutions as well, we just need to detach from the problem to see the solution. Observation allows us to detach from the emotion or problem and see what it is we are dealing with. The first step towards playing golf in The Zone is an honest assessment of where it is you are right now. Acknowledgment is our first step to clearing the obstacles.

> **Simple Secret Reminder # 28 – Acknowledgment**
> **Acknowledge your thoughts, emotions, and feelings.**
> **Observe whatever gives you a charge.**
> **Your outer world is a reflection of your inner world.**

One's initial reaction and response to observing and accepting oneself can at first seem quite odd or weird, most likely because you have never done it before. Perhaps it is because your subconscious brain automatically responds in self-defense mode. I invite you to treat this experience of observing and accepting yourself on the golf course like a game or a mission in itself—just do it! I like to call this game an experience within the experience itself. All I want to do is observe myself playing golf – how I am feeling, how I am reacting, how am I being with accepting each shot no matter if it is a good shot or a bad shot – take a mental inventory on everything that is going on inside of you and outside of you.

Your outer world is a reflection of your inner world. We learn an awful lot about ourselves simply by paying attention to what we see in the mirror, our thoughts, words, and actions. How are you being? How are you talking to yourself? Play that kind of game with yourself and you will be amazed at what you observe and experience. It's time to become acutely aware of your self. It's the next step on your path to playing better golf.

Observing our selves, and taking an honest assessment of our selves is an essential component paving the way forward. We really don't evolve too much until we get real with ourselves. And we have to know where it is we are in order to grow and evolve to where it is we are going. The Mental Edge Golf Assessment Form helps to get our thoughts on paper. It's kind of like organized journaling.

Just getting it all out there allows us to better understand ourselves. Chris is the guinea pig to offer his personal assessment as to how he sees his own golf game at this particular point in time. Follow along and fill in your own blanks to get an even greater perspective of your own golf game.

The Mental Edge Golf Assessment Form

Name: Chris Shepler
Date: 1/1/08

1) Golf Handicap / Index: My handicap is a 9 and my index is an 8.8.
2) Age: 45 Sex: Male
3) How long have you played the game and how often do you play? I have been playing golf for 11 years. How many rounds of golf will you typically play in a year? 80 rounds, nearly half of them are on his month-long vacation in March and part of April every year in Disney World, often 36 holes a day.
4) Range of your average (typical) scores: I usually shoot between 80 and 85.
5) How's your golf game? (Short description / first thoughts that come to mind) I am a passionate golfer. I read, watch, and think about golf all the time. Occasionally I get burned out but for the most part I am constantly thinking about golf. My game is not bad, I'm pretty happy with how things went in 2007. I'm satisfied, but I am not okay with it. I want to get better.
6) Describe yourself and your demeanor as a golfer? (Longer version with more clarity) I find myself racing to the course often feeling unorganized, especially when I don't have time to warm up properly or prepare myself. I have negative thoughts and think incorrectly at times, and I sometimes lose focus in the moment, not sure where my mind wanders off too, and I am working at this. I sometimes find myself getting ahead of myself focusing

The Fairway of Life

on what might happen if I par this hole or when I think I have to birdie this next hole to make up for my last blunder. I lack confidence and often play scared golf at least 80% of the time. I do get all jacked up around the bigness of an event – sometimes I play well, other times I'm grinding. I'm a social golfer who fits in well with others. I just wish I could play with more confidence and make it happen more often.

7) What are your strengths? (Driving, iron play, short game, putting, mental) The love of the game and I hate playing bad golf. One other thing is that I believe I am strong at is the fact I don't give up, whether it is a bad shot or a bad round, I will try to grind it out to the end. I think this year my strength of my game is actually my putting. I got into a good mental game with my putting and that hasn't always been the case.

8) What are your weaknesses? (Driving, iron play, short game, putting, mental) The biggest thing I believe is a weakness of mine is my shot length. The second thing that is a weakness of mine is that I get too far ahead of myself . . . thinking of the outcome or the score instead of thinking about my routine. On Monday, when I shot a 77, I was completely in the moment and on the 16th tee box I found myself thinking about the outcome, and I went bogey, bogey, bogey to finish.

9) In your opinion what is the biggest obstacle in your way of playing your best golf right now?
I believe that the biggest block is the time factor. With my job and the time it involves, I do not have the necessary consistent time that it takes to practice. When I say "practice" I mean practice with the mental side (clearing my mind, with my work I bring a lot of that "noise" to the golf course with me) as well as the physical side, practicing the shots I will encounter when golfing, physical range time and the putting green.

10) What kind of thoughts do you have in overall general terms (before, during, and after your round)? Are

you feeling confidence, doubt, feelings of potential embarrassment, fear, joy, eager anticipation, beat myself up, recall my good shots, recall my bad shots?

Before my round I have everything from A to Z. Sometimes I play games and I don't even want to be there.

During my round I have everything from A to Z. I could chip one in and be higher than a kite or I could dunk one into the water on hole #13. The key is to get confidence early and ride that confidence as long as I can.

After my round I beat myself up a little bit even if I win or don't win money. I could bogey or birdie / eagle hole #18. I remember my last shot or my last hole, or my last round. I think about where, when, or why did I start to lose my shit – usually the next day. I also look at my whole year after it is over and see how successful I was and what I need to work on – like hitting to a spot versus just hitting it. I learned how to putt better and chip to a spot when I needed it. I know my routine works.

11) How do feel when you think of playing golf? Are you excited, confident, eager, joyful, nervous, scared, depends upon who I'm playing with?

I am all over the board A to Z. But most of the time I am very excited to play. Ninety-five percent of the time I get jacked to play.

12) How do you feel when you are on the golf course playing? Are you excited, confident, eager, joyful, nervous, scared?

My thought process is definitely different depending on who and what is at stake. Call it the bigness of the event. Sometimes my thoughts are scared of the round because I have not played all that well lately and sometimes I feel confidence when it comes to my round. Generally, when I am confident I don't always play that well because my thoughts get too far out in front of me. Meaning, I start out feeling a little too confident and get in trouble because I start to think on the outcome (I can birdie this hole because I did it yesterday and I should be thinking about the routine and the shot at hand) instead of the moment. Sometimes I go to the golf course scared as hell and shoot a good round because I stop worrying about all the things that make up a golf swing (i.e. shoulder turn, weight transfer and the million other things that make up the swing) and just focus on keeping my eye on the ball and amazingly I start to hit good shots. I also think that no matter how well you are hitting on the range (just prior to the round) you still have to navigate the golf course and every day the golf course is different. Meaning, if I can get "into the groove" quickly on the golf course then things will be okay no matter how bad or good I was hitting on the range.

13) How do you respond when you miss hit a shot? How do you feel when you hit a bad golf shot? Are you accepting, angry, embarrassed, embracing, frustrated, irritated, upset with your self, with little or a lot of emotion? How do you show your body emotions (verbal / non-verbal language)?

Frustrating – my mental side will go immediately to "what in the hell was I thinking?" just prior to the shot. Most times I can define what I was thinking and generally find that I was thinking about something other than the task at hand. I am doing a much better job of not getting pissed about a bad shot and immediately trying to figure out what caused this bad shot. The bigger the event the more focused my mind is on fixing the problem. I would also add this new mindset I have now is because of the strategies and techniques in this book have rubbed off on me. I used to be horrible when I hit bad golf shot —all pissed off, which only ruined most of my rounds before. Now I am more accepting and saving more rounds, believing I can right the ship. I very rarely get livid with myself anymore like I used to on a regular basis. It's very rare that I get too pissed at my golf game anymore – most often it could be slow play or that some other guy I am playing is always jibber jabbing – and I allow that to get into my head. And allowing that to get into my head pisses me off. Not the golf swing or my shot. Why I am getting pissed off at a comment someone else made? It's my job to control that and I haven't been very good at that.

14) How do you respond when you execute a good shot? How do you feel when you hit a good golf shot? Are you accepting, happy, elated, embracing, proud, thrilled, with little emotion or with a lot of emotion? How do you show your body emotions (verbal / non-verbal language)?
Confident – I become energized and this energy could change the whole round and build confidence very quickly. Confidence is what it is all about. Making a birdie putt from 30 feet sometimes can change a round that was headed in the mid 80's to a round into the high 70's.
I don't show too much body emotions. On occasion I give a fist pump. You're only as good as your next shot. I generally pull my ball out of the hole and say thank you and get on to the next hole.

15) Where in your body do you feel pressure, tension, or stress (abdomen / butterflies, chest / breathing, head / confidence, heart / negative thoughts in my mind, jaw, throat, shoulders, sweaty palms, weak knees)?
In my shoulders, hands, and in my mind–lacking confidence and negative thoughts, playing scared.

16) When do you have self-doubts? Describe your self-doubts.
I have self-doubts when I stand over a shot and all of a sudden I forget how to hit that shot. I have no idea why this happens. Maybe lack of practice or lack of mental focus . . . not sure why.

17) When do you have confidence? Describe your confidence.
I feel confident when I see a spot where I have to hit it and it will go in. I gain confidence when I say that's where I have to hit. I'm pretty confident I'm going to make it. In order for me to get to that confidence I have to go to this green with a game plan –I can't let my mind wander.

I have to have a routine walking up to this green with a game plan, like I am going to war – and that's hard to do.
18) What part of your game (performance) do you dislike? Inconsistent golf – whether it is a 45 on the front 9 and 35 on the back 9, or I am playing a great round and all of a sudden I pull one into the woods. These consistencies are questions that I cannot figure out. Sometimes I think about what's for dinner or what's my next event that draws me out of my routine.
19) What part of your game (performance) are you the most challenged with? What kinds of shots do you feel you can't hit or are required to do yet you just don't feel you have the ability to pull them off? What part of your game do you consider out of reach or practically impossible to achieve (short game, putting, short-sided lob shots, bunker play, driving accuracy, long iron, etc.)?
Could be the driver one day or the 60-degree wedge the next day—inconsistency is what kills me the most.
20) What kind of golfer would you like to be? How would you be if you were playing your most ideal or best golf (confident, focused, relaxed, letting it happen, having fun)? Carefree, confident, focused on one thing at a time, and make it happen.
21) What is the first thing or two you'd like to change to make you become a better golfer? What do you think is holding you back from being your very best (time, practice, routine, confidence, belief in myself, anxiety, worried, fear of not making it happen, the bigness of the event, who I am playing with / against, too much focus on the outcome / result, trying too hard, pleasing others)? Time.
22) What is the best thing that could possible ever happen to you as a golfer? What kind of golfer do you want to be? (Dream big)
Playing competitive golf on the Professional Golfers Senior Tour.
My immediate thought is to break par.

Long term would be to understand how to be more consistent and develop a plan (or check list) that I would refer to so that I can consistently get my mind in the right place (or a more consistent place). What can I do mentally, to give me the best opportunity to play golf at a higher level? So, when I am driving to a golf course to play golf, what can I do mentally to prepare myself to be a more consistent? Now I get into my car and drive to the golf course with no mental routine, no thought process, just "I am going to go and play golf today" and that is it. The game will give to me what it wants to give to me today. Why can't I control this with a mental check list or mental warm up and give myself the best possible advantage to be as consistent as I possibly can?

I want to be carefree golfer, focused on one thing, calm, and I want to make it happen.

23) On a scale of 1 percent to 100 percent how committed are you to making question # 20 your new reality? Yes, 100% possible. Why can't it happen? Cause it hasn't. What outrageous goal / intention are you setting for your new handicap? 5 or lower By When? The end of summer 2008.

24) Is there anything else you would like to share about yourself as a person or as a golfer? To keep your mind clear do you intentionally do anything that would resemble being superstitious (like the kinds or number of coins you place in your pocket, how you mark your golf balls, how many tees you start out with, or your favorite ball mark repair tool)? How do feel now that you have completed this form and assessed your self? Is there anything you would go back and change – add or delete? Any other questions you'd like to ask about how to become a better golfer?

I struggle with, swinging at an exact target versus "just get it on the green". Sometimes if I don't try to and be exact . . . "just let it happen" versus "I got to get this close" then good things usually happen. Trying to get it close screws me up.

For me it's all about the routine. Stay in a solid routine versus oh my God I've got to get this close.

This assessment has been a special treat. I'm learning a lot about myself. I'd like to know how I can better organize myself and bring a positive mental mindset to the golf course each and every time that will allow me to play good consistent golf to my full potential.

Here's some feedback I had for Chris:

The number one goal or intention for Chris is for him to dream and visualize what kind of golfer he desires to be twice a day for ten to fifteen minutes, for as long as it takes and to keep on even after that. Our ultimate adventure is to create a champion's self-image within his subconscious mind, getting him to believe in himself playing golf and life to his fullest potential. The intent is to break him out of his comfort zone. The rest of the coaching is removing the obstacles one at a time making the necessary changes. Little by little and piece by piece Chris will add to his bag of tricks. It's all a process and it evolves as we do.

Here are twelve emotional energy-draining issues I pulled out of Chris's initial golf assessment that I am currently working on with him:

1) Pre-round racing thoughts, feeling disorganized
2) Feeling a lack of time to prepare mentally and on the range
3) Staying present, losing focus
4) Shot length
5) Getting ahead of himself (effort vs. outcome)
6) Confidence to hit the shot he wants, getting the ball to go where he wants it to go. Is it making it happen or letting it happen?
7) The perceived bigness of the event
8) Playing scared
9) Hates playing bad golf

10) Belief in himself on the course
11) Specific golf shots or key moments in the round that produce tension and fear
12) Priorities (we all have them). There is always something else we'd rather do than work on the things we know will make us better. We choose the things that we like to do versus the things we don't like to do. There is always something else going on. We're more committed to something else. How committed are we really? Where are we spending our time?

I mention priorities because I observe them as they came up in our coaching session. I simply point them out to him and he can reflect upon his own commitment to becoming his best. How often do we really practice mentally? Where are our priorities? It takes a lot of self-discipline to keep your self on target and on schedule. Yet that is what great champions are known for.

Here are the three things I am working on with Chris as he takes his month-long spring vacation to Disney World. We are also working on lowering his comfort zone of scoring, and creating a champion's self-image.

1) Practice preparation (mental and range)
2) Present moment effort vs. outcome (we are responsible for our effort)
3) Visualizing and focusing on the target (what do you want)

I would also suggest that Chris keep a copy of the Serenity Prayer nearby and read it to himself several times and allow this wisdom to sink in. God, grant me the serenity to accept the things I cannot change; the courage to change the things I can; and the wisdom to know the difference.

My suggestion to Chris on the topic of racing to the golf course and feeling out of sorts and unorganized would be to relax and reflect upon his inner knowing. Stop trying to control the situation. Chris, here is your mental checklist:

The Fairway of Life

1) Repeat the Serenity Prayer to yourself and feel its wisdom. You know what is within your control, and what is not.
2) Learn to let go and let God. Go with the flow versus trying to control. Let it happen versus trying to make it happen. There is such a thing as trying too hard.
3) Reflect upon your options of how you wish to be and set an intention to be calm, clear, relaxed and focused.
4) Pay attention to your body. Slow down your thoughts and your breathing. Are your muscles relaxed or tense? Is your energy flowing or is it blocked? Connect with yourself. Practice these thoughts away from the golf course as well.
5) Your body knows what it feels like to feel good. Align your body with good feeling thoughts. Your body is the source of your life-blood, your vitality, your inspiration, enthusiasm, zest for life, and most importantly your intuition. It is best to be aligned with your intuition when venturing to the golf course. Listen to your intuition.
6) Keep reaching for the best feeling thoughts.
7) Remember golf and life are supposed to be fun.
8) All is well and you are loved. So there really is no reason to beat our selves up.

I would also practice some emotional freedom mental edge golf techniques with Chris around the emotions of racing to the golf course feeling disorganized and unprepared, and specific emotions of playing scared. The intention is to clear these negative emotions, accept ourselves exactly as we are, forgive ourselves for feeling this way, and replace these negative energy draining emotions with a new more powerful mindset—like being calm, relaxed, focused, clear, centered, having fun enjoying our NOW. The only moment we ever have.

The ultimate goal is to remove the obstacles that block his way to The Zone. Any emotions that stand in his way of playing golf to his full potential can be cleared and replaced. Likewise, whatever new issues pop up as we go through this process we address as well.

We end playing better golf within ourselves as we resonate with peace, harmony, and joy within. We end up falling in love with the game and ourselves just like it is all meant to be in the first place.

Chris Six Months Later...I Get It!

Often this is how it really works. Not everyone comes out with complete understanding right out of the box. Not everyone gets "it" right away. It's a process. It's called keeping on. And as soon as you think you "get it" you realize there will always be more. Here's a breakthrough example described by Chris' own words. I've been working with Chris on and off for nearly three years now and on Friday, September 26, 2008 he said he finally got it, "It's as clear as day." He gave me his story of how he got off to such a poor start on his first nine and again on holes #10 and #11. He said:

> "I was pressing so hard, grunting and shit, feeling like I'm in a basketball game. I brought it all back. It was as clear as day. I caught myself consciously not having any fun. I said to myself 'stop pressing so hard' and it worked and it worked fast. I said (screw) this; enjoy it. Look at the trees, the beautiful course; I'm with my friends playing golf. It's a great day. That's what I thought about. I stopped myself and forgot about my golf score, my golf swing, the game. I started to enjoy myself with my friends, laughing and not being so uptight. I was engaging in the conversation instead of being livid. It's the first time I really got it and could see it so clearly." I asked Chris what was "it"? He said, "It – is the feeling, the knowing what I wanted to do. It wasn't that I wanted to make a par; it was my knowing that I wanted to enjoy the day. So many people just don't know where to go, then they get more pissed off. Me, I knew what to do."

I asked him, "Then what happened." "I pared out thinking I was shooting a 45-46 on that nine and ended up shooting a 41 after a double, double start. I birdied the last hole. Yes, I banged in a 25-footer." "Anything else?" "Not an extreme, but I'm a lot better this year than I was last year. And yes, I still need to practice. I didn't practice as much as I did last year."

That is a big wow! I love this stuff. And there will always be more. I invite you to appreciate the growth process, embrace exactly where you are, and eagerly look forward to where you are going. Whenever you'll feeling out of sorts or in a funk – stop for moment – catch yourself – and turn downstream. All the good stuff and everything that you desire are all downstream. Getting mad, feeling you're supposed to be better, worried about outcome, embarrassed what others might think are all upstream thoughts. Appreciating the day, allowing the Well-Being in, being present, licking your chops are all downstream thoughts.

The Mental Edge Golf Technique

Introduction to Emotional Freedom Technique (EFT)

Understanding and Applying The Mental Edge Golf Technique

The Mental Edge Golf Technique (MEGT) is a specific method or technique designed to remove the obstacles, the emotional turmoil, that lie in the way to playing golf more often to our fullest potential and more often in The Zone. The MEGT is meant to clear those stubborn emotional blocks that have caused us all the chaos within ourselves, and its outward manifestation on the golf course. It clears or significantly lowers the emotional intensity of the situation that is causing us emotional distress. We apply this technique to whatever fears or emotional charges we are experiencing on the golf course. As a side benefit there is often a carry-over affect to other areas of our life as well.

I provide a variety of examples common to most golfers throughout the rest of this text, from simple to complex, from the yips to specific golf-related issues. These exercises are designed for every kind of golfer, from the beginner, to the intermediate to the very proficient and skilled golfer pursuing dreams of playing the PGA Tour and even to the world's #1. Yes, even Tiger Woods and Lorena Ochoa can benefit from this technology. It is your job to be aware of your most challenging emotional issues and develop your own language in your own voice when applying these incredible techniques. Simply acknowledge what you are feeling and tell your truth.

While this might sound a bit fooey at first, I found the experience extremely beneficial getting right to the heart of the matter. These techniques can save a lot of time and they work. I started using EFT and the MEGT whenever I experienced any specific emotional issue that I was experiencing on the golf course. I am amazed at how quickly the process works. So, I used it some more in other areas of my life. I love it! It's easy, it works, and it makes a lot of sense once you experience it. It's like a reminder.

I understand that some may not resonate with this "New Age" tool that really has its roots in age-old wisdom. This is not your grandfather's sports psychology or old school positive thinking method, where you just go *make it happen*. It is another way, another tool to put into your bag of tricks. Plus, it's extremely simple and beneficial. As with anything in life, find out what works for you. Don't believe any of this, know . . . just know what rings true for you.

The Mental Edge Golf Technique is a very specific form of Emotional Freedom Technique (EFT), which is about bridging the gap between emotional turmoil (clearing or removing the negativity or stress), applying the spiritual law of acceptance and self-forgiveness, and replacing the old pattern with a new more powerful belief. It is powerful beyond words, and it works. Once understood, you can actually perform it on yourself. Our whole intention in becoming a champion and going with the flow is to weed out old beliefs that no longer serve our best interest and replace them with new more empowering beliefs that do. Every technique that is presented in this book has its roots firmly planted in this understanding. Just keep reaching for better feeling thoughts, which will give way to more empowering beneficial beliefs. If the negative issues are so deep and so stuck inside us, then we must clear them first, otherwise they will be competing with our positive focus and we know that the two cannot co-exist in the same space.

We must have the courage to face things exactly as they are. We can't heal what we cannot see, and likewise we cannot heal what we cannot feel. And too often the pain from our past and our fears of the future keep us stuck and unable to see our lives as a whole. Our blurred vision prohibits us from being in the present and opening up to higher levels of awareness.

> *"It is only when we have the courage to face things exactly as they are, without any self-deception or illusion, that a light will develop out of events, by which the path to success may be recognized."*
> I Ching: Hexagram 5, Hsu – Waiting (Nourishment)

Acceptance comes when we step out of denial and judgment and are willing to see the present exactly as it exists in this moment, without any drama or story line. Drama keeps us stuck in an endless spiral of excuses that prevent us from being able to distinguish between fact and fantasy. Our drama serves as a defense mechanism designed to protect us from the pain of our past. When we're all caught up in our drama, we are no longer living in the present moment.

Distinguishing between your story and the facts can be a life-changing experience. It presents the opportunity to find freedom. "Divine detachment is when the lower self steps away from the drama it has created and allows the higher self to observe and comment without reservation," explains Neale Donald Walsch, author of *Conversations with God*. He goes on to say, "You will know when this process is working for you because there will be no negativity, no judgment, no anger, no shame, no guilt, no fear, no recrimination or sense of being made wrong—just a simple statement of what is so. And that statement may be very illuminating."

> **Simple Secret Reminder # 29 – Practice Divine Detachment**
> Allow the lower self to step away from the drama it has created and the higher self to observe and comment without reservation. Observe yourself through detachment. There I am playing golf, how am I showing up?

This next technique will help ground yourself in the process by changing old, stagnant, repressed, negative emotional beliefs and blocked energy—the ones that no longer serve us, into a more fluid, flowing, and natural state of being—the kind that does serve us. I am reminded to inform you that like most things, the process is only as effective as you are committed to playing full out. The techniques and strategies work in a very high percentage of cases, you may have to keep applying them as new issues arise. Take it one step at a time, be patient:

- Acknowledge your emotion or issue exactly as you feel it and see it
- Accept yourself exactly as you are even though you feel this way
- Forgive yourself even though you are feeling this way
- Replace your old negative emotion with new positive focus and belief
- Recreate yourself anew into a grander version of yourself. Create a new champion's image!

In simplest terms the Emotional Freedom Technique is a bridge from challenging emotional issues to personal peace. Originally EFT was developed for those individuals returning from war who expressed extreme emotional Post Traumatic Stress Disorder (PTSD) – haunted with emotional scars from the intensity of war. From there it spread to practically every imaginable emotional ill or dis-ease that one can possible imagine. Yes, EFT does work with a variety of disease within the body. It is all stored emotional energy and it all begins with a thought. Everything is psychosomatic. Everything starts with a thought.

For a further explanation and more comprehensive view regarding the benefits of EFT, please read this condensed open letter below by EFT founder, Gary Craig, Ph.D., and research more of it on your own. Dr. Craig wishes to give away this understanding to anyone interested in receiving its benefits. Please visit www.emofree.com for a deeper understanding. If this technique can heal PTSD, it certainly has merit in helping golfers overcome first tee jitters or their putting yips. Many golf professionals are using this technique quietly and silently behind the scenes. I mean, I will have to admit, it's kind of weird, but it works – so the heck with the critics and naysayer. Since EFT can become a significant tool, we feel that you too should have a better working understanding of how it works. We use it whenever a stubborn emotional block begins to show itself. It serves a variety of purposes as we explore the core of who we really are.

The Mental Edge Golf Technique, based on EFT, is an easy to follow step-by-step format. This is as real and as unique as it gets. There is nothing else quite like it. You become the Master of your own reality. You become a powerful creator in charge of your own golf game.

An Open Letter

To all Emotional Freedom Techniques™ students that sets the stage and tells the "why" of this course.
"Together we will build within you a bridge to the land of personal peace."
EFT: Alternative healing that often works where nothing else will

Dear Friend,

As I write this I'm at home . . . alone . . . on a Tuesday evening. There's a light rain outside making gentle noises on the window. After two years of writing and filming, EFT is complete. We are almost ready to "go to press."

And five minutes ago the tears came rolling down my

face. And then I knew why I authored this course.

What I mean is, I always knew why . . . but I didn't know how to say it. And now I can put it in words. Here's the story.

Five minutes ago I was reviewing a video that my associate, Adrienne Fowlie, and I made at the Veterans Administration in Los Angeles. We spent six days there using EFT to help our Vietnam vets get beyond the horrible memories of war. You will see that DVD as part of this course.

They had Post Traumatic Stress Disorder (PTSD), which is among the most severe forms of emotional disorders known. Every day these men relive the catastrophes of war . . . like being forced to shoot innocent civilians (including young children) . . . burying people in open trenches . . . and watching their own dear friends die or become dismembered. The sounds of gunfire, bombs and screams ricochet in their heads day and night. Sometimes only drugs ease the ever-present aches of war.

They sweat. They cry. They have headaches and anxiety attacks. They are depressed and in pain. They have fears and phobias and are afraid to go to sleep at night because of their nightmares. Many have been in therapy for twenty years . . . with very little relief.

I still remember how thrilled I was when the VA invited Adrienne and me to bring EFT to our soldiers. They gave us free rein to counsel with these men in any way we wanted. This would be the ultimate test regarding the power of EFT. If all it did was make a modest, but noticeable, difference in the lives of these severely disabled men, most people would have considered it successful. In fact, it did much more.

The Fairway of Life

The VA didn't pay us. They didn't have a budget for outside help like this. In fact, we had to pay for our own airfares, hotel bills, meals and car rentals. But we didn't care. We would have paid much more just for the opportunity.

So anyway, this video I was watching was a summary of what happened during those six days. One section was all about Rich, who had been in therapy for seventeen years for his PTSD. He had:

**Over 100 haunting war memories, many of which he relived daily.

**A major height phobia... aggravated by having made over fifty parachute jumps.

**Insomnia... it took him three or four hours to get to sleep every night –even under quite strong medication.

After using EFT with him, every trace of those problems vanished.

Like most people, Rich had a hard time believing that these rather strange appearing procedures would work. But he was willing to give them a try. We started with his height phobia and after about fifteen minutes with EFT, it was gone. He tested it by going several stories up in a building and looking down over a fire escape. To his amazement, he had no phobic reaction whatsoever. We then applied EFT to several of his most intense war memories and neutralized all of them within an hour. He still remembers them, of course, but they no longer have any emotional charge.

We taught the techniques to Rich (just as you are being taught through this course) so he could, by himself, work on the rest of his war memories. Within a few days they were all neutralized. They no longer bothered him. As a result, the insomnia went away and so did the insomnia medication (with the supervision of his physician). Two months later I spoke with Rich on the phone. He was still free of the problems.

That's real emotional freedom. It's the end of years of torment. It's like walking out of a prison. And . . . I had the privilege of handing him the keys! Man . . . what a feeling. This is the promise of EFT. Master it and you can do for yourself, and others, what happened for Rich.

You and I are about to travel together on a journey toward emotional freedom. It will be like nothing you have experienced before . . . I promise. It is not a mythical ride on a magic carpet that ends in illusion. It is a real ride destined to give you real results . . . just like it did for our veterans. You will, indeed, develop the ability to discard your fears, phobias, traumatic memories, anger, guilt, grief and all other limiting emotions. And it won't take years and years of painstakingly slow and financially draining sessions either. Often, even the most severe negative emotions vanish in minutes. But I'm getting ahead of myself. You will see all the proof you need as you learn this course and apply these techniques to yourself.

You will also learn of their limitations. EFT doesn't do everything for everyone. But what it does do will astonish you. It still astonishes me and I've been doing it for years. EFT, by the way, does far more than what is covered in this letter. I've just opened the lid a little here and let you peek in. The rest of it will unfold as you turn these pages.

My Best Regards,
Gary H. Craig

P.S. As a reminder, please recall from our opening comments that the emotional and energetic releases brought about by EFT frequently result in profound physical healings.

The Science behind EFT & MEGT

"EFT offers great healing benefits."
—Deepak Chopra

"Some day the medical profession will wake up and realize that unresolved emotional issues are the main cause of 85 percent of all illnesses. When they do, EFT will be one of their primary healing tools as it is for me."
—Eric Robins, M.D.

EFT falls under the umbrella of a wide range of therapies or life coaching called energy psychology, or emotional education. Energy psychology is based upon Einstein's discovery that all matter (including the human body) is actually composed of energy. Emotional education is based upon psychologist Carl Yung's extraordinary work with the shadow of personality aspects and his coined concept that what you resist, persists. You'll keep getting more of the same, and like Einstein you can't solve a problem with the same energy that created it. We will need to get at the root of the problem to release and clear the energy block. All forms of energy psychology deal with the body's energy and how it affects our emotions, and how it may even manifest in the body as pain, discomfort, frustration, disease, and worse, even death. Actually, once you understand that in reality you never do die, that you simply change forms back to pure positive energy, you can really begin to live again.

The short answer is that EFT and MEGT works by releasing and opening up the energy meridians within our body. Stored, stagnant energy moves along slowly. Pure positive energy flows naturally. The ancient art of acupuncture is designed to open the pathways and release any stagnant blocks or stored energy and restore balance to the system. EFT and MEGT is a similar experience except there are no pins to poke into your body. We simply tap on these energy points while acknowledging the issue that is causing us our frustration, irritation, or pain. We remove the obstacle, open up the free flowing pathways, and create a new belief in its place. Sounds simple, and it is. For a deeper exploration please see the EFT manual from the website I listed above. Just a little more groundwork before we get to it! I know you're feeling anxious about getting on with it – that's good!

Mental Edge Golf Technique: Its Function, Intention, Meaning and Purpose

The Mental Edge Golf Technique (MEGT) is a *simple* yet incredibly effective emotional and mental technique that induces calmness and relaxation, eliminates fears and traumas, replaces negative belief systems with new more powerful and inspiring beliefs, and allows you to play golf to your full potential – more often in The Zone.

The MEGT is an acknowledgement of an emotional or mental golf issue. It releases the resistance and opens the channels of life's energy system. It breaks up the fear and trauma lodged in the body. Therefore, the stress, little by little dissipates; it's gone. Bye-bye! MEGT allows us to return to our natural most inspired state of being, a state that supports us in becoming our personal best.

First of all let's acknowledge a new belief system that perhaps there is nothing "wrong," "bad", or negative about *any* emotion. Emotions, like life, just are. Emotions exist for our own benefit in navigating life. If we feel bad or mad it's probably a sign we're doing something that is not in alignment with who we really are. It's an internal guidance system to get us back on track.

The problem is not the emotion itself, the problem is because we have *perceived* a negative emotion to be "bad" or "wrong". Society teaches us this. Our parents and schools reinforce it. Before you know it, we end up believing this lie, and just like those before us we end up passing it on to our offspring. Our negative emotions end up stuck somewhere in our bodies and the fear keeps repeating itself, until it doesn't. MEGT seeks to clear this stuck energy and replace it with a new more powerful positive focus belief system.

Negative emotions become blocked energy and they get stored within our bodies in various places. But, here's the hitch. The real problem is that every emotion has a polar opposite. When you block the *perceived* negative emotion, you also block the positive emotion. When you suppress the negative emotion, this energy holds you in such a space that you have a most difficult time in expressing any of the positive emotions.

Let's take a closer look at a real "problem" or negative type of emotion that many of us experience on the golf course to see how this works. Let's take a look at anger and frustration. The only difference between the two is the amount or degree of intensity.

Anger and frustration are associated with aggression, conflict, powerlessness, fear, and poor golf scores. The polar opposites of anger and frustration are being calm and relaxed; two very positive experiences a golfer would like to have. Being calm and relaxed is associated with being centered, grounded, happy, confident, and enjoying oneself in the moment. If you are angry and frustrated you cannot possible allow the positive emotions of calm and relaxed to flow. You can't experience anger and calm at the same time.

But remember that when you block the flow of one side, you also block the flow of the other. What you resist; persists. It is best to be with all your emotions and allow them to flow and pass through you quickly.

MEGT dislodges the blocked emotions and makes them more fluid so they will flow through you leaving you open to experiencing your polar opposite and the wholeness of who you really are.

Tap Your Way into the Zone

Here are the essential tapping points to get you on your way. A tapping point is on an energy meridian line that exists within our bodies, akin to acupuncture. I am suggesting that you use ten points in a typical golf session. However, you are certainly welcome to use more or less. For instance, if you are on the golf course and are looking for a quick solution, we suggest you use one to three tapping points to immediately relieve and ground yourself to whatever is causing you stress and keeping you from playing golf to your full potential. After all, there is only so much time.

The ten points of interest are: side of hand (karate chop area), inside eyebrow, outside or side of eye, under the eye, under the nose, chin, inside clavicle near neck (either side), under the armpit, inside of double wrists, and the top of your head (your crown chakra area). A tapping point of interest is the inside of both wrists. We'll use this area when we don't have a whole lot of time out on the course – a quick fix, or solution so to speak. The quick ten-second technique while walking to your next shot feeling your feet on the ground, hearing the sounds of nature, smelling the air, being fully present is tapping on the inside of both wrists saying, "Let it be easy."

Coaches Notes: Please refer to the tapping point diagram when doing The Mental Edge Golf Technique. Grace E. Scott is the artist who gets credited for this illustration. Her work is copyrighted and appreciated.

Mental Edge Golf Technique Visual Diagram

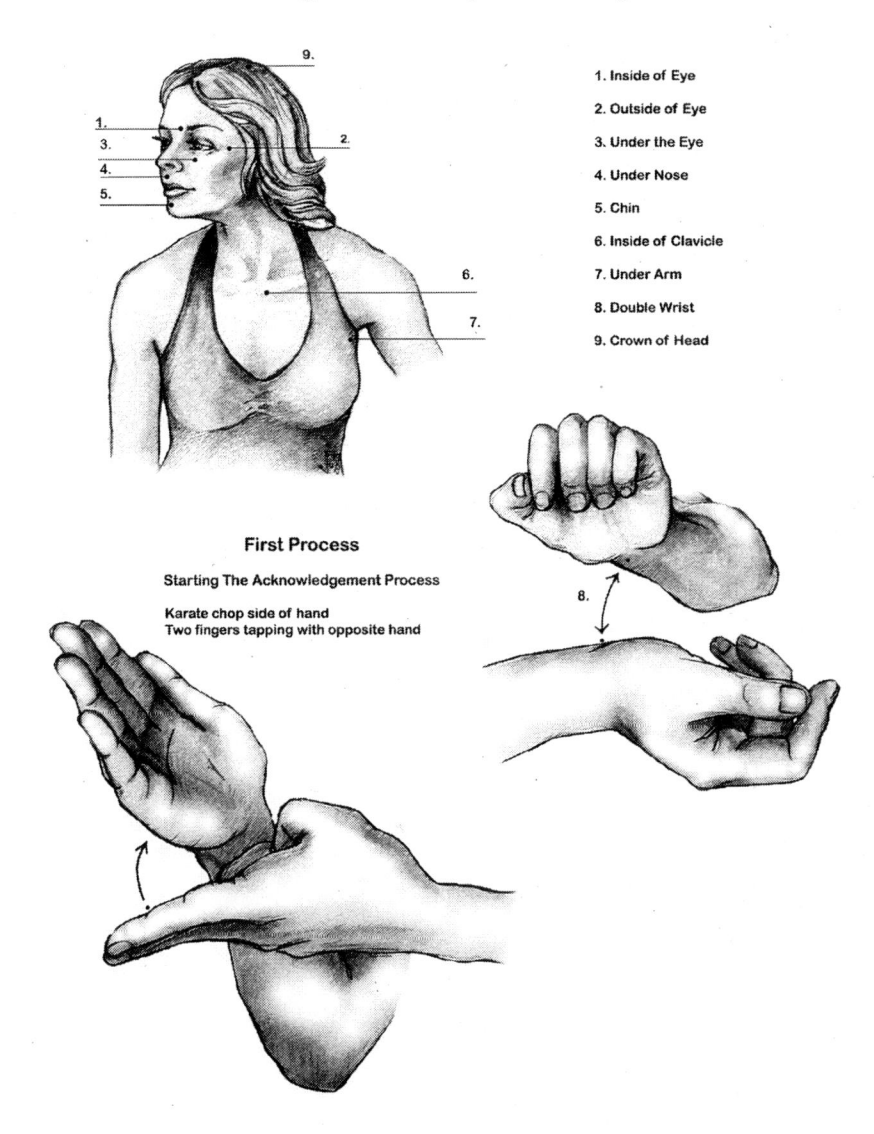

1. Inside of Eye
2. Outside of Eye
3. Under the Eye
4. Under Nose
5. Chin
6. Inside of Clavicle
7. Under Arm
8. Double Wrist
9. Crown of Head

First Process

Starting The Acknowledgement Process

Karate chop side of hand
Two fingers tapping with opposite hand

Applying the MEGT Process

The Mental Edge Golf Technique Process

I have created several MEGT processes as they relate to most everyone. In the next Chapter Say Goodbye to Your Fears, we keep on applying the process as we continue on with more specific exercises. After you learn the basics and practice the technique, you can create strategies that are tailor made for your specific mental or emotional issue. It's really easy once you go through it several times. Here is a general MEGT process for feeling scared and nervous on the golf course when playing golf with others.

MEGT # 1 – Worried About Playing Golf
Anxious, nervous, scared, and freaked out when thinking about playing with others

Connie is a fifty-one-year old woman who has tremendous potential as a golfer. She can hit great shots and less than desirable golf shots. For the amount of golf she plays Connie does extremely well. In our last Golf Is Supposed to Be Fun seminar Connie related that her biggest issue is her worry about playing with other golfers. Just thinking about playing with others that she does not know that well makes her nervous. She admitted that once she got going she would most likely settle into being somewhat comfortable. On a scale of 1-10 her emotional intensity level was at an 8 before we started tapping. I asked her to describe her emotions. Connie said she is worried about what others think, worried about not being prepared, worried about her comfort zone, worried about playing with others and others watching her, and being freaked out. Her body tensed up as she described these feelings.

My response is who hasn't felt these same kinds of feelings?

I remind the participants the proper protocol of the ten tapping points to consider and a minimum of four rounds within the process. Sometimes it may take more than four rounds to clear the negatively charged issue or emotional intensity feeling. The intention is to acknowledge, accept, and forgive our selves, which in turn, clears the issue, or lessens its intensity grip that is giving you the most charge. Next we offer and establish a new positive belief and focus which, in essence, frees you up to be calm, relaxed, and focused, etc. After the initial karate chop acknowledgment round of approximately 15-30 taps or approximately 20 seconds worth each successive tap will consist of 8-10 taps, or 6-8 seconds before moving on. Once you've tapped and told yourself the short description you move immediately to the next tapping point. The taps should be strong enough to make a thud sound, yet not too strong to hurt yourself. Each round will last approximately 3-5 minutes for a total of 12-20 minutes per session. Follow along with our first session and you will begin to understand why, how, and when the exercise ends. You can't get it wrong. You become the participant and you decide how long it lasts. The four rounds include:

1) Acknowledgment
2) Acceptance
3) Forgiveness
4) Establish a New Positive Belief & Focus

To begin the process, use your forefinger and middle finger of one hand to tap on the backside of your opposite hand while talking to yourself, honestly and openly, about how you are feeling. Focus on your emotionally charged issue and *don't hold anything back*. The clearer you state your emotion, the better your results. This will help you remember what you will be saying in the tapping points that follow. It might seem a bit awkward at first but it will get easier with a little practice. Just relax and remember that this does not have to be "perfect". Make it natural and in your words. Make it work for you!

First begin with an initial overall description of the emotional issue while you are tapping on the side of your hand (karate chop area), which may last 20 seconds at most, perhaps a total of 15-30 taps. All the other tapping points will consist of approximately 6-8 seconds or up to 8-10 taps in each location before moving on to the next tapping point. (Notice the last tapping point is your crown chakra, the top of your head. This point becomes more of a release and positive reinforcement area as the process evolves.) I provide typical dialogue of what to say and you are welcome to make it custom fit for you. There is no right or wrong way to do this. It is best to naturally use your own language. Just follow the basic procedures. Remember, the taps should be strong enough that you at least hear a slight thud sound. The tapping points are specific points designed to release energy. To find the exact spots, see the diagram above, or go to the website I mentioned above for deeper understanding, or do a search on emotional freedom technique – it's all free information to be utilized.

A one-round process might take about 3-5 minutes on average, for a total of 12 -20 minutes minimum per session. Obviously, additional clearing rounds will add to the overall time commitment. Some processes and sessions may take longer, and some processes you may have only a minute or two to put into place. It's up to you to decide how often, how long, and how effective the process is for you. I'm given you general guidelines to follow. It's your job to observe how you are feeling and how many rounds it will take and how often to use it? Use it whenever you're feeling an intense emotional issue – it's amazing!

Before and after each round give yourself an intensity rating level on a scale of 1–10, with 10 being the highest emotional level of intensity for each clearing issue. Ask yourself how strong is the emotion you are experiencing, one (1) being virtually non-existent and ten (10) being extremely intense. In Connie's case she is feeling a strong eight (8) before we begin.

Coaches Notes: We always begin with a negative aspect or emotion of the issue. Do not be concerned about *being negative.* Remember it is the acknowledgment and the clearing of the negative issue or emotion that is our objective. When the negative emotion is cleared you are more receptive (and it is easier) to replace or integrate the positive belief and focus. It's just that simple!

Step one – example of how to start the MEGT process or exercise. Notice how natural and effortless it is to speak your truth about what you are experiencing and feeling:

State out loud the issue that gives you a charge while tapping on the outside of your karate chop area of your hand, "I am worried, scared and nervous when playing golf with other golfers. I am very nervous and scared when I think before hand that I will be playing golf with others, especially those outside my normal golfing group. I get extremely anxious and worried when playing golf with others I don't know very well. I'm worried I'm not prepared. I'm worried I'll embarrass myself. I'm worried about the other people in my life. I get anxious just thinking about playing. I'm worried thinking that others are watching me. I'm worried about being outside my comfort zone. I'm scared to play golf. I'm freaked out!"

1) **Acknowledgment**
2) **Acceptance**
3) **Forgiveness**
4) **New Positive Belief & Focus**

Connie, 51
I'm anxious, nervous, and worried when I'm playing with other golfers
Intensity level – 8

1) Acknowledgment:
***Side of hand:** I'm worried thinking about playing golf with others. I get very nervous and anxious. I am worried and scared when I'm playing with other golfers. I get very nervous before I even get to the course. I'm worried that others are watching me. I get very nervous. I'm scared because I don't want to look bad or embarrass myself. I'm scared to play golf. I'm worried I'm not prepared. I'm uncomfortable. I'm freaked out.

* Use the side of hand is the beginning or when addressing a new issue. Then move into the other nine tapping points the rest of the way.

Inside Eyebrow: I'm nervous and scared when I'm playing golf with others.

Outside of Eye: I'm worried thinking about playing with others.

Under the Eye: Feeling worry and doubt.

Under the Nose: Nervous and scared.

Chin: Feeling anxious.

Inside Collar Bone: I'm anxious and worried when I golf with others.

Under Arm: I'm worried, nervous, and scared.

Double Wrist: Feeling freaked out.

*Crown of Head: I'm anxious, scared, and worried when playing golf with others and I am ready to release this fear; it no longer serves me.

*Notice the crown of head tapping point becomes a release of blockage.

Deep Breath: Breathe in and out.

We rate Connie's intensity level after Round 1: Connie – "I give it a 5, still feeling somewhat anxious, scared, worried, and nervous. I'm feeling better." After the breathing in and out and a quick self-rating move immediately to Round 2: Acceptance.

<u>**2) Acceptance:**</u>
Inside Eyebrow: Even though I am feeling worried and scared, I accept myself exactly as I am.

Outside of Eye: Even though I am feeling anxious, nervous, and scared when I am playing with others, I accept myself exactly as I am.

Under Eye: Even though I feel scared golfing with others, I accept myself exactly as I am.

Under Nose: Even though I am scared and worried, I accept myself exactly as I am.

Chin: Even though I am scared and nervous when playing with other golfers whom I may not know that well, I accept myself exactly as I am.

Collar Bone: I accept myself for feeling scared and worried.

Under Arm: I accept myself for feeling scared, nervous, and afraid.

Double Wrist: Even though I feeling freaked out, I accept myself exactly as I am.

Crown of Head: I accept myself for feeling scared, for feeling worried, and I'm choosing to release this fear and nervous energy and just be my true self while playing golf with others.

Deep Breath: Breathe in and out.

We rate Connie's intensity level after Round 2: "I give it a 4, a little better."

<u>**3) Forgiveness:**</u>

Inside Eyebrow: I forgive myself for feeling scared and nervous while playing golf with others.

Outside Eye: I forgive myself for feeling embarrassed that I might not play as well as I would like.

Under Eye: I forgive myself for being anxious, nervous, and worried on the golf course.

Under Nose: I forgive myself for being nervous and scared.

Chin: Even though I am feeling nervous and scared, I forgive myself.

Collar Bone: I forgive myself for feeling nervous and scared while playing with others.

Under Arm: Even though I am worried about what others think, I forgive myself.

Double Wrist: Even though I feeling freaked out, I forgive myself.

Crown of Head: I forgive myself for feeling nervous. I am choosing to be calm, confident, and relaxed.

Deep Breathe: Breathe in and out.

We rate Connie's intensity level after Round 3: "I'd say a 3. I have some emotion."

4) New Positive Belief & Focus:
Inside Eyebrow: I'm calm and confident while playing golf with others.

Outside Eye: I'm calm and relaxed.

Under Eye: Feeling calm and confident.

Under Nose: Calm and relaxed.

Chin: I'm calm and confident while playing golf.

Collar Bone: I'm calm and relaxed while playing golf with others.

Under Arm: I am calm and confident while playing golf with others.

Double Wrist: Feeling calm and relaxed.

Crown of Head: I am calm and confident while playing golf with others, I'm playing my best golf and I am enjoying myself.

Deep Breath: Breathe in and out.

We rate Connie's intensity level after Round 4: "Still feeling a 3. Maybe a little bit than before."

Notice how one simple exercise calmed Connie down from an 8 to a 3 in a matter of 15 minutes. This was a live presentation and Connie had never heard of this technique before. There was no prompting on my part and she brought up her own emotional issue. It takes courage to face your perceived fears. This technique is quick, easy, and it appears to work in many situations. Is it an end all or a cure, certainly not? Life is an eternal process and we never get it all done.

So, Congratulations on your first voyage to experiencing more emotional freedom and applying the Mental Edge Golf Technique. Here are just a few other case examples that you may wish to help you begin your process and that you can tailor to fit your circumstance:

- I have the yips. I'm nervous when I'm putting because I'm focused on the outcome. I want it so badly that I'm shaking in my boots. My body is nervous and tensed. Feeling locked up. Scared.
- I've got the first tee jitters. I have no idea where this ball is going and how I might play today. I'm scared as hell and I have no idea what I am doing.

- My short game is horrendous. I'm scared as hell with short chip shots and deathly afraid from just off the green.
- I don't want to let others down. I'm playing awful, and I am embarrassing myself. Feeling embarrassed.
- I'm afraid of what others might think if I hit a bad shot –I'm nervous.
- I'm stuck on reliving a bad shot or poor performance – I can't seem to get the past off my mind. I'm feeling doomed. I'm in an emotional downward spiral. Feeling disconnected and doubtful.
- I get ahead of myself and focus on what I might shoot – I give too much attention to my score and outcome. I get nervous thinking about what I might shoot. I'm scared to play. I make out the event to be bigger than it is – I'm scared and nervous.
- I play small so I won't disappoint myself—I hide behind my own insecurities. I'm disappointed in myself. Feeling a heavy burden and worry.
- I'm embarrassed to look bad – sometimes I just don't play. I'm just plain embarrassed because I can get so scared just thinking about playing.
- I'm not good enough – I'm a terrible golfer. Feeling discouraged.
- I'm too inconsistent – sometimes I play well and sometimes I play poorly. Whenever I play poorly it drives me crazy, plus I get depressed.
- Making swing changes – I get all caught up with analysis and I'm feeling extremely frustrated. Feeling disconnected and not as ease.
- I'm an idiot – I hit so many bad shots and lose my focus.
- I can't hit the ball very far and that pisses me off. I'm angry.

I've got the yips – I'm shaking, practically paralyzed over short putts I'm supposed to make. Woody Austin blew a potential win at the 2008 Buick Open in Grand Blanc, Michigan finishing in a tie for second place admitting he's prone to getting the yips. "I threw it away," he said. "I didn't hit the ball close enough to the hole the last two holes to counteract my yips that I have when it comes to putting…nobody's fault but my own, so that's two weeks in a row. So I've got to figure it out or I'd better quit."

MEGT # 2 – I've got the Yips

Tapping on the side of your hand several times say, "I've got the yips. I am nervous as can be when facing a dreaded 2½ to 4½ foot putt. I am scared; I can hardly pull the putter back. I have no control over my putter; I could push it or pull it badly. I am practically frozen still and scared out of my wits. My whole body freezes and tenses up. I am so scared over the putt. I've got the yips, and I am paralyzed with fear. My whole body is crumbling. I'm literally trembling in my boots."

On a scale of 1-10, rate the intensity of the emotion. Definitely a 10! I'm scared out of my wits.

1) Acknowledgment:

Side of hand: I've got the yips. I'm scared. I am nervous as can be when facing a 2½ to 4½ foot putt. I dread them; I can hardly pull the putter back. I have no control over my putter; I could push it or pull it badly. I am practically frozen still and scared out of my wits. My whole body freezes and tenses up. I am so scared over the putt. I've got the yips, and I am paralyzed with fear. My whole body is crumbling. I've got the yips and I am emotionally charged with an intensity level that is sky high. I'm scared over this short little putt. I'm trembling with fear.

Inside Eyebrow: I've got the yips and I am so nervous and scared.

Outside of Eye: I'm nervous and scared over short putts. I've got the yips.

Under the Eye: Feeling extremely nervous and scared over short putts.

Under the Nose: Nervous and extremely scared. I'm trembling with fear.

Chin: I'm feeling nervous and scared, short putts scare me.

Inside Collar Bone: I'm feeling anxious and paralyzed over short putts.

Under Arm: Anxious and paralyzed over short putts.

Double Wrist: Feeling anxious and scared.

Crown of Head: Anxious and scared, I'm ready to release this fear; it no longer serves me.

Deep Breath: Breathe in and out.

Rate your intensity level after Round 1: I'm down to an 8, still scared. Can this really work? I'll do anything. Still feeling a lot of emotions with the yips.

<u>2) Acceptance:</u>
Inside Eyebrow: Even though I have the yips, I accept myself exactly as I am.

Outside of Eye: I've got the yips, and I accept myself exactly as I am.

Under Eye: I accept myself even though I have the yips.

Under Nose: I accept myself exactly as I am even though I am scared and nervous over short putts trembling with fear.

Chin: I am scared and nervous over short putts, I have the yips, and I accept myself exactly as I am.

Inside Collar Bone: Even though I'm trembling with fear, I accept myself exactly as I am.

Under Arm: I accept myself even with all my fears around short putts.

Double Wrist: Even though I am scared because I have the yips, I accept myself exactly as I am.

Crown of Head: I'm feeling anxious and afraid and I am choosing to release this fear and putt with confidence.

Deep Breath: Breathe in and out.

Rate your intensity level after Round 2: I'm feeling only a 4, better.

3) Forgiveness:
Inside Eyebrow: Even though I have the yips, I forgive myself.

Outside Eye: Even though the yips have caused me fits, I forgive myself.

Under Eye: I forgive myself for having the yips.

Under Nose: Forgive myself.

Chin: I forgive myself for feeling embarrassed about having the yips.

Collar Bone: I forgive myself for having the yips.

Under Arm: Even though I am nervous and scared putting short putts, I forgive myself.

Double Wrist: Even though I am scared and trembling with fear because I have the yips, I forgive myself.

Crown of Head: I forgive myself. I am choosing to be a confident putter and I allow every cell in my body to resonate with that. I am choosing to be a confident putter.

Deep Breathe: Breathe in and out.

Rate your intensity level after Round 3: Feeling a 3.

4) New Positive Belief & Focus:
Inside Eyebrow: I am a confident putter.

Outside Eye: I am a calm and confident putter.

Under Eye: Calm, focused and relaxed.

Under Nose: Calm and confident.

Chin: Present and focused.

Collar Bone: I am a calm and focused putter.

Under Arm: Calm and focused.

Double Wrist: Feeling calm, confident, focused, and relaxed.

Crown of Head: I am a calm, confident and focused putter. I allow all the cells in my body to resonate with this energy. I am calm and focused.

Deep Breath: Breathe in and out.

Rate your intensity level after Round 4: Still a 3, I have some intensity.

I'm feeling there is more work for me to do in this area. I'm ready to experience myself on the golf course. Please note that focusing on outcome and results (getting a head of ourselves) may also be a key factor and possibly a deeper root cause versus staying present giving your best effort on this putt right here, right now. Like Tiger does!

MEGT # 3 – Racing to the Golf Course / No Time to Properly Warm Up

This is for Chris, from our earlier case study, and all the rest of us who find ourselves racing from work to the parking lot and off to the first tee with but only a few practice putts and swings and our minds filled with all kinds of other stuff. Earlier I offered a mental checklist and suggestion that if you find yourself in this situation that you practice using the Serenity Prayer. I also suggest that you find 3-5 minutes just to get still and allow yourself to be present and let go of all your thoughts and concerns of the day. Close your eyes and be present, even if it is in the parking lot at the golf course. Take a couple deep breaths and be still letting go of any thoughts or concerns and allow yourself to be present right here and right now. Intentionally set an intention seeing yourself as being calm and relaxed. Play a couple holes in your mind feeling and visualizing your ideal demeanor, tempo, and rhythm. We've got to take the time to center and ground ourselves away from all the mind noise from daily living.

Here is the Mental Edge Golf Technique to lower the intensity feelings that you may be experiencing on your way to the golf course and off to the first tee.

Chris: My intensity level of feeling anxious racing to the golf course is an 8.

Begin by tapping on the backside of your hand several times. I'm rushing from work. I don't have enough practice time. I'm feeling anxious about my performance. I'm feeling disorganized. My mind is racing in all directions. I'm feeling that I am not prepared. Not enough time to prepare myself mentally and physically. It's difficult to focus. I don't have enough time. My mind is racing and I am rushing to the golf course. Feeling disconnected and disorganized.

1) Acknowledgment:
Side of hand: I'm rushing from work feeling disorganized. My mind is racing all over the board and I am feeling disconnected. I'm feeling anxious about my performance. I'm feeling that I am not prepared and that bothers me. Not enough time to prepare mentally or physically. I'm not feeling focused or ready to play. My mind is racing and I am rushing to the golf course. I'm feeling anxious, nervous, and scared. I'm rushing and my mind is racing in all directions. It's difficult to focus and get my mind off my work and other issues. Feeling anxious. I hope I play well, I just don't know.

Inside Eyebrow: Feeling nervous and scattered.

Outside of Eye: Feeling anxious, my mind is racing all over the board. I'm feeling rushed and overwhelmed.

Under the Eye: Feeling anxious that I don't have enough time to warm up properly.

Under the Nose: Feeling anxious that I am not focused. There are too many other things still on my mind. Feeling disconnected.

Chin: Feeling rushed.

Inside Collar Bone: Anxious and scared.

Under Arm: Difficult to focus, my mind is racing.

Double Wrist: Feeling disorganized, feeling doubt.

Crown of Head: Feeling anxious and I am choosing to let this go.

The Fairway of Life

Deep Breath: Breathe in and out.

Rate your intensity level after Round 1: "I'm down to a 5."

2) Acceptance:
Inside Eyebrow: Even though I am feeling anxious and rushed, I accept myself exactly as I am.

Outside of Eye: Even though my mind is racing all over the board, I accept myself exactly as I am.

Under Eye: Even though it is difficult to focus and make this transition to playing golf, I accept myself exactly as I am.

Under Nose: Even though there is not enough time to properly prepare myself, I accept myself exactly as I am.

Chin: I accept myself exactly as I am for feeling rushed and unprepared.

Under Arm: Feeling disconnected, I accept myself exactly as I am.

Double Wrist: Even though I am feeling disorganized and doubtful, I accept myself exactly as I am.

Crown of Head: Even though my mind is racing, and I am not fully prepared, I am choosing to let this go and settle back into the present moment feeling calm and present.

Deep Breath: Breathe in and out.

Rate your intensity level after round 2: "A three."

3) Forgiveness:
Inside Eyebrow: Even though I am feeling anxious and rushed, I forgive myself.

Outside Eye: I forgive myself for feeling disorganized and disconnected.

Under Eye: Forgive myself for feeling unprepared.

Under Nose: Even though I am feeling a lack of focus because of all these other thoughts I have on my mind, I forgive myself.

Chin: Even though my mind is racing in so many directions; and I am feeling disorganized and rushed, I forgive myself.

Collar Bone: I forgive myself for feeling anxious.

Under Arm: I forgive myself for feeling rushed and unprepared.

Double Wrist: Even though I am feeling disorganized and doubt. I forgive myself.

Crown of Head: Even though I find myself racing to the golf course feeling rushed and unprepared, I am choosing to let this go and center myself back into the present moment. I have all the skills to perform to my very best and I am giving every cell of my body the wisdom to allow it to be.

Deep Breathe: Breathe in and out.

Rate your intensity level after Round 3: "Wow feeling a 2!"

4) New Positive Belief & Focus:
Inside Eyebrow: I'm feeling present and centered.

Outside Eye: I'm feeling calm and relaxed.

Under Eye: Calm, clear and relaxed.

Under Nose: Calm and clear.

Chin: I'm feeling focused and present.

Collar Bone: Focused and present.

Under Arm: I'm feeling calm, clear and confident.

Double Wrist: Feeling calm, confident and present.

Crown of Head: I'm calm, clear, confident and relaxed, I'm feeling centered, grounded, and in the present moment. I'm calm and clear. I'm feeling confident and centered.

Deep Breath: Breathe in and out.

Rate your intensity level after Round 4: "I'm feeling great, feeling a one (1). Amazing!"

The results speak for themselves. Those who have used the MEGT have had amazing results, finally finding a way to deal with their fears and emotions. More Mental Edge Golf Techniques will be integrated throughout parts of this book as we say good-bye to our fears. Now let's turn to another golf assessment area. Our intention is to get very clear about where we are right now so that eventually we can decide where we want to be next.

Analyzing Your Own Golf Game

The purpose of the journaling exercise that follows is to show you that life is about the yin and the yang. For every positive aspect there is a negative. For everything that works for us there is obstacle that stops us. For every up there is a down. For every here there is a there. The opposite of hot is cold. These things are good. How would you know and understand what hot is, for instance, if you did not first experience what cold is, or vice versa? We live in a land of illusions and polarity of energy. Inside each of us is a balance that is composed of opposites that complement one another. The intention is to show you that you have a brilliant side—natural gifts and talents— as well as the side that must work harder to achieve a desired outcome. Our objective here is to remind you of all the things that serve you well with your golf game and how to enhance those points as we work on those things that give you fits—that appear not to serve you well at the present moment, aspects of your game that you can improve upon.

In your journal please list at least twenty-five things that are not serving you well with your golf game. After you have done that, list twenty-five things that are serving you well with your golf game. I've listed twenty-eight.

Twenty-eight Things That You Can Improve Upon in Your Golf Game

Examples:

1) I'm nervous before I start.
2) I have too much expectation to perform well.
3) My putting can be dreadful. (I'm nervous when putting). My putting is inconsistent—sometimes good and sometimes really bad. I just don't know when the transition to feeling my stroke takes over versus feeling scared.
4) I hit a few "bad" golf shots. (I hit a few shots that really don't resonate with me, and this causes me stress. I get upset.)
5) I sometimes get the yips in the beginning of my round. I want to play good golf so badly; it's scary to think of missing short putts. It's hard to break the cycle of feeling the yips and putting scared.
6) It takes me a while to find the feel in my golf swing and putting.
7) My swing mechanics. I know I am not technically correct. My balance is off.
8) Inconsistency with accuracy. I can hit left or right.
9) Inconsistency with distance. I can hit it crisp and pure or weak and short.

10) Too emotionally charged to be myself. My body is full of nervous energy.
11) Windy or cold conditions can sometimes get the best of me.
12) When I am off my game and "forget" how to swing. Sometimes I just never seem to recover.
13) Just the thought of playing poorly keeps me stuck in a self-fulfilling prophecy.
14) My chipping and short game is a disaster.
15) Wedge shots from just off the green to 90 yards out. I give away too many strokes back to the course.
16) Sand and bunker play is abysmal. I really don't know what I am doing?
17) Breaking 70 is the critical point. I'm hung up on this comfort zone factor. It feels scary to be able to break 70.
18) Feeling if I don't break 80 or it looks like I won't then it feels like I've failed. It's an awful feeling if I don't break 80.
19) Not practicing enough.
20) Taking a long layoff.
21) Playing with new people.
22) Big tournaments when my score counts – I avoid them.
23) Embarrassment that I won't play to my fuller potential just because I'm afraid and scared. I'm embarrassed to look bad in front of others. I've got people pleasing and perfection issues.
24) Getting too enamored about my score.
25) Feeling the pressure to perform well to please others.
26) Fear of making a mistake.
27) Being a perfectionist.
28) Fear.

Twenty-eight Things That Are Serving You Well About Your Golf Game

Examples:

1) There are times when I am feeling confident on the first tee.
2) There are times when I get into a good feeling state and I play well.
3) When the light bulb goes on I can be an excellent putter.
4) Thinking it over, I do hit a ton of very good shots.
5) My putting in the latter part of my round is usually very good.
6) I know that I will eventually find my feel and learn to trust my swing.
7) My swing, albeit technically challenged, works for me a majority of the time.
8) I am a very accurate striker of the ball.
9) I am very consistent with distance with all my clubs once I find my groove.
10) I am calm and confident. I stay calm even when things don't appear to be going my way.
11) I actually do play well in all weather conditions. I adapt easily into a supportive mindset.
12) More often than not, I am on my game.
13) More often than not, I play well.
14) I can be an excellent short game player.
15) I can be very good with wedge shots up to 90 yards out.
16) My sand and bunker play continues to improve.
17) I am lowering my comfort zone and eagerly looking forward to breaking 70.
18) My game is consistent, very rarely do I fire a high number.
19) I play well even without proper practice.
20) I am confident I will find my game even after a long lay off.
21) I play well with new people.

22) I play well in the tournaments I enter.
23) I accept myself exactly as I am.
24) I give my focus upon enjoying the present moment.
25) I am only here to please myself. I am my own toughest opponent.
26) I am a good risk / reward golfer.
27) I accept myself perfectly imperfect – just as I am.
28) I am relaxed, and focused.

After doing this you should see your game from a whole different perspective.

The yin and yang, the balance, in your golf game should come into focus. The more aware we become of ourselves the easier we can find a solution to our problems. We also recognize and gain a greater appreciation for our innate talents and strengths. It's always important to be grateful for what you've got. Very often we tend to downplay our strengths, not giving ourselves as much credit as we really do deserve. It's interesting to note the irony of the antithesis how we can view ourselves in one breath as an awful putter and an excellent one just moments later. The ying and the yang exist within all of us.

What comes up for me in this exercise, is that certain areas or aspects of my game that give me a charge—like short game, putting, bunker play, perfectionism, pleasing others – are an opportunity to keep removing the obstacles that lie in the way and to work more diligently on my weaknesses in my golf game. I can also work on any unhealed aspects within me by acknowledging them. I can empower myself to play my best golf using whatever technique works for me. I can also give my attention and focus upon my strengths, creating a new shift in focus and belief.

As you become more aware of your golf game, you can take care of business one level or one process at a time. Eventually, the toughest decision you will have to make is: should I eat that Oreo cookie or ice cream for dessert, or not?

What Is Our Comfort Zone?

True growth begins at the end of our Comfort Zone and it is up to us to initiate it. It's up to us to step up to the plate and let go of old thoughts that kept us safe and playing small. It's time to set new goals and intentions that align with our new desires. Remember: if your goals don't scare you, then they are not big enough. It's time to start feeling that positive nervous energy again!

Our Comfort Zone is like our self-image; it dictates everything about our lives including the way we play golf. Often what we believe about ourselves and how we play golf is, for most of us, a lie. We've made up this lie because we've allowed ourselves to settle for less. For a multitude of reasons we stopped dreaming and setting intentions long ago. We don't want to dream and then disappoint ourselves any more. We resign ourselves to this *perceived* fate that this is just how it is. We end up rationalizing and justifying an existence that is often less than what we dreamed of or hoped to become. At this pace we end up settling for lives of quiet desperation and mediocrity. Same thing happens on the golf course – we end up settling for less than our full magnificence, our full potential.

Our Comfort Zone is something we make up. It's an illusion. It's the self-imposed limit we have placed upon ourselves over the years. Our Comfort Zone is most likely settling for something less, something mediocre. We play small for several reasons. We don't want to think of ourselves as great – that's too much to accept, too much bigness, too much wonderment, too much responsibility, too much to ask. Do you grasp the implications of this kind of thinking?

We tell ourselves we're not that good and it becomes a self-fulfilling prophecy. It's safe to play small and fly under the radar – no one will expect much from us and we won't be disappointed when we don't perform well. Some of us even manipulate our own handicap because somewhere deep down inside we believe we can't live up to those expectations. We're getting used to being mediocre and miserable. We've come up with all kinds of excuses and reasons to blame our pathetic "status quo" plight.

If that doesn't please you good...it's not supposed too! This is all meant to shake you up. It's meant to get you beyond the end of your self-imposed Comfort Zone. It's time to find out what is keeping you from playing golf to your full potential, just like I did –with a crushing blow, realizing that I had settled for much less. It's time to step over this imaginary boundary and play golf to more of your full expression. It's time to act on your goals, the ones that scare you the most. It's time to Think, Talk, and Play, Like a Champion Today!

Finding and Then Lowering Your Comfort Zone Score

"No one can make you feel inferior without your consent."
—Eleanor Roosevelt

Our Comfort Zone is actually comprised of a single score, while our general Comfort Zone in golf may on the surface appear to be three to four strokes either side of our actual Comfort Zone. It's easy to find this single score. Once we find this score, we acknowledge it, know longer are we disillusioned or in denial. Applying the MEGT to our Comfort Zone can be a very enlightening experience.

It's important for you to know your own Comfort Zone, without any self-deception, in order to start the process of lowering it. I also suggest you complete this procedure on a daily or perhaps weekly basis. How much time you invest in your own mental game is a direct match to what you reap.

Imagine lowering your Comfort Zone score by a few strokes, or even a single digit or two. In the world of professional golf, the difference between averaging 69.5 and 70 could very well be millions of dollars.

Here's how you find your Comfort Zone and apply the MEGT:

Case Study: Rand Marquardt, 48 coached by Michelle Burns, Prince Edward Island, Canada. Disappointed in knowing I have settled for less and mediocrity.

Step One: Pick a score that is several strokes higher than what you normally shoot on your home course. The idea being that the first time you finish the statement, you will feel confident; it will feel *true* for you.

Example: I would pick 83 and begin there. If I were to play only 9 holes I would pick 42.

Step Two: Complete the following statement and then answer yes or no.

Statement: "I am confident that I can consistently shoot _____83, answer (yes)."

Step Three: Keep on repeating this process, one stroke at a time lower and you will get a feel for your own game. Keep on doing this until you get uncomfortable and you can no longer with 100 percent certainty say that you can consistently shoot that score.

Example: "I am confident that I can consistently shoot _____83 (yes), I am confident that I can consistently shoot _____82 (yes), 81 (yes), 80 (yes), 79 (yes), 78 (yes), 77 (yes), 76 (ah . . . no, can't quite claim 76 consistently)." So, shooting 77 is my actual Comfort Zone number. The score just above where I could no longer say I can consistently shoot. Shooting a 76 (trombones) raised a doubt in my mind. I've just discovered my Comfort Zone. Have I shot 76 before, certainly? I also shot a few 70's, 71's, 72's, 73's, 74's, and 75's. Besides my Comfort Zone limitation, shooting in the 60's is also one of my self-limiting barriers that I wish to break through. I've only done it twice in my life.

Disappointment is the understanding that we have settled for less than what we *know* we are capable of. Knowledge of this is critical to your ongoing and ultimate success. Most people want to think they are better than what their Comfort Zone tells them. It is okay to feel that way. You're supposed to feel slightly upset with yourself that you are not quite playing golf to your full potential.

Because our Comfort Zone is such a big part of our lives and golf game you may find yourself using more than four rounds. You may find yourself using several rounds to unveil some really juicy stuff. In order to get real with your self, stay with it and allow yourself the full exposure to this technique. Whatever emotions or intensity you are feeling, whether feelings of complacency or disappointment, simply acknowledge them.

Coaches Notes: We always begin with a negative aspect or emotion of the issue. Do not be concerned about being negative. Remember it is the acknowledgment and the clearing of the negative issue or emotion that is our objective. When the negative emotion is cleared, then you are more receptive and therefore it is easier to replace or integrate the positive belief and focus. It's that simple!

I'm feeling a 9 on my scale of emotional intensity. Disappointed and upset with myself!

Step four: Tapping on the side of your hand (the karate chop area), repeat the following statements out loud, to yourself and fill in *your score* and *language* as it relates to you.

1) Acknowledgment:
Side of hand: I can't shoot 76 (your score) consistently. I don't believe I can shoot 76 (your score) consistently. I'm not good enough to shoot 76 (your score) consistently. I don't deserve to shoot 76 (your score) consistently. I can't do it. I'm not good enough. I'm too scared to shoot 76 (your score) consistently. I can't shoot 76 (your score) consistently.

Inside Eyebrow: I can't shoot 76 consistently.

Outside of Eye: I can't shoot 76 consistently; I'm not good enough to shoot 76 consistently.

Under the Eye: I don't deserve to shoot 76 consistently.

Under the Nose: I can't shoot 76 consistently.

Chin: I'm not good enough to shoot 76 consistently.

Inside Collar Bone: I can't shoot 76 consistently.

Under Arm: Can't do it.

Double Wrist: Not good enough.

Crown of Head: I can't shoot 76 consistently, I don't deserve it, and I'm not good enough.

Deep Breath: Breathe in and out.

Rate your intensity level after Round 1: Still feeling at least an 8 or a 9. Not feeling very good. Upset with myself.

Coaches Notes: Too early to replace with any positive belief or focus. I must clear and move through my negative belief and settling for mediocrity first.

Keep on with Round 1 type of language (Acknowledgment) and some new language, like "I still can't do it", or "I don't believe I can do it". Tell the truth versus being in denial. I can't do it. I'm simply not good enough. Acknowledge your truth of where you are. Let's break through it. We do it by acknowledgment, accepting, forgiving, and then we give ourselves a new positive focus. For now, you must stay here with your old self-limiting beliefs before our new champion beliefs will be allowed to break through. It very well could make you feel upset at yourself knowing you've allowed yourself to settle for less than your full potential.

1) Acknowledgment:
Side of hand: I still can't shoot 76 consistently. I'm not good enough to shoot 76. I still believe I can't shoot 76 consistently. I'm

too scared. I've settled for less. I can't do it. I still believe I can't shoot 76 consistently.

Inside Eyebrow: I still can't shoot 76 consistently.

Outside of Eye: I can't shoot 76.

Under the Eye: I still believe I don't deserve to shoot 76.

Under the Nose: I'm not good enough to shoot 76.

Chin: Still can't shoot 76 consistently.

Inside Collar Bone: I still can't shoot 76 consistently.

Under Arm: I don't deserve it.

Double Wrist: I don't think I can shoot 76 consistently.

Crown of Head: I still can't shoot 76 consistently. I still believe that I don't deserve it. I still believe I am not good enough. I've settled for less and I am upset with myself.

Deep Breath: Breathe in and out.

Rate your intensity level after Round 2: I am still at least an 8 or so, still feeling a lot of emotional intensity around my Comfort Zone.

2) Acceptance:
Side of hand: Even though I can't shoot 76 consistently, I accept myself exactly as I am. Even though I believe I am not good enough to shoot 76 consistently, I accept myself exactly as I am. Even though I have settled for less, I accept myself exactly as I am. Even though I have a hard time believing and accepting that I cannot shoot 76 consistently, I accept myself exactly as I am.

Inside Eyebrow: I accept myself exactly as I am, even though I cannot shoot 76 consistently.

Outside of Eye: I accept myself exactly as I am, even though I cannot shoot 76 consistently.

Under Eye: Even though I believe I can't shoot 76 consistently, I accept myself exactly as I am.

Under Nose: Even though I have settled for less, I accept myself exactly as I am.

Chin: Even though I am not good enough to shoot 76, I accept myself exactly as I am.

Inside Collar Bone: Even though I'm upset with being mediocre, I accept myself exactly as I am.

Under Arm: I accept myself exactly as I am, even though I cannot shoot 76 consistently.

Double Wrist: Even though I believe I can't shoot 76 consistently, I accept myself exactly as I am.

Crown of Head: I accept myself exactly as I am, even though I have settled for less.

Deep Breath: Breathe in and out.

Rate your intensity level after Round 3: Feeling around a 7. Not too pleased with knowing how I have settled for less with myself.

New thoughts come up for me at this stage. Therefore, I shall stay in the process of acknowledging and accepting before moving onto Forgiveness. I'm mad at myself for settling for less. Notice the slight change in my language.

Side of hand: Even though I have allowed myself to get comfortable shooting in the upper 70's when I know I am capable of more, and I get angry when I think about it, I am willing to accept this situation and my current level of performance, exactly as it is.

Even though I have settled for being mediocre when I know I am capable of being extraordinary, and I don't even like saying it, I'm willing to accept this situation, I forgive myself and I choose to realize my full potential as a golfer.

Even though I have allowed myself to get comfortable playing below what I am capable of, and I have allowed other people's opinion to influence how I play, I forgive myself and anyone else who has contributed to my limiting beliefs, and I accept this situation exactly as it is. I am now willing to admit to myself and to the world that I am not normal, I'm not average, I am capable of much more, and I am ready to break through to a new level of performance.

Inside Eyebrow: I'm frustrated that I have allowed myself to get comfortable shooting in the upper 70's.

Outside Eye: I'm angry that I've settled for being mediocre when I know I am capable of more.

Under Eye: I've settled for less than I am capable of.

Under Nose: I'm embarrassed that I've allowed myself to settle.

Chin: I've been playing below my potential.

Collarbone: I'm frustrated now that I realize I have allowed this to happen.

Under Arm: This is tough to accept, but I am willing to accept this situation and myself exactly as I am.

Double Wrist: Even though I have allowed this to happen, and it hurts, I accept this situation and myself exactly as I am.

Crown of Head: I can't believe I have allowed this to go on for so long when I've known I am capable of so much more.

Deep Breath: Breathe in and out.

Rate your intensity level after Round 4: Feeling around a 5 or a 6. I'm more accepting, yet still upset with knowing I settled for mediocrity.

Side of hand: Even though I'm still frustrated that I've allowed this to happen, and I don't' know how to accept it, I'm willing to accept it, and I'm grateful for this new level of awareness, I'm ready for a breakthrough.

Even though I'm still angry that I've settled for being normal and average when I've known all along that I am much better than that, I'm grateful for this new level of awareness, and I am ready to break through to a new level of performance, one that is in alignment with who I am.

Even though I still have resistance to playing at my best, I accept and forgive myself exactly as I am.

Inside Eyebrow: Still frustrated that I've allowed myself to settle.

Outside Eye: Having a tough time accepting that I've allowed this to go on for so long.

Under Eye: I feel anxious because I feel that it's too late, I'm getting older, and it's just another belief.

Under Nose: I'm embarrassed now that I realize I've let this happen.

Chin: Still frustrated that I've been playing below my potential.

Collarbone: Still frustrated that I've settled for being normal and average.

Under Arm: Still having a tough time accepting this.

Double Wrist: Can't believe I've allowed this to go on this long. I'm willing to breakthrough to a new level of performance.

Crown of Head: Releasing this resistance, willing to accept and move on to my higher Self.

Deep Breath: Breathe in and out.

Rate your intensity level after Round 5: Feeling a 4. I'm feeling much better, still stunned at myself for being less than I am.

3) Forgiveness:
Inside Eyebrow: Even though I can't shoot 76 consistently I forgive myself.

Outside Eye: Even though I have settled for mediocrity, I forgive myself.

Under Eye: I forgive myself for settling for less.

Under Nose: I forgive myself for believing I can't shoot 76 consistently.

Chin: I forgive myself for not understanding how this works.

Collar Bone: I forgive myself for feeling I don't deserve to shoot 76.

Under Arm: I forgive myself for feeling that I am not good enough.

Double Wrist: Even though I can't shoot 76 consistently, I forgive myself.

Crown of Head: Even though I have settled for less I forgive myself and I am ready for a new more positive empowering belief and focus, one that will support me in becoming my personal best.

Deep Breath: Breathe in and out.

Rate your intensity level after Round 6: Feeling much better, perhaps only a 2 or 3. I'm still disappointed with myself for settling for less. I can't believe I set these self-imposed limits within myself.

Side of hand: Even though I have been uncomfortable shooting in the mid to low 70's and below par consistently and I don't know why, I'm willing to get out of my head and in to The Zone where I belong.

Even though I know I belong in the 60's, but have not been playing to my potential, I forgive myself and accept myself and my current level of performance, exactly as it is, as I explore my full potential and establish a new comfort zone.

Even though I have allowed myself to shoot in the mid to upper 70's, I realize that I am not comfortable with this level of performance, I accept myself, I forgive myself, and I am ready to shoot consistently below par where I belong.

Inside Eyebrow: I've been uncomfortable shooting below par.

Outside Eye: I know I can shoot below par consistently but I have not been doing it.

Under Eye: I have been uncomfortable shooting below par because my mind gets in the way.

Under Nose: I get uncomfortable when I start shooting below par because I can't expect to play that good all the time.

Chin: I start getting uptight when I'm shooting below par because my mind gets in the way.

Collarbone: I know I can shoot below par consistently, but I get uptight because my mind gets in the way. I now realize that I have control over it, it does not have control over me.

Under Arm: I have not been shooting below par consistently and I am uncomfortable with that.

Double Wrist: I'm upset that I have allowed myself to be less than I am.

Crown of Head: I am releasing this resistance to shooting below par consistently, ready to let it go and play golf in The Zone.

Deep Breath: Breathe in and out.

Rate your intensity level after Round 7: Still feeling some emotion around this issue, perhaps a 2-3.

Side of hand: Even though I still have barriers to shooting 69 or below consistently, I know I can do it, this is where I belong, I am ready to enjoy the experience and realize my fuller potential as a golfer.

Even though I have resistance to realizing my fuller potential as a golfer and I don't know why, I'm starting to realize that it is just resistance, I am willing to explore other possibilities and bring my attention and my intention to shooting in the 60's on a more consistent basis.

Even though I have allowed myself to remain in a Comfort Zone that is not serving me because I wanted to belong, I wanted to fit in and be normal. I am now realizing that I am not average, I'm not normal, and I'm getting much more comfortable with that idea. I'm ready to step outside my Comfort Zone and shoot in the 60's more consistently, I've done it before, and I can do it again. It doesn't matter what anybody else thinks. I know what I can do. I am ready to shoot in the 60's consistently.

Inside Eyebrow: I'm ready to release resistance to shooting in the 60's consistently.

Outside Eye: I'm releasing this resistance to being the best I can be.

Under Eye: I'm letting go of these limiting beliefs, and it feels good to let go.

Under Nose: I'm releasing this resistance; it's safe to let go.

Chin: I'm ready to play like a Champion, in The Zone where I belong.

Collarbone: My new comfort zone is THE ZONE.

Under Arm: I feel much more comfortable playing in The Zone.

Double Wrist: Ah, playing in The Zone.

Crown of Head: The Zone is my new Comfort Zone. The Zone is my most natural state of being. Every cell of my body radiates in The Zone.

Deep Breath: Breathe in and out.

Rate your intensity level after Round 8: Feeling great, feeling inspired, feeling a 2.

Coaches Notes: Begin moving toward positive belief and focus.

Side of Hand: I'm no longer comfortable shooting in the mid to upper 70's, I'm more comfortable with the thought and idea of shooting below par on a consistent basis. I've been ready for this breakthrough and now I have all the tools at my disposal to let it happen.

Inside Eyebrow: I'm no longer comfortable shooting in the mid 70's.

Outside Eye: I'm more comfortable with the idea of shooting below par consistently.

Under Eye: I don't have to work harder, I just need to be in The Zone and allow it to happen.

Under Nose: Breaking 70 consistently is a possibility, and I'm ready to do it.

Chin: I have what it takes to break 70 consistently, I always have and I've always known it.

Collarbone: I've been waiting for this breakthrough. I've always known I could do better; it feels great to realize it. I'm ready, I'm excited and I'm in The Zone.

Under Arm: I'm very comfortable shooting below par.

Double Wrist: I'm grateful to be playing my best golf in The Zone.

Crown of Head: The Zone is my new Comfort Zone. Every cell in my body radiates and vibrates in The Zone.

Deep Breath: Breathe in and out.

Rate your intensity level after Round 9: Feeling Awesome. I'm at a 1.5!

4) New Positive Belief and Focus:

Inside Eyebrow: Playing to my full potential.

Outside Eye: Playing golf in The Zone.

Under Eye: I'm in The Zone.

Under Nose: The Zone.

Chin: Feeling...The Zone.

Collar Bone: Ah . . . The Zone.

Under Arm: Golfing in...The Zone.

Double Wrist: Playing Golf in...The Zone.

Crown of Head: I'm in The Zone.

Deep Breath: Breathe in and out.

Rate your intensity level after Round 10: Feeling Awesome, going with the flow. I'm at 1! I'm feeling eager, excited, and ready.

Action steps:

1) Do these exercises every day until you are consistently shooting your next lower Comfort Zone score. Say, "I consistently shoot (your score) or better on a regular basis." Then, lower the number even more, all the while being happy now, and loving yourself for being the magnificent you! Learn the sequence of tapping points so you can perform it on yourself whenever you desire.

2) Practice any MEGT on yourself and see for yourself how you feel. Take your new freedom to the golf course... and keep on!

3) Oh, by the way...shhh...you can also imagine yourself tapping and the process still works. If tapping in public makes you "feel" silly or uncomfortable then just imagine yourself going through the process in your mind.

Chapter 13

Say Goodbye to Your Fears

"Fear of any kind is the number-one enemy of all golfers, regardless of ball-striking and shot-making capabilities."
—Jack Nicklaus

How to eliminate and greatly reduce doubt, worry, or fear in your golf game?

You can only experience fear when you *pretend that you are not in control.* It's like "pretending" you can't dance, are not photogenic, or not loved unconditionally. It's all in your head. Remember: you are not your thoughts; you only think your thoughts. Chose to be as you wish to seem and allow everything that really is you become your experience. Learn to go with the flow of who you really are. When you are going with the flow of who you really are, you are in control, and everything clicks in to place including your golf game.

Fear is an illusion and it is the polar opposite of everything that you really are, which is joy, truth, and love. Fear exists so that we can know joy, truth, and love; otherwise we would not know what they felt like. As we discussed earlier life is the yin and yang; opposites exist in this realm of the relative to give us contrast, to complement each other, and as an opportunity to break through the illusion once we awaken to this understanding. Once we understand the illusion of fear, we can embrace our joy, truth, and love, since that's all there really is, and therefore let go of our fears, which we have perceived as fantasy experienced as real. Once we see and understand why the illusion exists we can return to that which we really are. How would we know what joy is like unless we first experienced despair? It's why the illusion exists in this world.

Once we acknowledge our shadow selves, our "negative" emotions, we can love, honor and integrate them, then there is no need for them to get our attention to show us our true path.

What exactly is FEAR?
Fantasy Experienced As Real
False Evidence Appearing Real

Our greatest obstacles on the golf course are not the sand traps or the water hazards: it is our own fear on the inside. I am certainly not going to dispute the quote by Jack Nicklaus that opened this chapter, because that is what I feel, on and off, practically every time I play golf. I wouldn't lie about that, which is why I still ask to overcome my fears and play golf to my more full potential. After having used the techniques and following the messages in this book I can honestly say I am getting much better at handling my fear. The gains I have made, including embracing my experience, being more connected, etc., has been a Godsend.

Look, a little bit of nervous energy is good for the soul. Golf professionals feel this nervous energy practically every time they tee it up. Yet when it crosses the line to being outright scared and afraid, then perhaps we have not embraced exactly where we are. Nicklaus also said, "That the difference between being nervous and scared is being prepared." Perhaps we should take a closer look at how prepared we really are? How much "focused and productive" practice time are you really putting in, both on the physical and mental driving range?

Why do we get so scared? Usually it is because we allow events to become bigger than they really are. Perhaps we want it so bad to impress another, or not look bad in the presence of others, wanting to show them how good we really are? Perhaps we allow our creative imagination to negatively spiral wildly out of control and get the best of us? Perhaps we get ahead of ourselves and out of the current moment of now? Perhaps our old beliefs, which we've allowed to run our self-image is no longer serving our best interest? *What are you giving your energy and thoughts upon?*

It is the illusion of fear that keeps us stuck in these repetitive patterns of negativity that are keeping us from playing golf to our full potential. So, let's break it all down and really observe what's going on. Let's dislodge the stuck and fearful energy and get back to being our natural healthy selves. Let's get just a little bit better than we used to be, shall we?

One of simplest techniques to utilize is to walk boldly with your fears fully experiencing them rather suppressing them, hiding from them, being all nervous and uptight with them. I want to show you how to do this. Whenever fear appears, notice it. Choose to walk with it. Choose to acknowledge it. Choose to own it. Own whatever fears come to you and really examine them. I find that many times what I thought I was afraid of melts away within moments. No reason to over analyze the situation, just simply notice and be with them.

In the words of Orison Swett Marden, *founder of Success Magazine* and father of the new success growth movement, "Most of our obstacles would melt away if, instead of cowering before them, we should make up our minds to walk boldly through them." As we walk we acknowledge our fears and in the same breath we acknowledge we want to feel better. I believe that by acknowledging our negative thoughts, clearing them first, we open the pathways to new focus and mental toughness. Tiger just didn't become the world's most mentally tough athlete overnight…so welcome the process.

The next time you're feeling slightly scared or afraid practice being with this emotion. It could be walking into a new home, a business, or the Clubhouse. Take special notes about why. Journal about what comes up for you? Is it because you're a people pleaser? Is it because you feel inferior or unworthy? Is it because you lack confidence in yourself? Instead of running, hiding, or suppressing the issue walk boldly with your fears and journal about the experience and see why it occurred and keeps on repeating itself – until it doesn't. Remember, what you resist, persists.

The real answer is to meet our fears head on, not to escape them.

Escaping our fears brings denial, which is a form of suppression, often lodging our fear in our bodies and then causing all sorts of physical and psychological havoc. Resistance builds up energy walls or blocks, and unless we allow these blocks to flow to us and through us we keep getting the same result on the golf course over and over and over again. Even worse, left unchecked our fears become suppressed deep down within us and can literally eat away at us causing outward physical dis-ease. These blocks are disowned aspects of ourselves that we haven't loved and integrated. Perhaps we thought we were supposed to run from them? Perhaps we thought we were supposed to roll up our sleeves and show them whose boss? Most likely we simply didn't understand how this process really works. Many will not want to love and integrate their fears and disowned aspects of themselves, the exact cause of all their "perceived" problems in the first place. Many think they can figure it out on their own by paddling even harder. The path is narrow for those who chose to really see. Our fears have been seeking to get our attention, so that we *can* walk boldly in being our highest Self. They are all part of our experience, yet they don't have to run our lives or our golf game anymore.

So, what do I do now? You're asking the 10 million dollar question. Good! Perhaps you'll find some relief and some wisdom within this question. The answer has always been...once awakened... to keep on. Some say to never give up, you're only 3 feet from gold. The answer and wisdom lies within you. It's up to you, to take back your power and control of your life. You get back into the game of life wherever you are now. The rest of the messages are simply tools you can use to sharpen your focus.

Learn to love, honor, and cherish yourself! Part of our work here is *too love* the parts of ourselves that we don't like, the parts that we keep beating up ourselves over – the anger, the nerves, the choking, our own negativity, and at the same time gain greater understanding of how this game of golf and life really works. Soften your stance, find some relief, stop paddling so hard, and your game will improve. As our perspective changes so does our understanding about life, which carries over into all aspects including our golf game. Sometimes at first it may feel exactly like God is pinching us or tapping us on the shoulder. God's real mission is to wake us up.

Any deeply rooted fear, like a stubborn wisdom tooth removal, may require additional assistance or another technique. I like to begin with telling my truth, becoming my authentic Self, owning my experience, understanding these new perspectives about life, followed by a MEGT or EFT clearing that supports me along the fairway of life. If your fears appear to be so deeply rooted like mine were, then keep on reading because there is hope. Where there is a will, there is a way.

Negative thoughts seldom have to do with reality. They are simply announcements about things that scare us, and the things that scare us seldom threaten us in the present moment. In golf we are afraid of what might happen later if we don't perform this golf shot right now. Imagine the insanity. All negativity is fear announced. That is true of anger as well. Negativity appears when there is something we want that we do not now have, or something we have that we do not want. We want to make eagles, birdies, and pars; and sometimes even a bogey can be extremely satisfying. When we are imagining an outcome in our mind before it even manifests (often before we even tee it up, or in the middle of the hole or our round) that we *might* make a high number, for instance, or when we are making bogeys, double bogeys, or even worse, these are things we don't want. Many of us allow these things to make us afraid and we become angry. Remember what we said earlier: you have a choice to be angry or not. You also have a choice to become afraid and project negativity into the future, or not.

Fear is when we are afraid of what might happen later and negativity appears when there is something we want that we do not now have, or something we have that we do not want. We want a par or a birdie so badly—something that we do not now have. Wanting something desperately ends up pushing it further away. Rather, eagerly anticipate the eventual expansion of it, feel the positive energy, let it go, stay present, and so shall it be. Let God and Let Go and be present now. "Want not" becomes a razor thin divine dichotomy. Or we end up with a bogey or double bogey and that is something we do not want. Wanting with pure intentions of the heart and attracting it is different than wanting and feeling a lack of not having it.

There are several strategies, techniques, or thought processes to eliminate negative thoughts based upon fear and anger. Our mission together is to present them; allowing you to choose and decide what works for you. The easiest thought process lies with its roots firmly planted in acceptance and embracing the moment, staying present, being aware, and understanding that everything is happening now. A true Master accepts all that comes to his or her gate. Can you accept all that comes to your gate? Can you feel good even in the face of adversity? Can you reach for a higher feeling thought no matter what? Can you take the punch in the gut and still feel good?

It's an amazing transformation when you simply begin to accept everything just exactly as it is right now – yes even if you may not like it. And it is the *not liking it* that continues to cause us problems and hold us in this space of golf purgatory—which in ultimate reality simply does not exist. But the illusion of it does, and for many the illusion keeps us stuck. Your negative emotions and fears appear as real as real can be, even if you know they are all illusions.

Sometimes it becomes the bigger the event, the greater the fear. Let me give you another analogy. If we were walking along side by side in a fairly straight route on a non-busy sidewalk it would be pretty easy right? You wouldn't even think about it, correct? If I asked you to walk across the floor within the confines of a four-inch parallel border for twenty feet without losing your balance, or without falling to the floor, it would pretty easy, right? Would you become a little more conscious—meaning left-brain thinking? Or would you trust the same process as before? Now if I asked that you walk across a four-by-four piece of wood on the ground it still would be pretty easy, perhaps a tad more difficult, right? Maybe a slight hiccup here and there, perhaps not. Now if I asked that you walk across this same beam suspended some twenty feet in the air, as in the case of a ropes course objective, how would you perform? The same as it was on the sidewalk or floor? No, when you think about what might happen if you lose your balance so high up you might start sweating, feel your heart palpitating and maybe even freeze up. That's exactly how many of us have played golf. The less conscious thoughts and fear we allow, the better we perform. We want to perform to artistic excellence without thinking too much. In fact, in The Zone no thoughts exist – just pure positive energy transcending self.

This same concept has a similar carry-over affect to everyone seeking to make a swing change as well. The two million dollar question is: should I make a swing change or not? Perhaps there are advantages and disadvantages. There's something to be said about the guy or gal who gets it down his or her way, even if it is less traditional looking. You don't have to look too far to notice this when you see Jim Furyk swing. It works for him.

Sean O'Hair is an upcoming big time contender who just recently finished second to Tiger Woods' incredible comeback victory in the 2009 Arnold Palmer Golf Invitational. Sean has recently changed his swing with his new coach, Sean Foley, to suit his game, something he can feel comfortable with rather then trying to look a certain way. Sean is also working on the mental game with Dr. Bob Rotella about getting away from being results-oriented. O'Hair describes it this way, "I want to concentrate on the process – having a good set-up and good alignment and then a good swing – but not worrying about where the ball's going to go. That really helped me out a lot this year as well." Sticking to what feels good to you *and* is fundamentally sound will help ease the process in making swing changes. And if you do decide to make a swing change, and it does cause you some frustration, or temporary choppiness in your swing the MEGT is a useful tool to ease the emotional transition.

The best way to describe making a swing change is through the use of other analogies. Let's say you just purchased or leased a new car. Everything is a little foreign compared to what you were used to; some differences are slight, some major. In your old car you naturally evolved to sliding the key into the ignition slot with relative ease without too much thinking. In your new car you've got to develop a new mind-muscle memory program—in this case it usually doesn't irritate you too much because that's just the way it is. Applying a new golf swing is a bit different because we might fear the outcome or, the first few tries, the results might not be apparent because we have not practiced the swing long enough. The same can be said about staying in a hotel, a relative's house, or a new condo – you're just not quite familiar yet where everything is—reaching for the light switch, walking at night in the dark, or how to operate the new remote on the television. If the transition to the new way of doing something is frustrating, try applying the MEGT to facilitate the ease of learning a new habit or golf swing. By simply acknowledging your frustration, doubt, worry, fear, hesitation, or choppiness in learning and integrating a new swing concept your anxiety level will be lowered greatly. You'll end up playing more confidently much sooner.

Another mental mindset strategy to help you understand the concept of negative thoughts is to not worry about your negative thoughts because they are par for the course so to speak. Change your thoughts when you can, but when the negative ones seem to overrun you, let them run. No matter how persistent they are, you can always spend five to ten minutes a day imagining your dreams coming true; seeing yourself happy, laughing, calm; confident; relaxed and smiling ear to ear—even if the negative thoughts creep in. Eventually, you'll find yourself gravitating toward joyful, better feeling thoughts, and internal peace of mind. Yeah, life is good. You're in the right place, at the right time, with the right juju. Carry that perspective with you and it will help lighten the load when things appear to be getting out of hand. There's no situation too great to handle. Relax and breathe. Sometimes we just seek to soften the edge and find some relief from all the mental stress. Imagine Boo Weekly playing Happy Gilmore galloping down the first hole riding his driver.

Two other powerful techniques to utilize in overcoming your fears are to practice the Infallible Formula and to remember that God is your best friend. Practicing the Infallible Formula, which means causing another to experience that which you wish to be yourself. In other words, if I desire myself to become a more mentally tough golfer then I look for opportunities to guide and support another into becoming more mentally tough. Just like the Phil Mickelson story back in the last chapter. It's an amazing concept; I invite *you* to be the teacher. Tell and show another how to be more mentally tough and you will become that yourself. Do it naturally and effortlessly.

Coaches Notes: Please teach others in a way that is not proselytizing, not giving advice. Do it in way that supports and guides another. Asking "what" type of questions is a place to start. Telling and showing another how you did it helps pave the way – what works for you. I also notice that many think that if they keep working really, really hard then they'll figure it out hardly paying any attention to what I am offering – some folks are just not ready for this kind of teaching right now – and you will get better on picking up that vibe as well. Reminds me of me for 30 years worth, ☺. So, don't get too bent out of shape if another is just not "getting it" right now. Remember, you and I didn't either some time ago. It's okay, our work here is really not to help or fix another; *perhaps* we get them to another level, perhaps not?

Understanding that God is your best friend is a powerful reminder to the life force that flows through you. The love you hold in your heart will manifest in all parts of your life. When I think of God being my best friend there is reassurance in my game. I'm able to carry on that much more. I feel the energy radiate throughout my body. I feel gratitude and appreciation. I feel relief – everything is going to work out.

Allow me to digress for a moment and tell a very powerful story that first happened when I started practicing these life principles on the golf course and causing another to experience that which I desired to experience myself. What's really at the heart of this concept is that when you are asking to get better yourself, opportunities will present themselves to help (guide and support) others in the most amazing ways once you are open and start paying attention. And sometimes it takes a bit of courage; trust that your sense of connection and intuition will guide the way. You cannot get it wrong when listen to your soul and you speak from your heart.

My Dad's Visit

From the time I was very young, my father and I have spent little time together. When we do get together, it is usually over a game of golf or a couple of beers, and usually, both. I still feel drawn to him. Even though a long distance separates us, I still feel the love; I still feel connected. I know now that everything happened as it did for a perfect reason. I chose my perfect parents, perfect in the sense that through them I was able to find my freedom to follow my own path, to experience my soul's desire to know it self. Sometimes it takes a certain amount of internal willingness to follow your own true path versus a path that you have been conditioned to live by others. Perhaps there is a blessing in divorce? This allowed me to awaken more fully to who I really am. Hmmm…back to the story.

Early in August 2005, I was excitedly preparing for a visit from my Dad and Kitty, his second wife whom he married some thirty years ago. They were to arrive on August 4th and stay for about ten days, though my father typically got the dates confused because Kitty made the travel plans.

The day before they were to *supposed to* arrive according to what I was told by my dad, my golfing partner Keith (Fitzee) called me to say our game for today is on at Charlevoix Belvedere Country Club with Bud Klooster at four in the afternoon. To my surprise, no sooner had I loaded my clubs into the golf cart then I saw Kitty and her sister, Nancy, in the parking lot. My first thought was, what are you doing here? I thought you guys were supposed to be here tomorrow? Kitty didn't appear a bit surprised because she knew of her itinerary. She commented on how my dad gets dates and names mixed up. Immediately I was hit with an internal adrenaline rush. Wow, Dad is out on the course! Can you believe it?

Anyway, we were off and running, having a great time. I was teeing off on the par five, fifteenth hole at Belvedere when Dad comes along riding up in his golf cart. This would be his typical behavior – here I am. Yep, that's my dad. I've learned to accept this kind of behavior. I mean, for the past thirty-five years, I'd only seen him about once every five years. He rode along in the cart telling us stories. He said that this exact trap (sand bunker) on hole number fifteen determined a significant part of a match in Michigan Amateur golf history. Dad told the story of how both players hit their balls into this bunker, and neither player could identify his ball. The first player, the player farthest away from the hole, the player first to hit, got to carve all the sand out around his ball in order to identify it and play it that way, but the other player who still could not fully identify his ball, could do nothing, because the rules officials determined that it must be his ball. One lie was vastly improved. It was the rules of golf. Like his father before him, my dad told us the exact same story the following year. Perhaps I will be doing the same thing myself someday. After 2005 my dad and Kitty decided to make annual two-week visits to Northern Michigan in the summer.

I was now about five weeks into my personal golf laboratory (playground) experiment, so I was handling my emotions a lot better. I play through my first few holes with some nervous energy that caused some resistance in my swing. But I settled down and played very well for the last fourteen holes.

Rick Grunch, the head course superintendent, came out to greet us on hole number seventeen—the par three with a big drop-off in front and to the left of the green. Rick observed our golf shots from a distance and invited us over to his house after our round. He said Bud—a club member and a strong five-handicap golfer (currently a two)—is probably playing the best. We all just kind of glanced his way and went about our business, leaving what we're thinking to his imagination. The game was pretty even. We'd all played pretty well. I shot 76; Fitz shot 75, and Bud was right around 78. Our fourth, Hal Price, a friend of Bud and Keith's, was somewhere in the mid 80s.

Dad and I decided that we would play my home course, True North Golf Club of Harbor Springs on Friday. Incidentally, True North is commonly known as a point on the compass, and finding your true north, which I was reminded once again from my friend Dan Henrickson, the architect for the True North Golf Club Clubhouse, and his wife Julie, that *True North* means aligning with your true path. And we continued chatting even more about your *True North* when I saw Dan on the driving range this past summer of 2008. As I've learned there are no coincidences, chance circumstances, or random events!

Courage to Talk to My Dad

On the day of our outing Dad, Kitty, Keith Grunch, an assistant golf professional at PBVCC, and I teed it up.

Let me explain something about my dad, John Marquardt. He is a classic curmudgeon at times on the golf course. I mean talk about a guy who has a hard time accepting what is. You almost feel sorry for him at times when he appears to be so frustrated on the course, and then love him to death in the next breath when he makes you laugh. However, to his credit he is a man's man. He had quite a group of friends he cherished. Life is a mirror: what you recognize in another lies within you, both the dark and the light.

Dad is seventy-five years old on (December 8, 2008), and he acknowledges that his best scoring days are behind him. It's difficult for him to reach the long par fours in two. Years ago, he played to about a six to eight handicap golfer, and he still manages himself pretty well. He can par or birdie any hole on the course. When he hits a good shot, he's pretty upbeat and happy; when he hits an okay shot, he's just so-so, kind of nonchalant; when he hits a shitty shot, he's one miserable bastard. Until recently, for the most part, I was just like Dad, aren't we all to some extent? Like the *Cats in the Cradle* song by Harry Chapin, I was growing up just like him—until I wasn't.

Keith Grunch is a great golfer. He is an aspiring head pro to be, and enters all the local tournaments. He's young, hits it long, and is really a nice guy. The day of our outing I was there to play the course and enjoy Dad, Kitty, and Keith's company. Dad and I rode together in the cart.

In order to make his A Team list, I always felt I had to prove to him that I could play decent golf. Well, I do play well; on that day I shot a 74. Keith shot a 75. Kitty also played well. She's always been a very gifted, all-around athlete, but not one to compete seriously.

Her dad, Keith Carey, played professional basketball with George Mikan. Dad played well too, and today shot in the low 80's.

However, my biggest move of the day was not my own golf game; it was when I started talking to my Dad. We were on the second hole after he'd just knifed and thinned his second shot from a downhill lie. He proceeded to fling his club to the ground, berating himself with, "God damn it John! What the fuck was that?" Well, that's the miserable bastard-ness I've been talking about. He does it in such a classic fashion that it's both humorous and kind of scary. I mean, what are you supposed to do while he does this? Feel bad for him or just let it be? So I did neither. My new awakened state wouldn't let me feel bad for him. After Dad cut loose with his tirade it took me about three seconds to realize I was called to deliver a message: it was time for a heart-to-heart talk.

Power in Your Message

I was a little nervous at first but I wanted to talk to Dad about the wonderful secrets of golf and life that I was beginning to integrate into my own life. I wasn't sure how he would take it. Maybe he would think I was weak. Maybe he didn't want to hear what I had to say. He might even get pissed off. I decided it was worth taking the chance. I had changed and I wanted to share that with him what was working for me. I felt the calling within my heart.

So I began. When Dad wasn't looking, Kitty kept on silently encouraging me—with glances and whispers that said, "Keep it up, Randy. Your dad needs to hear this; he doesn't listen to me." I told him about accepting the shot and seeing what it's trying to tell him. "After all, who hit it," I said. It's about embracing every shot and making your self better next time. It's about loving the game of golf. "Are you happy being a miserable bastard? How do you think others like playing with you?" I kept it up and I told him how these principles were working in my game. I mean, I'd been playing very well, and I was sure he saw that. I was thankful; who the hell listens to advice like that from someone who's playing shitty?

After the round, we went to my sister Kristi's for a barbeque, and out on the deck, I had another opportunity to share more with Dad. It was flowing, and he was listening and taking it in. I got inspired; the tables were turned and my dad was taking my advice, my guidance through my new understanding. He asked a couple of questions, and I responded. I reminded him of things he already knows deep inside, but it was time for him to hear it again. This kind of connection is my inspired state of being.

All the while, I was becoming more focused on my own intentions. More than helping him, I was giving myself back to me, just by announcing and declaring what was working for me in my life and how I was doing it. This was big stuff. I offered him a combination of all the work I'd done and invested into myself, and the experiments I'd done with these principles on the golf course the past month. Kitty heard just about everything I said, and I could tell that she, too, believed in these concepts.

Kitty's Dream

I found out about a week later that because my dad is such a miserable bastard on the golf course, Kitty can barely stand to ride in the same cart with him. She called me about a dream she'd had about me making a CD with these life principles and golf concepts. She said, "Just duplicate what you told your dad. People could pop it in their car just before playing golf. Your dad is a changed man because of you and what you told him." I was flabbergasted to some extent, yet I knew I was on to something pretty special; I felt empowered!

It took great courage to share with my dad how I'd stepped into my light to recreate myself anew but once I did it felt great! I finally walked through the revolving door, and I felt blessed. I received this letter from my dad soon after our conversations. It was unsolicited confirmation that this stuff really does work. If it can work on a miserable old curmudgeon like my dad, it can work for you, too!

Rand S. Marquardt

Unedited Letter from Dad

October 11, 2005

Randy,

Please allow your dad to personally thank you for the help you have given me, in such a thoughtful and caring way during our visit to Northern Michigan in August this year [2005].

The last four days in "God's Country," I was working towards your compassionate and loving suggestions of enjoying life and enjoying golf...and all that golf has meant to me.

As a result of your advice, and your counseling on attitude and demeanor...I am a better man. Through golf and those I love is the path I choose to take during the remaining years I have. Golf will always be (as Dorothy in the *Wizard of Oz* would say) my "hearts desire."

Naturally I wish I could hit the shots, make the putts, play the required fade, draw, stinger, recover, or whatever... like I consistently did as a 6 or 7 handicap player at age 30 or 40. But the reality is that I cannot. I can still hit some very good shots, and I can still string 5 or 6 pars and birdies together and still enjoy 4 hours doing what I love more than anything in life with the exception of my family. I will continue to follow your advice, to have fun, to enjoy nature, to keep under control, to manage my attitude, to be light and happy, to show others that I am a good sportsman.

Randy, it is working. I am improving my attitude. I do not throw clubs. I do not swear. I am enjoying it much, much more.

One final personal thought...when you were 10-11-12-

13 years old, I told you, "Always play to win. If you don't win then practice harder so you will win the next time." I know you remember this! However, I was wrong! If I could do it all over I would not tell you that. What I would tell you is the same as the Marine Corp slogan, "Be all that you can be."

And thankfully, you fit that description. I hope to reach that level on and off the golf course as soon as I can.

Thanks again,
Your Dad

"My father gave me the greatest gift anyone could give another person, he believed in me."
–Jim Valvano

Wow, my dad believed in me!

Removing/Greatly Reducing Fears and Obstacles

The Mental Edge Golf Technique that we learned about in our last chapter is based upon solid life principles. In review, we acknowledge and accept everything exactly as it is. We forgive ourselves for thinking and behaving a certain way. We integrate a more positive focus. We say goodbye to our fears by utilizing this powerful technique, which is founded in pure positive energy as we speak and honor our truth. We learn that in order to change, we change within.

Our objective now is to remove, and/or greatly reduce the actual fears (obstacles) on the golf course that are clouding our way to being in The Zone. These are all the fears and negative thoughts that crop up from time to time that cause us anything from a subtle lack of confidence to outright paralysis – from the first tee jitters to the putting yips; from closing the deal down the stretch to throwing up all over ourselves; from chunked chip shots to fear of the out of bounds to scary thoughts of performing a shot where there is a pond immediately right of the green; from scary thoughts about your score and outcome; to fearful thoughts about pleasing others; from embarrassment and humiliation; to believing we are not good enough to the lowest levels of self-esteem. These are the thoughts that cause us tension in our ability to perform to our full potential.

Golf Performance Coaching

Let's take a closer look at what's really going on in the mind of others, similar to and perhaps a tad different from what has gone on in the mind of myself, and perhaps in the mind of yours. Let's find out what others are really thinking about and going through even further. Let's find out what you are going through. It is my intention to provide a variety of coaching situations utilizing MEGT and other golf specific exercise techniques as they relate to most golfers. It is my hope and desire that with similar practice that you too will begin to notice and observe that you are feeling much better enjoying this wonderful game of golf. Slowly but surely the intensity level of nervous anxiety will begin to melt away. One by one our fears become a non-issue. Yet understand this, for some of you it may take continued repetition in doing the work. I know that is how it works for me. Wherever we begin is the perfect place to begin.

The following are some case examples with coaching clients that show how this really works for a variety of challenging golf related fear issues. I personally experienced most of these issues and discovered solutions to them on my own. I allowed three years of golf to pass and plenty of students to make sure that it does work. One of the most important steps as you begin this process is that you must recognize and acknowledge that there is a problem. Whether you call it frustration or just some nerves, you have to own it. In the beginning most people are unwilling to acknowledge they play golf scared – too much for the ego to admit. Many are mental closet freaks – they dare not admit to their best friends that they have a mental problem playing golf.

A couple years ago when Ernie Els admitted he was battling

his demons within, the golf world appeared shocked. Shocked at what, our humanness? Golf professionals are constantly working through these kinds of head problems and mental issues. This is where the sports psychologists, like Dr. Bob Rotella make there living. Dr. Bob is seeking to quiet Ernie's intense wanting to win again – keeping him present and enjoying himself. When we relax into it, one shot at a time, we play our best. By golly, Ernie just won again. Now he has Butch Harmon as his swing coach to give him a new perspective. Introducing new conscious thoughts into our golf game can be a bit challenging. Again let's acknowledge what we are feeling and experiencing.

How do we know that people have mental golf problems? How can you not notice? Our outer world is a reflection of our inner world. Outer body language is a direct reflection from inner thoughts and energy vibration. In all my years of observing golfers and asking them how there golf game is, rarely do I find that someone tells me they are playing great golf and enjoying every minute of it. Let me clarify what I mean. Most everyone wants to play better. That's not the issue. The issue is not accepting it. The deeper issues are ones of disappointment, frustration, fear, disconnection, or a lack of belief and camaraderie. So let's get real! Let's find out what is causing us all this chaos within.

How do we build this up and how do we find the freedom to be able to perform to our ultimate potential – to give our best effort in which we know we are capable? If the messages from a Ryder Cup Captain, Assistant Captains, and a Life Coach can bring out the best in the Ryder Cup players, it can bring out the best in you! Just tap into the abundant flow of Well-Being that is always expressing itself through you. Keep on building a champion's self-image!

Not Having Too Much Fun

Kelly is a forty-five-year-old brilliant woman and mother of an eight-year-old boy. Her son is enrolled in the First Tee Program and Kelly wants to be able to play golf for fun with him. Kelly quit playing golf four years ago because it wasn't any fun. Kelly is one of my coaching clients. She approached me because she had heard that I was writing a book about the mental, emotional, and spiritual aspects of golf. She ended liking what I had to say during an informal conversation. I asked Kelly to describe herself as a golfer. She said she hasn't played for so long partly because she was raising her son. She said now that he is getting old enough to play; she thought that golf would be a nice thing they could do together. I asked her why golf had ceased being fun for her. Kelly answered very directly and poignantly: "There's too much mental tension about being worried about what might happen. It wasn't fun! There was too much tension about the whole 18 holes before I even teed off. Just thinking about golf in that way is not much fun." I asked her what kind of thoughts she had out there on the golf course. Kelly answered, "I was thinking too much about what could go wrong instead of what could go right."

Earlier in the day Kelly, her dog Skeeter, our friend Chris, and I went for a snowshoe on the second nine holes at True North. We came upon golf hole # 13, a slightly downhill par 3 with water front right and all the way along the right side. There are tall pines lining the left rough area and a sand trap smack dab over the middle of the green if you go long. In that trap you're practically dead. The green slopes away and if the ball trickles over the edge off the green, you're back in the pond lying 2. I did make 3 from that trap once. On hole # 13 there are four tee boxes. We all were standing on the black, or far back, tee box. The golf hole plays slightly over 200 yards up to 220 with a most difficult deep pin tucked a few paces from the edge of the green. Miss it slightly right you're in the drink. Hit it a tad long you're in the long rough, pines, or the trap. Pull it left, tall pines again, and a most difficult out, where 4 would be a good score. I remember making a 7 in the Club Championship and winning the hole, and I still shot 75, which meant I posted 73. Remember: fair and honest handicaps for several reasons.

As I was standing on the tee, I imagined the Sunday pin location. I spoke out loud, "They call this hole TRUST." Kelly just kind of shook her head with a bewildered gaze. I said that I just named it, and it's called TRUST from the back tees because that is what you must do on this hole. The smart play by the tour professional, when the pin is back and tucked deep is one, or perhaps two plays: Unless

The Fairway of Life

you're really feeling it, really clicking along you hit the ball exactly into the middle of the green (know your exact yardage); take your two-putt, and move on. Obviously, a great risk reward shot can be had when you're on. A great shot from the back tee with a back pin is absolutely a moment of beauty to watch and capture.

Kelly admitted later that when I said I named the golf hole TRUST, in her mind came the words, "Oh God, Death Valley."

So, here's what we have with our friend, Kelly:

1) Kelly wants to play golf again.
2) Kelly wasn't having any fun, so she quit playing golf.
3) Kelly has too much mental tension just thinking about playing a round of golf. She is too worried about what might happen.
4) Kelly gives her attention to what could go wrong, instead of what could go right.
5) Kelly sees and names the trouble.
6) Kelly is giving her intention to negative outcomes (fear and worry living in the future) versus being present with her effort (enjoying her now).
7) Kelly only plays with those she knows avoiding any feelings of embarrassment. Her golfing partners know her game.
8) Knowing Kelly just a little, she is a magnificent woman who takes great care of her self, pays attention to all the details, is very helpful, very compassionate, loves her sports, especially the University of Michigan, and it is my observation she has a tendency to lean toward perfectionism.

So, you probably have a pretty good feeling by now about where we are going to begin. We start with acknowledgment of all these negative and fearful thoughts. We bring awareness into the equation. Our mission is to soften the edge and to make golf more fun again for Kelly. Let's apply our Mental Edge Golf Technique.

Coaches Notes: We always begin with a negative aspect or emotion of the issue. Do not be concerned about *being negative.* Remember it is the acknowledgment and the clearing of the negative issue or emotion that is our objective. When the negative emotion is cleared you are more receptive (and it is easier) to replace or integrate the positive belief and focus. It's just that simple!

MEGT – Golf is not fun
Too much mental tension
Too much worry or fear on what might happen or what could go wrong

Rate your intensity level around this emotional issue from 1-10. Kelly is feeling a strong 9.

1) Acknowledgment:
Side of hand: Tapping on side of karate chop hand with two fingers (index and middle), begin saying, I'm scared to play golf. Golf is not fun anymore. I'm not having any fun. I have too much mental tension and stress. I'm afraid to play. I focus on negative thoughts on what could go wrong. Not having any fun. Golf is a scary game to play. There's too much mental tension and stress. Not having any fun. I'm focused on outcome, ahead of myself. Not having fun. I'm feeling mental tension. I have too many negative thoughts. Feeling scared.

Inside Eyebrow: Feeling stress and mental tension.

Outside of Eye: Not having any fun.

Under the Eye: It's not fun.

Under the Nose: Scared.

Chin: There's too much mental stress. Not having any fun.

Inside Collar Bone: Getting ahead of myself. Feeling mental tension.

Under Arm: Afraid and scared to play.

Double Wrist: I've got negative thoughts about what might happen, about what could go wrong. I'm stressed and afraid. I'm focused on a negative outcome.

Crown of Head: Scared to play, there's too much mental tension. Not having any fun. Stressed about what might go wrong. I can't do it. It's no fun.

Deep Breath: Breathe in and out.

Rate your intensity level after Round 1: Feeling a 6.

<u>**2) Acceptance:**</u>
Inside Eyebrow: Even though I'm feeling too much mental stress and tension, I accept myself exactly as I am.

Outside of Eye: Even though I'm not having any fun playing golf, I accept myself exactly as I am.

Under Eye: Even though there's too much mental tension, I accept myself exactly as I am.

Under Nose: Even though it's not fun, I accept myself exactly as I am.

Chin: Even though I have negative thoughts, I accept myself exactly as I am.

Collar Bone: I accept myself exactly as I am for thinking these negative thoughts.

Under Arm: Even though I am stressed thinking negatively on the outcome, and it kills to think this way, I accept myself exactly as I am.

Double Wrist: I accept myself exactly as I am for thinking negative thoughts and creating unwanted mental tension.

Crown of Head: I accept myself exactly as I am for not having any fun and making a mountain out of a molehill. I am choosing to acknowledge my fears and accept myself exactly as I am.

Deep Breath: Breathe in and out.

Rate your intensity level after Round 2: Feeling a 3, silly me.

3) Forgiveness:
Inside Eyebrow: Even though I am not having any fun, I forgive myself for feeling that way.

Outside Eye: I forgive myself for creating excess mental tension.

Under Eye: I forgive myself for thinking about a future outcome that I have perceived to be negative.

Under Nose: I forgive myself for thinking that I had to be perfect.

Chin: Even though my mind is racing with negative thoughts I forgive myself.

Collar Bone: I forgive myself for not having any fun and getting all worked up over a game that is supposed to be fun.

Under Arm: I forgive myself for having fearful thoughts about what could go wrong.

Double Wrist: Even though there's too much mental tension and I'm not having any fun, I forgive myself for thinking this way.

Crown of Head: I forgive myself for getting all worked up over a game that I love to play. I am choosing a new way to play this fun game. Golf is a great game and I am choosing to enjoy myself and have a better mindset. I'm choosing to believe in me.

Deep Breathe: Breathe in and out.

Rate your intensity level after Round 3: Feeling a 3.

4) New Positive Belief and Focus:
Inside Eyebrow: Golf is fun game.

Outside Eye: I love the game of golf.

Under Eye: I am focused and present in the moment.

Under Nose: I'm feeling calm and relaxed. Golf is a great game.

Chin: Calm, confident, relaxed.

Collar Bone: Feeling joy. I'm enjoying the moment.

Under Arm: Focused and present.

Double Wrist: Having fun. Having fun playing golf with my son.

Crown of Head: I love the game of golf. Golf is a fun game. I let every cell in my body resonate with good feeling thoughts. I enjoy the game of golf. I'm relaxed.

Deep Breath: Breathe in and out.

Rate your intensity level after Round 4: Feeling somewhere around a 2. I'm hopeful and I will practice this exercise again.

Coaching an Old Dog to Do New Tricks

Bill is a seventy-five-year old, fit-as-a-fiddle, ferryboat captain who works really hard on his game whenever he gets the opportunity. He works really hard when he is working at his job as well. He devotes 100 percent of his time and energy to whatever he is doing. He is a stubborn, relentless, and a never-give-up kind of gentlemen, which is most likely why he is so successful in business. He is also very gracious, giving, and hospitable to those closest to him. Family is very important to Bill. Bill has adopted a "Disney School of Service Magic" mentality having been a Disney school participant and one who integrates these exact concepts into his own business. He likes things to be done a very certain and particular way. Hence, perfectionism is an attribute he would like to bring to the golf course as well. The family motto is "PERFECT."

Bill would like to improve his length on certain shots, his golf scores, his confidence with certain clubs, his confidence with certain challenging lies, and his fear of not making the shot. He gets frustrated over his current level of play and his score. Bill is constantly thinking about how to play golf (even on the course); he's thinking about where his body should be; making the perfect shot, he's a paralysis-by-analysis type. I certainly can relate – been there a thousand times. Bill often plays two balls and hits a mulligan in trying to figure it out while on the course; little does he know how that is defeating his purpose, and this action is not making him a better golfer.

Coaches Notes: Although I certainly admit that *sometimes* a little practice on the course can be extremely beneficial. Find your balance between practicing on the course and playing the actual game of golf, which is played one stroke at a time. Sometimes we just have to bite the bullet and work through our challenges at another time, or like the professionals do – after their round is over. In other words, although re-do's would be nice, the rules of golf don't allow them, unless you count penalty strokes.

Bill also feels he sways too much and does not stay behind the

The Fairway of Life

ball at impact. He feels he sometimes has a poor swing. He wants to improve and he also understands that his age will not allow him too much time to reach his goals. And yet he adamantly refuses to believe his age is a deterrent to achieve the intended golf, which is to play better golf. Bill loves the game of golf.

So here's what we have with our friend, Bill:

1) Doesn't hit long enough. Feels if he hits it longer, he will lower his scores.
2) Wants to improve his golf scores.
3) Wants to have more confidence with certain clubs and certain shots.
4) Has some fear in not making the shot.
5) Gets frustrated over his current level of play and score.
6) Is constantly analyzing his swing on the course. Too many swing thoughts to mention.
7) Feels he sways too much and does not stay behind the ball at impact often enough.
8) Thinks he has a poor swing. Overly critical of himself.
9) There is an overwhelming drive of perfection that drives him to be perfect.
10) He is trying too hard. He sometimes struggles with his golf game.

I invited Bill over for a forty-five-minute coaching session and we ended up chatting well over three hours. The last half of our talk was about Service Magic. A topic we are both passionate about. I wanted to give Bill three things to begin working on and a couple action steps. Although I would like to do a round or two with him on the MEGT around his shot length, disappointment around his current level of play, and his score, I'm feeling that it is too early to go there right now.

Bill is like the majority of us. He likes to be in control and feels he can work it out, but maybe he'll *have too* "invest" in golf lessons. What I observe is that his thinking is mostly cerebral – left brain thoughts about his golf. And like most, when he plays well, 43 for

9 holes and below, he's happy, 44-46 he's okay; 47 and above he's not happy.

The three things I thought deserved attention were:

1) Set an intention to what kind of golfer you desire to be
2) Only one swing thought
3) Visualize your target and let it happen

The two action steps I suggested are:

1) Play one ball by the rules and post an honest score
2) Establish a handicap so we see exactly where we are

After some success in Florida over the winter Bill decided that he would go see Brian O'Neill, a well-respected PGA teaching professional. Brian taught with and under the tutelage of Jim Flick and uses video for show and tell. He then teaches each student practice exercises and the feeling of what that is like according to what he sees would benefit them. Bill was amazed at what he saw and knew why his swing had produced less than desirable results, i.e. shot length and inconsistency. Now in his mind he knows what he must do. He feels if he swings better he'll hit the ball better, he'll make better contact. "And once I feel it I can depend on it and then it's there. I've got to concentrate better, stay focused, and really see the ball instead of just looking at it. When I do all of these things I have better tempo and a slower backswing. I've hit some really good shots and it just feels good." Bill said he had not invested his time into lessons before and now his desire and willingness to get better is at an all time high.

I asked Bill if he is having any more frustration issues? Immediately he said, "I'm frustrated that I allowed myself to not concentrate, not have the correct thought process, that I get lax and lazy in my swing and sometimes I just lose my focus." I said and what do you think it will take for you to concentrate and focus? "I think dummy remember your swing, focus, see the ball, and keep concentrating." Subtly I asked him if calling himself a dummy or idiot does him any good? Remember the Phil Mickelson episode? He said, "Yes, but with me it's just a habit. It's not that big of a deal. It's over in a few seconds." So be it, then I asked him if there were any other frustrations? He said yes on certain kinds of shots. "The demons come back whenever I recall my bad experiences that I had on a particular hole or a particular shot. I tend to tense up and lose my focus and flow to my swing again." I asked him for specific shots that cause this. Immediately Bill went to two challenging approach shots where there is a hazard lurking. His frustration level increases whenever he's faced with a challenging shot where you absolutely have no room to bail right or left (the second shot on hole #2 at True North) or when you can't hit it right and going left is not so good either (the approach shot on hole #9 at True North). We also talked about similar examples on the par 3's. On certain holes of the same length he feels good over and usually gets good results. On other par 3's where there is more of a challenge (obstacles like water or sand traps) he tends to get poor results. The intensity of his emotions over these kinds of golf shots is very high. He's unable to swing fluidly because he has negative thoughts swirling around his brain prior to execution.

Since Bill is old school I proceed with the Mental Edge Golf Technique in surrogate form while sitting at the Thanksgiving dining room table turning down the volume on the television set having just watched the Detroit Lions take on another thrashin' this time by the Tennessee Titans. I tap he follows.

MEGT – Frustration on certain challenging shots, demons from past experiences

Rate your intensity level around this emotional issue from 1-10: Feeling an 8.

1) Acknowledgment:
Side of hand: Frustrated with challenging shots. Frustrated I lose focus. Frustrated with past demons. Frustrated with bad experiences on certain holes. Frustrated with my current level of play. I'm not good enough. Frustrated with my golf scores. It's not

good enough. Frustrated I can't play better. Frustrated with shot length and inconsistency. Feeling frustrated with my golf game.

Inside Eyebrow: Feeling frustrated with my golf game.

Outside of Eye: Feeling frustrated with challenging golf shots.

Under the Eye: Frustrated with my golf scores.

Under the Nose: Frustrated with my demons from past experiences.

Chin: Frustrated I lose focus.

Inside Collar Bone: Frustrated that I get lax and lazy.

Under Arm: Lax and lazy.

Double Wrist: Frustrated with my current level of play. I lose focus.

Crown of Head: Feeling frustrated with on certain shots. Feeling frustrated with past failure with my demons. Frustrated with my current level of play, and my golf scores. Feeling very frustrated.

Deep Breath: Breathe in and out.

Rate your intensity level after Round 1: We did not rate intensity levels until after we finished.

<u>**2) Acceptance:**</u>
Inside Eyebrow: Even though I'm feeling frustrated with my golf game, I accept myself exactly as I am.

Outside of Eye: Even though I'm feeling frustrated on certain challenging golf shots, I accept myself exactly as I am.

Under Eye: Even though I am not happy with my current level of play, I accept myself exactly as I am.

Under Nose: Even though I lose focus and concentration, I accept myself exactly as I am.

Chin: Even though I get lax and lazy and lose focus, I accept myself exactly as I am.

Under Arm: I accept myself for feeling frustrated over my current level of play.

Double Wrist: Even though I am feeling frustrated with certain challenging shots, I accept myself exactly as I am.

Crown of Head: Even though I've allowed the demons to get the best of me and I tense up and lose focus, and even though I am frustrated with my current level of play, my shot length and inconsistency, I accept myself exactly as I am.

Deep Breath: Breathe in and out.

Rate your intensity level after Round 2: Noticing acceptance.

3) Forgiveness:
Inside Eyebrow: Even though I lose focus on challenging golf shots I forgive myself.

Outside Eye: Even though I am not happy with my golf scores, I forgive myself.

Under Eye: Even though I am extremely frustrated with my current level of play, I forgive myself.

Under Nose: Even though I lose my concentration and forget to see the ball, I forgive myself.

Chin: I forgive myself for being frustrated with my golf scores.

Collar Bone: I forgive myself for being frustrated with my current level of play.

Under Arm: I forgive myself for trying to be perfect.

Double Wrist: I forgive myself for being frustrated and upset with myself on the golf course.

Crown of Head: I forgive myself for being frustrated over my shot length, my golf scores, and my current level of play. I forgive myself and I am choosing to experience myself in a much better way, a way that supports me for being more of who I really am.

Deep Breath: Breathe in and out.

Rate your intensity level after Round 3: Going along and following.

4) New Positive Belief and Focus:
Inside Eyebrow: I am focused.

Outside Eye: I'm playing golf to the very best of my ability.

Under Eye: I love the game of golf.

Under Nose: My technique continues to improve. I know what I have to do.

Chin: I'm calm and relaxed.

Collar Bone: I focus on my effort and being my best in the moment. I allow it to happen.

Under Arm: I play golf to the very best of my ability. I'm focused in the moment.

The Fairway of Life

Double Wrist: I enjoy the game of golf.

Crown of Head: Golf is a fun game and I being my absolute best.

Deep Breath: Breathe in and out.

Rate your intensity level after Round 4: Staying focused.

* I suggest one more round of New Positive Belief and Focus.

<u>**4) New Positive Belief and Focus:**</u>
Inside Eyebrow: I play golf to the very best of my ability.

Outside Eye: I get the most out of every shot.

Under Eye: My swing is fluid and has great timing and rhythm.

Under Nose: I concern myself with my effort.

Chin: My shot length is perfect for me.

Collar Bone: I'm in The Zone.

Under Arm: I'm playing to my full potential and I love it.

Double Wrist: Golf is a great game. I'm being my very best.

Crown of Head: I'm in The Zone and my swing is awesome.

Deep Breath: Breathe in and out.

Rate your intensity level after Round 5: Feeling much better. I do some of these things in my own way.

    With Bill we combined some of his issues in one and we could easily have created a separate technique for each issue. I suggest he does that on his own and I can help him create that. The more specific we are, the better the results.

Choking Down the Stretch

Chris is a forty-five-year-old golfer of ten years with high ambitions. He wonders why he chokes down the stretch, unable to finish the deal. Chris is a classic case of focusing too much on the outcome versus being present with his effort. His mind is racing too far ahead of himself as his hopes and wishes are to finish well, well before he has finished. He has taken himself out of The Zone. He's too concerned about finishing while he is still playing. He thinks: "If I par out or make a birdie, then I could shoot this score." Whenever that score is out of his Comfort Zone, more than likely he'll sabotage himself and return to what he is comfortable shooting. Chris plays impatient golf, often pressing too hard and wanting it so badly. My suggestion to him is to be more humble and more accepting. Playing golf in a more acceptance mode will actually help Chris achieve his goals more quickly.

Chris also plays golf against his opponents and allows this form of friendly competition to take away from him playing in the present moment against the course and within himself, doing his personal best and giving forth his best effort. Both of these scenarios, playing ahead of him self and playing against his opponents rather than against the course and himself, are outcome-based. A better scenario would be for him to give his best effort, focusing on this one very special play right here and right now. Instead, Chris finds himself getting sucked into playing against another with $5.00 or so on the line. And he actually relishes the side bet and feels it will make him a stronger golfer. I have no qualms with the friendly side bet unless the side bet gets the best of you. When winning or loosing the Nassau becomes the game, golf in the present moment takes a back seat. Soon you'll find yourself straying further away from The Zone and in to the game of ego.

MEGT – Effort versus Outcome

Rate your intensity level around this emotional issue from 1-10: I'm feeling at least an 8.

1) Acknowledgment:
Side of hand: Feeling concerned and nervous about my score. I think too far ahead of myself. I'm getting ahead of myself. I'm worried and concerned. I've taken myself out of the present moment. Worried and concerned about my score. I'm focused on the outcome. I get ahead of myself. I want it so badly. I want to win and score well. I'm scared.

Inside Eyebrow: I'm focused on my outcome.

Outside of Eye: I'm concerned about my score.

Under the Eye: Feeling worried and concerned about my score.

Under the Nose: I'm racing too far ahead of myself.

Chin: I'm not in the present moment. Feeling anxious.

Inside Collar Bone: Feeling anxious and nervous. It's too big.

Under Arm: Feeling anxious and scared.

Double Wrist: I'm way ahead myself; my mind is racing. I want it so bad.

Crown of Head: I want it so bad I end up pushing it further away. I'm concerned about my score. I get ahead of myself. I've taken myself out of the present moment and out of my zone. I'm focused on the outcome.

Deep Breath: Breathe in and out.

Rate your intensity level after Round 1: Feeling about a 5. I know I do this and it pisses me off.

2) Acceptance:
Inside Eyebrow: Even though I am so focused on the outcome, I accept myself exactly as I am.

Outside of Eye: Even though I am so concerned about my score, I accept myself exactly as I am.

Under Eye: Even though I am worried and concerned about my score, I accept myself exactly as I am.

Under Nose: Even though I feel nervous and scared about what I might shoot, I accept myself exactly as I am.

Chin: Even though I am nervous and scared and I get way ahead of myself, I accept myself exactly as I am.

Under Arm: Even though I take myself out of the present moment, I accept myself exactly as I am.

Double Wrist: Even though I get way ahead of myself wanting to do my very best, I accept myself exactly as I am.

Crown of Head: I accept myself exactly as I am for feeling nervous and scared and wanting to do my very best. I accept myself for getting too far ahead of myself and taking myself out of The Zone. I am accepting myself for being this way and not understanding how it works. I will be choosing another way that supports me in being my best.

Deep Breath: Breathe in and out.

Rate your intensity level after Round 2: Perhaps I'm feeling a 3-4.

3) Forgiveness:

Inside Eyebrow: Even though I am racing too far ahead of myself on the golf course, I forgive myself.

Outside Eye: Even though I find myself getting so focused on the outcome I forgive myself.

Under Eye: I forgive myself for being too far ahead of myself.

Under Nose: I forgive myself for being so anxious and nervous.

Chin: I forgive myself for being out of the present moment and so concerned about the outcome.

Collar Bone: I forgive myself for being so concerned and worried about the outcome.

Under Arm: I forgive myself for racing so far ahead of myself.

Double Wrist: Even though I find myself focusing on outcome and score, I forgive myself.

Crown of Head: I forgive myself for being all caught up in my score and feeling so anxious about it. I am choosing to stay present and to let it happen naturally. I am allowing myself to slow down and enjoy the present moment.

Deep Breathe: Breathe in and out.

Rate your intensity level after Round 3: Feeling a 2.

4) New Positive Belief and Focus:

Inside Eyebrow: I am responsible for my effort, not my outcome.

Outside Eye: I enjoy the present moment.

Under Eye: By enjoying the present moment, my score will take care of itself.

Under Nose: I am present.

Chin: I am focused upon my effort in the present moment.

Collar Bone: I am focused and present.

Under Arm: Feeling calm, focused, and present.

Double Wrist: I am responsible for my effort.

Crown of Head: Calm, focused, and present. I am enjoying my present moment. I am focused on being my very best in this very moment. Every cell of my body is present and functioning with maximum effort. I am present and focused upon my effort in the NOW. I play golf in the present moment and that feeling radiates throughout my body in a most glorious way. I am present and focused upon my effort right now.

Deep Breath: Breathe in and out.

Rate your intensity level after Round 4: Feeling a 1 to 2.

The Wind

Michael is a forty-five-year-old tennis player turned golfer. I played with Michael over Labor Day weekend in 2007 and we had a great time chatting on the course, more than Lee Trevino and Peter Jacobsen if you can imagine. Michael was Up North to do a Challenge Day Program for Petoskey High School. I invited him to be my guest at True North. After we came off hole # 13, the tricky par 3, I asked Michael, "How's it going, how are you feeling about your game?" He said something like, "I'm having fun, could be playing a little better, the wind is bothering me." Within moments I receive a call from Michelle, a performance coach from Canada. I introduce her to Michael and after he tells her the wind is bothering him some, she goes into a quick MEGT acknowledging Michael's frustration with the wind. I tap along over the speakerphone on my cell phone. After a short chat, we tee off on the next hole and we're off.

When we come off the green on hole # 17 I asked Michael about the wind. His response, no kidding, is, "What wind?" And we all get a big laugh. You see EFT and the MEGT has so many uses and it works on so many issues. Michael's response about the wind confirmed my belief even more.

Incidentally, it was interesting to hear what Paul Azinger and Tom Watson had to say about the wind at the 2008 Open Championship at Royal Birkdale with gusts over 40 mph. Azinger made reference to embracing the wind otherwise you're in for a long day, and Watson said to make the wind your friend.

Chipping Yips

Cary is a forty-four-year-old former University of Indiana collegiate player. He admits that his biggest weakness is his chipping and his short game just off the green. Cary often uses one hand on the club to play this shot, just to avoid his disappointment and embarrassment with his chipping. He's actually taught himself to play fairly well using the one-handed technique. His dad also plays one-handed golf because of a doctor's negligence at birth that severed a tendon in his shoulder. My suggestion is that Cary keep using this tactic in his practice, kind of like how you see John Daly and Loren Roberts practice putting. Perhaps we will someday slowly integrate the two-handed move back into his game, with the feeling that he is using one hand and the other is just a guide. Regardless, our intention is to help clear the mental block and emotional chaos within, freeing up and allowing a new more empowering belief and focus to take root.

Cary hesitates to admit he is deathly afraid of his short game. This fear is why he learned that in order to score well in college he *had* to hit practically every green in regulation to avoid the dreaded short chip around the green. He developed a fear and a belief that he simply could not get up and down to save his ass. He could skull it, chunk it, leave it short, pull it, push it, and practically any other scenario you can imagine. For Cary we delve deep into his emotions around his frustration and disappointment with this short game and once again apply the MEGT, feeling scared and anxious over my short game around the green. Although I am feeling extremely anxious with my chipping, I accept myself exactly as I am. Although I am feeling extremely disappointed with my short game, I forgive myself for allowing myself to feel that way. I am choosing to let go of this fear with a new more powerful, positive focus and belief: feeling confident, calm, and present with my short game.

When I performed this technique with Cary he actually enjoyed it. His intensity level dropped from a 9 – 8.5 down to about a 1.5. He also wanted to make a point that that was then and this is now. Back when he was playing highly competitive golf his emotions were all over the board and he would have done just about anything to improve himself. He says he's pretty content with how he now plays and to him golf is all about having fun. Therefore, he doesn't get too worked up over his golf.

Cary went on to make some interesting additional comments just after we finished the process. He made a point about how putting technique has changed over the years and no one really questions the confidence factor in these kinds of changes anymore. People putt cross-handed, craw-gripped, with belly-putters, and other forms of anchoring and steadying the putting stroke and no one talks about how these new forms of playing the shot are embarrassment issues anymore. I reminded Cary that the only thing that matters is to find out what works for you. He agreed and went on to say, "This is really about positive reinforcement. Since you are basically stuck with yourself, there's no sense for blame, guilt, or destructive feelings; you might as well embrace who you are and get out of your own way and let it happen. If I can hit the shot one-handed then I can hit the shot two-handed."

Pressure to Perform

Trish Garber is a fifty-five year-old business owner who has been playing golf since she was 11 years old. She's an avid golfer, very intense, and takes the game very seriously. She's a member at two clubs and her main goal is to become the club champion. Trish currently plays to 10-handicap, and the lowest she's been is a 7. She's all in when it comes to working through her demons. Trish also understands the principles of personal growth and success in her professional life. "I heard them before many times, now I just have to apply them to golf."

Trish's Story: "Sometimes I get so aggravated. Sometimes I get so nervous and scared; I end up choking and "throwing up" all over myself, especially in a big match – usually coming down the stretch, most often on the very last hole. It's all nerves. I can't seem to control my emotions. I'm a mental basket case. I beat myself up. I don't often forgive myself. I need help…lots of help. I just don't know what to do?"

I asked Trish to set an intention as to what kind of golfer she would like to be. At first being the club champion popped into her brain. Something she wants so badly that she ends up pushing it further away. She feels the lack of it too much. I suggested perhaps another intention. Trish said, like you, **"I'm going to drop my handicap to a 7 or less by July 4th."** Immediately she felt some trepidation. "It's like a chicken laying an egg or a pig going to slaughter," she said wittingly. Trish has a new commitment. What Trish really needed is a push outside her comfort zone, where new growth begins. Perhaps this will allow her the focus to stay on this goal of becoming a better golfer than she used to be, and let everything else take care of itself. As we enjoy, the scoring will take care of it self…and so will the championships. Play for the fun and joy, being clear and fully expecting – a vibrational match between your asking and allowing…and then let the results speak for it self after the match is over. What you're really asking from your self is to become the fullest expression of who you are as a golfer...your personal best! What does being your personal best look like? Go be that! And go show and tell another how to become their personal best.

Coaches Notes: I honor Trish for her honesty and willingness to put herself out there on the line. I recognize many of her traits that also lie within me. While words can only take us so far I am reminded of the greatest discovery in psychology in the 20th Century: We Become What We Think. "If you think you can or think you can't, you're both right," Henry Ford. What you give your thoughts and energy upon you become.

What Trish truly wants: "I want to play mentally tough golf and keep my nerves under control. I want to play like I know I can play."

What you're saying: Give me what I want...then I'll feel good.

What the universe *has been* hearing from Trish: I can't play to my full expression and potential because it's so hard.

How can I change: Trish has got to start telling a new story. Trish has got to start giving more "airtime" to what she prefers. She's got to first find some relief and soften the discomfort. Once she does find some relief (drop the oars so to speak), then she can find the space to celebrate her struggle realizing it was an opportunity for growth and move into the direction of what she prefers.

How can I do this: First acknowledge the idea that you've thought some thoughts that are hindering or sabotaging your desire to play well. In other words if you keep thinking about "what is" you keep getting more of "what is." Understand that you cannot deactivate a negative thought or belief. Trying to deactivate a negative thought only draws more of this experience into your life. Thinking more about "what is" only gives you more of "what is" and on and on and on we go.

How it works: You have to give more "airtime" to what you do desire or prefer, eventually squeezing out the old self-image lodged within our subconscious mind, which runs everything in our life, including our golf game. Be careful with how you are telling yourself a new story…any yeah, buts, yet, or I can't when ending your vibrational thinking or speaking kills the whole deal before it even has time to take root.

What can I do now: First, drop the oars. Stop paddling. Find some relief – soften your stance. Move into the direction of what you prefer. Tell a new story. Perhaps not the ultimate story of you playing in the final group and winning a major, just soften your stance, like it's okay that I'm not perfect, that I'm not all the way there yet. I'm choosing to enjoy this day, my friends, and simply be my best today. I'm choosing to allow the Well-Being in. I allow myself to be with whatever comes up – without judgment. Today I am an objective detective. I'm observing and learning from myself. No sense to take this too seriously, after all, no one else is taking me seriously. Life and golf are supposed to be fun. Today I am choosing to not get angry and simply enjoy. It's okay just the way it is and it's getting better.

What else can I do: Practice the art of feeling good no matter what. Practice the art of feeling good with eager anticipation. Practice the art of being fully present and enjoying this moment. Master the art of feeling good with your desire and the universe will give it to you. Feeling good = playing good…not the other way around. Practice the art of feeling good, no matter what. In other words, can I take the punch in the gut and still feel good? And please lighten up and don't take anything too seriously. It's about feeling good. Don't believe me, just be it for yourself and take notice. Lighten up, lighten up, lighten up – and not one ounce of competitor fire will ever leave you, perhaps your focus, joy, and going with the flow will increase. Let it happen versus trying too hard to force it to happen.

Observe, accept, and embrace all of your golf thoughts – just notice them, every golf lie – it's just a lie, and every golf shot – it's just a shot that I created from my own vibrationally energy. Shrug your shoulders more often, smile at what just happened, and laugh at your obstacles. Think like Tiger, how can I become better tomorrow, while enjoying today?

Mental Edge Golf Technique: I am working on several MEGT practices with Trish, teaching her how to do it on her own. Clearing the emotional chaos helps to pave the way for what Trish truly does desire. She can also stand a bit of acceptance and forgiveness. This is yet another form of softening your stance, clearing some of the stuck emotional energy lodged in her body, while integrating new more powerful beliefs and focus. What Trish is really aching for is to experience what her soul already knows – the grandest version of the greatest vision of who she really is. On the golf course she wishes to experience the freedom and her fullest expression, embracing the highs and lows along the fairway of life. Off the golf course Trish is an absolutely wonderful women showing respect and compassion in her business and personal life leading by her example.

Long Term Strategy: Keep dreaming your dream, visualizing and gravitating toward the picture you are painting. Long term and on-going strategy is training your subconscious mind into being mentally tough with positive focus and belief. We keep on depositing more positive mental thoughts squeezing out the old beliefs that no longer support us.

Trish sent me a quick e-mail from her recent golf match experience in Florida. "Well, living proof that it works. I won both my matches this weekend. I had to tap...because I had to get my nerves until control. I don't know which was responsible for the turnaround (the tapping or setting my intention)." As with everything, I remind Trish that it's all a process. Sounds like she is finding some relief and softening the edges. I'd still like her to focus more on the process; good set up; good alignment; good swing, and not worrying about where the ball is going, which is too much results-oriented. Once you get away from being results-oriented and more in tune with enjoying the process, then simply allow the shot to produce the swing. That's it – just this swing right here and right now. For now, I invite Trish to take some insights from the things Sean O'Hair is working on. One swing, one hole, one round at a time. Then after the year is over give your self some more feedback. It's a process Trish, one in which we go through the experience on our own. Relax and go with the flow.

- Good set up
- Good alignment
- Good swing

Sometimes, these gentle reminders take off the edge; they keep us more in the present. Sometimes we just have to keep it SIMPLE.

Becoming a Better Golfer – an Epiphany

"Hi Rand, I'm excited to share a breakthrough I've recently experienced. First, thank you for your commitment to yourself, the game of golf, and to this amazing website and golf blog…I am inspired and it's time for a change!

My game has been the same for 10 years or more, as you know, pretty stagnant. Sure, I've had a few decent rounds, but for the most part I've hovered around the low to mid 90's. Through your guidance, however, I've chosen to step out of myself to observe who and how I've been being, on and off the course. Like most, I've always wanted to score better, but I can see now that my approach to the game is what has hindered me. Every time I've played in the past, I've gone to the course carrying my baggage (not my golf bag); fear, doubt, worry and pride. 'What if I play bad? I don't want to lose money! Will people get upset if I suck?' Sometimes I could hide these inevitable landmines, and begin with a couple pars, possibly even a birdie, but sooner than later the demons would surface and get the best of me...all because of my "concern" of being able (or not) to shoot a low score. The focus of my game was always the score, never on really enjoying myself, the camaraderie of friends and being grateful for the beautiful surroundings. Even when I tried to tell myself to relax and enjoy, my subconscious was constantly talking about score, score, score! I had to "look good" and thought I could only be happy if I played well. Consequently, every bad shot, bad hole and bad round left me disappointed, again.

I remember playing an outing with 8-10 guys at Pine Knob, and being so disgusted with my game that afterward I got in my car and left without a word to anyone...what a loser! Another round I threw my 4-iron into a 40 ft. pine tree surrounded by Junipers, and never found it. I couldn't have been a good sport if I tried.

The last couple years though I've found peace with letting go of worrying about the outcome, even when I knew I wanted to "look good" but couldn't. My mind was made up that 'my score is my score, so I'll just accept it.' This did give me relief, although it didn't lower my score. I simply resigned myself to the fact that I sucked no matter how hard I tried, so I might as well get used to it and enjoy myself anyway. I decided to just give up on even trying as soon as my game went to hell (which was usually on the front nine), and drink away my misery on the back.

That was then, this is now. As we talked about last night, I've never been so inspired and excited about my game. Your guidance and wisdom hit me like a brick Rand, and I got it. I got that "Going With the Flow" means going with the flow of life, realizing and understanding that we are all connected to the omnipotent Energy of the Universe/God, and by virtue of the Law of Attraction and Deliberate Creation, we are creating our own reality every day! Our thoughts, words, feelings and emotions are all energy, so that which we radiate draws back to us an equal energy in response. So, I get now how I can harness this amazing power that we all have, and use it to my advantage in my golf game, as well as in life. I'm vibrating like crazy, knowing now that I can go out to the course with confidence, and play a game with myself, inside of my game and actually have fun.

I heard Jack Nicklaus say, during an event a few weeks ago, something I had never considered in my 25 years of playing, something you've also suggested. He always first visualized the end result of every shot, and then the flight or the roll of the shot finishing, and then let the picture create the swing. Wow, what a concept. I've felt that my visualization was good, but I never let go and surrendered my swing. I always tried to control it, and there in fact was the problem.

I had an epiphany, in realizing the problem and understanding the power of the solution. Never before have I had the genuine confidence to say that I could break 80, and now I know that I can and I will, this summer. The idea for me is to play a game with myself, within my game. I'm excited knowing that all I have to do is let go of the "score" and trust that my visualization and alignment with Well-Being will lead the way. In this knowing, I accept that I will have good shots and bad, I am where I am and it will take time to improve...and I will! So each round will be a game for me to become aware and observe myself in action, focus on each shot (not even the hole), accept the outcome without attachment and practice being grateful, for my friends, the surroundings and my growth. Feeling good and accepting the results will naturally lead to a better game, and the better it gets the better it gets. I already know it's going to work because I remember clearly instances in the past when I called shots beforehand (being cocky), and to my amazement they manifested...instantly! Had

I only understood the power that's been harnessed and patiently awaiting to assist...but that's okay, I'm perfectly fine with it. I've come to the realization that being happy is more important than being a "low score" whether I accomplish it or not, so my key to enjoying golf and life, is to unconditionally accept my game exactly as it is, and exactly as it is not. And for that, I am grateful.

Thanks my Friend, you're the best!"
David Zmikly

"The will is greater than the skill!"
—Muhammad Ali

Wow! Isn't that the truth! I'd say for the most part, like Crosby, Stills, Nash, & Young, we have all been here before. Deja Vu. Espavo David! Thank you for sharing so candidly, honestly, and openly. The intention is to allow others the opportunity to begin their own process of becoming better than they used to be - no better than anyone else. What a wonderful epiphany to start the 2009 golf season!

Incidentally, after completing our 2009 7-week Mental Edge Golf Coaching Program, David went on to shoot the best round in his life, an 82. He tapped in to the abundant flow of Well-Being and went with the flow. He says, "It's amazing how easy it is; I can't believe I didn't do this, or think like this before – applying these spiritual laws and life principles to the game of golf. This is awesome. I am so grateful Master." And that's exactly how it happens, it just sort of sneaks up on you when you align, connect, and commit to Source Energy through your higher Self...tough to sometimes explain miracles too – yet, everything is a miracle. This understanding is paradigm shifting. It's a complete transformation in the way we perceive our world and our selves. Thank you David, your confirmation is so appreciated in more ways than one.

Ultimate Coaching

In ultimate reality it is not our job to help or fix anybody. Perhaps we get them to another level...perhaps not. Yet we are always planting a seed. What I find most gratifying is when I have worked with another and they take on the responsibility of their own growth experience. For it is not the one with the most students, but the one who creates the most Masters.

True non-bias coaching simply guides and supports another allowing them to choose and pick whatever comes up. The session starts out with everyday common language like, "What's up with you golf game dude?" That's how my coach Jim Fritz began his life coaching sessions, "What's up dude?" From there it just evolves to wherever the coaching unfolds naturally – the coach asking "what type" questions and the student simply going within answering with whatever is coming up. If ever you get stuck, remind yourself or another with the phrase, "But if you thought you knew...what would that be, what would that look like?" It's about keeping on...

Whatever specific issue is bothering you and giving you fits of frustration, merely apply EFT or, if it is a golf specific issue, apply the MEGT. You will be amazed at how the intensity level drops and you can return to the state of being that supports you in being your very best. From the first tee jitters to the yips MEGT greatly reduces the emotional intensity freeing us up to play our best. I invite you to apply this technique to your specific issue and experience the difference. It's quick, it's easy, and it's simple to use. You can even shorten the session when out on the course.

Whenever I am beginning to feel anxious over a tee shot, a second or third shot, a tough chip, or an upcoming putt, I simply do a quick ten to twenty-second fix.

MEGT – The quick ten to twenty-second fix

Step 1: First, take two deep breaths. Inhale from lower abdomen area up to your upper chest and let it out slowly. Pay attention to your breath. This begins the process of grounding and bringing yourself back to the present ... calm mind, calm body...calm body, calm mind.

Step 2: Walk slowly and feel your feet firmly planted on the earth. Pay attention to the heel-toe movement and feel yourself in the present moment.

Step 3: Listen for sounds through the air. Hear the wind, the trees swaying, the leaves rustling, a squirrel playing, birds chirping or any other voices that allow you to become fully present.

Step 4: Feel the temperature of the air. Pay attention to your body being fully present.

Step 5: Notice and observe your environment. See the beauty all around you. Become fully present.

Step 6: Begin a short ten-second MEGT. Tapping on the side of your hand say, **"Let it be easy."** Tapping on the side of your eye, **"Let it be easy."** Tapping on your collarbone, **"Let it be easy."** And finally, tapping on your double inside wrist, **"Let it be easy."**

If tapping visually in front of others is embarrassing, imagine you are tapping in your mind and it still works the same.

There you have it; a quick ten to twenty-second technique that will reduce the intensity level of feeling anxious over any particular shot. Is it a perfect science? Will it reduce your anxiety levels of intensity? Will it allow you to be a better golfer and shoot lower scores? You be the observer of that. All I know is that I would pay big money to use whatever allows me to be more calm, confident, relaxed, and having fun allowing the Well-being in. Remember either you are allowing the Well-being in or you are resisting it.

And just remember: everything in life and on the golf course is temporary (this too shall come to pass) and if we allow ourselves the opportunity we can move quickly through the negative experience and back up the scale of our emotions back to being more content, optimistic, appreciative and joyful. Any move up the scale feels better than where you were before. Little by little we end up clearing these negative emotions and replacing them with new more empowering beliefs and focus. Little by little we end up catching ourselves much sooner before we dip into negativity. Little by little we create more of a champion's self-image. We play more consistent and better golf.

Tiger's golf psychology: Very similar to what I just told you above. Perhaps because Tiger practices this it may add even more credibility.

One of the golf psychology methods used by Tiger and Steve is something so simple and can easily be practiced by anyone. Now, remember don't just try this once and say it doesn't work. These methods need to be practiced and employed on a regular basis just like the golf swing.

Have you ever played in a big tournament or money game and found it harder to hit the same quality shots you hit playing with friends or with no pressure on? Even tour players do, and to overcome this, here is a method I've found Tiger and Steve use. Now remember you need to practice this golf psychology just as if you were practicing your swing. In fact while practicing your swing is a good time to employ these methods.

What happens under pressure is we tend to get in our own way, we over think. What needs to be done is allow the subconscious mind to have control and leave the conscious mind out of the swing. Even though few of us if any, have the ability of Tiger, we will all achieve better results by staying more relaxed over shots and not over thinking.

Here is one method Tiger uses. The one thing Tiger and Steve do after Tiger hits a shot is to never discuss golf or the golf swing between shots. The one thing golf psychology teaches is to take the conscious mind out of the swing. Instead they may talk about a movie, sports event; they even talk about people in the gallery while walking to their ball, anything but golf.

The first thing Tiger does when he gets to the ball is to check the lie. He looks to see if the grass is wet or dry, is there grass around the ball or is it on hardpan. In his eyes there is no such thing as a good lie or a bad one. The lie is what it is and he accepts it in this order but first he will listen to noises around him, sometimes both near and far.

After evaluating the lie he begins a process that involves all his senses. Maybe it's a bird chirping or a train whistle blowing in the distance. Next he will smell odors in the air, the fragrance of flowers or burgers cooking on the grill. He feels the air, is it moist or dry, warm or cool, and last he will visualize the shot. Not only does he visualize it in the air, he visualizes where it will land and where it will roll out too. Now he is ready to hit the shot.

Talk to Yourself Quietly

Another short positive tactic that I use whenever I am feeling a bit out of sorts, or I wish to ground myself, is that I will talk to myself without anyone hearing me. I might say something to the effect of my appreciation to God or Source Energy, such as: "Thank you for allowing the Well-being in"; "I allow the Well-being in"; "feel the Well-being." What this does is ground myself back into the present and allows me to hopefully break down any resistance that I am feeling. I know I am either allowing the Well-being in or I am resisting it. I did this over a long 45-foot putt for birdie on golf hole #8 at True North, a long uphill par 5, and I ended up making the putt. My golfing partners did not see the putt go in. As I was walking up to take my ball out of the hole, Matt said, "Did you just make that?" With appreciation I certainly did. I gave thanks and off I went shooting a 75 and winning some money for my score and my skin on hole #8. That's part of the secret. I was feeling good and I gave thanks and appreciation…thank you God.

Many times I will find myself saying, "Let it be easy." Sometimes I use the Muhammad Ali mantra whenever I'm feeling slightly nervous. Just before stroking my putt I'll say to myself over and over, "My will is greater than my skill." Breathe deeply and stroke your putt after you have let out your breath. It's how the Army teaches you to pull the trigger on your M-16. You're more relaxed at that moment. Whatever you do, breathe; there is no reason to hold your breath unless you're swimming under water or practicing a breath exercise for meditation.

Use whatever tactic you can to keep yourself in the present moment and feeling good. I always seek to reach for a better feeling thought whenever my mind noise is wreaking some havoc within. No, it's not a perfect science, yet I am becoming better than I used to be. Imagine where Tiger is with his mindset and mental toughness. We can all aspire to become better than we used to be. It's a process . . . it's called keeping on.

> **Simple Secret Reminder # 30 – My Will is Greater Than My Skill**
> **Think of Ali being a champion!**

Expect to Win

Lee Janzen has used the mantra, "I will win again; I will win again" between his U.S. Open championships. Lee won the U.S. Open in 1993 and again in 1998. It's essential to think I can and I will. The universe delivers to us a perfect match every time. We end up believing our own expectations we have of ourselves. Some pros just want to make the cut; some want to finish in the top whatever, others want to win majors, and still others want to win every time going away by a large number – that's Tiger.

What is your expectation and vibration that you are offering? What is it that you believe it is possible to become? It's all relative to you. There's BIG stuff here. In your wisdom lies the answer. It's no secret anymore. I am, I can, and I will. Visualize and become it. You draw into your experience more and more momentum of thought from visualizing upon your desires. Soon you simply become that.

Visualize

Tiger Woods will visualize his entire round in his mind before he even plays. He will plan his course management and strategy before he even puts a tee in the ground. Each and every hole he will play out in his mind's eye and he will involve all his senses and intuition. I am suggesting you do the same. Play an entire round of golf in ten to twelve minutes, or however long it takes. Have fun with it.

Visualize and see where you want the ball to go. Involve all your senses. Feel the wind. Feel the weather. Smell the grass. Feel your body actually making that athletic move. Feel the contact as you drive through the ball. Hear the sound of a well-struck shot. Feel your balanced finish. Hear the sounds of nature. Hear your voice talking quietly to yourself. Involve your intuition. Feel the positive vibrational energy and alignment. Allow the Well-Being to flow to you and through you. Feel the appreciation. Feel the joy. Feel the love.

Coaches Notes: If by chance you find yourself with doubts or fears of what you cannot achieve in your visualization, practice MEGT and clear those emotions as well. If you find yourself in denial or thinking you are only fooling yourself, identify and clear those emotional issues. They are all in your mind and they are only illusions that you have allowed to be part of your experience. Replace them with positive beliefs and a new focus. You can be, do, or have whatever you desire.

Once you've played out your entire round and you are feeling good, keep on holding the vision. Visualize, visualize, visualize. Involve all your senses and keep feeling the good feeling thoughts. Good feeling thoughts create good, feeling swings. This exercise will not only ground you in the present, it will keep you calm, confident, and focused.

When it is time to play your round you are now eagerly anticipating a great day. Carry that positive attitude with you the entire round. Embrace and accept all your golf shots. Believe in yourself. Believe your feel is always there and allow the Well-Being in. Always believe your Well-Being will flow and get better throughout your round. Open the floodgates.

Visualize each shot a good five to ten seconds before each shot.

The Fairway of Life

Visualize where you want the ball to go. Visualize the type of shot. See the ball flight and ball landing. Feel the energy within you. Feel your confidence. Believe in yourself. Allow your body to just let it happen. It's easy. You're in The Zone...licking your chops.

Play games with yourself. Imagine a freeway and see your ball racing down the fairway. Imagine the goal post of trees and see the field goal. Pick a spot, like a tree, a 150 pole, or a mound and play to it or over it. Pick a spot on the green, see the path, feel the stroke, and let it happen. Talk to yourself with belief and trust. Let it happen. You're feeling it. You're in The Zone. Golf and life is good!

Pre-Shot Routine

Your consistent pre-shot routine is yet another strategy to visualize, to calm, and relax yourself. It sets the tone for your state of being, and also keeps you grounded and centered in the present. Nick Faldo speaks about this mindset all the time. Here are a couple examples from golf professionals as they describe their pre-shot routine.

Jack Nicklaus has won eighteen majors and numerous golf tournaments. He's one of the greatest golfers ever to play the game. Nicklaus has shared his mental game of golf in numerous interviews, books and among his friends. His mental toughness is what kept him playing like a champion for six decades. He passes this mental wisdom on to us as well. Nicklaus states four things he did while playing each shot:

1) I never hit a golf shot without having a sharp picture of it in my head.
2) First, I "see" where I want the ball to finish.
3) Then I "see" it going there, its trajectory and landing.
4) The next "scene" shows me making the swing that will turn the previous images into reality.

In his book *Golf My Own Damn Way: A Real Guy's Guide to Chopping Ten Strokes Off Your Score,* John Daly reiterates the importance of a pre-shot routine as well. He says, "Never, ever hit a shot without going through your pre-shot drill. Not on the practice range, and certainly not on the golf course either. Your pre-shot drill is critically important to your golf game because it focuses your mind on all the keys to putting a good swing on the ball." He goes on to say:

1) Stand behind my ball and set my target line. Mr. Harvey Penick said it best, "Take dead aim."
2) Visualize my shot soaring through the air exactly on line and trajectory that feels best for the situation.
3) Walk up to my ball and take my stance: square alignment, feet parallel to target line.
4) Check my ball position: off inside left heel for driver, more towards the center as the club I'm using gets shorter.
5) Check my upper body: arms hanging straight down from shoulder, hands in perpendicular line with chin and ground.
6) Check my ball position by imagining a line straight up at a 90-degree angle from the ground: if it touches inside my chin, it's too close, outside my forehead, too far away.
7) Check my grip: the V's formed by my thumbs and first fingers are pointing just right of my chin.
8) Look/Waggle. Look down the target line, then back at my ball, and waggle my club head over it. Four looks, three waggles. No waggle after fourth look. Time to let 'er rip.
9) Exert slight (slight!) increase in grip pressure on fourth look. I'm reluctant to include this, because I've made such a big deal of you relaxing your grip. But for me, an ever-so-slight increase in grip pressure is my way of saying it's time to get down to business. You know, Grip It and Rip It.

Daly continues, "As I said, that's my pre-shot drill. Looks like it takes forever, but it really doesn't, you will soon learn to do it without thinking but one must always remember to do it. And while I might shorten my pre-shot drill some with middle and short-irons, I always follow it to the letter when I hit driver. You don't have to copy it. Prefer three looks and two waggles? Two and one? Be my guest. It all depends on what you're comfortable with. Just don't try to get away with, say, ten looks and nine waggles. If you were to do that at the Lion's Club in Dardanelle (Ark.), I'd have to get someone to politely ask you to remove your butt from the course – unless your playing partners hadn't already come up the side of your head with a 2-iron. But whatever mix you settle on, go through your pre-shot drill every time. Trust me–grooving your pre-shot drill will help your groove your golf swing."

Enhance Your Visualization with Affirmations
Let It Be Easy

We become even more powerful in the face of our fears or doubts or even when we are feeling extremely confident when we have a sense that we make a difference in the world. Affirmations of purpose or intent communicate the truth that we are all meaningful, valued, and worthy participants in the game of golf and life. We are here to appreciate life, enjoy our chosen experiences, and give and receive love.

We can enhance and expand our experience on the golf course through all inclusive visualization techniques with life and specific golf affirmations:

1) Thank you God, let it be easy.
2) I know that I am valued, let it be easy.
3) I spread peace, harmony, and joy, let it be easy.
4) I see it, feel it, and trust it, let it be easy.
5) I am a healing force; let it be easy.
6) I read it, roll it, and hole it, let it be easy.
7) I spread warmth and love everywhere I go, let it be easy.
8) I believe in me, let it be easy.
9) Thank you universe; let it be easy.
10) Thank you guardian angels; let it be easy.
11) I feel the joy, let it be easy.
12) It is easy, and I am loved, valued, and worthy.
13) It is easy, and I make a difference.

14) It is easy, and my life has meaning.
15) It is easy, I see it, feel it, and trust it

It will all seem far easier, when you keep in mind, all of the time, that it is easy. Life is supposed to be fun and visualization is the surest, fastest, and most ingenious way, between here and there. Let it be easy.

Okay, we've come a long way and now I'm thinking about your game. I've been thinking about it a lot. I've been thinking about how you are being with all of this. Yes, I am speaking to each and every one of you. I am even considering how all of this will affect other aspects of your life in wonderful, unforeseen ways as well. Do you realize how magnificent you really are? I even imagine you already own it; you're already on your way becoming it. I vividly see you enjoying your golf game and life outside the ropes; your heart racing with joy; your friends and the pro talking; your playing partners gawking. I can hear their ooohs and ahhhs. I can feel the high-fives and the knuckles, and I can taste the thrill of success on your lips. Yes, life really is good and you are so magnificent.

Visualize all of it NOW. It's about feeling good NOW. We gravitate towards what we feel, vibrate, visualize, and think. We become what we think about ourselves. Reach for the best feeling thoughts you can. Not necessarily the ultimate of the ultimate, just the best feeling thought you can right now. Get yourself up to speed with who you have become.

Visualization works in so many ingenious ways. We can visualize our dreams, our intentions. We can visualize our entire round before we play. We can visualize each shot seconds before we actually play. We can visualize vividly how we desire to play involving all our senses and really feel and taste the good feeling thoughts. We can visualize what we desire while being in the present with eager anticipation. We become what we think. Good feeling thoughts; create good feeling swings. It is all a process and visualization is yet one more tool to put into your bag of tricks. VISUALIZE!

"When you visualize, then you materialize. If you've been there in the mind you'll go there in the body."
—Denis Waitley

> **Simple Secret Reminder # 31 – Visualize Good Feeling Thoughts**
> **Good feeling thoughts; create good feeling swings.**

Understanding a Golfer's Scale of Emotions

Remember while playing golf in The Zone we are playing without emotions, we are being practically, if not completely, emotionless. We are simply being. We are being calm, relaxed, confident, joyful, present, and fun-filled. When we are in The Zone we simply experience our own bliss and Well-Being, our natural state of being. We transcend our personal self into our higher Self. We move from ego, personality, fears, and mind noise into a higher state of consciousness bliss where life becomes effortless, oneness, with ease, peace, and all motion becomes artistic and graceful, like Jordan, Gretzky, Ali, or Woods; the opera singer or the waitress. This is a place where we get out of our head and into The Zone. It's our most heartfelt talent or gift that flows to us and through us. There is an internal knowingness and a flow as we step back into The Zone, our natural state of being; it is a place that is always shining. It clicks.

"I'd say, 'Tiger, I promise you,'" Earl says as we look upon his son's unmistakably steely gaze, '"That you'll never meet another person as mentally tough as you in your entire life.' And he hasn't. And he never will."
— Earl Woods

"I refuse to give into fear, real or imagined, or to be afraid either consciously or unconsciously of anything or anyone."
—Tiger Woods

Pretty strong!

Golfers Scale of Emotions

Our golfer's scale of emotions is simply another tool to appreciate how life really works if we allow that to be. I observe so many hanging on to their frustration that they simply will not allow themselves to move up the scale. They are so angry and frustrated with their golf game; they hold themselves in this space for far too long, often ruining more golf holes then necessary, sometimes the rest of their entire day. In the worse case scenario people quit playing golf because it's so damn frustrating, and they're just not going to take it anymore!

I invite you to accept, embrace, and allow yourself to move through your frustrations if you find yourself in whatever space you are currently residing that just doesn't feel good. Simply be with wherever space you are in right now; notice; observe; and witness yourself. As you do, you will move back up the scale. As you move up the scale perhaps you will find yourself playing better golf. Perhaps you will find yourself playing in The Zone once again, simply another tool to embrace your emotions and say good-bye to your fears. Remember: change is inevitable, nothing is permanent, do not be attached to anything for this too shall come to pass. Embrace all of it – Namaste!

> **Simple Secret Reminder # 32 – Choose To Feel Better**
> **Choose to feel better and you'll move back up the scale.**
> **Change is inevitable; nothing is permanent, let go of your attachments.**

Coaches Note: This list of twenty-two emotions on a scale below comes from Esther and Jerry Hicks and their wonderful book, *Ask and It is Given*. The same principles apply to golf as they apply to life. Simply allow yourself whatever moments you need and then move up the scale. What I found amazing in life and on the golf course was that it actually does feel better when moving up from say, feeling doubt, to being disappointed. Emotions, like anything in life, are short-lived and these too shall come to pass. The more you practice these principles throughout this book (which are just reminders), and with all the knowledge and wisdom you have been born with, the more often you reside in the top side of this scale. The more often you feel good. Not to say that I never find myself in the lower half on occasion from time to time. Whenever I find myself in the lower half I know now that my soul is urging me on to get back up to speed with who I have become, to choose better feeling thoughts and to get back on my own true path, the one I have chosen for myself, the path that I have asked to experience myself as. There is joy in knowing that! Your emotions and feelings become your internal guidance system, and they are a perfect compass to give you direction and purpose and meaning to life. Yes, your purpose is to create your purpose. The mystery is solved in one feel swoop. And you can take that to the bank!

1) Love/ Joy / Empowerment / Freedom / Knowledge / Appreciation
2) Passion
3) Enthusiasm
4) Positive belief and expectation
5) Optimism
6) Hopefulness
7) Contentment
8) Boredom
9) Pessimism
10) Frustration / Irritation / Impatience
11) Being Overwhelmed
12) Disappointment
13) Doubt
14) Worry
15) Blame
16) Discouragement
17) Anger
18) Revenge
19) Hatred / Rage
20) Jealousy
21) Insecurity / Guilt / Unworthiness
22) Fear / Despair

Action steps:

1) Walk with your fears. Practice being with your negative emotions and observe yourself moving up the emotional scale. If and when your fears arise, I am inviting you to allow yourself to be with your fears. Acknowledge your fears. Accept your fears. Own your fears. Be with your fears and forgive yourself for feeling afraid. Walk with the roar of the lion in your face and your fears will disappear. It is only when we run away from that which we perceive is scary will it persist. We are to learn about fear, not how to escape it. Escaping fear is only a temporary bandage fix. Walking with our fears rather than resisting them, allows them to be acknowledged and welcomed showing us the way to our true higher Self. You can be, do, or have whatever you desire. It's all about keeping on.
2) Practice and experience whatever technique or pre-shot routine works for you, both on the range and on the golf course.
3) Visualize, visualize, visualize!
4) Keep on creating your internal champion's self-image.
5) Practice choosing to feel better.
6) Have fun!

Chapter 14

Let Time Serve You

"Time is the most precious element of human existence. The successful person knows how to put energy into time and how to draw success from time."
—Denis Waitley

How do you spend your time?
Do you serve time or does time serve you?

In my work with clients and in the observation of my own life, I've discovered that the concept of time affects us all. Now, how are we going to handle it? What choices are we going to make? How many times are we going to hear, there's no time? I don't have the time. How many times are we going to hear about all these excuses about where you're going to find the time because you have all of these other commitments?

Look, I do not have any easy answers for you because, quite frankly, the answer and wisdom lies within you. However, if you do use time as an excuse, then your thoughts "about" time is what you will get! If you think you don't have the time, then you won't. If you think that time is holding you back, then it will. If you truly want to do something...*you will find the time*. What is it that you are more committed too? Perhaps a better way to look at time is to ask your self, how can I spend my time more effectively, more productively?

It sounds ironic but often if we are not doing something that we think we want to do, we are actually more committed to doing something else. So, let's be clear about that. Everyone's got excuses, justifications, rationalizations, and often an outright defense mode when discussing the subject and apparent "scarcity" of time. Everyone has the same amount of time. There are twenty-four hours in everyone's day, another one of our man-made constructions, ☺. You might say, "But, my job is different can't you see, I don't have the time!" Yeah, you're right, you just told me so! Get up earlier, practice later, change your schedule, change your job, peel yourself away from the computer or the television screen, or better yet, change your mindset. Get *really* clear about what you desire and you will find the time.

Coaches Notes: Guess what is the biggest illusion about time? Time doesn't exist. WHAT? Yep, time is here right now, standing still, going nowhere. It is us who are moving through time. Just imagine yourself in a big sphere going about your business moving through each experience. Time goes nowhere, you move through time, like corridors through a hallway. Each corridor represents how you spent your time, whereas, time did not go anywhere. Well enough of the esoteric, even though quantum and metaphysics is one of my favorite subjects. The idea is to wake you up! Let's see if we can get time to serve you better. Are you open?

Is the concept that you don't have enough time giving you a charge, making you feel important, like you've got to get things done – the garden needs tending, the kitchen floor, the television, stock market, exercise, kids, etc.? If it does then that's the problem. Look, I'm not saying these things are not important, yet isn't there a little bit of drama created around how busy, busy, busy you seem to be – always feeling like there's not enough time? If you like what you are choosing then don't complain about *there's just not enough time*? Either find the time to do what you say you want to do *or* make peace with how you are choosing to spend your time.

You have the power within you to choose the way you spend your time. You have the power to choose your work, your career, your mate, your family, your home, your health, and your fun and leisure. Nothing is keeping you stuck except yourself. If you think you can't change, then you're right. "What about my house, my mortgage payment, my kids, and my retirement; don't you see there's no time!" Remember, you chose all of it. You can choose again. You can serve time or make time serve you. Like I said, I don't have your answer, yet I do know that if you truly do want something bad enough you will find the time. And you can be, do, or have whatever you want. And all of this dialogue around time is yet another subtle reminder to be at peace with our self.

How do you change your attitude and belief around the concept of time? How do you find the power to change? First, you have to be honest with yourself. Let's cut through your important priorities. Let's cut through rationalizations and justifications. Let's get real, shall we? Once we can see and observe ourselves exactly as we are, taking full responsibility for our decisions, choices, wants, and desires we melt away the illusion of our internal drama. Once I finally got the understanding that it is my choice in how I spend my time and it is my choice whether I am more committed to what I "kind of" of want (becoming a better golfer, more loving husband, taking better care of my health) or what I actually do like doing (cutting my grass, weeding the garden, tinkering with other projects, watching TV), then I can honestly go about my business without any blames, excuses, or poor me's. Most likely we don't do certain things because we really don't want too, and we are more committed to other things. In other words, if you want your cake and to eat it too – then make a commitment and let time serve you. There's always enough time. The same goes for the amount of "time" you spend preparing mentally and with all the techniques or practices you very well could put into place that will make you a better golfer. You know the old saying, think what you've always thought and you will get what you've always gotten. So instead, get really clear about your intention and you will become much more productive in being it, practicing it, and living it.

Finding Time

Karen is in her forties, raising three kids on her own. Her dream of running in the Olympics has passed but now she has new aspirations. Karen trains for fitness competitions. Either she gets up at 5:30 A.M. to get in her workout, or she trains in the early evening, just after her kids are all fed and settled in. Karen finds the time. She doesn't complain nor is she not getting in her proper workouts. Let her example be a guiding light. Most often people who say they don't have time really don't want to do whatever it was in the first place, otherwise they would. How committed are you?

Chris is a busy ferryboat captain. His job requires him to work a lot of hours in the summer months and he's exhausted after his day is done. He stills finds the time to practice his putting or work on his game for an hour or two in the evening just before dark. He's committed to becoming a better golfer.

Rob is a schoolteacher who works at the golf course cutting cups in the summer. He gets up early, which allows him to play later. Or he gets up early to play golf on his days off and be with his family later. He finds the time to practice, to play golf, be with his family, and do what he loves to do. He makes it work.

Clean Up the Emotional & Physical Clutter

One of the first strategies I recommend to people who don't seem to find the time is to clean up the clutter within their life, which allows them to get up to speed with the present moment. The clutter in our life can be past events in which we can make peace with, or it can be the clutter in our immediate vicinity – the things we see everyday that drain our energy. Our clutter can be emotionally draining when we procrastinate and it can take some physical work, like cleaning out the closets or basement. Find one project and complete it before moving on. There's tremendous wisdom in this one simple concept.

Find a way to make peace with all your emotional clutter of the past – the things we chatted about in the Introduction and in the beginning of this book, things like our shadow, our past detrimental behaviors, and our relationship issues – not a small task, yet it can be done with one person or one issue at a time – just understand that all of it is leading us to higher ground.

I also invite you to begin the process of cleaning the clutter in your house. That's right, all those old clothes you never wear anymore, all those boxes filled with stuff you'll never use, your closets, your garage, your workroom—clean it *all* up. Have a garage sale or give it to charity. Once we get ourselves up to speed with being in the present, we can turn old negative draining energy into new more powerful living in the now.

According to the Chinese philosophy of Feng Shui, all this clutter does is block our *chi*, our vital life energy. We don't need all this "stuff" holding us back. So de-clutter around your home and get yourself up to speed, feeling good living in the present. Old unfinished projects and clutter keep us stuck in a rut. Find one project to work on, and when you finish it, just notice the way you feel. Perhaps one positive change may lead to another?

Another tenet of Feng Shui is to create peace, harmony, and joy in our life through the energy of where we live and who we are. Put out candles, plants, and objects that uplift you. Listen to inspiring music. Rearrange your room so that it is more uplifting, which gives you more energy. It could be as simple as putting old coats or shoes away from the entrance to your home or more complex like a new counter top or coat of paint? I've learned about Feng Shui by keeping my ears open and listening to others who are in the business or have read books on the subject. There are several books on this subject and experts who work in this field. Most life coaches suggest cleaning the clutter and getting up to speed as a foundation to move forward in the present – less clutter equals more freedom to create anew. My objective is to bring this concept to your awareness. Perhaps this is the message you've been waiting to hear and you will not have to think but for one more second why you received it. Let time serve you rather than being a servant to time. Choose how you wish to spend your time and you will melt away the negative emotion that you felt around time. Become a creator of your own reality.

Create a Plan

Those who have a plan succeed. Those who do not have a plan . . . plan to fail – they get what they get. Here are few suggestions on how to allow time to work for you. It all starts with a clearly defined purpose, a dream, or a goal, that becomes the number one driving force to keep us going. We literally move mountains and climb over obstacles with a definitive purpose and a single, one-minded focus. However, that purpose must be so strong that is resonates within us all the time. Without definiteness of purpose it is easy to put off today what we can do tomorrow. Remember to dream and clearly visualize your purpose with a one-minded focus. Those who succeed zero in like a laser beam. They love what they do. It's this high-octane energy that gets them out of bed in the morning.

10 Steps to Let Time Serve You

1) Have a dream (a definiteness of purpose).
2) Set an intention (an overall statement of what you will be, and by when).
3) Set one goal at a time—too many goals means we may never start any of them because we have too much dispersed energy; it's going in too many directions, which essentially leaves us with no energy for any useful purpose. When we feel overwhelmed we end up dropping the ball and very often do nothing. And to remember that doing nothing is still doing something. Remember one goal, one vision, and one-minded focus.
4) Make sure you really want it (hold the vision – does it feel good?).
5) Reduce your time commitments to things that don't serve your best interest (get rid of and cut out those things that do not serve your best interest).
6) Stay focused and committed—(remind yourself about your dream, intention, goal).
7) Make time in your daily schedule by physically writing it down. Make it a mantra.
8) Stick to your time commitments like you do for your dentist appointments.
9) Tell others how committed you really are (now there's no way out).

10) Keep your eyes on the goal, intention, or dream (keep holding the vision).

Are You Still Feeling Anxious Over Time?

Definiteness of purpose (having a dream, a goal, an intention) is what keeps champions going. They know *what* they want and *why* they want it and *why* they believe they will have it. Keep on telling yourself these things, and like all great champions you will not be denied. Champions also understand that how, where, when, and with who takes care of itself because they find the time. It happens because we gravitate towards the picture we paint. In our asking towards the picture we paint it does take a little bit of time to catch back up with our selves. That is why it is imperative to enjoy exactly where we are right now and to just keep on. It's called acceptance, which is a higher form of patience, while we continue to persevere. And it doesn't have to be such a struggle, like most of us were conditioned to believe.

Most of us were told by our parents, our schools, and our society at large that hard work and struggle is the key to our success. Why? Because someone told them that hard work and struggle is good. And I say, "Why?" Why not go with the flow? Why not align and connect with who you really are and enjoy this journey by pointing your kayak downstream and going with the flow. It's the struggle, which is a form of resistance that keeps many stuck. Many people believe they have to struggle mightily to get to where they are going. Believe it or not, there are those who thrive by going with the flow. That's what I'm practicing, and that's the key to my breakthrough. I struggled mightily and I beat myself up over this concept a million times. Talk about struggle. The solution: you've got to find relief, relax into it, soften your demeanor, allow the Well-Being in, and enjoy the journey—then and only then will you evolve and grow and become a better golfer. Champions thrive by going with the flow. And yes overcoming adversity is a common thread.

Coaches Notes: Once you understand that struggle is a form of growth, and yes it can be and usually is messy, you can move through this experience with greater awareness, with greater appreciation, and perhaps less arduously with ease and grace. It's how life works. Now you know the secret, and nothing is a secret because you have known it all along. Once again, I am just reminding you. It's a paradigm shift in perspective, one in which you must choose to see life through new lenses, or not?

As we go back in life and connect the dots, time becomes a non-issue because it's all a perfect plan. Choose joy when choosing how you wish to spend your time and live the life of your dreams. Let joy be the standard of success for anything you desire or wish to achieve. Let joy be the standard of success with your intention to play better golf. All it takes is a simple shift in perspective.

> **Simple Secret Reminder # 33 – Find Relief**
> **Soften your demeanor and let joy be the measure of your success.**
> **Go with the flow.**

As you let go and begin to go with the flow you begin to understand that everything is a perfect plan just the way it is and that the key to your success is the amount of joy you are feeling. Let your standard of success be your achievement of finding joy in all that you do on and off the course, and everything else, like time and practice, will fall exactly into place. Be joyful in the pursuit of creating your purpose. Be joyful on the putting green, on the practice range, with your mental driving range, and on the course. Let joy be the measure of your success.

As an amateur, if you are still feeling anxious about time with all of your other commitments, then try practicing mentally before you play physically. This will alleviate most of your anxiousness, and you will ground yourself back to center, back to the present moment. Spend ten to fifteen minutes visualizing just prior to actually playing how you wish to play before you hit the course. Become fully present and actually feel and see yourself playing.

Then when you are playing it will be a gateway to being more centered and more grounded, and you'll feel a softer stance around the emotional intensity – more internal peace. Talk to yourself in a more positive tone, even when things appear to be challenging: "It's a beautiful day. I'm here with my friends. I'm going to enjoy myself. Life is good." Usually when we finally relax and find relief, a big sigh if you will, we end up playing better. Why not capture that feeling right from the get-go instead of much later in our round? We are not ever taking away from being our best; we are simply shifting our energy to better feeling places versus being all caught up or uptight in our emotional struggle. Soften the edge of emotional chaos and align with the stream of Well-Being.

> **Simple Secret Reminder # 34 – Stop and Catch Your Self**
> **Whenever you are drifting away from what you intend…**
> **STOP and remind yourself.**
> **I'm here to have fun!**
>
> **Simple Secret Reminder # 1 reiterated again**

If you are still feeling a charge around any of these issues then practice EFT or MEGT. Rate your intensity level around this emotion before you begin. Remember we clear the negative emotion to make room for the positive belief.

1) Not feeling ready
2) Scared to play
3) Don't have enough time to practice
4) Don't know what I'm doing
5) Have no clue how to hit it
6) Afraid to play
7) Not feeling prepared

MEGT – Anxious Over Time

All of the above feelings are common experiences that most

golfers face from time to time. If this still applies to you then begin tapping with two fingers against your opposite karate chop hand: feeling anxious, not ready to play, I'm scared to play, not enough time to practice, feeling scared, have no clue what will happen, afraid to play, not ready to play, feeling anxious and scared, feeling unprepared, not enough time, feeling anxious, tension in my head and neck.

MEGT simplified format

1) Acknowledgement:
Inside Eye: Feeling anxious

Outside Eye: Not ready to play

Under Eye: Scared to play

Under Nose: Not enough time to practice

Chin: No clue what will happen

Inside Clavicle: Afraid to play

Under Arm: Not ready to play

Double Wrist: Feeling anxious and scared

Crown: Feeling unprepared and anxious

Deep Breath and rate your intensity level

2) Acceptance:
Inside Eye: Even though I'm feeling anxious, I accept myself exactly as I am

Outside Eye: Even though I'm feeling not ready to play, I accept myself exactly as I am

Under Eye: Even though I'm feeling scared to play, I accept myself exactly as I am

Under Nose: Even though there's not enough time to practice, I accept myself exactly as I am

Chin: Even though I have no clue what I'm doing, I accept myself exactly as I am

Inside Clavicle: Even though I'm deathly afraid to play, I accept myself exactly as I am

Under Arm: Even though I'm not ready to play, I accept myself exactly as I am

Double Wrist: I'm feeling anxious and scared and I accept myself exactly as I am

Crown: Even though I'm feeling unprepared and anxious, I accept myself exactly as I am. I am choosing to let this go and allow my body to resonate in peace, harmony, and joy.

Deep Breath and rate your intensity

3) Forgiveness:
Inside Eye: Even though I'm feeling anxious, I forgive myself for feeling this way

Outside Eye: Even though I'm feeling not ready to play, I forgive myself

Under Eye: Even though I'm feeling scared to play, I forgive myself

Under Nose: Even though there's not enough time to practice, I forgive myself

Chin: Even though I have no clue what I'm doing, I forgive myself for feeling this way

Inside Clavicle: Even though I'm deathly afraid to play, I forgive myself

Under Arm: Even though I'm not ready to play, I forgive myself

Double Wrist: I'm feeling anxious and scared and I forgive for feeling this way

Crown: Even though I'm feeling unprepared and anxious, I forgive myself. I am choosing to let this go and allow every cell in my body to resonate in peace, harmony, and joy. I'm feeling calmness come over my body and I am allowing the Well-Being in. I'm feeling present and in the now. I'm feeling joy resonate throughout my body.

Deep Breath and rate your intensity

4) New Focus and belief:
Inside Eye: Feeling calm and relaxed

Outside Eye: Feeling peace and joy

Under Eye: Feeling present

Under Nose: Relaxed and calm

Chin: Ready to play

Inside Clavicle: Feeling joy

Under Arm: Calm, confident, and present

Double Wrist: Feeling appreciation

Crown: I'm allowing the present moment to be. I'm allowing the Well-Being in. I'm feeling calm. I'm feeling joy.

Deep Breath and rate your intensity

Our work is to find relief, find relief…find relief. Stop beating the drum of emotional chaos. Stop paddling against the current. Stop paddling altogether and let your kayak go with the flow of the stream for just a moment. Breathe deeply. It's silly to be all caught up in this foolishness. When you find relief you can start paddling with the current and with a positive mindset, with joy, and with eager anticipation. All it takes is a simply shift in perspective.

Coaches Notes: Catch yourself in your experience whenever you appear to be going against the flow. It could be before you start, while on the course, or after you just played. Notice, observe, and become aware of how you are showing up. Catch yourself whenever you sense you are resisting the Well-Being and remind yourself to get back on your true path.

As you begin the process of catching yourself in the beginning you might feel a little guilty or foolish of why you have gotten yourself all worked up and how you may have acted. Make peace around all of this—you are loved and all is well. Let go of all of that. Stop the judgment process and remember God loves you—and never judges you—period! As you catch yourself more and more, the less you will find yourself in this godforsaken state of creating your hell on Earth, and the more you will find yourself in this divine state of creating heaven on Earth. Ever wonder why some see joy and others see gloom and doom? We live in the same place.

Once again time does not exist. It is you who are moving through time. It is an illusion to think you do not have the time. You are perfectly imperfect just the way you are. Actually life is always unfolding in the most perfect manner all the time. If you desire something you will find the time. Thinking you don't have the time will only perpetuate the illusion of worry, which is an expression of fear. Make peace with your time and let time serve you. Now if you have other commitments that you have chosen to spend your time on, then accept it. Have serenity to accept the things that you cannot change. Find the courage to change the things you can. And have the wisdom to know the difference. Practice the serenity prayer and make peace with where you are right now.

Action Steps:

1) **Find your definiteness of purpose.**
2) **Let time serve you.**
3) **Stay committed to your goal and dream.**
4) **Cut out the unnecessary things that chew up your time.**
5) **Clear any negative emotion you have around time.**
6) **Catch yourself whenever you stray from your true path.**
7) **I invite you to find relief, find relief...find relief.**
8) **Let joy be the measure of your success.**

Part III – The Inner Game of Golf ... and Becoming a Champion

Chapter 15

Creating a Champion's Self-Image

"There is only one corner of the universe you can be certain of improving, and this is your own self."
—Aldous Huxley

A step-by-step reminder to what we've already done…

Golf is an amazing game and our joy along the fairway of life should be a magnificent adventure. You and I are God's greatest creation and we are meant to thrive. We are born to win, and there are enough prizes to go around for everyone. We are capable of being, doing, and having anything. Do you know what separates the champions from the wannabes? It's the perception of them selves. It's what and how they think. Champions are aware of their authentic (higher) Self and they draw upon it continually. They allow this life force, wisdom, clarity, this ever-abundant stream of Well-Being, which is pure positive energy to flow to them and through them. Unfortunately, not everyone views the world, life, or there golf game the same way.

There is nothing you *have* to do; yet there is so much you can *choose* to be. And the only thing that you have to be is exactly what you are being right now! However, if you truly desire to build a healthy champion's self-image, you create it through the power of your thoughts, which form your beliefs, which manifests into action and behavior, which produces your results. Want to change your action, behavior, and results? You need to change the way you think—become keenly aware of your thinking and what you allow to sink into your subconscious mind. For man becomes what he thinks of himself.

Which thoughts do you hold of yourself? "There is a thought in your mind right now. The longer you hold on to it, the more you dwell upon it, the more life you give to that thought. Give it enough life, and it will become real. So make sure the thought is indeed a great one," said Ralph Marston, author of *The Daily Motivator*. Every thought that exists in our subconscious mind got there through a conscious decision to accept that thought. Yes, we literally become what we think. Hold a thought for more than seventeen seconds and it may very well become part of us. Our subconscious mind becomes a library of practiced thought and beliefs about ourselves, which runs everything in our life, including our own golf game and comfort zone.

Coaches Notes: I have a thought that I am struggling with technique in my golf swing right now. I have my demons and doubts because I forgot how to swing in my round yesterday. It costs me several strokes compared to what I know I am capable of performing. This takes me back to many years ago when these same thoughts deterred me from pursuing my dream at the time. One moment I'm on top of the world, the next I'm a no good, worthless bum. Now it is time to go within and heal this wound.

My work is to change that thought, give it new meaning, bless it, and shift my attention to what I prefer—to my dream and focus my attention upon the new champion's vision I hold about myself. See how easy it is to get caught back up in negative thinking! A belief that is stored in our hidden self-image runs its course from time to time. It is the experience right now within the experience itself that deserves my immediate attention. Become aware of how you are being and thinking right now.

I am suggesting and inviting you to think only the thoughts that uplift and inspire you, the thoughts of being and becoming your dream: how you think, talk, play, and carry yourself, how you see yourself, the things you imagine, the kind of golfer you desire to be. Whenever you find yourself sinking back into your lower self, shift your attention back onto your higher Self. I am suggesting that you become fully aware of both your thoughts, dreams, and self-talk so you consciously allow only positive focus and belief to take root. Our goal is to shrink the negative self-limiting beliefs by replacing them with new more empowering beliefs and focus, simply giving more "air time" to uplifting good, feeling thoughts and more beneficial beliefs that support us in being our personal best.

The universe delivers all the tools and resources, allowing you to create a most amazing you, and life is supposed to be a magnificent adventure. You have the power and free will to choose the identity and self-image you love and desire. The process of creating a champion's self-image requires awareness, diligence, persistence, desire, and repetition. James Allen said, "Man is made or unmade by himself. In the armory of thought he forges the weapons by which he destroys himself. He also fashions the tools with which he builds for himself heavenly mansions of joy and strength and peace." All is takes is but a simple shift in focus.

While not necessarily a pre-requisite (because life just is), the Law of Attraction works with or without your understanding and it may help to be reminded about the powerful creator in that which you really are. Everything is happening because of the Law of Attraction. Everything is energy in motion following an exact science of vibrational cause and effect in this simultaneous moment of now. That's all it is, all that was, and all that will ever be, which basically defines God and Life.

Who You Are

You are an extension of Source Energy. You are a divine aspect of All That Is. You are a Leading Edge powerful creator. There is a never-ending supply of pure positive energy that is always flowing to you and through you. Your soul, non-physical, or Inner Being, is pure positive energy and is like a crystal clear mountain stream always rushing forward, seeking its next continuous joyful expression of itself. This is our lifeblood, the energy that gives us life, the energy calling us forth to experience the grandest version of the greatest vision we ever held about who we really are. Your Inner Being is always guiding you in the direction of your heart's desire. Your work is to hear, listen, and let go of any resistance, aligning and connecting with Source, allowing and going with the flow. You cannot get too far off your true path because your Inner Being is always calling and guiding you to the next most glorious moment of yourself. Are you listening? Your Inner Being is guiding and supporting you, bringing you back to your true path. You cannot get it wrong. Your feelings are the language of your soul meant to guide the way.

As we awaken we find new levels of expansive knowledge and understanding. Again appreciate this awe-inspiring wisdom; yet do not take it too serious. Life just is and there will always be more. Your job is to ask and to get yourself up to speed in an allowing mode. Life is like a never-ending upward expanding circle once we get in the game and decide to play full out and connect with whom we really are. We may neglect ourselves temporarily. We may abandon our dreams and hopes along the fairway of life. We may stall or appear to slow down here or there. We start up again. And there is no judgment in any of it! There is no one right way and there are plenty of paths.

Eventually, we are drawn to heed to our calling that says something like, 'Please return to your higher Self, please return to living the life of your dreams, please return to your true path, please return to the highlighted route, please surrender or connect to who you really are. Please Let God and Let Go.' Can you feel the depth in all of this? Our dance with life is to awaken to our higher Self, follow our bliss, live our joy through expressing and experiencing who we really are. Trust life and let life know it can trust you and you will find that it all works in perfect harmony. And when we've had enough we simply croak and return once again to pure positive energy. In essence we never do die we simply change forms. Now that you know this, there's nothing to be afraid of, you can begin to fully live again. Flesh-eating monsters turn into paper tigers.

Change Your Thoughts and You Will Change Your Golf Game

Playing the game of golf can be our fun and leisure or it can be our career and our source of income. Yet the principles are the same for everyone: creating a healthy self-image of ourselves, really believing in ourselves. The difference between good players and great players is a belief in them selves. Internal vibrations don't lie, and neither does body language. Golf analysts like Johnny Miller, Paul Azinger, and Nick Faldo observe and make note of this all the time. Creating a champion's self-image for ourselves involves feeding our subconscious mind with new positive focus and belief, eventually squeezing out the old beliefs that no longer serve us. That's why there is usually a process to this madness unless you're fortunate enough to be Tiger Woods, who got many of the goods from the get-go. Yet even Tiger has gone through his fair share of growth experiences. All champions do! Even George Washington, the father of the United States, experienced his fair share of setbacks and disappointments...yet he persevered. The secret is keeping on...

Our mission together is yet another reminder to keep on. Our intention has been to become aware of our beliefs, emotions, feelings, and focus. We do so by becoming aware of our outward manifestation, what we see in the mirror, how we are showing up in the world. If we like what we see we keep on building upon that. If we don't like what we see, then we change our internal program inside and replace it with new more powerful belief and focus, one change at a time.

Like a plane on automatic pilot we perform to the signals and frequencies that are punched into our computer. This automatic pilot is akin to our self-image, our comfort zone we have settled on in our golf game. Our stored beliefs (self-image) effects and runs every aspect of our lives, including our golf game. Your comfort zone is where you subconsciously feel that you "belong." Now we understand that the only corner of the universe we can be certain of improving is our self. We change our world when we change our internal self. How do we really see ourselves? What does this question provoke within you? Are you ready to make the commitment to playing full out?

> *"You will never consistently perform at a level which is inconsistent with how you see yourself."*
> —Zig Ziglar

We have learned that our comfort zone is a safe place we have decided to temporarily settle for mediocrity, a place in which we consistently perform because we have allowed ourselves to see ourselves as such. Our internal patterns of behavior come directly from our deep-rooted beliefs about life and ourselves lodged directly in our subconscious brain from years of influence from others and the world around us. Some of this has served us very well and some of it may no longer serve our best interest. In order to change your outer world, you must first change your inner world. Our outer world is a direct reflection of our inner world.

You want to change your life then change your thoughts. You can change your immediate thought about something within about fifteen to twenty seconds and immediately change your behavior. You can decide right here and right now that you are quitting smoking and so shall it be. You can decide right here and right now that you desire a better demeanor on the golf course and so shall it be. However, for a more lasting and permanent change it may take a little more time to keep reinforcing the positive change. Most ingrained beliefs and focus that you would like to change takes anywhere from thirty days to slightly more depending upon your work on applying them. Sometimes it may take a year or two to clear the negative stubborn belief that you keep holding onto. Sometimes the real issue lies deeply hidden and it may take a fair amount of time to find it, let alone deal with it. The freedom comes from just knowing this understanding and having the ability to do something about it—or not. The choice is always yours and yours alone. It's about getting in the game exactly where you are, enjoying the process of announcing and declaring, expressing and experiencing, becoming and fulfilling who you really are...and keeping on! There will always be more.

The Fairway of Life

So really there are two issues at hand: 1) Clearing the negative emotion or limited belief within our self-image (removing or shrinking it), and 2) Replacing, or remaking, and rebuilding a new more positive belief and focus into our self-image. The way to do this is give more "airtime" to all the good things that you do want.

Clearing the negative stuck energy is simply a process of acknowledging that you have thought some thoughts that don't resonate with who you are now becoming. Our purpose here is to open the energy field within our body, mind, and spirit allowing everything to flow naturally, being healthy and at ease with our selves. It's okay to simply experience our thoughts, emotions, and our feelings letting them pass through us instead of clamping down on them keeping us hostage. Like Tiger, if you must, release the anger or disappointment in a healthy way and let it pass through. Tell your truth if it was a grind and choose to become better than you used to be. Learn from the experience and become an objective detective. Rebuilding our positive champion's self-image is the process of gravitating towards our vision, our dreams, and how we wish to see ourselves now. Act as if it is so.

Turning Fantasy into Fact and Dreams into Reality

Turning fantasy into fact and dreams into reality is a choice. Really contemplate that. Pause for a moment and go inside. How are being and doing so far? How do you really see yourself? You see, this really does expose our selves to ourselves – appreciate the wake up call, because your life really is waiting. Life is always showing us about life itself. Now, it's just a matter of what are we going to choose to be, and do next? Is this just another book that you pick up and read or are you making some very profound changes? Is there more that you desire? Are you willing to become what your heart desires? Some will hear and really make some significant changes, some will only listen, and some will do nothing at all. Our stay here on Earth can be and really should be a magnificent adventure. There is so much goodness and joy to experience, and you are meant to win. Golf and life are supposed to be fun.

Unfortunately, not everyone sees it that way. Master Life Success Coach Bob Proctor, as seen in the movie *The Secret,* provides us with a compelling and inspiring message in creating a winner's image of ourselves. It is my calling to offer this similar message as it relates to our own golf game. I acknowledge his personal blueprint for success that he obtained when The Secret was passed on to him, and he passes it on to all who are drawn to hear this message. The Secret is revealed when one is open to hearing it. While in the beginning it may have been suppressed by others who did not want others to know about it, it is now available to all. Just as Jesus went around teaching, "To all who have ears to ear, let them hear."

No one is reinventing the wheel; we are just re-packaging the wisdom of the ages. We've done great work so far; just remember one of the most important keys in recreating ourselves anew is repetition. Repetition is good for the soul and keeps us focused on task. Repetition helps to burn positive belief and fantasy into reality and fact. God also loves repetition through his multifaceted and never-ending communication. His messages come to us in many unique forms: you may read it in a book, hear it in a song, feel it in a meditation or prayer, or see it in the eyes of a beloved or the beauty in a flower...all of it is inspired by God. Let God work miracles through you, as you inspire another with your unique gift. And so shall it be.

10 Steps to Turning Dreams and Fantasy into Reality and Fact

I am going to condense this material into ten steps with a few questions, and a handful of exercises to keep you grounded and on task. Print these out, and follow them on a daily basis and I guarantee your life and golf game will become better than it was. The process works the same with relationships, career, money, or your health. Remember: We Become What We Think!

Step One: Have a Dream, a Thought, a Fantasy

It all starts with a dream, a thought, or a fantasy. You must have one to even begin the process. Become very specific about your dream and definiteness of purpose. Examples: Henry Ford had a dream, so did Alexander Graham Bell, and the Wright brothers. They changed the world. Tiger Woods has a dream to become the greatest golfer ever. His focus is nineteen majors – the measure of success in his mind for professional golf. His mindset and persona is changing the game by introducing so many youths and those with diverse ethnic backgrounds to the game of golf, not to mention the income that professional golfers are reaping. People are watching and playing golf all over the world because of Tiger.

My dream is to play golf to my full potential as I enjoy my journey. My unique gift is to awaken all those who are drawn to hear this message that have struggled just as mightily as I have—perhaps making this a better world...one more enlightened golfer at a time. I'm using the golf world as a platform to give away my message. Golf is a stage to launch a grander message about being, doing, and having a better life, making it more playful, and more joyful...becoming better than *we* used to be. That's what this is really all about. By playing better in life, we end up playing better golf. I keep asking, is what I am being and doing making me a better me? Notice again the asking...you must ask! And when the answer comes hold the voracity of it.

Step one is having a dream, a fantasy.

Step Two: View the Game of Golf in a Positive Way

How do you view the game of golf?

- Is it harsh and cruel?
- Are you struggling and frustrated?
- Do you love to hate the game of golf?
- Do you feel like you are going nowhere never taking the time to enjoy where you are?

Or

- Is golf one of the greatest games you have ever played?
- Is it fun and enjoyable?
- Is it a thrill just to be out there?
- Do you look forward with eager anticipation to play this wonderful game?

I re-invite you to see the beauty and joy that golf really does have to offer and begin shifting your focus to that. Turn and point yourself in the direction of what you really do desire and go with that. Go with the flow!

Step two is how you view the game of golf. It's your perception and perspective.

Step Three: Become Aware Of and Connect with Your Authentic (Higher) Self

Our authentic (higher) Self is what differentiates the champion's self-image from the masses. We talked about awakening to your magnificence right from the get-go in Chapter 1. There is an image of perfection within your soul that is forever attempting to express itself in a greater way. Champions draw upon this image and connect with their authentic (higher) Self in order turn their dreams into reality. There is a transcendence of personal self into our higher Self. It is the same feeling we get by going with the flow and being in The Zone.

Connecting with our authentic (higher) Self is where we find our magnificence within ourselves, and our unique gift for everyone else. Fall in love with the idea of following your bliss. Show up big and give service; abundance and riches will flow to you effortlessly. You will be rich in all aspects of your life.

Here are some examples of those who have done exactly this:

- Arnold Palmer brought the game of golf to television and inspired millions. He lets his golf do the talking. Palmer is an ambassador for the game.

The Fairway of Life

- Gary Player keeps himself fit as a fiddle and he brings a level of awareness to staying active and fit to millions of others.
- Jack Nicklaus gave us a competitive and gracious spirit. His focus and will to win is etched upon the minds of all golfers.
- Annika Sorenstam inspired millions of girls to take up the game of golf and play it with compassion and spirit to be their best.
- Lorena Ochoa brings us hope and perseverance. Her work ethic will inspire millions of golfers across a wide spectrum.
- Tiger Woods inspires millions of kids to play this game and become better human beings from a wide diversity of ethnic backgrounds. His full gift to humanity is in the process of being realized.

You and I are just like them. The only difference is our perception of our selves. Becoming aware of our higher Self is the first place to begin. How do you see yourself?

You and I are blessed with unlimited possibilities and infinite potential. We have the same mental mindset or blueprint from which to draw upon as Jack Nicklaus, Lorena Ochoa or Tiger Woods. The same Source Energy or power that flows to and through them flows through all of us. The difference between our success and failure is our hidden self-image.

Step three is to connect with your authentic (higher) Self.

Step Four: Understand Your Self-Image

Everyone has a self-image. It controls and runs our lives just as our mind controls our breathing and heartbeat. All our behavior and the results we get in life come from this perceived view of ourselves.

Are you wondering about what kind of self-image you have? Look at the kinds of actions and results you are getting on the golf course. Our outer expression is a direct match to our inner self-image. Want to remake your life on the golf course? Change or alter your inner self-image and everything on the outside begins to change.

Most people will attempt to change everything on their outside versus on the inside. We practice more of the same bad habits. We beat balls and ourselves up until we are bloody. We think that hard work and struggle is the key to being a success. We take lessons. We attempt to be a good sport. We read about and study the game of golf. We watch it on television. We try new things and fall back into old behaviors. Trying to change our golf game this way is like trying to change our reflection in the mirror without changing our clothes or appearance. It's not going to happen. People attempt to change what's going on outside without changing what's going on inside.

Step four is in the understanding our own self-image, and how it runs everything in our life, including our golf game. All we have to do is to look at our actions and results we are getting.

Step Five: Build a Champion's Self-Image

In order to build a champion's self-image we must alter our inner image. We are in essence, remaking or rebuilding our hidden self-image. Since we are working with our mind, we have a challenge: no one has ever seen the workings of the mind. So immediately confusion sets in as to how our conscious and subconscious mind really works. Therefore, we have to build an imaginary picture in our mind's eye. Imagine your brain being divided into two parts: your conscious mind (which thinks and gathers all the information like yardage, lie, wind, visualization, etc.) and your subconscious mind (which controls your behavior, your swing, your action, and your results). Our old self-image is lodged in our subconscious mind. Our subconscious mind influences our behavior like an airplane on automatic pilot. Our subconscious mind operates within the range of our comfort zone and very rarely deviates too much from our set point of perspective within our self-image. Once in a while we'll put together a string of some very good golf and shoot an incredible score, or conversely once in a while we'll have a string of some not-so-good golf, and shoot a horrendous score, yet more often than not we end up settling right back into the image or comfort zone we have created for ourselves. In order to create better behavior and results we've got to create a better self-image in our subconscious mind.

When playing golf we tend to fall comfortably into consistent behavioral patterns. If we are playing extremely well beyond our comfort zone, or extremely poor, more than likely our nervous system with its set point of coordinating mechanism kicks in until we are back on course. We may have an occasional great round or awful round here and there, yet our automatic pilot self-image will pick up on this deviation and through thick and thin we generally play consistently to whatever self-image we have. So, naturally, you ask, "How can I alter my old self-image and create a new more empowering one?" You've been doing this throughout this book. Your work is to keep on imprinting the greatest vision of your highest Self into yourself. That's your dream in how you desire to see yourself. Keep visualizing how you would like to see yourself and you will gravitate toward that.

Step five is to begin building a champion's self-image by imagining what it is we desire to be.

Step Six: Turn Your Fantasy or Dream into Reality

Before you can turn your fantasy or dream into a fact or reality you have to turn it into a workable theory. A theory is a general proposition or explanation whose status is still conjectural, in contrast to well-established propositions that are regarded as reporting matters of actual fact, like Newton's theory of gravitation. The dreamer must ask himself a couple questions (and a whole host of more questions as this process evolves) and fully commit before providence (divine inspiration and guidance) actually moves to you and through you. We talked about providence before. Providence moves through us when we say yes to a few questions and *fully* commit—playing full out. Ask yourself:

1) Am I able to do this? Can I turn my dreams into reality?

Yes or no? Remember dreams are the things you have not yet accomplished and are beyond what you even know exist. They are in the realm of the unknown. If you answer yes, then your authentic (higher) Self realized a higher innate awareness that you are able to do this.

2) Am I willing? Yes or no? In this question lies a long list of tests and more questions. Am I willing to endure the ridicule? Am I willing to endure the setbacks? Am I willing to accept the failures (all the times I found in how not to do it)? Am I willing to climb over my obstacles or illusions? Am I willing to pay the ultimate price and do whatever is required? Am I willing to move? Am I willing to sacrifice certain time commitments and give up the things that may not serve my best interest? Am I willing to do what is best for me? Is this choice making me a better me? Am I willing to do whatever is asked of me— that I know is best for me?

Answering yes or no to these questions will tell you a lot about yourself. Let's assume you say, "Yes, I am able and willing to all of this." The second you answer in the affirmative you've created your theory. Providence moves. It never dawned on Tiger Woods that he would not ultimately realize his dream even though I am quite sure he had his many challenges along his path. All great champions in all walks of life had to ask themselves these very questions. You, too, must go through exactly the same process and line of questioning, as do all champions.

Step six is turning our dream or fantasy into reality by answering a couple questions and making a commitment to our workable theory.

Step Seven: Overcoming the Stumbling Blocks

Before you turn your fantasy (dream) into fact (reality) you first have to turn it into a theory. Before you turn your dream into reality there are a couple of tests that you must pass:

1) **The test of ability**. Am I able to do this? You don't have

to know how; you just need to know that you *are capable* of being and doing anything. The truth is you can, once you understand that you are God's greatest creation, and you are a spiritual being living a physical existence, and that all things are possible. So yes, we can and we are able. We don't have to know *how* right away; just knowing we *are* able and willing opens up the how.

2) **The test of figuring out "how?"** The universe opens up to our unlimited potential as soon as we commit to ourselves. The truth isn't always in the appearance of things. All obstacles, all demons, all of our fears, are illusions. Our obstacles and fears cause us to have doubt in our minds. We ask ourselves if we are we really capable of doing this. Once we realize that every obstacle is an illusion we are able to figure out how to get around them, over them and walk boldly with them. Then we are on our way to where we want to go. Yes, we know we are quite capable of doing anything.

3) **The test of willingness.** Am I willing to do whatever is required to realize my dream? When you answer yes to that question, with the snap of your fingers you've built a theory in your mind and you are on your way.

Simple Secret Reminder # 35 – All Obstacles Are Illusions
Every fear, demon, obstacle are all illusions.
Once you fully commit and say, "Yes I can," and take action down *The Fairway of Life* the how's will show themselves.

Step seven is in overcoming the fear or obstacle.

Step Eight: Review

1) We've built our fantasy
2) We've admitted we are able to do it
3) We said, "Yes I am willing."
4) We've got a theory, a dream, and a champion's self-image

in our conscious mind. Notice I said *conscious mind*. Our thoughts, dreams, and fantasy begin in our conscious mind *first*. Next, we imprint our empowering new beliefs and focus upon our *subconscious mind.*

Now our objective and mission is to firmly plant the seed into our subconscious mind and let it take root so it will change our behavior and the results we are getting in our life. In order to properly deposit your new champion's self-image into the treasury of your subconscious mind remember the first law of learning: repetition. Repetition is how we burn our new focus and belief into our subconscious mind.

Step eight is our review on how to burn our new focus and belief into the treasury of our subconscious mind: repetition.

Step Nine: Practice Visualization

It is vitally important to spend at least ten to twenty minutes, two times a day, visualizing how and what you wish to be. Here are some suggestions:

1) **Create a vision board.** A vision board is a picture you have painted in your mind's eye of how you desire yourself to be. You can use poster board or cork board. Put pictures and ideas that inspire you on your vision board as you gravitate toward being that collage. Act, think, and feel if it is so.
2) **Begin to visualize how you wish to be.** Take a couple deep breaths and let it out. Practice a "falling still" exercise where you completely clear your mind and let go of any thoughts or concerns of the day or in the near future. Allow those thoughts and concerns to melt away off you and into the face of the Earth. Tell them you will deal with them later, because now you desire to be fully present and clear. Allow yourself to be totally relaxed and present, while connecting with your Inner Being

The Fairway of Life

and authentic (higher) Self. Practice a form of guided meditation or visualizing on how you wish to be.

3) **Begin to see yourself actually living this experience.** Allow yourself to imagine your dream, your fantasy, or your intention. See yourself being the champion you want to be. Involve all your senses. Act as if it were so.

4) **Let all these beautiful pictures and images soak in.** Allow these images to penetrate deeply into every cell of your being. Add a lot of emotion. Feel the energy around all of it. These are the feelings that match your desire.

5) **Visualize living the life that you want.** Feel yourself living it.

6) **Write it all down.** Now that you have a good visual image of what you want, make a written description of your dream and visualization. Now freeze it, stand back and take a good look at how different your dream is compared to what you are actually living. The difference between your dream and visualization, and what you are currently living allows you to see the changes that have to be made.

7) **Begin making those changes.** Make the necessary changes one at a time. There are hundreds of changes you could make. Start with something small and simple. Say, for instance, your personal appearance: how you dress, how you carry yourself, how you present yourself to others. All of these things send a strong message to everyone and a powerful message back to your self. Present yourself outwardly with an image that is consistent with this new champion's image you are developing internally – be as you wish to seem. A second change you can immediately make is your choice to get angry or stay calm. You can immediately change your demeanor. Another change you can start applying is giving your focus and attention to what you want in your golf shots versus what you don't want.

8) **Go inside to get an understanding of how you perceive yourself.** Allow your inner eye to get a good solid picture

and perception of yourself. Are we beginning to see ourselves from within as the champion that we really want to be? For example: remember the optical illusion photo of the ugly old lady and the beautiful young lady in the same photo? It just takes a simple shift of focus. How do see yourself? Do you see yourself as a chump or as a champ? See the differences and begin making the changes one at a time.

9) **Transition into being a champion.** In the transition period process of implanting your champion's self-image into your subconscious mind there will be two people you perceive. One, the old you, and two, the new you (the champion). Every time you see yourself as a failure or lacking in some way, simply begin shifting your focus (like on the beautiful young lady) until you see the new beautiful you. Likewise, do you see internal conflict or peace and harmony within? How do you perceive your world? One of struggle, frustration, and being difficult? Or one of abundance, flow, and Well-Being? A champion is never in conflict with her world and allows harmony in all situations and lets it work in her favor. All it takes is a simple shift in focus. Point yourself into the direction of your desires and good feeling thoughts and remember to go with the flow.

Step nine is practicing visualization and recognizing what changes we want to make. It's about how we perceive our world and how a simple shift in focus allows us to get us back on track.

Step Ten: Final Review

1) We've built the dream.
2) We've admitted we're able.
3) We said we're willing.
4) We've built the theory.
5) We're committed to our program
6) We've completed the exercises.

7) We're working towards making the changes.
8) We're visualizing with emotions at least twice a day.
9) We're planting and burning the champion's self-image upon our subconscious mind.
10) Our old image fades, our new image becomes stronger.
11) Our new champion's self-image becomes our new self-image.
12) We experience the reflection of our new champion's self-image in our behavior and in our results. It is obvious for the whole world to see, and for us to enjoy.
13) We're actually living our fantasy. Look at yourself.

We've created a better world for ourselves and everyone else to enjoy. What you're looking at is a reflection of your own champion's self-image. You can do it and it can be done. Turn your world into absolute beauty, an image of excellence. Keep on developing that champion's self-image!

Action step:
1) **Review this champion's self-image process at least two times a day for the next ten weeks and keep on visualizing...**

Chapter 16

Keep Dreaming Your Dream

"Our truest life is when we are in our dreams awake."
—Henry David Thoreau

Keep on keeping on...

Once you understand the secret to life, the mystery is over. The veil is lifted. There's no more separation theory (we're all one), no more blaming (we're responsible), no more excuses (we've created it), no more fear (love is all there is), and no more ignorance (we understand). Life is unfolding just perfectly, just the way it is.

It's time to take responsibility; you and I really become the creator of our lives and our reality. We become what we think, and believe, and feel in our vibration...in the messages that we are sending. We are energy in constant motion, vibrating. All of life is energy in motion responding to the Law of Attraction. Everything responds to your vibration, which is the way you feel. Change the way you feel about something and you change your life. Change the way you respond to your golf game and your golf game changes. You are becoming the powerful creator that you have always known. You are becoming the grandest version of the greatest vision ever you held about who you really are. You are embracing life, living in the gap of unfulfilled desires, and you continue to ask for more, because there will always be more—and it never ends.

You ask, the universe responds, and you allow the Well-Being in. Everything begins to make perfect sense. It all makes perfect sense just by observing others and now it all makes perfect sense in your own life. You now understand why everything works out as it does. It all makes perfect sense. Your thoughts, words, feelings, and actions create your reality. You become what you think and what you dream about. I invite to keep following your dream, to keep following your bliss. I invite you to keep living your dream all the while being happy exactly where you are, eagerly anticipating your next new rocket of desire, and you know there will always be more, and this dream we are living never ends.

> **Simple Secret Reminder # 36 – We Become What We Think**
> **We become what we dream about.**
> **We become what we give our attention upon.**
> **Change your thoughts and you will change your life.**

Life is about enjoying the journey, not the destination. It is the experience, not the result. It's about enjoying the moment, letting the scoring take care of itself. Once you embrace the joy in the present moment you will end up playing the best golf of your life. Everything will effortlessly fall into place and take care of itself and you will end up enjoying the abundance and riches of what you truly resonated with in the first place. It's just that simple.

The secret lies in the never-ending continuous moments of now, and each new moment can be just as wonderful as the last or even greater than the previous. The secret is that the dream never ends. It is the dream, our joy that drives our life. It is the dream, our joy that motivates us. It is the dream, our joy, that inspires us, and it is having and living our dream moment-by-moment that brings forth joy and our reason for being.

The secret is in having and living our dream without any particular need for an outcome or a result. The dream is not in the accomplishment, it is in the journey of each moment. Then one day we wake up realizing we've become what we gave our imagination, thoughts, and vision upon after all. We've become what we gave our attention upon, what we thought about. You're being it and doing it right now. What you gave your thoughts to in the past you are living now, that's the miracle of life. Can you see this? Can you understand this? Can you feel this? This subtle and profound understanding changes everything. There is nothing you have to have, do, or be—except exactly what you are being right now. And if you want to change that and recreate yourself anew, all it takes is a simple shift in perspective. Change your thoughts and you change your life.

As you live within your dream you can slow down, you can smell the roses, you can relax now, and you will play better golf. With a persistent keeping on attitude you will naturally and joyfully keep gravitating toward your dream, toward the picture you have painted, and more will be drawn unto you. While you may feel a bit challenged in any new endeavor (because the exact opposite enters our experience first), there is also the opportunity to turn fear into feelings of joy and inner peace as we awaken to our true magnificence following our *True North*, our true path. Listen to the language of your soul. How glorious it is to live the life of your dreams and to keep following your bliss.

I honor your journey, and it my sincerest hope and desire that your life will be blessed with riches and abundance, and that you, too, will enjoy the greatest game ever played.

Action Steps:

1) **Just be who you really are.**
2) **Listen to your feelings – the language of your soul. Go with the soul.**
3) **Keep dreaming your dream.**

Part IV – The Golf Swing

Chapter 17

The Golf Swing

"All my muscles felt 'involved' in the swing."
—Ed Kelbel, Sr.

Some nuggets of wisdom from the Master...

As you well know this is a book about Life; it's a book about enjoying the golf journey down the fairway of life. It's not a book about the technical workings and intricacies of the physical golf swing through illustrations, video tape, concepts or practice drills as taught by the PGA teaching professional on the driving range or on the golf course in how to make those swing changes – you can do all of that on your own if you so choose.

That being said, it is important for me to include a short chapter on The Golf Swing for several reasons. First, you get a bite size taste of the golf swing from one of the best, if not *the best*, player(s) in the state of Michigan at one moment in time – professional or amateur. You also get to hear the voice of one of the best golf teachers, someone who could easily diagnose anyone's swing in a matter of moments without the aid of a video camera. He was one of my golf teachers and a good friend of mines' dad. He's got a lot of golf knowledge to share, and it is my desire to capture some of those nuggets of wisdom and pass them on to you. Oh, did I mention according to him that he's now living his last few years like, "A poor movie and I'm in it." I feel like I living Saturday's with Ed similar to how Mitch Album told his story in Tuesday's with Morrie. It's important for me to share this chapter for all of these reasons and more. God bless Mr. Kelbel. He gave so much to others, all he asked was for excellence in return. The amazing thing is, it worked.

> "We turned the corner emotionally from being on a road of constant sadness over my dad's condition to a new road of 'gladness' in knowing that he was properly recognized for his accomplishments both on and off the golf course. What made him an outstanding educator is the same thing that made him an outstanding golf instructor and that is he 'demands improvement' and even more important... receives it, from all who come under his influence."
> —Ed Kelber, Jr.

Ed Kelbel, Sr., seventy-one, has suffered a stroke, and is in the latter stages of Parkinson's disease. He is entering his sixth year in a nursing home. In spite of the apparent physical affects of his stroke and the disease, his mind is as clear as ever. He speaks in a slower soft-spoken manner. He's been a devoted family man and was an avid golfer, one of the best. Although he can't play anymore, and would like too, as he swings his hands and arms back and through in the wheel chair, he still thinks about the golf swing all the time. Every time he hears a "new concept" he feels as if the golf swing is coming back full circle. His wife brings him golf magazines to read, though he typically comments, "I already know this stuff. I taught it and practiced it." The new term of trapping the ball, where the ball is trapped between the clubface and the turf is an age-old concept that many practiced in 1960, calling it shut-face golf. Yes, your nine-iron actually turns into a seven or a seven and a half iron by de-lofting it at impact – you hit down on the ball, which allows it to spin up the clubface with optimum launch angle, spin, and trajectory. It's an explosive blow at impact and the ball penetrates through the air with precision and accuracy like a missile seeking its target.

Ed has a lot of golf knowledge in his mind. His three boys are all golf professionals and he had the privilege of teaching a young twelve-year old Tom Watson while Tom's family vacationed in

The Fairway of Life

Walloon Lake, Michigan in the summer months. In his soft-spoken manner, as I ask him about Tom Watson, Ed goes on to say, "Stan Thirsk was Tom's primary teacher, (along with Byron Nelson) but I had the privilege of working with him. Tom was electrifying." Just hearing the words makes me shiver. Ed proceeds to quietly change the subject and talk humbly about all the other students he taught at Walloon Lake Country Club and that *many of them* went on to become pretty good players themselves. He literally taught thousands of lessons to hundreds of golfers over a lifetime.

As a player Ed Kelbel, Sr. was one of the best in the state of Michigan. It wasn't until his recent induction into his Alma Mater's Aquinas College Athletic Hall of Fame did we really get a grasp on how good he really was. He peers recall his domination through all the tournaments he won and course records he set. Ed never talked too much about himself. He was a humble man with meager beginnings and gave his life to supporting his family. Now his son, Eddie, Jr. understands, "I just wish dad could have been able to see how good he really was instead of providing for us. What he did as a player I took for granted until I tried to do it myself. His goal was to hit every shot from 150 yards in within 8-10 feet every time. And he did."

I remember playing in the mid 70's with Ed, his son Eddie, and another golf pro named Joe Hirsch. They all played so well, I was in awe bringing up the rear shooting in the mid to upper 70's, whereas each of them were playing par golf or better. While I never got a chance to see Ed play in what he calls his "prime" I could tell by his swing and the stories that people told that he's one of the best. The pictures of Ed with Tom Watson and Tom's dad Ray and the articles on the wall in Ed's room at the nursing home tells his story: Ed Kelbel shoots 65 for course record. He goes on to tell me that he ended up breaking his own course record, shooting a 63 five times. Yes, he's that good. Why didn't he pursue the big tour in those days? "Because I come from a pretty conservative upbringing and raising a family meant more to me."

Rand S. Marquardt

The Golf Swing

Since I ran into Mr. Kelbel coming off the 9th green at True North Golf Club in August 2008 while he was getting out with his daughter, son-in-law and their kids, I've been visiting him on a regular basis at Bay Bluffs Nursing Home with a notebook in hand. This mutual get together is healthy for both of us. Remember, there are no accidents or coincidences. The universe is always providing us the perfect match for our desires at just the perfect time. We just have to listen and follow our intuition when guided.

In our first "official" golf meeting on Labor Day 2008 at the nursing home I wheel Ed outside and we find a nice place to begin talking golf. I notice another gentlemen in a wheelchair following us outside. He stops by and proceeds to talk, and talk, and talk some more. Eventually, in kindness and respect, I mention we have some work to do. My intention is to be present with Mr. Kelbel and listen, perhaps allowing for any nuggets of wisdom to come forth.

I mention to Ed that isn't it interesting that everything comes full circle with the golf swing. I'm curious about what he has to say about this. Forever, the ultimate teacher, he is eager to discuss this and says, "It all starts with the fundamentals, the preliminaries of stance, grip, set up, and alignment. And maintain your spine angle, that's crucial." Soon he's grabbing my hands telling me about position, being parallel, toes pointed out for easier rotation, a stronger grip, and a feeling of the right hand being compressed down into the left (a shorter distance of the hands on the club), and a reminder about keeping the triangle within the swing. He tells me about the importance of a pre-shot routine and how to keep it simple, to have fewer thoughts, and go more with the feel. I ask him about the take away and what he's thinking. He says, "I don't think about it, I turn it into feel. I like to imagine like I'm reaching for the sky. At the top of the swing (the shelf) get your hands at least eight inches above your shoulder. When I played my best I would have my hands fifteen inches above my shoulder." We talked about finishing low, medium, or high depending upon what type of golf shot you wanted to hit. He says, "Marry your grip to the rest

The Fairway of Life

of your stance and set up depending upon what kind of shot you want to hit."

Ed goes on to say, "The golf swing is like a mirror. What happens on the backswing mimics the follow through. At the top of the swing I like to see a crease in the skin of the left wrist with a right-handed golfer," as he manipulates the back of my left hand making sure the crease is in the absolute correct place. We talk about Hogan's move at impact and how the arms and wrists come into the ball allowing the right elbow to rotate over the left after impact for a draw, and holding the right elbow under the left for a fade.

"The golf swing is really an attempt to swing in a coordinated fashion with the hands, wrists, arms, and shoulders. The better you set your swing, the better balance, and the better nerves you will have. When I reach for the sky in my backswing, I'm in a position to drive the ball like a homerun hitter. It's more of a feel thing. When I hit my hole in one at PBVCC in the early 60's all my muscles felt involved." Feeling sure of himself with a slight smile he says in his soft-spoken voice, "That's a pretty good quote." He used a pitching wedge from 150 yards slightly downhill and watched it suck back into the hole. "There's a sense of feel that would be coming through you." Hmmm . . . Ed talks an awful lot about feel. "Feel is as important, or more so, than mechanics."

I think the secret is in your feelings and the way you feel about your golf game. Because think about it, scientifically speaking if you have to "think" too much about how to hit the ball (paralysis by analysis), and all the mechanics, then it's simply not natural. We're not feeling it. Now spiritually speaking when we just go with the flow (a feeling) of our swing, the one that feels natural, something clicks and we just play better. Hmmm...which one would you rather choose...brilliant deduction Einstein? You've got to turn those mechanics into feel. And then there is a knowing when you are feeling it. That's why Ed Kelbel stuck so many iron shots within 10 feet of the flag. It's why he could crush his drives long distances. He felt it. Putting is also very much a feeling and letting it happen. Think about it, when do you putt your best? "When you're feeling it," as I read Mr. Kelbel snippets of the final stages of revising his chapter. "It's true," he acknowledges over lunch at Bay Bluffs. "You know (he says) the game of golf is similar to the game of life. Play the game with your unique personality. My biggest weakness in golf was my putting. Sometimes I just lost my touch. I remember losing my touch playing in the Michigan Amateur and giving my match away."

Ed went on to talk about so many old golf stories with the Watson's, his relatives, and his good friends. For the most part I just listened soaking it all in. He talked about absolutely crushing and smashing the ball while shooting a 28 on the upper nine at PBVCC. He could hit it very long. He shows me as he rolls his right elbow over his left in his follow through on how he hits it so long and also gets the right to left extra roll while sitting in his wheel chair. He described hitting his Wilson Staff 1-iron on several occasions. I said, "You hit your 1-iron 260 yards." He said, "Yeah, more than that." He said he drove the green on a par 4 hole #7 at Walloon Lake Country Club (which plays slightly less than 300 yards) with his 1-iron twice in one day and went on to three putt both times for his par. He'd drive par fours with his 4-wood. "You'll be surprised at what you can do if you think you can." We go on to talk about this exact energy of what you're feeling prior to the shot and how that ultimately influences your execution. Yes Mr. Kelbel. Thank you for reiterating that point.

> **Simple Secret Reminder # 37 – Feel Your Golf Swing**
> **Get out of your head; get out of your way,**
> **and into your feel.**

Trapping

We talk some more about "trapping" the ball because all good players do it. I proceed to tell him about how you've got to hit down on the ball with a bent right wrist at impact versus the dreaded go nowhere bent left wrist at impact producing a scooping effect for the right-handed golfer. The left wrist has to be solid and straight at impact with perhaps some slight curve outward, like a bow effect. That's how Tiger hits it, a strong left wrist coming down into the ball at impact. The loft of the iron then gets de-lofted or shut down; hence the old term shut-face golf. Agreeing, Ed grabs my left wrist and makes sure my grip is solid on the club and the back of my left wrist is in the correct position while I'm imitating impact position.

Dropping into the Slot

"This is when the club head drops into the same plane as the arm is swinging," Ed, Sr., describes. He goes on to say, "The slot is likened unto the derailleur of a bicycle. The club gets fed into its perfect slot just prior to impact and then follows its exact position at impact to produce a powerful blow. It's the point where the club drops back into the last part of the swing path arc." 'I asked what is the drop, is it gravity?' "It's when you start high and come in low – that constitutes the drop."

Stacking Over Your Left Side

Then I ask, "What is this concept we hear now called 'stacking the left side?'"

Ed answers, "This is a three-quarter swing when you put all your weight on the left foot on both the backswing and the follow through. Actually, we've been practicing this kind of swing since the 60's and before as well. You just create a feeling of more accuracy with your wedge. In this case you don't transfer your weight from your right side to your left side, which is ideal for full swings. For the most part, I teach transferring the weight from the right side on the backswing to the left side on the follow through holding the finish for the right-handed golfer."

His Life

I'm extremely grateful for the opportunity to visit with a man filled with such golf wisdom and knowledge, one who can back up his words with his golf game as well. This letter that his son Eddie wrote to the editor of a local newspaper speaks volumes about

Ed Kelbel, Sr. I received Eddie's e-mail on October 2, 2008, just prior to his dad's induction ceremony into The Aquinas College Athletic Hall of Fame. First, I include his induction comments from the evening program on October 3, 2008. Ed Kelbel was inducted into the Hall of Fame from the class of 1959. As stated in the program:

> Ed Kelbel was an outstanding golfer from 1954-1958 who led the squad as its number one golfer and captain. During this period, the Aquinas teams set the standard of excellence for all AQ golf teams that followed. At one time, Ed held course records at numerous golf courses from Kalamazoo to Petoskey. Kelbel is held in high esteem by his peers from the Aquinas golf community who recommended him as a "must" for induction into the Aquinas Athletic Hall of Fame. He was always around par at the Grand Rapids Elks / Highlands course where Aquinas hosted its meets. He taught and coached golf for nearly thirty years at Harbor Springs High School developing outstanding squads. He served as head golf professional at Walloon Lake Country Club as well as head professional at Harbor Point Golf Club. Ed and his wife, Mary Lou (Malec '59), have six children (three boys and three girls). All three sons are head golf professionals while two of their daughters are kindergarten teachers and a third is an accountant. Following his retirement from education, Ed suffered a stroke, but recovered enough to have ten additional quality years of playing and teaching the game he loves. Ed and Mary Lou reside in Harbor Springs.

Here is my correspondence with his son Eddie.

Hi Randy,

Below is what I wrote a few weeks ago about my dad. You and he have some similarities, both learning to play at Bay View! Enjoy. If my emotions will allow me, I plan on reading this at his Induction ceremony this Friday. Congrats on your upcoming speech and new book. You and my dad both love golf at a higher level than most anybody I know. Thank you for the kind words on dad. It means a lot to him that you would visit him like you are.

>Eddie
>Ed Kelbel, Director
>PGA Golf Management Program
>College of Business
>University of Colorado-Colorado Springs
>Colorado Springs, CO 80918

From Ed Kelbel, Jr. to Charles O'Neill, editor of the Harbor Light Newspaper:

Hi Chaz,

As far as college, I don't know that much other than he was the #1 player on a team that I have been told was undefeated for four years. My mom has Dan Pupel's phone number and he has everything you need to know and is a wonderful guy to boot. Please get with my mom on his contact info if you can. My dad may tell you different but that is what I have been told. He started at Walloon Lake CC in 1960-68, Harbor Point 1969-75, Back to Walloon 1976-88? Pine Hill 1988-94? The last stints at Walloon and Pine Hill are a bit fuzzy to me memory wise.

His Petoskey St. Francis High School 1953 golf team won the state championship with at least four Kelbel's on the team with his older brother Bill and cousins Steve and Jimmy. Dad was always known for how far and straight he could hit his driver, and how high and accurate he could hit fairway woods and 1 and 2 irons. Also, his accuracy from 150 yards in was mind-blowing. I used to caddy for him a lot and he rarely hit a shot outside of 10 feet of the pin from 150 yards in. I didn't know how special that was until I tried to do the same thing and found it very difficult, ha! Also, dad was the best sand wedge player both in a bunker and around the green that I have ever seen to this day. There simply was not a shot he couldn't hit close to the pin. He had an old PowerBilt Citation sand wedge that my son Ted has now that might as well have been a magic club. Perhaps Brian (O'Neill, a PGA teaching professional) will remember his skill around the greens as well. Dad was a streaky putter; he ran very hot or very cold. He was an aggressive putter, which made for a lot of one putts or three putts. That aggressiveness fit his personality to a tee. He hated to lag anything and he hated to lay up off the tee with an iron. He would much rather smash his driver and usually did so very accurately. He was a very good "clutch" player as well. He could almost always successfully pull off a shot with a lot of pressure on him. In fact, he truly thrived under those kind of pressure situations.

So, when I read what I just wrote above, you can see his game really didn't have any weaknesses and that is why he is headed to the Hall of Fame. He was a fierce but fair competitor. He hated to lose but would shake a person's hand if they beat him. As you know, he loves the game of golf and is nothing short of fascinated with the golf swing. Much more than I ever was or am. He was preaching the technique of using a 3/4 type knockdown wedge swing that he used with so much success about 20 years before it become and still is the preferred method on tour for hitting wedges. As far as golf instruction goes, he was truly a visionary teacher. Well before any video equipment or training aids ever came along, dad could look at your swing for less than two minutes and have your diagnosis down to a tee. Remarkable when you think about it! Brian will attest to all of this I'm sure. So will all of the other thirty or so pros he used to help with their games in the Northern Michigan area. It says something that for many

The Fairway of Life

years, he was the instructor most of the other pros in the area would go to for help. Of course, he would never collect a dime from them but was simply happy to help them out. But, he was excellent with all skill levels of players and both genders. Ladies loved the way he taught them to play golf. His background in Education obviously helped him communicate in a way that people could better understand.

With a wife and six kids and working both in teaching and golf, he simply did not have the time to compete as much as I would have liked him to. After all, I knew how well he could play. Par was just a mediocre round for him for many, many years. This despite a chronic bad lower back. He was thinking of supporting his family first. Dad really never had much of an ego either about his playing ability or his teaching ability. There were never any self-promoting words that came out of his mouth. He simply let his actions speak for themselves. He was and is what I call "old school" all the way. He has always thought that talk was cheap and until you proved something to him with your deeds or actions you would not win his respect. That probably was the result of how he himself was raised. Their family of five children and parents lived in "Kegomic" in the old Tannery Co. housing where Glen's Market in Bay View is today. His and all the other tannery houses had no indoor plumbing, nor insulation, just an outhouse and warm blankets. He said there were many winter mornings when he woke up there was snow covering his bed blanket from the wind blowing the snow in over night. All they had was a pot bellied stove for heating and cooking.

Petoskey-Bay View Golf Course however was right across the street and he and almost all the "tannery kids" caddied and learned how to play at Bay View. Caddy initiation consisted of the older kids literally taking the clothes off the younger kids and then throwing them in the bushes with pickers and thorns. The young kids then had to "dive in" to the bushes to retrieve their clothes in order to be possibly considered "initiated". The tougher you were the less they bothered you. This was in the 1940's when times were tough and the "Kegomic tannery people" were certainly that way as well. But, I have had many conversations with my dad and uncles over the years and to this day they say they loved how they grew up and wouldn't change one thing.

My dad was the first person in his family to graduate from college. He then went right out and got his Masters from MSU as well. That of course became the expectation for his own kids. In short, he has always set the bar very high for himself and for others. Any student who had him in class in Harbor knew they were going to learn a lot from my dad whether they think they wanted to or not, and that they darn well better behave, ha! I think between him and Charlie Paige that they have spanked half of the Harbor Springs local residents who attended school there at one time or another, ha!

Chaz, I don't know how much of this you can use, but I have had fun reminiscing about my father and I thank you for giving me that opportunity. Have a great weekend.

Eddie Kelbel

I paid another visit to see Mr. Kelbel on Saturday, October 4, 2008. I asked him how he was feeling. He said, "I'm weaker than a fart in a hailstorm." Although he speaks his truth, Ed Kelbel, Sr., still has his humor and classic one-liners.

We talked more about golf and about some of the old days. He talked about how Ray Watson, Tom's dad, befriended him and how wonderful that was. He said, "He had so much money, but he still enjoyed my company." He mentioned his other son (there are three), Mark who is the head golf professional at The Broadmoor in Colorado Springs, Colorado, site of the 2008 Senior PGA. Mark had about a half-hour conversation with Tom Watson, telling some old stories about his dad. Pretty cool stuff.

When I told Ed that I was going to be the keynote speaker at the annual Phi Epsilon Kappa, a Professional Physical Education and Sport fraternity initiation event at Central Michigan University, he asked me about the audience I would be addressing and what my topic was going to be. I told him I would be speaking to about forty students and some faculty on The Power of Intention and The Zone. I chatted to him about my belief about The Zone and it sparked his interest. I asked him what thought. He said, "I think you got something. I'd keep it up. You should teach all the local golf professionals."

I was thinking "yes," recalling one local pro suggested I teach a class where they can earn credits. When I asked him about the title and message to my book, *The Fairway of Life,* and I discuss all the mental, emotional, and spiritual aspects about the game of golf. He said, "That's exactly what it is! Why not call it that?" And so shall it be.

Action steps:

1) **Be present for another and you will not have to think but for one second about why you received this message.**

2) **God will bring you the exact message with the exact person. Just open your eyes.**

Conclusion

"The game of golf is played mainly on a five-inch course, in a space between your ears."
—Bobby Jones

Yes…the game of golf really is a game played between the ears

Bobby Jones said that and he was right. What this game of golf and life really comes down to is our personal perspective within the space between our ears and our connection to life itself. Life is always showing us about life itself. We just have to listen to that calling, align with our *True North,* and go with the flow.

I have learned through experience, and you have too after reading this book, that the way you play golf is in the reflection of own your life lived. While golf is very much a mental game, it is also a very physical and spiritual experience—it is all connected. Blending the ingredients of your mind, body, and spirit in perfect harmony creates the ultimate adventure. The intent here is to remind you of what you already know. It is a road sign to guide you back to your own true path and perhaps enhance and expand your fuller potential even more.

As you have been reminded in this book, the ultimate message is to awaken you to more of whom you really are and to give you back to yourself. Golf is a metaphor for life. Playing the game of golf is *one* with the game of life; it is an opportunity for you to announce and declare, express and experience, become and fulfill your true brilliance and magnificence both on and off the golf course.

The benefits to playing golf as you intend for fun and more joy with a new awakened state are mind-boggling. And not once does it ever take away any burning desire within to be your personal and "competitive" best; it only enhances and expands it! I am forever amazed by the insights, ah ha moments, and outrageous joys along this journey we have come to know as *The Fairway of Life*. Once we come full circle and realize that the main event in life is not about the manifestation or reaching a mountaintop or winning a golf tournament we can begin to real live again. The main event has always been about the way you feel moment by moment, because *that is* what life is. Lighten up, let it in, and have fun with all of this. This perspective changes everything. And since we are all eternal beings there is never going to be a time in which we do not exist. So, there's no point in rushing. It's why the message of enjoying the journey is reiterated everywhere you go. Now perhaps you will have an even deeper understanding of this amazing life principle.

> *"People say, 'The joy is in the journey,' but they rarely understand what they are saying. You are in this focused time / space reality with goals and objectives that call you because as you identify a desire it literally summons life through you. Life summoning through you is what it's all about, not the completion of anything."*
> —Abraham through Esther Hicks

The joy is in the journey in each step along the fairway, with each glance into the beauty of nature or into the eyes and heart of another, with each shot in every moment, in every putt, and the journey never ends. By embracing the good, the perception of the bad, and the illusion of the ugly along *The Fairway of Life* the more good stuff almost magically becomes a part of our new experience and there will always be more. The moment we accept and embrace every thing as it is, then we allow ourselves to move into better feeling spaces, and the better it gets…the better it gets. It's the way we allow ourselves to feel about it. It's in how we give it meaning. It's realizing we are making it all up and nothing really matters, except what we decide to make matter. It's in that five-inch space between our ears that connects to life itself. It's the way we embrace life unfolding as a most precious and sacred experience. As soon as we give up the notion of getting somewhere or thinking we are supposed to be complete in our swing, in our golf game, in our mental mindset, or in our life is the moment (which by the way has kept us stuck in the repetitive cycle of anger, frustration, and never getting any better) we can relax into the outrageous moment of joy that has existed all along.

The real question to ask yourself when you're feeling frustrated or out of sorts, off your game, choking when it seems to count is, can I be with this and can I take the punch in the gut and still feel good? As we evolve along the fairway of life perhaps we become a more mentally tough golfer simply by first dropping the oars or paddle, our struggle and finding some relief. Next, we plant the seeds of belief and focus that supports us. We evolve into a more mentally tough mindset when we allow the Well-Being to flow to us and through us. Awaken and fall in love with the magnificent and simultaneous moment of now, where cause and effect become one. It's all in the law of attraction. It's karma unfolding deliberately or by default depending upon where we are giving our thoughts and attention.

While growth can be messy at times, and I felt like giving up and falling back into my old ways, which I did many times – it's easy to fall back into a safe zone of mediocrity, I am still happy I kept on through the thick and thin and all the juicy stuff in between. With internal fortitude, desire and enough repetition, I made it to what seems, like the other side, and what feels like a test. I could have given up very easily, yet it was my ex-wife that sent me a message of hope that allowed me to keep on growing in this direction. I am certainly most grateful and appreciative that I have asked, and I am most grateful to everyone who I have drawn into my life that helped to awaken me, so that I can tell my story of asking to become a better person and a better golfer, delivering my unique gift and message in this form to a whole new audience. I give gratitude to all those who awoke the sleeping giant within me. In a sense life is like the game of dominoes. Each new awakened soul awakens another through an expression of their gift within. I can only pray and hope that perhaps my message has inspired you in some way, big or small. That's really what this all about.

What I am telling you here is nothing new. I did not invent it. I am not taking credit for it. I honor the collective consciousness of God and the universe, where this clarity and wisdom exists. Everything that is here has always existed. It's just a matter of reaching into your cupboard for the ingredients you desire and launching new rockets of desire. The only thing new is our ever-expanding spiraling upward consciousness.

What I reached for was the courage to heal myself to connect with life, to be authentic, to be real again. It was not an easy first step to take. I pondered it for many years not quite fully understanding its magnitude or full significance. Wow, and in the process of healing and transforming myself, I asked for more guidance and wisdom. These things came to me one layer of understanding at a time. And the more I know or appear to "get it," the less I do. And the cycle continues – not knowing leads to knowing and I know now there will always be more. More levels of deeper consciousness, more levels of new understanding, more levels of greater authenticity, and more levels of transformation. This kind of transformation is never finite, with an end point; instead it is an eternal process, with incremental steps that build upon each other in a spiral that keeps going—up and up and up—as far as you wish to go. With growth and new transformation comes the responsibility of keeping yourself up to speed with that which you have now become. And what you now have become is simply a series of just taking the next logical step, going with the flow, listening to your intuition, connecting with life getting yourself up to speed with what your soul already knows. Life becomes pretty joyful, authentic, and intoxicating experience. And as you get yourself up to speed with who you have now become, life makes even more sense. Just take the next logical step.

I have gone far enough to present the messages that I've come to understand. I have observed them working in my life both on and off the golf course, and I have observed them working in the lives of others. I know that there are deeper levels of awareness, understanding, and unlimited potential and beliefs. I know there will always be more. I remind you that my way is merely one way and that there are plenty of paths. Now you can take your own life as far as you desire. I invite you to let go of your limited beliefs and open up to a new dimension of infinite possibility.

I remind you also that I am making this all up. We all are. So, why not reach for the highest and best feeling-thought of joy and happiness that you can possibly muster? Why not recreate yourself anew and become the next grandest version of the greatest vision ever you held of who you really are? The lessons I have presented in our journey along *The Fairway of Life* are nothing more than reminders, and you are the creator and leading edge extension of Source Energy.

We began our journey with my personal life story, my intention being to bring the human element into the equation. We all have gone through our fair share of life challenges. It is my hope that, by bringing you to reflect upon your own life and golf game, this book has brought you more joy and more understanding than before.

I invited you to make a commitment to play full out. I presented the understanding of how providence moves through you once you fully commit. I've suggested that you learn to love, honor, and cherish yourself and to believe in the brilliant and magnificent person that you really are. I've reminded you about the message to trust life and to let life know that it can trust you. We began our journey by dreaming our dream and setting an intention. We've been exposed to thoughts that we've allowed to filter into our subconscious mind and how to input new more empowering beliefs and focus. Like a computer, our subconscious mind creates our own reality with the information it is given that we allow to be. We've discussed the concept to change your thoughts is to change your life.

We talked about the power of role models and how the qualities that you observe in others lie within you. I invited you to integrate those qualities into your life.

We spoke of the Universal Laws of Creation. You ask; you intend; you receive; you allow; you expect it to happen. And so shall it be.

We discussed the concept of honesty and how the truth shall set you free. Telling the whole truth about everything will transform your life.

We embraced the spiritual law of acceptance.

We reminded you about the present moment of NOW. We reminded you to become fully present and suggested ways to center yourself.

We understood that our toughest opponents are ourselves.

We awakened more to our own magnificence.

We became the change we wished to see. We were exposed to the Infallible Formula: cause another to become that which we wish ourselves to be.

We experienced it all in our greatest joy.

We are becoming more of who we really are. We are giving ourselves back to ourselves.

We are constantly giving our subconscious the positive focus and belief in creating a champions and winner's self-image of ourselves.

You have done great work here, I honor and I acknowledge *you*... and I invite you to keep on. While life and golf may not always be smooth and effortless, we can certainly enhance our experience while we are here. All it takes is a simple shift in focus. It's all a matter of perception, which creates our perspective. Life is like a circle – and it never ends. You can relax because you never do die – you just simply change forms – back into pure positive energy when you shift back into the realm of the absolute. And perhaps you and I will choose to come back and play this game again and again. Imagine that – a journey that never ends.

Can these mental, emotional, and spiritual golf concepts actually improve your game? After all the writing, processing, reflecting, and integrating, the only thing I know for sure is that my handicap is lower than ever before, my attitude and demeanor better than ever before, I have changed my thoughts and perspective—and I am making it . . . all ... up.

I invite you to make it work for you, and tell another how you thrive in this joyous co-creative game: as in golf, so in life. I invite you to keep on living the rest of the secret by aligning with your *True North* letting your feelings guide the way.

Play inspired golf with outrageous joy!

Icing on the Cake

On Sunday, August 13, 2006, I won the second annual True North Golf Club Championship, beating David Ketterer in the finals 2 & 1. Here is the note he left for me that day:

> Scout,
>
> I am so positively compelled to thank you for being such a solid and gracious competitor today. Congratulations on winning our Club Championship. I will never forget what a great match we had today and I will always think fondly of it.
>
> Your "ole" brother,
> Ketts

Looking back fondly upon this experience I realize how much it means to me to be seen as a gracious competitor and how my example left an impression upon my opponent, my playing companion for the day. There is always an exchange of energy taking place whenever two or more people gather and it can either be positive or negative. It is up to each of us to set the tone by the clarity of our example for the experience.

What really matters? There is a bigger message in all of this. I could easily get esoteric and say nothing really matters because we are making it all up, therefore make it work for you. Yet, what really matters is my growth and personal connection to life—to really appreciate the joy and challenges, or growth opportunities that life offers. You have done this for me, allowing me to write this book and share it with you.

The game of golf is simply one more avenue to express this message. Yes, I'm grateful I've won the Club Championship a couple times, I'm grateful to be more free to express my full potential in golf and life, and I am grateful to be more aligned and connected with life itself. I am grateful to be awakened. Even though I do not always get it "right" or "perfect" and I still fall down, get uptight,

The Fairway of Life

tense, nervous, and scared…I do know I will be "all right" embracing my stroll along *The Fairway of Life*…and so will you. I am grateful that you have been drawn to hear this message and trust that perhaps you will also put some of these spiritual "woo-woo" laws (wink, wink), and universal life principles back in to play…both on and off the golf course. I look forward to hearing about your new adventure.

As we come full circle once again in this wonderful game of life, perhaps the greatest message of all is universal. It is heard by many in various forms, and taught by all Masters throughout the history of time: do unto others, as you would have them do unto you. As you treat others with love, kindness, respect, and compassion – seeing their light within them, as you become the grandest version of the greatest vision ever you held about who you really are…you let your own light shine, and you give permission to let others do the same. Namasté – the god in me sees and honors the god in you!

> **Simple Secret Reminder # 38 – The Secret is in our Alignment**
> **…and in the full expression of who we really are.**
> **Allow the Well-Being to flow to you and through you.**

References and Resources

1) *Golf in the Kingdom* by Michael Murphy
2) *Bagger Vance* by Steven Pressfield
3) *The Majors* by John Feinstein
4) *The Greatest Game Ever Played* by Mark Frost
5) *Way of the Peaceful Warrior & The Warrior Athlete* by Dan Millman
6) *Zen Golf* and *Zen Putting* by Dr. Joe Parent
7) *Playing To Win* by Dr. Bob Rotella
8) *Power vs. Force* by Dr. David R. Hawkins
9) *Journey To Center* by Thomas F. Crum
10) *The Power of Now* by Eckhart Tolle
11) *Ask and It Is Given* by Esther and Jerry Hicks (The Teachings of Abraham)
12) *Conversations with God* by Neale Donald Walsch
13) *Radical Honesty* by Brad Blanton
14) *The Secret of the Shadow* by Debbie Ford
15) *A Return To Love* by Marianne Williamson
16) *Autobiography of a Yogi* by Paramahansa Yogananda
17) *The Power Pause* by John Harricharan
18) *TUT (Totally Unique Thoughts) Universe* by Andy and Mike Dooley
19) For daily inspirational messages visit: http://www.TheDailyGuru.com
20) To participate and view *Simple Secret* golf blog reminders, mental, emotional, spiritual coaching programs, seminars, events, or newsletters please visit: http://golfissupposedtobefun.com/ or http://www.randmarquardt.com/